THE STRUCTURE
OF EARNINGS

THE STRUCTURE
OF EARNINGS

BY

HAROLD LYDALL

OXFORD
AT THE CLARENDON PRESS
1968

Oxford University Press, Ely House, London W. 1

GLASGOW NEW YORK TORONTO MELBOURNE WELLINGTON
CAPE TOWN SALISBURY IBADAN NAIROBI LUSAKA ADDIS ABABA
BOMBAY CALCUTTA MADRAS KARACHI LAHORE DACCA
KUALA LUMPUR HONG KONG TOKYO

PRINTED IN GREAT BRITAIN

FOR
MARGARET

PREFACE

THIS book was started in Adelaide; but most of the work was done while I was on sabbatical leave during 1966–7. The first half of that year was spent at the Institute for International Economic Studies, Stockholm, of which the Director at that time was Professor Gunnar Myrdal; and the second half at the Center for Advanced Studies in the Behavioral Sciences, Stanford, of which the Director was Dr. Ralph Tyler. I am greatly indebted to both these institutions, and to their Directors, for the generous help which they gave me. My work at the Stockholm Institute was made possible by a grant from the Wenner-Gren Foundation.

I derived much benefit from comments and suggestions made by the staff and research workers at each of these institutions. A paper containing many of the essential ideas developed later in the book was discussed at a seminar in the Stockholm Institute. At the Center, I received most valuable advice on statistical problems from Mr. David Peizer, who also programmed many of the computations. Professor Arthur Jensen, of the Institute of Human Learning, Berkeley, very kindly read an early draft of Chapter 4 and gave me suggestions for its improvement. At the University of Adelaide I also had helpful discussions with Professor Alan James about certain statistical aspects of the analysis.

The collection of data from a large number of countries necessitated correspondence with a great many government statisticians, and university and other research workers, all over the world. They were all most generous with both information and advice and I wish to thank them collectively. Many of them are mentioned personally in Appendix 8.

Mrs. Hildegarde Teilhet, of the Stanford Center, and Mrs. Gillian Morgan, of Adelaide University, did a first-rate job on the typing of the manuscript. But my greatest debt is to Mrs. Helen Wickens, who was my research assistant throughout the project. She undertook a very large programme of graphical work, as well as other research tasks. Without her careful and accurate attention to detail the project could never have been completed.

The book was entirely written before I took a post with the United Nations.   H. F. L.

Geneva, February 1968

CONTENTS

NOTATION

References to books or journal articles in the text are given with the name of the author and the year of publication. Further details can be found in the bibliography on pp. 377–85.

Statistical sources are listed in Appendix 8, pp. 371–6. They are referred to in the text and tables by their code letters and numbers, e.g. AL 1, SW 4, sometimes followed by a page number or by a table number, e.g. T20.

Country tables, given in Appendix 7, are identified in an analogous manner. Each country has a two-letter code, and its tables are numbered in the usual way thereafter. A hyphen separates the code letters and table numbers, e.g. AL–6, SW–8.

In all tables a figure in brackets, such as (25), means a less reliable estimate.

.. means not available.

1

INTRODUCTION

THE essential problem of economics is how to increase economic welfare. In a broad sense, this problem can be divided into two parts: how to increase total output from given resources; and how to distribute the resulting goods and services in such a way as to give the community the most benefit from them. These two aspects are sometimes described as the problem of 'production' and the problem of 'distribution', respectively. The two parts are not, of course, independent; and many of the most difficult questions arise out of the interdependence of production and distribution. Nevertheless, it is possible to identify some influences which bear primarily on the side of production and others which primarily affect distribution. No progress could be made in the discussion unless we abstracted, at least temporarily, from some of the considerations which might eventually be shown to be relevant to one or other side.

This book is concerned mainly with the problem of 'distribution'. In its most general sense, the problem of distribution is to discover what causes determine the shares of total output taken by the various members of society—men, women, and children. In an exchange economy these shares are composed partly of payments for the use of productive services owned by the members of society—that is, factor incomes; partly of net payments made by the public authorities through fiscal channels—net transfer incomes; and partly of net transfers made privately through gifts, charity, and family income-sharing. This third group of payments, though rarely discussed, is almost certainly of greater aggregate importance than the more obvious group of government transfers, since more than half the population has no other significant source of income. Until fairly recent times —which in most countries means within the past twenty or

B

thirty years—very little was known about the ultimate reci-
pients of income; and even today we know hardly anything
about the distribution of income within families. Partly for
this reason, and partly perhaps because what happens within
a family is generally not thought to be of much concern to
economists, attention—even in recent years—has been confined
to the distribution of income between families, households, or
spending units.

In earlier times it was not possible to go even that far. Until
the arrival of income taxes, less than a century ago in most of
western Europe, and within the past half-century elsewhere,
scarcely anything was known about the distribution of income
between families, even at the top of the income scale; and it
required the development of systematic censuses and sample
surveys, within the past thirty years or so, to complete the
picture for all strata of society. Thus, in the nineteenth century
the problem of distribution, which the classical economists
recognized to be a crucial one, had to be handled in a very
approximate fashion. Adam Smith, Ricardo, and Malthus took
it for granted that landlords were rich, labourers were poor, and
capitalists were somewhere in the middle. If this was so, it was
possible to discuss the problem in terms of the distribution of
the total product between wages, rent, and profit, that is, the
aggregate shares of the factors of production.

Much of the discussion of the problem of distribution is still
carried on in these terms, despite the fact that it is well known
that many landowners are poor, many employees earn more
than some capitalists, many property-owners work and many
workers own property.[1] There is, of course, a positive correlation
between ownership of property and level of income; but it is not
as close as often seems to be assumed, at least in the more

---

[1] For example, Hicks (1935, p. 33), while recognizing that 'the abilities of
the different labourers in a trade are probably distributed according to something not far removed from the normal curve of error', proceeded to develop
his theory of wages on the assumption that labour is a homogeneous factor
with a single price. Modern 'neo-classical' model-builders generally do not even
bother to mention that labour is a heterogeneous factor, let alone consider the
implications of this fact.

developed countries of western Europe, North America, and Australasia. Moreover, the assumption that the distribution problem is essentially a problem of factor shares overlooks the very considerable dispersion of income amongst individual workers, property-owners, and entrepreneurs. Even in the communist countries, in which income from property and private entrepreneurship has been much restricted or even eliminated, there is still a considerable degree of inequality of earnings, both amongst employees and between employees as a group and collective and individual farmers.

Thus, if we are really interested in the distribution of income between *persons*, it is necessary to study the distribution *within* factor shares as well as *between* factors. A complete picture would also require a study of the ways in which factors are combined in the ownership of individuals, of the clustering of individuals with different amounts of income into family groups, and of the voluntary redistribution of family income amongst its members.

The Importance of Employment Incomes

In any such study one of the crucial steps is the analysis of the distribution of earnings of employees. Employment income—income from wages and salaries—represents in the developed capitalist countries one-half to two-thirds (or in come cases more) of total personal income; in the Soviet Union and parts of eastern Europe the proportion is probably higher. In some of the developing countries employment income is not yet a large proportion of total personal income, but it is growing rapidly and its distribution is of considerable economic (and in some cases political) importance.

Moreover, the study of the distribution of employment income is relevant not only to the traditional welfare problem of equity but also to two important aspects of production. The structure of earnings in a competitive market can be expected to reflect both the conditions of supply of labour services of different qualities and the conditions of demand, which, in turn, depend on the level of technique, the supply of other factors and the

pattern of market demand for the products. It is to be presumed, in such a market, that the structure of earnings will be
one which maximizes output from given resources, given also
the pattern of ownership of those resources. In practice, however, the structure of earnings is not determined by such a
purely competitive market. There are many frictions, imperfections, and deliberate interferences by collective bodies, such
as governments, employers, trade unions, professional organizations, and educational institutions. Although it may well be
impossible to discover the 'ideal' structure of earnings from a
production point of view, a comparison of the structure of earnings in different countries and at different periods of time may
reveal some of the effects on distribution of changes in market
conditions, institutional structure, government policy, and the
like. Some light may thus be thrown on the nature of the inter-
relationship between productivity and the structure of earnings;
and so enable us to predict some of the repercussions on productivity and growth of different distribution policies.

A further problem, which is relevant to both output and
equity, is the relationship between the structure of earnings and
inflation. If we wish to avoid inflation, experience seems to show
that either we must be prepared to have less than full employment or there must be a socially directed incomes policy. But in
a democratic society an incomes policy cannot be established on
a purely aggregative level, since much of the activity of trade
unions and others is specifically directed towards redistributing
income shares, both between factors and within factors. Although the idea of a voluntarily accepted social incomes policy
may turn out to be an illusion, it is an aim of great importance;
and some effort should be made, by studying the causes determining the distribution of income between and within factors,
to give guidance to those attempting to establish or to adminis-
ter such a policy. Since employment income is such a large proportion of the total, and since movements in money wage-levels
seem to play an important role in inflation, there is a good case
for giving special attention to the relation between the structure
of earnings and inflation. One hypothesis which it may be useful

to consider, for example, is that wage drift is at least partly a consequence of attempts to impose artificial constraints on the dispersion of earnings.

The Need for a Theory

Thus the study of the structure of employee earnings is relevant to issues of equity, productivity, and inflation. But, apart from these 'practical' considerations, the structure of earnings is a subject of considerable intrinsic scientific interest. Why, the question arises, should some people earn so much larger incomes than others ? Are we not taught that we are born equal ? What, then, are the sources of inequality of observed earnings, even if we set aside incomes from property, which may be largely inherited ? Are these differences the result of inherent differences of 'ability' ? What parts do inheritance and environment play here ? Or is it all, perhaps, merely a matter of luck ? Can the whole thing be explained as the outcome of a stochastic process, repeated over and over through time, in which each individual follows a random path, leading him to the point at which we happen to observe him ?

Many different hypotheses have been put forward to account for the observed distribution of incomes. In some cases such hypotheses are relevant only to a particular type of income ; but many of the hypotheses are general, not specifying what type of income they are intended mainly to explain. One reason for this is that the information available in most countries about the personal distribution of income has often been rather limited, so that it has not always been clear exactly what it was that was to be explained. As we shall see, a number of hypotheses have been built up to explain particular shapes of the income distribution which are either not typical or not universally applicable. It would be much easier if all income distributions were essentially of the same shape, as Pareto and others have believed. Then we would know exactly what had to be explained and we could concentrate on the job of finding appropriate hypotheses. In fact, as will become clear below, the curve of income distribution, even for employees separately, can follow many different paths; and this in itself suggests that we are unlikely to find a single simple hypothesis to explain all distributions.

But the scientific problem remains, and is closely bound up with the 'practical' problems mentioned above. In the later chapters of this book we shall examine many hundreds of different income distributions, drawn from over thirty countries, and in many cases from varying periods of time. Both the similarities and the differences between these distributions present a challenge. Why are so many so similar? And why are others so different? Are there consistent patterns relating differences in income dispersion in different countries to differences in other aspects of their economic or social conditions? And why, over the past twenty years or more, has the degree of dispersion changed in some countries but remained relatively unchanged in others?

Outline of the Subsequent Chapters

The arrangement of the discussion will be as follows. In Chapter 2 we shall review existing theories of income distribution, and attempt to assess how far they have been, or could be, successful in explaining the shape of the distribution of earnings from employment. Some of these theories will be shown to have been based on misconceptions about the typical shape of the curve, so that they have tried to explain the existence—even the inevitable existence—of something which often does not in fact exist. Others can be shown to make use of assumptions which are either untrue or inadequate. But nearly every theory contributes something to our understanding of the forces underlying income distribution; and the review will help us to identify the most important considerations which should enter into a more complete theory.

From this discussion it will become clear that one of the first tasks is to discover precisely what shape, or shapes, the distribution of income from employment does in fact take. This forms the subject of Chapter 3. Here we show that the shape of the employment income distribution depends very much on the way in which income is defined, and on the types of employees covered by the distribution. There are many thousands of different possible definitions, of which quite a large number are actually used in constructing the distributions available in different countries. It is necessary, therefore, to try to reduce this variety of distribution types to some kind of order, and to estimate the influence which differences of definition or coverage have on the degree of dispersion and on other parameters of the distribution. For this purpose a special system of classifying the distributions has been developed.

But in order to go further than this, and to make systematic comparisons between countries and over time, it is necessary to select one particular distribution—preferably a 'typical' distribution—as the Standard Distribution. The particular distribution which has been selected as the Standard is the distribution of full-time male adult employees, in all occupations and in all industries except farming, classified according to their pre-tax money wage or salary earnings. It is this distribution, also, which our basic theory will be designed to explain. Detailed examination of a number of examples of this distribution from several countries reveals that it has certain typical characteristics, namely, that it is unimodal, positively skew and leptokurtic in the logarithm of income, and that its upper tail generally follows the 'Pareto Law'. These are, then, the characteristics which our theory must be able to account for. Chapter 4 is devoted to the construction of such a theory.

An adequate theory must be based not only on a careful study of the facts which are to be explained, but also on a combination of realistic and relevant assumptions about the explanatory factors. Any attempt to explain a set of prices, which is what a structure of earnings represents, should take into account both the demand and the supply conditions underlying the market. But, while conditions of demand may be important in determining the earnings of particular types of labour in the short run, when the supply of such labour is fixed or very inflexible, in the long run the predominant influence is likely to be the conditions of supply, since there are at most only a few occupations for which the long-run supply is strictly limited in relation to demand. Attention has, therefore, been concentrated on discovering the factors which determine the supplies of persons to each occupation, and—within each occupation—of the distribution of people of different levels of effective ability.

It is shown in Chapter 4 that many factors are responsible for the dispersion of the effective abilities of young people who have completed elementary education but have not yet become differentiated according to specific occupations. These factors include inherited 'intelligence' and other qualities, early environmental influences, both from the family and from the wider social environment, and formal education. It is suggested that the interaction of these various factors would itself be sufficient to generate a distribution of general effective abilities which would be both skew and leptokurtic in the logarithm of income.

It is next shown that, on reasonable assumptions about the forces influencing the allocation of young people to different occupations, it can be expected that the distribution of the average earnings of occupations will also be skew and logarithmic leptokurtic. Hence the combined distribution of earnings of all employees is likely to be of the same form. Moreover, as time passes, adult abilities change, in most cases reaching a peak some time before middle age and then declining. When allowance is made for these variations, the over-all dispersion of earnings of employees of all ages is further increased and the kurtosis of the distribution is likely to grow.

But these factors alone cannot account for the Pareto tail of the distribution. The hypothesis which is offered to explain this phenomenon is that large organizations—which dominate the upper tail of the distribution—are organized on a hierarchical principle. On fairly plausible assumptions about the relationship between earnings at each level of the hierarchy and the earnings of employees in the grade below (as well as about the average number of persons supervised by each grade), it is shown that the distribution of earnings in a firm organized on such a pattern would be 'quasi-Pareto'; and that a distribution of supervisory employees in all firms in the population could conform approximately to a Pareto distribution. Some further implications of this hypothesis are deduced and submitted to empirical tests, which are found to give the hypothesis a measure of support.

In Chapter 5 we move to consider available evidence from different countries on the shape of the Standard Distribution. Distributions of many different types have been collected from over thirty countries. Estimates have been made of certain characteristics of each distribution, which permit comparison between countries and over time, and which reveal differences both in the degree of dispersion of the distribution and in its shape at various points. Our special classification code is used for identifying the different types of distribution according to the definition of income used and the coverage. After reviewing the evidence from all available distributions, an estimate is made (for most of the countries) of the degree of dispersion of the Standard Distribution. This permits us to arrange the countries in order of their estimated degree of dispersion, and these estimates are compared with estimates of dispersion which can be derived from skill differentials.

Chapter 6 is devoted to the study of changes in dispersion within countries over time. Earlier discussions of this problem have usually been based on an analysis of the skill differentials, information on which in some countries goes back half a century or more. But skill differentials are not very satisfactory indicators of the degree of dispersion. At best they may reflect changes in inter-occupational dispersion, which is, however, only a minor part of the total. But even for this purpose it is shown that they are likely to be a biased indicator, especially over long periods. In spite of these qualifications, the evidence which is available from the skill differentials is used, in conjunction with other evidence from over-all earnings distributions, to discuss changes in dispersion in a number of countries over the past twenty to fifty years. The results show that a radical shift in dispersion occurred in the United States and Canada between 1940 and 1950 but that changes in dispersion in other countries have, on the whole, been relatively small over the periods for which information is available. In some countries there was a considerable widening of dispersion during the Great Depression, which was later corrected; and in several countries there seems to have been a trend towards wider dispersion during the 1950s. Recent changes in dispersion in Japan are also examined in some detail.

Having reviewed the evidence on both differences in dispersion between countries and changes in dispersion over time, we attempt in Chapter 7 to account for these differences and changes on the basis of the theory propounded in Chapter 4. Our theory suggested that the dispersion of effective abilities is much influenced by differences in the environmental circumstances of different sections of the population, and especially by differences in the degree of formal education. The inter-country comparison showed that, amongst the non-communist countries, the degree of dispersion is generally less in the more highly developed countries and much wider in the very poor countries. But the association between dispersion and *per capita* income is not found to be particularly good; and, in any case, our theory does not suggest that it necessarily should be so. What matters is the *inequality* of environment and education, not its average level. Some data exist on the distribution of education in different countries, and these, so far as they go, are broadly consistent with our theory. But education is not the only factor; and a relevant indicator of environmental inequality—for most countries—seems to be the proportion of the labour force engaged in agriculture. In fact, inequality of education is also found to be closely associated with this indicator. In any event, the proportion of the labour force in agriculture seems to offer the best available statistical explanation of the differences in dispersion between countries.

When the same reasoning is applied to explain the changes in dispersion in the United States and Canada and—more recently —in Japan, it is found that the great shift in dispersion in North America coincided broadly with a sharp fall in immigration (of mainly poor and ill-educated peasants and workers), a rapid decline in the proportion of the population engaged in agriculture, and the mobilization of millions of men into the armed forces during the Second World War. All these factors would

tend towards reducing inequalities of education and effective
ability. In Japan, also, the recent decline in dispersion seems to
have been associated with a fall in the supply of farm workers
to industry and the culmination of Japanese efforts to provide
every child with at least a full elementary education.

Finally, some thoughts on policy are discussed in Chapter 8.
Here we attempt to relate the theory developed in Chapter 4,
together with the supplementary hypotheses developed in
Chapter 7, to the issues that were raised at the beginning of this
chapter. Although no firm conclusions can be reached at this
stage about the possible impact of short-term changes in government and institutional policies, it seems clear that—at least in
the long run—the most effective way to reduce inequality of
earnings amongst employees is to reduce inequalities of early
environment and formal education.

2

EXISTING THEORIES OF THE SIZE DISTRIBUTION OF INCOMES

1. Introduction

SCIENTIFIC theories arise in many different ways; but two limiting cases are common. The first is to start from a set of observed phenomena which exhibit a regularity or pattern of behaviour. A theory is then constructed to explain these phenomena. The theory draws on some higher generalizations, or 'assumptions', from which the observed phenomena can be logically deduced. The verification of a theory of this type takes the form of tests of its predictive power in other circumstances, including possibly tests of the predictive power of individual assumptions taken separately. This is the classic approach to scientific theorizing.

An alternative approach, however, is also possible, and is often followed in economics. In this case we do not start from a set of phenomena requiring explanation, but from a set of assumptions, which for some reason are thought to be valid. They may be axiomatic ('self-evident'), they may be based on elementary observation, or they may be assumptions established in the course of earlier theories. From these assumptions certain conclusions are drawn and a prediction is made. At this point, however, there is sometimes some confusion about the purpose of the exercise. If, as is often the case in economics, the prediction is one which it is difficult, or even impossible, to verify, the 'theory' is left high and dry as a pure piece of deduction from given premises. If the premises themselves have been verified in other contexts, there may be some confidence in the conclusions drawn from them; and this sort of reasoning plays a large part in normative economics. But from the standpoint of positive economics little or no progress has been made. On the other hand, if the prediction is subject to verification, then both the assumptions and the logic of the theory are put to an empirical test, and a contribution has been made to positive theory.

Theories of income distribution are of both these types: those which start from observations about the nature of the distribution, and those which start from assumptions about human qualities, or human behaviour, and deduce what sort of distribution of income one might expect to find. But the most common theories are those of the former type, and the most convenient way to divide our discussion is not according to which 'end' the theories start from, but according to the shape of the distribution which the theory is designed to explain. At various times economists have suggested that the distribution of income conforms to one or other of three main types of distribution. These are: the Pareto distribution, the normal distribution, and the lognormal distribution. We shall, therefore, develop our discussion under these three headings. Within each section we shall distinguish classes of theory according to the main assumptions on which they draw.

2. The Pareto Distribution

The first important and systematic observations of the character of the size distribution of income were made by Pareto (1897). From a study of a number of distributions, drawn principally from various European countries and mainly from the nineteenth century, he found a regularity of pattern which struck him as remarkable. Pareto's 'Law', as it has been called, is as follows. Let N be the number of incomes exceeding a given income level X. The the following function provides an almost perfect fit:

$$N = AX^{-\alpha}$$

where A and α are constants. Pareto estimated the value of α for each of his distributions and found that it was generally in the region of 1·5. He was very excited by this discovery and wrote:

These results are very remarkable. It is absolutely impossible to admit that they are due only to chance. There is most certainly a *cause*, which produces the tendency of incomes to arrange themselves according to a certain curve. The form of this curve seems to depend only tenuously upon the different economic conditions of the countries considered, since the effects are very nearly the same for countries whose economic conditions are as different as those of England, of Ireland, of Germany, of the Italian cities, and even of Peru. (1897, vol. 2, p. 312.)

Davis (1941*a*, p. 435) even went so far as to suggest that substantial deviations of α from its equilibrium value of 1·5 would lead to revolution or civil war.

There are clearly two parts to Pareto's law: first, the universality of the functional relation; and secondly, the constancy of α. Few economists have placed much faith in the latter. Even Pareto's own sample of distributions shows a variation of α from 1·24 to 1·89;[1] and subsequent observations have shown an even wider range, with α often increasing above 2.[2] But much greater faith is generally placed in the Pareto *function* as an adequate description of the upper tail of the income distribution.

Pareto originally believed that his function would describe the whole income distribution.[3] His measurements, however, were confined to the upper tail, since it was only for these incomes that statistical information was available at that time. If the Pareto function is extrapolated backwards—towards the lower end of the income range—it will reach a 'maximum' at zero income, where the cumulative frequency will be infinite. And the same is true of the frequency density. Since the frequency density of a Pareto distribution is the negative derivative of the Pareto function, namely,

$$-\frac{dN}{dX} = \alpha A X^{-\alpha-1}$$

it can be seen that the density function is itself of the Pareto type. To overcome this difficulty, Pareto assumed that the

---

[1] Excluding the City of Augsburg in 1526, for which Pareto estimated a value of 1·13. But this was one of the cases which he regarded as being based on rather uncertain data (pp. 311–12).

[2] See, for example, Clark (1951, pp. 533–6).

[3] But by the time of his *Manuel* (1927) he admitted that the income curve probably was hump-shaped (p. 384).

frequency curve terminated at some positive income, corresponding to the amount needed to provide the physiological minimum. Since it was impossible for human beings to exist with an income of less than this minimum, the distribution could not exist below this point. By implication, therefore, the modal value of income was also at this point. Thus, Pareto's conception of the frequency distribution of income can be illustrated by the curve in Fig. 2.1.

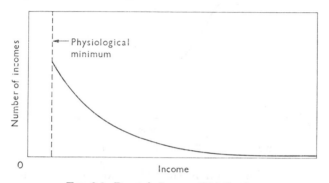

Fig. 2.1. Pareto's Income Distribution.

Experience has shown that in very many cases the upper tail of distributions of total income of individuals or families conforms fairly closely to Pareto's function.[1] There is, of course, no case of a 'perfect' fit, and the degree of closeness of fit varies a good deal; but, as an empirical approximation, and within certain limits, the Pareto function does remarkably well. But the Pareto law has two important limitations. The first is that it applies only to the upper tail of the distribution, in a region which embraces usually not more than about 20 per cent of the total number of incomes. We now know, from the more comprehensive statistics of income which have been collected since Pareto's time, that the frequency curve of income is not hyperbolic throughout its whole length, but is hump-shaped, with at

[1] The easiest test of the function is to transform it to logarithms, namely,

$$\log N = \log A - \alpha \log X$$

and to test the regression of $\log N$ on $\log X$ for linearity. This can be done reasonably well by eye, if the values of N and X are plotted on logarithmic paper.

least one maximum, or mode. A fairly typical distribution of family incomes is illustrated in Fig. 2.2.[1] In these circumstances the Pareto function can be of no assistance in describing the whole distribution of income, although it may still be of value as an aid in interpolation, or even in extrapolation, within the upper tail.

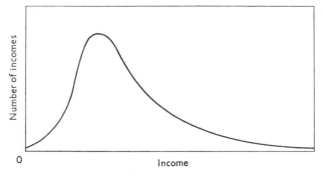

FIG. 2.2. A 'Typical' Distribution of Family Incomes.

The second limitation is that the Pareto law applies most satisfactorily only in cases where income from all sources is included in the income variable. This would be true, for example, of the tax-assessed income of individuals, or of the total income of households. But when income from a single source is considered separately, the Pareto function is sometimes less useful. This fact was well known to Pareto himself. He wrote (1897, pp. 307–8): 'When it is a question of income from work or from capital, taken separately, one does not find any more a straight line in the logarithms, or at least in the few cases which we have been able to examine.' His tests showed that the curve of income from work was concave from below and the curve of income from capital was convex. It was only when all sources were added together that the curve became a straight line (1897, p. 308). My own experience, however, from plotting several hundred distributions of employment income, is that often the Pareto law operates fairly well for the top 15 or 20 per cent of

[1] Since some households whose main source of income is from entrepreneur-ship have a negative income, the curve should strictly extend to the left of the vertical axis and approach the income axis asymptotically.

employee incomes; and that the deviations from log-linearity are not always in the same direction. Despite the fact that Pareto limited his law to the curve of income from all sources, it has often been assumed to apply equally to income from employment taken separately. Hence, we shall consider below all theories designed to account for the Pareto distribution, unless the author implicitly or explicitly excludes the distribution of employment income from the scope of his theory.

Theories Designed to Account for the Pareto Distribution

Pareto theories fall into two groups. One group consists of theories which rely on a stochastic process as the principal force generating the distribution. The second group is much more heterogeneous and includes (1) a theory which depends on assumptions about the distribution of abilities, (2) a theory which is based on assumptions about the diminishing difficulty of raising one's income as income increases, and (3) a theory which regards the structure of employment income as reflecting the hierarchical structure of organization inside enterprises. It will be convenient to consider this latter group of theories first.

Miscellaneous Theories

Davis (1941*b*), who asserted that 'no one . . . has yet exhibited a stable social order, ancient or modern, which has not followed the Pareto pattern at least approximately' (p. 24), traced the origin of the income pattern to a 'law of the distribution of special abilities', and suggested that 'it is reasonable to assume that the ability to accumulate wealth is an ability not dissimilar to those which appear in games of skill and in the production of scientific literature' (p. 50). The underlying explanation must, therefore, be sought 'in the mysterious realm of human psychology' (p. 51). Davis quotes some examples of the distribution of achievement in various fields—including the playing of billiards —but he does not produce convincing evidence that all special abilities are distributed according to the Pareto law, nor that the 'ability to accumulate wealth' is a 'special' ability. His theory takes no account of other factors besides natural ability, and, in particular, he ignores the influence of inherited wealth on the income distribution.

Zipf (1949), like Davis, finds that the Pareto law applies to a wide range of phenomena, including individual word frequencies, sentence lengths, sizes of cities, and so forth; and he attempts to provide a unified explanation of all these phenomena, including the distribution of income, by his 'Principle of Least Effort'. It is not clear, however, how this principle is supposed to operate in the sphere of incomes (or indeed elsewhere). According to Zipf the value of α should be exactly 2. But the fact that it is not so does not seem to worry him unduly.

Lange (1959) suggested that the Pareto law would operate if 'the relative decrease (screening) in the number of persons as the income increases is smaller and smaller and diminishes in proportion to the income' (p. 192). He seems to assume that incomes are continually pressing upwards and passing through finer and finer filters. 'The situation is similar to that of examinations in the various years of study. The relatively largest "screening" during the examinations occurs during the first year of studies, is smaller during the second, still smaller during the third, etc.' But Lange concludes that this theory is not applicable to wages and salaries, since the over-all distribution of incomes of Polish employees is not log-linear. (In fact, the Pareto function is quite a good fit for the top part of the upper tail of the Polish distribution of 1955 to which he refers.) Lange's conclusion is that the 'screening' theory could apply to property incomes, so that the Pareto function might apply under capitalism, while incomes under socialism are more likely to be normally or lognormally distributed.

Some years ago I offered another possible explanation for the Pareto distribution of higher salaries (Lydall, 1959). The suggestion was that employing organizations—firms, government organizations, and so on—have, more or less inevitably, a hierarchical structure; and that the incomes of employees in a given stratum are related to the average number of persons supervised by them in the stratum below, and to their average income. On the assumption that the number of persons directly supervised is everywhere the same, and that the proportion which the supervisor's income bears to the aggregate income of the people he directly supervises is also constant, the resulting distribution of salaries would follow the Pareto law.[1]

This is a very simple theory which, I believe, is based on assumptions with a good deal of empirical validity. So far not very much has been done to verify the theory, although it would not be too difficult to collect relevant data. In Chapter 4 I make use of this theory as an ingredient in a general theory of income distribution, for the specific purpose of explaining the Pareto section of the upper tail of employee income distributions. We shall see there that some empirical observations are easily accounted for by this theory and could not well be accounted for by any alternative theory.

Stochastic Process Theories

The preceding theories all rely to some extent on empirically based assumptions about relationships—arising either from the demand side or from the supply side or from some feature of the institutional structure—which are thought to generate the observed distribution of income. Stochastic process theories, however, attribute the observed pattern of incomes entirely to the operation of the laws of chance. Theories of this type, leading to a Pareto distribution, have been put forward by Champernowne (1953), Simon (1955), and Mandelbrot (1960, 1961). The essence of each theory is the assumption that the incomes of individuals follow a Markov process, the change in income during each interval of time being a random variable. For example, it may be assumed that
$$y_{t+1} = y_t + \epsilon_t$$
where y_t = income in period t and ϵ_t is a random variable uncorrelated with y_t. If, further, $E(\epsilon_t) = 0$ and σ_{ϵ_t} is constant for all t, indefinite repetition of the process will generate a distribution asymptotic to a normal distribution. Similarly, if y_t is the logarithm of income, the ultimate distribution will be

---

[1] A similar theory was put forward earlier and independently by Simon (1957).

lognormal; and, if particular assumptions are built into the process, it is possible to produce a Pareto distribution.

Champernowne's theory

The best-known example of this type of theory is Champernowne's (1953). Champernowne starts from the assumption that income distributions approximate closely to the Pareto law for high income levels, and the purpose of his article is to seek theoretical reasons for this. He assumes that the income scale is divided into ranges of equal proportionate extent and that incomes move stochastically from one range to another over time. In his basic model, incomes are assumed to be eternal, each income being passed on to a new recipient when the old one dies. He then demonstrates that, if the matrix of transition probabilities is of a particular type—namely, that 'no income moves up by more than one income range in a year, or down by more than n income ranges in a year', that there is a lowest range below which no income can fall, that, for each income range, the average number of ranges shifted during a year is negative, and that the transition probabilities are the same at each level of income—then the indefinite repetition of the transition matrix will generate a distribution approximating the Pareto distribution.

This, of course, gives only the right-hand tail of the distribution; but Champernowne suggests an extension of his assumptions which will generate what he calls a 'Pareto tail' for the lower incomes. The upper tail is a negatively sloping straight line on a double-logarithmic scale, while the lower tail is a positively sloping straight line on the same scale. The two tails approach each other at the lower boundary of the bottom range of the upper tail, which is also the upper boundary of the topmost range of the lower tail.[1]

Champernowne relaxes some of his assumptions in order to make them more realistic, but continues to succeed in generating distributions asymptotic to a Pareto distribution for the upper

---

[1] The position of this boundary—which is also the mode of the distribution —is quite arbitrary; and no justification is given for the assumption that the probability of crossing this boundary is less than the probability of moving across any other range boundaries.

incomes. He also suggests a way of allowing for the existence of semi-autonomous 'colonies' within his over-all distribution, consisting, for example, of particular age or occupation groups, each of which has a distribution asymptotic to a Pareto distribution in the upper ranges, even though the parameters vary between colonies. His conclusion is that his examples 'illustrate the theory that the approximate observance of Pareto's law . . . is not an illusion or coincidence, but has its explanation in a similarity at different high income-levels of the prospects of given proportionate changes in income' (p. 346).

Champernowne's theory is an extremely ingenious attempt to account for the observed distribution of income on purely stochastic assumptions. But it suffers, in my opinion, from a number of weaknesses. The first is that only the top 20 per cent or so of most income distributions can be said to approximate at all closely to the Pareto law—and even here there are many cases where the logarithmic regression line is not linear. Thus, at the best, Champernowne's theory could explain only a minor part of the distribution. His suggestion of fitting a 'Pareto tail' to the lower part of the distribution is a surprising one, since no one has ever suggested that the lower tail follows the Pareto law. Champernowne's two-tailed Pareto distribution would presumably look something like Fig. 2.3; but it is not clear how the two tails would be connected.

The second objection to Champernowne's theory—which applies also to all the stochastic theories, including those which lead to a normal or lognormal distribution—is that too much reliance is placed on the laws of chance and too little on specific factors which are known to influence the distribution. Stochastic theories can generate a given theoretical distribution merely by the indefinite repetition of a specified matrix of transition probabilities, *irrespective of the initial distribution*. The income or other characteristics of the individuals entering the stochastic process are irrelevant to the final outcome. Of course, if one makes the assumption that incomes are eternal, the 'initial' distribution is clearly irrelevant. But this is too large a departure from realism. In fact, the greater part of income dies with its owner, and, in many countries, a good deal of the remainder is transferred to the government. A more realistic model would have to recognize the existence of cohorts of income receivers of limited life, the initial endowments of whose members exercise considerable influence on their lifetime patterns of income.

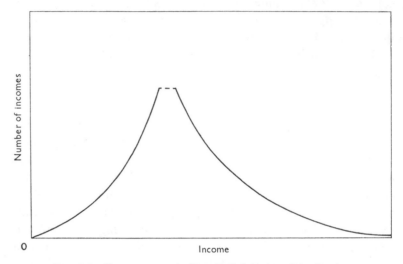

FIG. 2.3. Champernowne's Two-Tailed Pareto Distribution.

This point has been emphasized by Rutherford (1955), whose theory will be considered separately below.

The third objection to Champernowne's theory, which also applies to other Markov chain theories, is that the probability of a given income in time $(t+1)$ is made to depend solely on y_t. This means that, for example, a young person whose income is y_t^* in year t is assumed to have the same probability of moving to y_{t+1}^* in year $(t+1)$ as an older person; or that an individual with only an elementary education is assumed to have the same chances of given changes of income as a university graduate. But empirical studies show that factors such as age, education, occupation, and experience are influential in determining the transition probabilities. It is true that, in principle, Champernowne's system of 'colonies' could be used to deal with this: but then the crucial question becomes how the transition probabilities vary between 'colonies'. It is the differences between colonies which become the dominant influences on the over-all income distribution rather than the stochastic processes within each colony.

Champernowne assumes that empirical data on the relation between income in year t and year $(t+1)$ reveal the transition probabilities of a Markov chain. But this is not necessarily so. Suppose that each person's income, y_t, consists, as Friedman (1957) has suggested, of two components, his 'permanent' income, p, and his 'transitory' income, t_t. Then

$$y_{t+1}-y_t = t_{t+1}-t_t.$$

The observed differences between y_t and y_{t+1} will measure $(t_{t+1}-t_t)$, but the distribution of these differences does not represent the distribution of transition probabilities in a Markov chain. If $E(t_t) = 0$, σ_t is constant for all t, and $r_{p_t t_i} = r_{t_i t_j} = 0$, then it is easy to show that

$$\sigma_y^2 = \sigma_p^2 + \sigma_t^2$$

The variance of the distribution of income will contain only these two components and only the proportion $\sigma_t^2/(\sigma_p^2 + \sigma_t^2)$ will be attributable to chance.

A final difficulty with Champernowne's theory is that it gives no clue to the factors responsible for the existing degree of inequality of income in different countries, or which have been responsible for changes in the distribution within a given country over time. Indeed, since the transition probabilities are assumed to operate indefinitely, the theory seems to rule out the possibility of change. Presumably, differences in economic or social conditions can be thought of as affecting the transition probabilities; but the theory does not help us to identify what these economic or social factors are, nor how long it would take for changes in them to affect the income distribution.

Other stochastic process theories

Other theories involving Markov processes, and leading to a Pareto distribution of the upper tail, have been suggested by

Simon (1955) and Mandelbrot (1960, 1961). Simon's theory is essentially the same as Champernowne's for the upper tail. Simon does not attempt to account for the distribution of incomes around and below the mode; nor does he give any empirical justification for the stochastic mechanism which he assumes to operate. He makes no distinction between different types of income distribution, e.g. income from property and income from labour, and offers no explanation for variation in the value of α between distributions.

Mandelbrot, on the other hand, has attempted to explain the shape of a two-tailed skew distribution, of which the upper tail is of the Pareto type. This is the right sort of target. He bases himself on what he calls the 'Pareto–Lévy law'. This distribution results from the repeated application of a *weighted sum* of independent random elements. The normal distribution is a special case, which is approached when the value of α approaches 2. The Pareto–Lévy function is, therefore, only relevant when $1 < \alpha < 2$. Mandelbrot has opened up an interesting line of inquiry; but at the present stage his theory is of little practical use in the study of employment income distributions, for which the value of α is almost always greater than 2.

Conclusion

A number of different theories have been suggested to account for the Pareto distribution of the upper tail. Some of these also attempt to explain the shape of the whole distribution. But none of these is at present very successful. Indeed, apart from recognizing that the distribution *has* two tails, little has been done, even by those who take account of the lower tail, to examine the shape of empirical distributions over their whole range. The major fixation has remained the Pareto 'law', which is really only a small part of the problem. It is true that changes in the elongation of the upper tail have an important effect on most measures of inequality; but these are not the only changes which are important. Even with a constant value of α, there can be large changes in the degree of inequality of income, in any meaningful sense, as a result of changes in the shape of the bottom 80 per cent of the distribution.

Stochastic process theories, perhaps because of their mathematical elegance, have attracted a great deal of attention. But these theories rely at present, in my opinion, too much on the stochastic element and too little on the economic and social factors underlying the distribution of income. Perhaps because of the cogency of mathematical logic, stochastic process models seem to create a bias towards believing that the existing distribution of income is inevitable and unchangeable. Since we know that the inequality of income has changed in some countries very considerably over the past fifty years, any model based on the perpetual repetition of a constant matrix of transition probabilities (such as the typical Markov chain model) is at variance with the facts.

It is not suggested that stochastic processes are irrelevant. There is reason to believe that there is a Markov chain component in the distribution of income, although it probably operates on permanent income rather than on measured income. But this component is not measured by observed changes in incomes over time, since these mainly reflect variations in the transitory component of income. Nor is it reasonable to assume that all changes in permanent income are Markov processes. Part of the change in permanent income is predetermined by the social and economic characteristics of the individual concerned, and only the residual can be attributed to chance.

3. The Normal Distribution

Some economists have suggested that, if reasonably homogeneous groups of employees are taken separately, the distribution of earnings *is* or *should be* normal. This group of theories, unlike the previous group or those which follow, tends to start from *a priori* considerations rather than from observed facts. Generally, however, some observed distributions are introduced in order to support the predictions of the theory.

The basic assumption underlying these theories is that 'ability' is normally distributed. This assumption is not usually derived from any objective measurements of 'ability', which of course would be extremely difficult. The assumption is made by analogy with observed distributions of a number of physical characteristics of man, which have been shown to approximate the normal distribution. Moore (1911), for example, put forward the hypothesis that 'industrial ability—general capacity and energy—is distributed according to the normal or Gaussian law' (p. 74). He justified this assumption by referring to 'a great number of measurements of physical characteristics' by Quetelet and others, and by Pearson's comment that: 'We have very definite evidence that the normal curve suffices to describe within the limits of random sampling the distribution of the chief physical characteristics of man' (p. 76). Galton had earlier assumed that 'mental and moral qualities of man are distributed according to the same law as are physical qualities', and Pearson, making the same assumption, constructed his scale of intelligence so as to make the distribution of intelligence follow the normal law. Moore argued that since 'industrial efficiency is dependent upon physical, mental, and moral qualities', and since 'there is good reason for regarding [these qualities] as being distributed according to the Gaussian law', the distribution of 'industrial efficiency' should be normal. This conclusion is justified by reference to a theorem by Edgeworth that 'if a variable thing obey the normal law, a function of that thing will obey the normal law' (p. 77).

The expectation is, therefore, that wages of a homogeneous group of workers will conform to the normal distribution. Moore applies his theory on the assumption that workers in industry are divided into two groups—skilled and unskilled—who are assumed to represent the top and bottom halves of the entire distribution. In this way he is able to construct 'expected' distributions which are of varying degrees of skewness, depending on the parameters of the observed distributions. But his assumption that the over-all distribution can be neatly divided into two parts, one for skilled and the other for unskilled workers, is quite unrealistic. In practice, there are very large

overlaps between skilled and unskilled workers, and the most
probable arrangement is one in which each distribution by skill
is hump-shaped and of a different degree of skewness. The data
needed for testing the hypothesis that 'industrial efficiency' is
normally distributed are, therefore, distributions of workers of
fairly narrowly defined levels of skill in a given industry (or even
firm) in a particular locality. In fact, as we shall see later, it is
very difficult to justify the assumption that 'abilities' are normally distributed, and even less so that 'industrial efficiency',
which is a complex function of basic abilities, is so distributed.

Pigou (1932) also wrestled with this problem. After stating
that 'there is clear evidence that the physical characters of
human beings—and considerable evidence that their mental
characters' are normally distributed, he proceeded, 'on the face
of things, we should expect that, if, as there is reason to think,
people's capacities are distributed on a plan of this kind, their
incomes will be distributed in the same way' (p. 650). But in
practice incomes are known to be skew. His answer to this
inconsistency was that (1) people are not homogeneous, but
divided into groups 'among which the principal division is
between manual capacity and mental capacity', and the normal
distribution operates only *within* groups; and (2) 'income depends, not on capacity alone, whether manual or mental, but
on a combination of capacity and inherited property'; and
inherited property is highly concentrated. Part of this property
also may be invested in the owner's person by 'improvements
in capacity by training' (p. 651). Pigou recognized the importance of 'investment of capital in people', and showed that a
change in its distribution 'must tend directly to alter the distribution of earned income, even though original capacities are
distributed in accordance with some (the same) law of error'
(p. 654).

Thus Pigou succeeded in building a bridge between the (assumed) normal distribution of abilities and the observed skew
distribution of incomes, including earned income. But it would
follow from his argument that *within closely defined occupations* one would expect to find earnings normally distributed.

In practice, even this does not seem to be true, although it is
closer to the truth.

Bowley (1933), in an attempt to discover the economic forces
underlying the distribution of income, started with 'the working
hypothesis that aptitudes, so far as they are measurable, are
normally, or sub-normally, distributed' (p. 359). He continued:
'If, then, persons all had the same education, environment, and
opportunity, were paid by piece-rates, and worked with equal
zeal, their earnings in a stated time would be normally distributed, with possible gaps at the extremities if the least efficient
were not employed and the most efficient had passed on to a
higher type of work.' Such conditions, he maintained, were
approximately true (at that time) in cotton-weaving in Lanca-
shire, where 'records of earnings show at least a tendency to this
normality' (p. 360). He does not give the data on which he bases
this conclusion, but he does present some distributions from the
New Survey of London Life and Labour of wages of males and
females in east London. The male distribution relates to adult
male time wages for a normal week, mainly based on 'standard
rates agreed by the employers and workmen'. It is fairly close
to normal but significantly different on a χ^2 test. On the other
hand, distributions of adult women's wages in two selected
boroughs of east London are very close to normal.

Bowley's results are inconclusive, although his hypothesis
that hourly earnings of a very homogeneous group of workers
would be normally distributed is an important one. But he is
inclined to extend his hypothesis more widely than this, and
even suggests that 'in a community in which resources were used
to their best advantage, persons would, at maturity, arrive at
the work for which they were best fitted, and if the net efficiency
earnings were equal—as may be expected in certain conditions
—these earnings would again be normally distributed' (p. 360).
The concept of work for which one is 'best fitted' is not made
clear, but it seems to imply that people with higher abilities
would receive more education or training. If this were so, it can
be stated unequivocally that efficiency earnings would *not* be
normally distributed.

In a very perceptive paper, Staehle (1943) pointed out that 'a direct comparison of the assumed shape of the distribution of abilities, or aptitudes, and of the known distribution of total incomes' assumes perfect mobility between the various strata of society. But 'such mobility, obviously, does not exist, partly on account of social barriers, partly because of the fact that certain occupations require costly training and thus are not accessible on the strength of mere ability' (p. 81). This, of course, was Pigou's point. But Staehle goes on to draw an important distinction between full-time earnings and part-time (or part-period) earnings. Within a narrowly defined occupation group 'if wages are paid by the piece, the distribution of abilities will, with an equal piece rate for all, translate itself directly into a distribution of incomes of the same shape', provided that the degree of employment is the same for all members of the group (p. 82). And the same will be true when wages are paid by the hour, if there is a sufficient degree of competition within the group. But when the degree of employment varies, total earnings for a given time period, e.g. a year, will depend on both ability and the degree of employment. If the degree of employment were uncorrelated with ability, this alone would introduce skewness into the distribution of total earnings, but 'there is every reason to believe that a positive correlation between the rate of wages and the degree of employment would develop'. Employers would tend to cut down the employment of their least efficient workmen first and this would accentuate the degree of skewness of total earnings.

Staehle does not produce any evidence to support his belief that hourly rates and the number of hours worked are positively correlated; but he does publish some very interesting diagrams showing that the annual earnings of workers in specified occupations on the United States railroads are almost symmetrical, when only workers employed in each of the twelve months in the year are included, and highly skew (J-shaped) when those employed in less than twelve months are taken separately. From this he argues that, in periods of low employment, the inequality of wage incomes will tend to increase (p. 85).

When we turn from considering a given occupational group to the aggregate of wage incomes, we have to take account not only of the dispersion *within* occupations but also of the dispersion *between* occupations (or non-competing groups). Staehle gives an example (p. 86) to show that, even if the distribution of incomes within each of several occupations is fairly symmetrical, the over-all distribution may be skew because of differences in the means of occupations. But he does not discuss the conditions under which the distribution of occupational means is likely to be skew, nor produce adequate evidence to show that this is the typical situation. In practice, as we shall see below, the means of occupational earnings often approximately follow a lognormal distribution—a finding of considerable interest in itself.

Miller (1955) and Lebergott (1959) have both suggested that the observed distributions of earnings of certain broad classes of employees in the United States are more or less symmetrical. Using 1950 Census data, Miller divided employed males into blue-collar workers, white-collar workers, and other non-farm non-service persons, and he expressed the opinion that the distribution of total income of each of the three groups was 'essentially symmetrical' (p. 28). He did not subject the distributions to any statistical tests and it seems that he based his judgement on a rather cursory examination of the three frequency polygons. A more careful study reveals that each of the distributions is positively skew (and leptokurtic) and can better be represented—at least in the upper ranges—by a lognormal than by a normal distribution.[1]

It seems probable, also, that census data tend to underestimate skewness. Several studies have shown that there are substantial individual discrepancies between reported income in censuses and surveys, when their results are compared with the results of other surveys of the same group of persons for the same period, or with tax or other official data.[2] In the aggregate,

[1] See also Kravis (1962, p. 164).
[2] See, for example, National Bureau of Economic Research (1958, p. 198), Lansing, Ginsburg, and Braaten (1961), Miller (1966, p. 206), and Bureau of the Census (1964).

such discrepancies often cancel out, so that estimates of average income, for example, are very similar. But the existence of individual discrepancies shows that there are substantial measurement errors. Since these are probably symmetrical, the distribution of measured income will tend to be more symmetrical than the distribution of true income. If measured income were equal to true income plus the measurement error, the variance of measured income would be greater than the variance of true income, unless there were a negative correlation between true income and the error. In practice, it seems likely that the variance of measured income is *less* than the variance of true income, and this suggests, either that there is a negative correlation between true income and the error, or that the major component of measured income may not be true income but some estimate of 'typical' income, the variance of which would be less than the variance of true income. In fact, both these tendencies may be at work, and both would tend to reduce skewness.

Lebergott (1959) criticizes the theory of non-competing groups and points out that the average turnover of labour in the United States is 'well over 200 per cent' per annum. 'Given such an enormous volume of labour market choices, entrances, exits, and shifts, our initial expectation would be that here, if anywhere, the classic conditions for producing a normal distribution must exist' (p. 334). It is not at all clear why this conclusion is thought to follow. The figures for percentage turnover are misleading, since they represent mainly the movement of a relatively small 'stage army' of the young, the unskilled, and 'chronic movers'. Their circulation may help to improve the competitive market for relatively low-paid jobs but has little effect on the market for more highly skilled jobs. Reynolds (1951) and others have shown that labour markets are highly imperfect and that widely varying rates may be paid for what seems to be the identical job, even by firms in the same locality. Even if this were not so, there is no reason to believe that a perfect adjustment of earnings to 'ability' would result in a normal distribution of earnings. As will be shown in Chapter 4, the distributions of both 'effective ability' and of 'quantity of work' are likely to be positively skewed.

Lebergott proposes that all females, and males aged less than 25 years and 65 and over, should be excluded from the over-all distribution of incomes, because they tend to work less than full-time (or full-period). When the United States 1951 distribution is restricted in this way to males aged 25 to 64 he considers that it 'is clearly much more symmetrical than the typical Pareto curve', although still showing 'distinct skewness' (p. 340). In point of fact, his figures for the top four classes of incomes (there are only eight classes altogether) are very close to a Pareto function; and the small deviation of one point is not towards downward concavity, which would represent less skewness than in the Pareto case, but in the opposite direction.

Conclusion

The theoretical case for believing that employment incomes 'should' be normally distributed rests on the assumption that 'ability' is normally distributed. Those who have followed this line of reasoning have usually recognized that some further assumptions are necessary in order to reconcile the theory with the facts of actual employment income distributions. The principal additional assumption is that the labour market is broken up into non-competing groups, so that the pure influence of ability can only be expected to operate *within* occupations. Here, too, it is necessary to exclude variations in the number of hours worked, which tend to obscure the effect of ability as such. Empirical tests of the hypothesis have been rather few and unsatisfactory. In all cases, distributions within occupations (of hourly earnings or of full-time income) have turned out to be significantly less skew than distributions of employees in all occupations or of incomes for varying numbers of hours. But there has been no convincing evidence that these distributions are normal; and in no case have these authors examined the alternative hypothesis that the distributions are lognormal.

My own opinion is that most distributions of employment

incomes, even for the most precisely defined occupational categories and for a clearly specified length of time, have an element of skewness, which can often be represented reasonably well by a lognormal curve. Some interesting examples are given by Aitchison and Brown (1957, pp. 118–19). Their data relate to the earnings of full-year male workers in several fairly narrowly defined agricultural occupations in Britain (such as, tractor drivers, stockmen, horsemen and cowmen). All the distributions are remarkably well fitted by the lognormal function, at least if one is to judge by the plots on logarithmic probability paper. Plots of similar data for a later year (1964), examples of which are given in Figs. 2.4a and 2.4b show that the lognormal fit is extremely good—though not perfect—while the normal distribution is definitely curved.

A further test was made on United States distributions of wage and salary income of a number of fairly narrowly defined occupations in 1959 (based on the 1960 Census). The occupations chosen were blacksmiths, cabinetmakers, compositors and typesetters, pattern and model makers (except paper), plumbers and pipefitters, barbers, elevator operators, and labourers (not elsewhere classified). Only male workers working 50 to 52 weeks in the year were included, but this does not, unfortunately, eliminate all variation in hours worked. Cumulative percentage distributions for each occupation were plotted on both natural and logarithmic probability paper and examined for linearity. It was found that the normal distribution gave a good fit for the bottom 90 per cent of the distribution in each case; but a few per cent at the top curved away from the straight line, indicating skewness. On the lognormal diagrams, on the other hand, the top 50 per cent or more was often, but not always, well fitted, while the bottom part of the distribution showed curvature. Examples of the diagrams for one occupation—plumbers and pipefitters—are given in Figs. 2.5a and 2.5b. In this case it will be seen that the normal distribution gives a good fit for the bottom 98 per cent of the distribution; but this is exceptional. This test gives more support to the normal hypothesis than the British data; but in no case does the normal distribution fit the

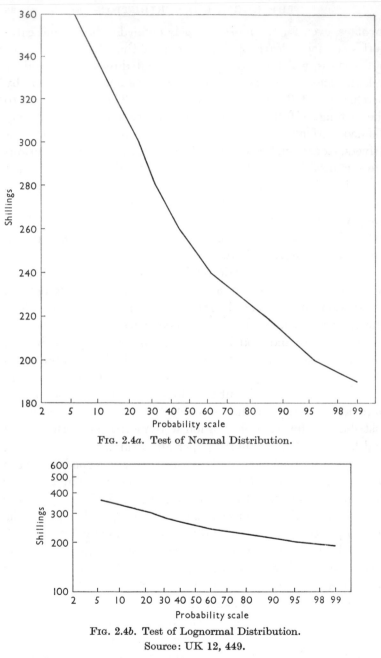

FIG. 2.4a. Test of Normal Distribution.

FIG. 2.4b. Test of Lognormal Distribution.

Source: UK 12, 449.

UNITED KINGDOM: WEEKLY EARNINGS OF TRACTORMEN IN AGRICULTURE,
THIRD QUARTER OF 1964

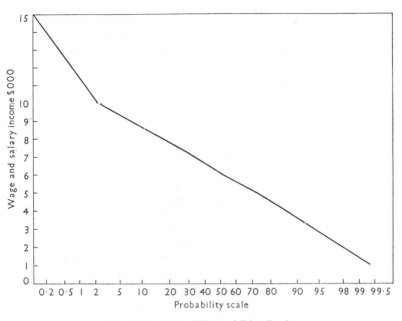

FIG. 2.5a. Test of Normal Distribution.

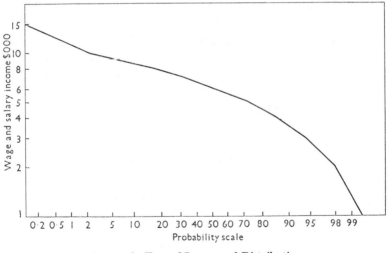

FIG. 2.5b. Test of Lognormal Distribution.

Source: US 3, Table 28.

UNITED STATES, 1959: WAGE AND SALARY INCOME OF MALE PLUMBERS
WORKING 50–2 WEEKS

upper tail, and, as we have mentioned above, there is some reason to believe that census data underestimate skewness.

Thus, the normal hypothesis is not well supported by empirical tests. Moreover, a basic difficulty with the hypothesis is that there is, in fact, no good reason to assume that 'ability' is normally distributed. 'Ability' is a very complex concept, which we shall examine more closely in Chapter 4. It will then be shown that 'ability' must be a function of genetic ability, home environment, education, training, age and experience, and of other less tangible variables, such as energy, will, and ambition. Even in the case of 'pure' genetic ability there are no solid grounds for believing that the distribution is normal, and some of the other variables are clearly not normal. Moreover, we do not know exactly how these variables combine. If some of them are multiplicative and intercorrelated, as seems very likely, the distribution of 'effective ability' will almost certainly be skew. Moreover, when we separate out specific occupations, in order to avoid the problem of non-competing groups, while we may remove some of the skewness resulting from variation in education and experience, we cannot be sure that each occupation includes a normally distributed sample of genetic abilities. Indeed, since there are good reasons for believing that genetic abilities are correlated with occupation, the distribution of genetic abilities *within* an occupation could conceivably be either positively or negatively skew, even if the over-all distribution in the population were normal.

4. The Lognormal Distribution

The widening coverage of income statistics during the first few decades of this century, until they began to embrace the whole population, made it clear that theories to account for the Pareto-like tail were inadequate and that it would be necessary to find an alternative distribution which, in the typical case, would be hump-shaped and positively skew. An obvious candidate was the lognormal distribution.

The lognormal distribution is a distribution which is normal in the logarithm of the variable. If X is a positive variable and

$Y = \log X$ is normally distributed, then X is said to be log-normally distributed. Clearly, in this case, Y will be symmetrical and X will be skew. The lognormal distribution has two tails asymptotic to the X-axis, of which, in the usual case, the positive tail is the more elongated. Thus the distribution has an immediate appeal as a possible description of a distribution similar to that depicted in Fig. 2.2.

The theory of the lognormal distribution was first stated by McAlister (1879) and much publicized by Galton, whence it is sometimes called the Galton–McAlister distribution. The theory was further developed by Kapteyn (1903) and van Uven (1917), and by others. Its first substantial application in the field of income distribution was made by Gibrat (1931), followed by Fréchet (1939, 1945), Kalecki (1945), Roy (1950, 1951), Aitchison and Brown (1957), and others.

Using probability paper, Gibrat plotted the cumulative per-centage of incomes above each given level of income against the logarithm of income. In some cases the points were found to be close to a straight line (thus confirming that the distribution was lognormal). In other cases the line was found to have signifi-cant curvature, especially at the ends. Gibrat discovered that by shifting the origin of the income variable he could improve the linearity of the log-probability plot, and he argued that this strengthened the case for believing that income distributions are lognormal. But his conclusion is doubtful, since the extra para-meter (the shift in the origin of X) is introduced arbitrarily. The important fact is that the great majority of income distributions are leptokurtic (have an excess of frequencies in the tails com-pared with a normal distribution) even after transforming to the logarithm. So far as the upper tail is concerned, this is reflected in the Pareto law, since a Pareto tail is more elongated than a lognormal tail. The excess of frequency in the lower tail in many cases is the result of including in the distribution persons whose working period is much below normal (part-time and part-period workers), but even distributions of 'straight time' hourly earnings are often characterized by this same excess of low income frequencies.

In spite of these qualifications, the lognormal distribution generally gives a much better fit than the normal, and of course has the considerable advantage over the Pareto distribution that it covers the whole income range. These facts have encouraged the development of a number of interesting theories to explain the lognormality of income. All these theories derive from one fundamental idea, namely, that income is a *product* of a large number of independent random variables.

The Central Limit Theorem shows that if $Y = \sum_{i=1}^{i=n} X_i$, where the X_i are independent random variables, the distribution of Y tends to the normal distribution as $n \to \infty$.[1] It follows that, if $Y = \prod_{i=1}^{i=n} X_i$, the distribution of Y will be asymptotic to lognormal. The next step in the argument is to decide what are the factors which combine multiplicatively to yield observed income. Here two types of theory have been developed: one which assumes that income is the product of an infinite stochastic process acting multiplicatively, and the other which assumes that income is the product of a number of independent factors operating simultaneously. These two assumptions are not, of course, mutually exclusive, but so far no one has attempted to use both.

Stochastic Process Theories

Kapteyn (1903) first developed the idea that an observed variate may be the outcome of a discrete random multiplicative process through time. If, for example, we have for all points of time t

$$X_{t+1} = \epsilon_t X_t$$

where $\{\epsilon_t\}$ is a set of mutually independent random variables, each of which is also independent of the set $\{X_t\}$, then the distribution of X_n for large n tends to be lognormal. This is the so-called 'law of proportionate effect'; the intuitive basis for which is that the effects of the many random factors causing

---

[1] For a more precise statement of this theorem and its implications see Appendix 2.

changes in the income of an individual over time are likely to be proportionate to his pre-existing level of income. This might well be true, for example, if all income were derived from capital, and if the factors at work were changes in prices or interest rates, which affected each individual capital by an amount proportionate to its size.

This version of the theory has been adopted most notably by Gibrat and Kalecki, and, in a modified form, by Champernowne and Rutherford. The simplest assumption is that the matrix of transition probabilities (the distribution of ϵ_t) is constant for all t, although this is not essential. But, in order that the distribution should approach the lognormal form, it is necessary for the time series to be long. Moreover, of course, there must be no inter-correlation between the $\{\epsilon_t\}$. These assumptions are empirically difficult to justify, since human lives are finite and changes in income in one year are often negatively correlated with changes in the following year (as would be implied, by Friedman's concept of 'permanent' income).

A further practical difficulty is that, if the $\{\epsilon_t\}$ are uncorrelated with the $\{X_t\}$, the variance of the logarithm of income will be continually increasing, by an amount equal to σ_ϵ^2 in each time period. Since this is contrary to the evidence, Kalecki introduced a negative correlation between X_t and ϵ_t just sufficient to maintain $V(X_t)$ constant. He was able to show that, even with this additional assumption, the distribution of X_n for large n remains approximately lognormal. Champernowne, in his analogous model, was also obliged to introduce a similar assumption, that 'for all incomes, initially in any one of the ranges R_n, R_{n+1}, R_{n+2},..., the average number of ranges shifted during the next year is negative' (1953, p. 324). But these are mere artifices to make the mathematics come out right.

A much more realistic approach to this problem is that of Rutherford (1955) who pointed out that, at least in some occupations, the variance of income tends to increase with age, but that this factor is offset by the continual entry of new earners at the younger end and the exit of older ones through death. Thus, if we recognize that the population consists of cohorts, it

is easy to reconcile steadily widening variance of income in each
cohort with constancy of variance of the whole population.
Rutherford assumes, again fairly realistically, that new entrants
to the income distribution are distributed lognormally and that
their 'income power', i.e. the logarithm of income, is subjected
to additive independent stochastic shocks in successive years.
On these assumptions, the distribution of income of each cohort
will remain approximately lognormal, but its variance will
increase with time. He assumes that the number of survivors
in each cohort declines exponentially (without limit), that the
mean and variance of income power of each cohort is the same
at the date of entry, and that the shock system has zero mean
and constant variance. He is then able to integrate over all
cohorts and over all years from $-\infty$ up to the year of observation, and obtains a Gram–Charlier Type A distribution.

The principal difficulty with Rutherford's distribution lies in
the estimation of the parameters. But his model has, in my
opinion, some excellent features; and it results in a distribution
which is not unlike many observed distributions, especially in
being leptokurtic in the logarithm of income. In Chapter 4
I shall discuss the variation of income with age and consider
how far Rutherford's model is necessary or useful in explaining
the facts as we find them.

Simultaneous Multiplicative Theories

Although the law of proportionate effect was originally con-
ceived as a dynamic process through time, and still retains over-
tones of this conception, there is no logical reason why the same
law cannot be applied to a large number of independent factors
combining multiplicatively at a given moment of time. Roy
(1950a) was the first to see the significance of this idea in relation
to income distributions.[1]

Roy accepts, for the sake of argument, that 'abilities' are
normally distributed, but he points out that the outputs of

---

[1] At least he was the first economist. As we shall see in Chapter 4, the
psychologist Burt (1943) had arrived at the same conclusion some years earlier.
See also Boissevain (1939).

THE LOGNORMAL DISTRIBUTION   41

workers employed on a given task depend not only on a single 'ability' but on several. He mentions, for example, speed, accuracy, age, education, health, and hours worked. Even if the last factor is omitted, there are likely to be a number of 'ability' factors on which output per hour will depend. The crucial assumption is now made that these various factors, each of which is a random variable, combine together, not additively but multiplicatively. For example, ill health may be assumed to decrease the output of workers at all levels of skill by a given *proportion*, rather than by a given *amount*. If, then, the underlying factors are stochastically independent, the distribution of output will tend towards lognormality, for the reasons given above. If the underlying factors are correlated but their distributions are normal, and the coefficients of variation are approximately equal, then the distribution of their product will still tend to lognormality (Haldane, 1942). However, if the coefficients of variation are unequal 'the existence of an association between the variates tends to exaggerate the asymmetry and the humpedness of the distribution of their product. This would mean that more individuals would have very high outputs than would be indicated by a lognormal distribution' (Roy, 1950a, p. 493).

Roy argues that 'as far as simplicity is concerned there is no reason to place multiplication lower in the scale than addition' (p. 493). He proceeds to test his hypothesis by examining distributions of outputs in twelve rather small samples. On the assumption that the two mutually exclusive hypotheses are normality and lognormality he eventually concludes (1950b, p. 836) that 'the evidence is overwhelmingly in favour of the hypothesis of a lognormal distribution and that the chance that we have been misled is only 1 in 100'.

Conclusion

Roy's hypothesis is a very fruitful one. But, although it has been used briefly by Mayer (1960) and referred to approvingly by Aitchison and Brown (1957), little progress has been made in applying it. Roy's hypothesis gives us the essential clue to understanding the distribution of earnings of *new entrants* to the work force. But in order to develop the hypothesis it is necessary to make a more systematic study of the factors underlying 'effective ability' and the 'volume of work'. I shall outline in Chapter 4 the results of my own explorations in this field, from which it will appear that there are good grounds for believing that 'effective ability' is a function of a number of underlying factors, several of which are likely to be intercorrelated. A study of these factors will also reveal some of the important economic and social influences on the shape of the income distribution, such as home environment, quantity and quality of education, length of training for skill, and good health. We shall thus be able to find connections between the distribution of income and factors over which social control can—at least partly—be exercised. But before we proceed with this discussion we must look more closely at the actual shapes of income distributions as they are found in practice. To this task we devote the next chapter.

3

THE SHAPE OF THE DISTRIBUTION

IN the previous chapter we have seen that theories to explain
the size distribution of personal income have focused on three
main conceptions of its shape—the Pareto, the normal, and the
lognormal. In each case there has been some empirical basis for
the belief that the distribution conforms to one or other of these
ideal types, and more or less plausible hypotheses have been
advanced to explain why the distribution should follow a particular mathematical law. We have also seen that the empirical
basis for these beliefs is, in fact, inadequate. In this chapter we
shall take a preliminary look at the kinds of distribution of
employment income which are found in practice. We shall find
that a wide variety of types of income distribution can be obtained on different definitions of income and of the population
covered.

1. The Desired Type of Distribution

Before we enter the forest, however, we should pause to ask
ourselves what sort of tree we are looking for. What do we mean
by the size distribution of employment incomes ? The answer
will clearly depend on the purpose for which we intend to use
the information. We may, for example, be primarily interested
in comparing the welfare aspects of income inequality in different countries. In that case perhaps we should aim to include in
our distribution *all* employees of every age, sex, race, occupation, industry, and so forth. Should we also include people who
work part-time ? If the reason for working part-time is the lack
of opportunity to work full-time, e.g. because of unemployment,
then probably we should include them. But if part-time work
is the result of voluntary decision by the employee, e.g. in the
case of women or elderly workers who prefer to work part-time,

then perhaps we should *not* include them. Or we could include them but measure income at a rate per hour, so as to bring all employees on to a comparable basis. Clearly, however, these are debatable decisions, since we do not know how much of part-time work is voluntary and how much involuntary.

Similar problems arise in deciding whether to include over-time earnings in measured income, since it is arguable that employees who work for longer hours than normal are giving up leisure in exchange for their extra earnings. If the overtime is voluntary they must be presumed to be better off; but not to the full extent of their extra earnings.

Thus, it may be argued that the type of distribution that is relevant for a study of welfare is one in which hours are stan-dardized, since this will tell us how much each person earns in exchange for the *same* number of hours of work. Even this, however, is not entirely satisfactory, since some sorts of work are more exhausting than others. Ideally, perhaps, we should like to know the earnings obtainable by each person for an 'equal' amount of real sacrifice—of leisure, or effort, or loss of health. But this is clearly beyond our means.

So far we have been discussing ways of ensuring that the earnings we measure shall be received for an equivalent amount of real sacrifice. On the receipts side, also, we must try to ensure that all real earnings and benefits are included. Money earnings should ideally be grossed up for income in kind and fringe benefits, and taxes should be subtracted. Income in kind, in the sense of free or cheap supplies of the goods produced by the employing firm, is usually not very important except in the case of farm workers. Since the distribution of such income is gener-ally unknown, the best solution seems to be to exclude farm workers from the analysis. But other fringe benefits, such as free meals, transport, clothing, insurance, holidays, and the like, are of much more widespread importance, especially in the richer countries. There are reasons to believe—and some evidence—that fringe benefits are relatively more important at higher income levels, so that their inclusion would alter the picture of the degree of dispersion of real income. Unfortunately, it is quite impossible under present conditions to estimate the distribution of these benefits.[1]

In many countries it may be possible to make *some* estimate of the incidence of direct taxes on wage and salary incomes. The estimate cannot be at all precise, because income taxes are not usually levied on wages and salaries as such, without regard to other sources of income, family circumstances, and so forth. The best that can usually be done is to estimate average effective rates of tax on income ranges, as defined for tax purposes, and to assume that these apply to individual employee incomes. It will depend on the particular tax system whether the results of such a calculation should be regarded as meaningful or not.

But it is clearly not sufficient to estimate the incidence of direct taxes (and of other deductions such as social security contributions). Indirect taxes also affect the real value of earnings, and their incidence may easily be non-proportional. In most capitalist countries indirect taxes are probably regressive, while in the communist countries they are usually progressive. But in trying to make the matter more precise we enter very difficult waters, both because the differential impact of indirect taxes on different income groups is in principle hard to define, and because the information required for such an exercise is very difficult to obtain. Since indirect taxes are taxes on expenditure, the most that can usually be done is to allocate them to spending units or families, classified by income or expenditure classes. It makes very little sense to try to apply such estimates to the wage or salary incomes of individuals, without regard to their family circumstances. But perhaps a rough adjustment could be made in those few countries where such calculations have been made.[2]

A similar problem arises in making allowance for differences

---

[1] A small amount of information which has been collected on fringe benefits is presented in Appendix 1. No systematic attempt has been made to collect all the available evidence on this subject from all countries, but it can safely be assumed that very little is known about it. See Rubner (1962) and the bibliography given there for further references.

[2] See, for example, Barna's (1945) and Nicholson's (1964) estimates for the United Kingdom.

in the cost of living. It is well known that prices vary between large and small towns, and between different regions of a given country. These differences are often reflected, or at least are supposed to be reflected, in differences in wage and salary rates in different areas. Some countries in which central bargaining is the rule, such as Sweden and the United Kingdom, have well-defined cost-of-living zones, between which wage rates vary according to a prescribed formula. In other countries there are *de facto* differences in earnings between regions, which probably at least partially reflect differences in living costs. If we aggregate money earnings for a country in which wide differences in living costs exist, without adjusting for such differences, the dispersion of money incomes will overestimate the extent of the dispersion of real incomes. In practice, however, it is very difficult to make such adjustments. The nominal differences in cost of living, even if they are laid down, are often quite arbitrary, and cannot legitimately be applied throughout the income scale. Moreover, we are faced again, as in the case of indirect taxes, by the fact that prices affect family expenditures, not wages and salaries as such. Only a very rough adjustment would, therefore, be possible; and this has not been attempted below. An alternative, which goes some way towards removing the influence of differences in cost of living, is to confine the analysis to fairly compact regions. We shall use this alternative approach in some cases.

This discussion so far has been in terms of rates of income for a given short period of time—at the most for a year. But, as Friedman (1957) and others have emphasized, the more appropriate criterion of welfare distribution might be income for a longer period, perhaps even over a lifetime. Since, according to Friedman, part of current earnings are 'transitory', in the sense of being chance deviations from some longer-term trend, the inclusion of these in measured income exaggerates the degree of dispersion of underlying ('permanent') income levels. Apart from this, even the underlying income itself varies over life, and its pattern is different for different occupations. For example, the average income for unskilled manual occupations varies much less at different ages than the average income of managers or professional employees. So a distribution which measures income for a year will include a wide dispersion of managerial incomes, part of which reflects merely the changes in income over life.

It would certainly be instructive if we could study the distribution of lifetime incomes. But so far very little has been done to collect figures on the actual lifetime earnings of individuals.[1] Even when such figures become available there will be great conceptual and practical difficulties in analysing them. Adjustments should clearly be made for changes in prices, and presumably something should be done to bring incomes of different years into a single reckoning. Theoretically, this involves discounting; but what rate of discount is appropriate? And in which direction should the discounting be done? Because of uncertainty, as well as for reasons of personal taste, many people may have very high private rates of discount of future earnings, far above the average rate of return that could be obtained from investment of surplus income. Should one rate of discount be used for all? Or should it vary between persons? And what contribution to lifetime earnings is made by premature death?

These difficult questions can perhaps be left to be resolved when more data on lifetime earnings become available. In the meantime, we are limited to studying distributions of, at the most, annual earnings, although some information is available on earnings for a few longer periods in one or two countries.

To summarize, then, if we leave aside the problem of measuring lifetime incomes, the preferred distribution for a study of the dispersion of welfare seems to be one which is limited to full-time (and full-period) employees, unless there is a significant amount of involuntary short-time working; or, better still, one which is based on 'straight time' hourly earnings (from which overtime premiums have been eliminated). The distribution should ideally be gross of income in kind and fringe benefits, and net of direct

---

[1] The only ones known to me relate to the incomes of 121 men in the Norwegian town of Sarpsborg over the thirty-three-year period 1928–60. See Soltow (1965, p. 102).

and indirect taxes. And if the cost of living varies significantly between towns or regions, an adjustment for this should also be made. In practice, there are not many countries for which even full-time distributions (or hourly earnings distributions) are available and none in which all the adjustments to convert money to real earnings can be made. We must, therefore, do the best we can with the distributions actually available to us, making such allowances as seem reasonable for the deficiencies in the data.

When we turn to the production side of the problem, we can find arguments for further restrictions on the type of distribution. While from an equity point of view there is much to be said for the assumption that all men (and women) are equal (in the sense that they should count equally), the problem from the production standpoint is to discover whether differentials in earnings reflect underlying differences in productivity. If women are less productive than men in the same occupation, then either they should be given a different weight, corresponding to their relative productivity, or the distributions of men and women should be examined separately. Similar arguments can be used to justify the exclusion of young people from a general distribution of employees, or, even further, of considering each age-group separately. There may similarly be a case for examining the distributions of particular occupations separately, as also the distributions within particular industries.

Detailed studies of this kind serve the purpose not only of making comparisons between countries of like with like but also of helping us to analyse the structure of earnings. As we shall see in Chapter 4, there are strong theoretical grounds for breaking up the over-all distribution into separate distributions by age, sex, occupation, and other characteristics, in order to understand its over-all shape.

2. Actual Differences in Definition

We have seen that arguments can be made for studying employment income distributions of various kinds. We now turn to consider the varieties of income distribution which are available in fact. There are a great many; and in order to keep the discussion in some order we shall develop a systematic scheme of classification.

There are two major ways in which definitions of employment income distributions may vary: first, according to the definition of income; and, secondly, according to the population covered by the distribution.

The Definition of Income

Under this heading we have four main classification criteria.

1. Sources of income included

So far as possible the income should relate to wage and salary income only. In practice, available statistics are not always in this form. Quite frequently we have to use data on the total income from all sources of wage and salary earners, these being usually defined as persons whose major source of income is from wage or salary. Such distributions are often prepared by taxation offices; only rarely do they make special tabulations on the wage and salary income variable itself. Distributions of persons by pure wage and salary income are, however, generated in some population censuses (e.g. United States, Canada), in some household surveys (e.g. United Kingdom, Hungary, Yugoslavia), in social-security and wage-tax statistics (e.g. France, Germany), and in special inquiries to enterprises.

In some cases, where no information on the income distribution of individual workers is available, the only alternative is to examine distributions of household income of households of which the head is a wage or salary earner. This is a last resort, to which we have been obliged to turn for information on some of the less-developed countries. Such statistics must obviously be used with exceptional caution.

2. Income before or after tax

In nearly all cases the statistics available are for income before tax. For reasons already mentioned, only very rough estimates of income after tax could be made, and these would usually take account only of direct taxation. In one country (Spain) the basic statistics of wages include family allowances, which are paid through the employer.

3. Income in kind and fringe benefits

Income in kind is sometimes included, at least in principle; but generally it is not included. Practically no information is available about the distribution of fringe benefits.

4. Period of measurement of income

Distributions are available for periods of time varying from an hour to a year. The year is the most common period; but wages are frequently measured for a week or an hour. In the latter case, the wage per hour is really an *average* rate per hour for some longer period, usually a week or a month. Average hourly earnings—or in some cases average daily earnings—can be computed either directly, by dividing total earnings for a longer period by the number of hours or days worked, or after eliminating (partly or wholly) the effect of overtime premiums. In the United States hourly earnings rates which exclude overtime premiums are known as 'straight time' hourly earnings.

The Population Covered

Under this heading there are seven further classification criteria.

1. Sex

Distributions may refer to males, females, or to both combined. Since, on the average, females are invariably paid less than males, it is very desirable to have separate distributions for the two sexes.

2. Age

Young people generally earn considerably less than adults; and even amongst adults there are consistent variations in mean income by age. Detailed distributions for a number of age-groups are available in a few countries, especially those in which income data are collected in the population censuses (United

States, Canada, Sweden, and New Zealand). In many other cases, however, only distributions of adults are given separately (and they may be differently defined in different countries).

3. *Occupation*

In many countries separate distributions are available for manual workers.[1] In some cases, distributions of salaried workers, or 'employees', can also be obtained; but, since salaried workers form a rather heterogeneous group, ranging from low-paid clerks and sales assistants to the highest-paid executives, little use has been made of such distributions. For the most part, only distributions of all employees (wage and salary earners) and of manual workers have been studied separately.

4. *Industry*

For some countries distributions can be broken down by industry in great detail. In others, only aggregates are available, or, at best, a few sub-groups. Under this heading many different combinations are possible; but for the most part we have concentrated on fairly broad aggregates, excluding where possible farm incomes, and sometimes personal services and other sectors.

5. *Area*

Here also there is scope for great variation in definition. On the whole, we have used data for whole countries; but, where regional differences are known to be important, and where suitable data are available, we have looked at distributions within regions or other defined areas.

6. *Full- or part-period working*

We can distinguish between full-period and full-time working. A part-time worker is one who *normally* works for less than the standard number of hours in the day or week. A part-period worker is one who has worked for less than the normal number

[1] It has been assumed below that the following descriptions are virtually equivalent: wage earners, manual workers, *arbeiter, ouvriers, obreros, arbete,* and 'physical' workers.

of days in the week, or of weeks in the year. A part-time worker may work for the full period if, for example, he normally works 30 h a week and has worked in every week in the year. But in the final analysis both categories (part-time and part-period) involve some reduction in hours worked compared with the 'normal'. If the distribution includes all categories of worker it will be more unequal than if it is confined to full-time workers only. Some distributions are available for workers who worked for only the normal number of hours, plus or minus a small margin. Others are given on an hourly earnings basis. Both these latter types are naturally less dispersed than more comprehensive distributions.

7. *Other limitations*

In some cases distributions are available only for taxpayers, or for persons assessed for tax. Such distributions may be truncated, or at least incomplete, in the lower income ranges. Some distributions, also, in multi-racial countries cover only one race, or exclude one or more races. Distributions of employees in Africa often distinguish between Africans and others, since the earnings of non-Africans are or have been at a much higher level. Distributions by race (or colour) are also much analysed in the United States.

3. Effects of Differences of Definition on the Degree of Dispersion

In order to make a systematic classification of employee distributions by type it was necessary to develop a code. Details of this code are given in Appendix 6. The code allows for four types of area, nine definitions of industry, two age classifications, three sex classifications, five occupations, three classes of source of income, three intensities of work (full or part-time, etc.), five income periods, and five special categories (taxpayers, race, etc.). It is obvious that, if every theoretically possible combination were to occur (even on this restricted classification), we should have many thousands of different definitions of income distribution.[1] This is perhaps enough to show that no single mathematical function is likely to fit all distributions, and that no simple theory is likely to be sufficient. But there are some common features of all distributions, and there are systematic differences between distributions of different types. In this section, therefore, we shall review the main types of distribution which occur in practice and consider the principal effects of the differences of definition on the shape of the distribution.

The Effect of Intensity of Work

We shall start by considering the most dramatic case: the difference between a distribution which covers *all* employees, or more specifically all persons who have received any wages or salaries at all during the period (say, a year), and a distribution confined to employees who have worked 'full-time' and for the 'full-period'. Both these latter terms, of course, need more precise definition. For example, in the British Ministry of Labour inquiry into wages in 1960 a full-time worker was one who normally worked for 30 h per week or more; and in the 1938 inquiry separate tabulations are available for men who worked 47–8 h. In the United States Census of 1960 separate distributions of wage and salary earnings are given for employees who worked 50–2 weeks in the year 1959. German wage-tax statistics distinguish between employees working for the 'full year' and others. The 'full-year working' employees are those who were employed in 11 months or more, but not necessarily full-time. In France, statistics have been published for 'permanent' employees, who are defined as those who were employed for the whole 12 months in the year, and full-time. (In recent years this definition has been amended to read those who were *paid* for the whole 12 months.) In Czechoslovakia the only available distribution is for employees who worked for at least 180 h in the month (or for at least 160 h in certain industries). In the Belgian distribution earnings for a quarter are divided by the number of days worked and multiplied by 25 to represent a monthly rate. In effect, this is a distribution of average daily earnings.

[1] In fact, nearly a quarter of a million.

In many other countries no such distinction between full-
period and part-period workers can be made, and it is clear that,
where this is so, the shape of the distribution will usually be very
different. The distribution of full-period earnings for a reasonably homogeneous group of employees, e.g. all males, or, better
still, male employees in a given industry or occupation, is always

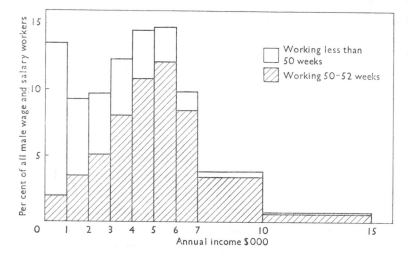

FIG. 3.1. United States, 1959: Frequency Distribution of Males with any
Wage or Salary Income in the Year, by Wage and Salary Income.
Source: US 5, Table 25.

hump-shaped, with a single mode. But the distribution of part-
period employees is highly positively skew, and in many cases
J-shaped. When the two groups are put together in a single
distribution the result may well be to produce a distribution
with two modes, or at any rate, one which has little shrinkage
in the lower tail. An example is given in Fig. 3.1. It shows
separately the distribution of wage and salary earnings of males
aged 14 and over who worked for 50–2 weeks in 1959, and the
effect of including those who worked for less than 50 weeks. This
is an extreme example, because any person who received $1 or
more of wage or salary in 1959 is, in principle, included. Other
United States distributions are confined to persons who were

'in the experienced labor force', which means those persons who had a job, or were looking for one, during the calendar week prior to the date when they filled in their census form. This group excludes people who had only casual earnings from odd jobs during the year and it has a much less pronounced secondary mode.

The census data for the United States and Canada are exceptional, in that it is possible to derive from them distributions which include everyone with annual earnings of as little as $1. Many of the distributions in other countries are by-products of tax assessments and these usually exclude people whose earnings are below a specified minimum. Although the effect is not to exclude all part-time or part-period workers, those with the lowest incomes are eliminated. Hence such distributions are generally not bimodal; but they often have a very thick lower tail, which is more like a gently sloping plateau than a normal or lognormal tail.

Males and Females

Only slightly less important than the intensity of work is the difference between the sexes. It seems to be almost a universal law that, on the average, women receive only between half and two-thirds of the pay of men. So distributions which cover both sexes are generally less symmetrical and more leptokurtic (with fat or elongated tails) than those for each sex separately. An illustration is given in Fig. 3.2 with data which are drawn again from the United States. In this figure only employees in the experienced labour force who worked 50–2 weeks in 1959 are represented, and farm workers and those whose occupation was not reported have been omitted. It will be seen that the male distribution has a fairly 'well-behaved' lower tail, but the addition of the females thickens out this tail considerably. The females make relatively little difference to the upper tail.

Of course, if we had included part-period workers in the distribution the lower tail would have disappeared completely, being replaced by a high mode in the under $1,000 class, consisting largely of femlaes.

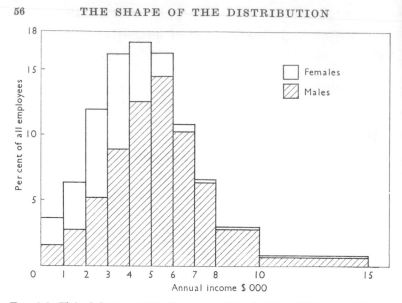

FIG. 3.2. United States, 1959: Frequency Distribution of Wage and Salary
Workers in the Experienced Civilian Labour Force who worked 50–2 weeks
in the year, by Wage and Salary Income.

Source: US 3, Table 28. Excludes farm workers and those with occupation
not stated.

Mixtures of Occupations

Occupation distributions vary in both their means and variances. Unskilled workers have a low mean and a low variance;
and both these parameters tend to increase as the level of skill
or responsibility increases. Consequently, a distribution which
includes all occupations will be more dispersed and more skew
than one which is confined to a single occupational group.
Fig. 3.3 shows the effect of dividing the total distribution of
United States male full-period workers into three broad occupational groups. It so happens, in this example, that the mode for
the 'white collar' group is in the same class as for the skilled and
semi-skilled 'blue collar' group ($5,000–6,000), so that this is
also the modal class of the whole distribution. If we had shown
the professional, technical, and managerial group separately, its
mode would fall in the $6,000–7,000 class; while the mode of the
household and service sub-group is in the $3,000–4,000 class.

It is obvious from Fig. 3.3 that most of the upper tail comes from the white-collar group, and much of the lower tail from the household, service, and unskilled group. As we shall see in Chapter 4, the leptokurtic character of the over-all distribution

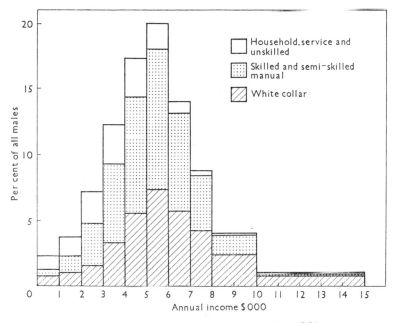

FIG. 3.3. United States, 1959: Frequency Distribution of Male Wage and Salary Workers in the Experienced Civilian Labour Force who Worked 50–2 Weeks in the Year, by Wage and Salary Income.

Source: US 3, Table 28. Excludes farm workers and those with occupation not stated.

of income can be partly explained by the mixing of different occupations (and other categories) with different internal variances.

Effect of Age

The inclusion of young people in a distribution increases the numbers in the lower income groups and produces greater dispersion of the over-all distribution. In most occupations mean income tends to increase with age up to a maximum in the 30s or 40s and then to decline again. The variance of income also tends to increase with age, at least during the first half of working life. Hence aggregate distributions tend to be more dispersed and more leptokurtic than distributions for specific age-groups. This is a point of importance in explaining the over-all distribution of income; and we shall return to it in Chapter 4.

Area and Industry

Whenever the means or variances of distributions are different for different areas or industries, aggregate distributions will be more dispersed and also more leptokurtic than distributions for the individual areas or industries. In practice, these influences are not usually very great, except in the case of distributions which include farming. In agriculture, and hence in country areas, mean employment income is often much lower than elsewhere, partly because income in kind is not usually included in measured income.

Components of Income

Pure wage and salary income is generally less dispersed than the total income of wage and salary earners from all sources. It is not possible, however, to make any clear prediction about the likely dispersion of household income (from all sources) of households headed by wage and salary earners compared with the other two types of income. Inclusion of fringe benefits would probably increase dispersion; but little is known about this. Income before direct taxation is usually more dispersed than income after direct taxes (except in the communist countries, where income taxes are often proportionate). If social-security contributions are also subtracted, however, the effect may be to increase dispersion in some parts of the distribution—at least in cases where such contributions are a fixed amount per head. Income after all taxes, transfers, benefits, and costs—i.e. 'real' income—may be quite differently distributed from pre-tax money earnings; but it seems reasonable to assume that, except where large differential effects are known to operate, the distribution of pre-tax money earnings would be at least a rough guide to the relative distribution of real earnings.

Period of Measurement

If distributions were available for the *same* group of people, in which their earnings were measured for various periods of time, e.g. for a month and a year, it could be expected that the annual distribution would be less dispersed than the monthly one. This result, which Friedman has especially emphasized,[1] arises because in any period of time there are chance fluctuations of income ('transitory' income) which tend to increase the dispersion of measured income compared with its underlying trend ('permanent' income). Over longer periods, Friedman assumes, the transitory component tends to cancel out, so that it contributes less to the dispersion of measured income than in shorter periods. There is some evidence to support this hypothesis.[2]

In practice, however, distributions of employment income for different time periods are almost invariably for *different* groups of people, even though they may have the same title. For example, a distribution of employees on a monthly basis will usually exclude people who were not employed at all during the month, while an annual distribution of the same *type* of employees will include people who worked for only a few months in the year. While the transitory component will be smaller for the longer period, the wider coverage of the annual distribution will bring in more low incomes, so that the dispersion of income, as measured by some coefficients at least, may not be any smaller. Moreover, since the transitory component is probably not very large amongst the higher salaried employees, the dispersion of the upper tail of an annual distribution is likely to be very similar to that of a monthly distribution.

The variation in the time period of measurement in different distributions is a nuisance, especially since it is uncertain what effect it has on the measurement of dispersion. In making international comparisons we are at present obliged to assume that variations in the time period of measurement are not very important, and—which is not quite the same thing—that the

---

[1] See Friedman (1957) and Friedman and Kuznets (1945).

[2] See, apart from the two previously cited works, Hanna, Pechman, and Lerner (1948), Kravis (1962), and Soltow (1965).

transitory component of measured income is roughly the same in different countries.

Special Definitions

Distributions which are confined to taxpayers omit some of the lower incomes and hence are less dispersed than distributions of all employees. Sometimes they are truncated. Distributions for one race in multi-racial societies are usually less dispersed than for all members of the society, at least where racial differences are important, as they generally are when such distributions are published separately.

4. A Standard Distribution

Amidst all this variety of different distributions it is convenient to choose one Standard Distribution, which can be made a point of reference. This distribution should, if possible, be relevant to our aims and should occur fairly often in practice. After careful consideration, I have chosen for my Standard Distribution the following combination of characteristics:

Male adults, in all occupations, in all industries except farming, in all areas, working full-time and for the full period. The income measured should be money wages and salaries only, and before tax.

This choice can be criticized on a number of grounds. It can be argued that males and females are all members of the same work force and should both be included in any study of the over-all structure of earnings. Against that, it can be said that men and women seem to a large extent in most countries to be non-competing groups. In any case, whenever possible, we shall examine both types of distribution to see whether they tell the same story.

It can also be argued that aggregates of industries and areas are misleading—because of market imperfections—and that the analysis should be made on an industry-by-industry basis, and for fairly narrowly defined areas. There is something in this argument, and to some extent the point will be met in our detailed comparions between countries in Chapter 5. But to meet the point completely would require an enormous expansion of this study. For the time being, we must see what can be learned from broader comparisons, the basis for which is the assumption that differences between countries are large enough to be revealed even when the countries vary in their industrial composition and regional homogeneity.

The biggest weakness in our standard definition perhaps is that it is based on income before taxes and benefits. This is an unfortunate practical necessity and it is difficult to see at present any way of getting round this problem satisfactorily.

The Shape of the Standard Distribution

The Standard Distribution serves a twofold purpose. On the one hand, it is the type of distribution on which our international comparisons will *primarily* be made. In addition, the Standard Distribution is the distribution which we shall principally be trying to explain. It is clear that we cannot hope to find a simple hypothesis to explain all varieties of income distribution; but it may be possible to build a theory to explain one predominant type of distribution. The other distributions may then be seen as variants of this central type, for which special explanations may need to be put forward.

What then is the typical shape of our Standard Distribution? It will be instructive to consider some examples; and three are considered below, which are drawn from the United States, France, and Hungary. None of the three distributions exactly corresponds with the definition; but they are close enough to it to give us some guidance about the answer to our problem. Fig. 3.4 is a frequency distribution of males, aged 14 and over, who were recorded in the 1960 Census as whites living in the central cities of urbanized areas of the United States, and who worked for 50–2 weeks in 1959. The distribution is for reported wages and salaries only, and it includes all persons who reported $1 or more of wage or salary, irrespective of whether they were classified as wage or salary workers at the date of the census. In order to display the shape of the distribution as clearly as

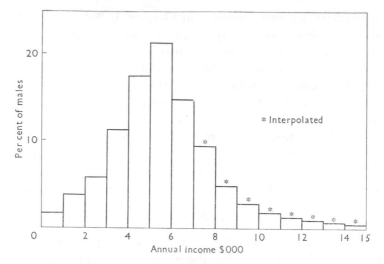

FIG. 3.4. United States, 1959: Frequency Distribution of White Male Wage and Salary Workers aged 14 and over, Living in Central Cities of Urbanized Areas, who Worked 50–2 Weeks in the Year, by Wage and Salary Income.

Source: US 5, Table 25.

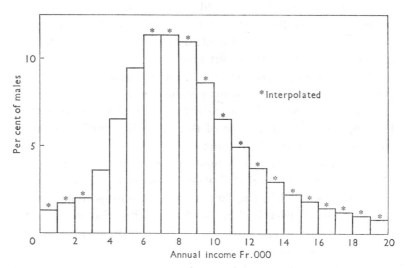

FIG. 3.5. France, 1963: Frequency Distribution of Full-Time Male Employees in the Private and Semi-Public Sectors, by Wage and Salary Income.

Source: FR 11, 56.

possible, estimates have been made of the division of the classes $7,000–9,999 and $10,000–14,999 by $1,000 intervals. These interpolations can be made fairly reliably by graphing the cumulative distributions on logarithmic paper. It will be seen that the distribution is hump-shaped and positively skew. The left-hand tail is truncated and the right-hand tail, which is not

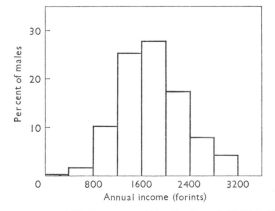

Fɪɢ. 3.6. Hungary, 1962: Frequency Distribution of All Male Employees by Wage and Salary Income.
Source: HU 1, 29.

shown beyond $15,000, presumably extends for a considerable distance, e.g. up to $100,000 or more.

The next example, in Fig. 3.5, is for France in 1963. This shows wages and salaries of male full-time employees in the private and semi-public sectors, excluding agriculture. The earnings of employees who were paid for less than a full year have been adjusted to an annual basis, so that the distribution is virtually equivalent to a distribution of full-year employees. Young people and apprentices are included. This distribution is very similar to the United States distribution in general appearance. It is, in fact, more widely dispersed than the American one, but the dispersion is exaggerated by the particular scale used in the figure.

Thirdly, in Fig. 3.6 we have a frequency distribution for Hungary in 1962. This refers to wages and salaries of male employees of all ages in the whole country. Most workers in agriculture are collective farmers and hence are excluded; but the distribution does contain some farm employees—presumably working on state farms. The distribution is not specifically limited to full-time or full-year employees, but it seems likely that nearly all Hungarian male employees are of this type.

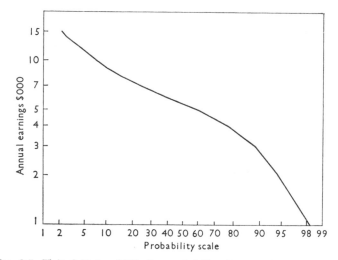

FIG. 3.7. United States, 1959: Logprobability Curve of Data in Fig. 3.4.

The distribution appears to be more symmetrical than the other two distributions, although it is clearly positively skew and probably has a fairly long tail to the right (about which we have no information).

It is obvious that none of these three distributions could be represented accurately by a normal curve. But, superficially at least, they might be represented by a lognormal curve. In order to test this hypothesis more rigorously, the cumulated distributions have been plotted on logarithmic probability paper; and the results are shown in Figs. 3.7, 3.8, and 3.9. If the distributions were exactly lognormal the line through the points on each diagram would be straight, its slope representing the standard deviation of the distribution of the logarithms. It will be seen that all three lines have a characteristic S-shape, although the

Hungarian line exhibits this tendency to a smaller extent than the lines for the United States and France. The meaning of this particular shape, with the lines bending away from the income

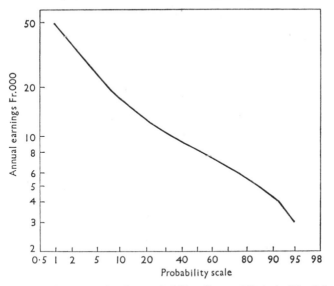

FIG. 3.8. France 1963: Logprobability Curve of Data in Fig. 3.5.

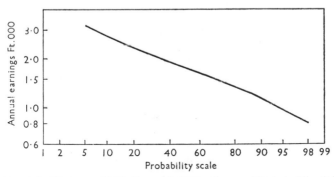

FIG. 3.9. Hungary, 1962: Logprobability Curve of Data in Fig. 3.6.

axis at each end, is that the numbers of earners in the tails of the distribution are in excess of the numbers which would occur if the distributions were exactly lognormal. In other words, the distributions are *leptokurtic* in the logarithm of income, with too high a peak around the mode and too many cases in the tails in comparison with a lognormal distribution. This is a characteristic feature of many income distributions, and it appears to be generally true of all distributions approximating to our Standard Distribution.[1]

Of course, a distribution with a Pareto tail would have an excess of frequencies in its upper tail in comparison with a lognormal distribution, since a Pareto tail is 'longer'—or dies away more slowly—than a lognormal tail. It is relevant to ask, therefore, whether our Standard Distribution tends to have a Pareto upper tail. A convenient way of answering this question is to plot the cumulated frequency distributions on double-logarithmic paper. Fig. 3.10 shows how our three distributions behave in this respect. So far as can be judged from the limited number of income classes in the upper tails of these distributions the French distribution is a good Pareto fit for the top 35 per cent of earners, the United States distribution is a fairly good fit for the top 25 per cent of earners, but the Hungarian distribution is concave towards the origin throughout its length. Tests of many other distributions suggest that the Pareto function generally provides a good fit for approximately the top 20 per cent of earners, at least in non-communist countries.

Conclusion

From the evidence of these three distributions, and from many others which have been studied but which cannot be presented here, it seems safe to conclude that our Standard Distribution has the following characteristics:

1. It is hump-shaped, and, if the distribution is strictly confined to adult males working full-time and throughout the measured period, the left-hand tail is asymptotic to the income axis. If the left-hand tail meets the vertical axis at a positive frequency, this suggests that the distribution contains some young people or part-time workers; or there may be some pure errors of measurement.

2. The central part of the distribution, from perhaps the tenth

---

[1] As we have seen, Rutherford (1955) noted this feature of income distributions and built his model around it.

to the eightieth percentile from the top, is close to lognormal. But the tails of the distribution contain an excess of frequencies in comparison with the lognormal.

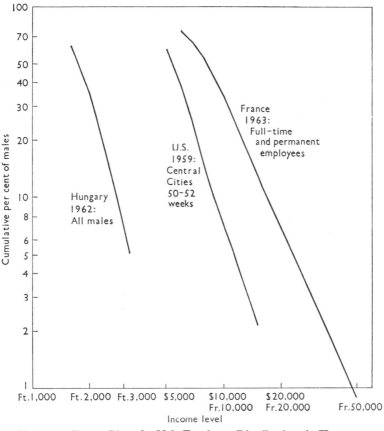

FIG. 3.10. Pareto Lines for Male Employee Distributions in Hungary, United States, and France.

Source: Same data as in Figs. 3.4, 3.5, and 3.6.

3. The upper tail often approximately follows the Pareto law, for at least the top 20 per cent of the aggregate frequency.

In the next chapter we shall address ourselves to the problem of explaining the Standard Distribution. After we have developed a theory to explain this distribution, it will be relatively easy to explain the other distributions.

4

PROPOSALS FOR A NEW THEORY

THE task before us is to account for the shape of the Standard Distribution, which is approximately lognormal, but with an excess of frequencies in the tails, the upper tail usually following the Pareto law. To begin with, we shall set aside purely stochastic process theories and attempt to explain the distribution with the help of economic and social factors alone.[1] At a later stage, we shall make some allowance for stochastic processes, but within fairly narrow limits.

Perhaps we can start our inquiry by posing the following question: Why is it that human beings, all of one species and starting at birth with fairly equal endowments, should develop by middle age a dispersion of earnings with a proportionate range as wide as fifty or even a hundred to one ? Let us substantiate the assumptions that lie behind this question. It is not asserted that all men are born equal, although this opinion has been held in the past and may even still be held.[2] We cannot measure differences in ability at birth ; but tests of ability made later yield coefficients of variation of the order of 15 per cent. To some extent, as we shall see, the coefficient of variation of ability is an artefact of the method of measurement, although this is not true of tests which have a natural scale of measurement, such as memory for digits, or the number of capital A's crossed out on a page. By the time children are able to be tested at all seriously for 'ability' they are 4 or 5 years old, and a certain (but unknown) proportion of the variation in their ability is

---

[1] Each of these factors, however, will itself be a random variable, as is inevitable in dealing with human populations, so that stochastic *effects* will still be present, even though stochastic *processes*, in the dynamic sense, will not.

[2] Descartes wrote at the beginning of his *Discourse on Method* that 'the power of judging aright and of distinguishing truth from error, which is properly what is called good sense or reason, is by nature equal in all men'.

attributable to environmental influences. Yet by middle age the earnings of wage and salary earners alone (apart from the self-employed or employers) have spread out to such an extent that the coefficient of variation, for men employed full-time, may easily be 50 per cent or more, and the range may run—in the United States, for example—from $4,000 to $200,000 or even more, and to a corresponding degree in many other countries. It may be suggested that much of this ultimate dispersion is the result of inheritance of property, or the 'pull' of family influence, which give opportunities of earning very high salaries in private business; but even if we concentrate on people of the same class background, or if we consider the situation in the communist countries, where inheritance of property has been largely abolished, we still find very wide variations in adult employee earnings.

1. Causes of Variation in Human Capacities

Over the first forty or fifty years of life, then, there is an enormous dispersion in the apparent capacities of human beings, especially in their economic capacities. This growth in dispersion can be divided into three phases: first, there is the growth and spreading out of general abilities from birth until the end of elementary education. During this period there is little differentiation between children on a vocational basis. With the commencement of secondary education, however, there is usually the beginnings of such differentiation, with separate schools for children of the more academic type and others for those wishing to obtain technical qualifications. Further specialization on the development of *occupational abilities* occurs both before and after the end of secondary education. Many children —in most countries—leave school fairly early and receive little or no further training for a specific occupation. Others continue through college, or university, and may require several years of postgraduate specialization before they are ready to enter the work force. This whole phase, running from the completion of elementary education to the time of fully entering the work

force, can be thought of as the phase of occupational specialization. This phase should be thought of as including any period
of on-the-job training, when there has been partial but not
complete entry to the work force.

At the end of the phase of occupational specialization the
original group of children will have been split up into hundreds
of different occupational sub-groups, each of which is more or
less non-competing with the others. It is a process analogous to
the manufacture of types of machinery. At first all is raw steel,
but at the end we have more or less specialized machines. By
this time it is no longer possible to talk about an over-all 'distribution of ability', since we have many different types of ability,
each of which sells in its own market. At best we can study the
distribution of ability within an occupation, since the distribution *between* occupations is not a distribution of a single ability
variable. Nevertheless, we can study the distribution of average
occupational earnings, and suggest reasons for this distribution
taking the shape it does.

Earnings commence at the end of phase two (the extent of
which for many children may be very short or negligible), and
the distribution of full-time earnings can be analysed into two
components. The first is the distribution of mean earnings
between occupations; and the second is the distribution of
individual earnings within occupations. We shall examine each
of these aspects separately below.

But variability of capacity does not cease at the age of entry
to the work force. Abundant evidence shows that human
capacities vary with age, typically increasing up to some point
in the 30s to 40s (depending on occupation, education, and basic
ability level) and then declining. During this 'ageing' process
there are not only changes in mean earning capacities but also,
at least in some occupations, a tendency towards wider dispersion. The combined effect of differential rates of change in mean
earnings by age in different occupations, and of changes in the
degree of dispersion within occupations, is to produce the maximum absolute dispersion of earnings for the whole population
of employees in late middle age. Relative dispersion, however,

in some occupations seems to continue to grow up to the age of retirement.

Thus, when we study the dispersion of earnings for all full-time male employees (the Standard Distribution) we can distinguish the effects of: (1) variation in mean earning levels of occupations, (2) variation in initial abilities of individuals within occupations, and (3) variation of individual abilities with age within occupations. We shall see that the stochastic combination of these sources of variation is sufficient to account for the existence of a leptokurtic lognormal distribution of earnings. But it is not sufficient to account for the Pareto distribution of the upper tail. For this we must turn to a different source of variation, not in the supply of abilities as such but in the need for men to take responsible managerial positions in organizations. We shall explain how this happens in detail below. We now proceed to consider each of the sources of variation of ability, starting with the variation of general ability.

2. Variations in General Ability

We are concerned in this section to explain the variation in general ability at the end of elementary schooling, that is, at the point up to which children have been subject to non-vocational education. The influences at work in the first few years of life are the following: (1) genetic inheritance, (2) home and social environment, and (3) schooling. Let us consider them in turn.

Genetic Inheritance

Psychologists divide genetic inheritance, apart from purely physical characteristics (which, of course, can also affect ability in the economic sphere), into 'general ability'—or 'intelligence' —and other personality traits, such as emotional stability, ambition, aggressiveness, willpower, and the like. In attempting to measure 'general ability' the main concentration has been on the construction of intelligence tests. There has been much controversy over the concept of 'intelligence' but it is now generally accepted that there is some general quality of mind, which can be defined, following Burt (1955), as 'an innate, general, cognitive ability'. It is believed that this general ability is of dominant importance in most problem-solving, memorizing, calculating, linguistic, and other 'intellectual' activities, and that it can be measured, at least approximately, by applying a battery of tests of various types. Although there may be disputes about the appropriateness of particular tests, and about the predictive value of measures of intelligence, there is general agreement that intelligence tests are measuring something significant. What is not yet resolved, however, is the great debate on how much of measured intelligence is genetically determined and how much is determined by environment.

The issue of 'nature versus nurture' is too large and too difficult for us to consider it at length, but we are obliged to devote some attention to it, at least briefly, because of its relevance to the question whether intelligence is distributed symmetrically or not. Unfortunately, as we shall see, intelligence cannot—for the most part—be measured on an objective scale: the scale itself is an artefact of the psychologist, and hence the shape of the distribution of intelligence, as given, is largely arbitrary. So we need to examine how measured intelligence itself arises and what sort of distribution we should expect to obtain.

Modern psychologists argue that intelligence contains a substantial genetic component, and that this component is multifactorially determined. That is, intelligence is not a quality like eye colour, which can be attributed to a single pair of genes, but is the outcome of the interaction of a large number of genes. The essential point is that intelligence is a continuous variable, and this suggests that it is the result of stochastic combinations of genes, each of which has an effect which is small and cumulative. If these effects are additive, then the expected distribution of intelligence, according to the Central Limit Theorem, will be normal.[1]

There is not much empirical content to this theory and most of it seems to be based on argument by analogy. Attention is usually drawn to the fact that physical measures, such as height,

[1] See Burt (1955, pp. 169–71).

are found to be approximately normal. But it is also known
that other characteristics, such as weight, are not normally
distributed. In theoretical terms, the outcome will depend on
whether the cumulative small effects from many factors are
additive or multiplicative. If they are additive, the distribution
of their sum will be asymptotically normal, while if they are
multiplicative they will be asymptotically lognormal.[1] There is
no *a priori* reason for rejecting the latter hypothesis in favour
of the former.

Let us, however, accept, for the sake of argument, the pre-
sumption that genetic intelligence is normally distributed. The
next question that arises is the influence of environment on
measured intelligence. How important is this influence, and
how does it combine with the genetic component?

Genetic Ability and Environment

Because intelligence cannot be tested satisfactorily until a child
is 4 or 5 years old, it is impossible to measure the genetic component directly. Measured intelligence always contains some
element of environmental influence. But something can be
learned from a study of the measured intelligence of identical
twins reared together and apart, and of unrelated children
reared together. Burt (1955) has summarized the results of two
such studies in a table which is reproduced here as Table 4.1.
It will be seen that the measured intelligence of identical twins
reared together is highly correlated, although not quite so highly
as some physical characteristics. There may be slight differences
of environment which account for this, but most of the difference
between this correlation coefficient and unity may be attributed
to measurement error. The correlation of characteristics of unrelated children reared together tells us something directly about
the effects of environment. If the children placed in a foster home
were selected at random from the whole population, we should
expect a zero correlation for all genetic factors; and this seems
to be broadly true of measured physical characteristics, such as
eye colour, which are independent of environment. Hence, on

[1] See Appendix 2 for a further discussion of this point.

TABLE 4.1

Correlations between Tests of Mental, Scholastic, and Physical Measurements

Measurement	A. Burt and Conway						B. Newman, Freeman, and Holzinger		
	Identical twins reared together	Identical twins reared apart	Non-identical twins reared together	Siblings reared together	Siblings reared apart	Un-related children reared together	Identical twins reared together	Identical twins reared apart	Non-identical twins reared together
Mental									
Intelligence:									
Group test	0·944	0·771	0·542	0·515	0·441	0·281	0·922	0·727	0·621
Individual test	0·921	0·843	0·526	0·491	0·463	0·252	0·910	0·670	0·640
Final assessment	0·925	0·876	0·551	0·538	0·517	0·269	—	—	—
Scholastic									
General attainments	0·898	0·681	0·831	0·814	0·526	0·535	0·955	0·507	0·883
Reading and spelling	0·944	0·647	0·915	0·853	0·490	0·548	—	—	—
Arithmetic	0·862	0·723	0·748	0·769	0·563	0·476	—	—	—
Physical									
Height	0·957	0·951	0·472	0·503	0·536	0·069	0·981	0·969	0·930
Weight	0·932	0·897	0·586	0·568	0·427	0·243	0·973	0·886	0·900
Head length	0·963	0·959	0·495	0·481	0·536	0·116	0·910	0·917	0·691
Head breadth	0·978	0·962	0·541	0·507	0·472	0·082	0·908	0·880	0·654
Eye colour	1·000	1·000	0·516	0·553	0·504	0·104	—	—	—

Source: Burt (1955, p. 168).

the assumption of random selection, any substantial correlation of measured intelligence of unrelated children reared together suggests that environment has an influence on measured intelligence. Burt and Conway's estimate of 0·269 for this correlation is based on 287 foster children and is clearly significant.

Some calculations, made in detail in Appendix 3, suggest, on the basis of these figures, that, of the total variance of measured intelligence, about 5 per cent may be attributable to measurement error, 20–30 per cent to environment and to the interaction between environment and genetic ability, and the remaining 65–75 per cent to genetic inheritance. These figures are very rough, and they are based on a very simple assumption about the interrelations between heredity and environment. But they are not completely out of line with Burt's somewhat sweeping conclusion (1955, p. 175) that 'in all at least 75 per cent of the entire variance must be due to genetic influences, probably far more'.[1] The important point, for our purposes, is that measured intelligence is partly determined by environment. It can also be seen from the table that scholastic attainment is heavily influenced by environment; but we shall return to this later.

The Distribution of Measured Intelligence

Now, if genetic ability is normally distributed, but measured intelligence is only partly genetically determined, what shape can we expect for the distribution of measured intelligence? The answer depends on the shape of the distribution of the environmental factor, and on the correlation between heredity and environment. There is every reason to think that environmental influences reflect the socio-economic class of the parents, and, as things stand in most countries, this distribution is highly skew. In addition, we know that there is a positive correlation between measured intelligence of children and social class of parents. Some figures illustrating this correlation are given in Table 4.2.[2] Burt (1943, p. 84) found a correlation between

[1] See also Bloom (1964, p. 71) for a summary of a number of estimates of the proportion of the variance of I.Q. attributable to heredity, ranging from 60 to 88 per cent.
[2] See Conway (1959) for similar data for Britain.

TABLE 4.2

*United States, Estimated Average I.Q.s of Children
for Different Occupations of Parents*

Occupation group	Terman-Merrill Study	Duff and Thompson Study
1. Professional	116	115
2. Semi-professional, managerial	112	113
3. Clerical, skilled trades, retail	107	106
4. Rural owners, farmers	95	97
5. Semi-skilled, minor clerical	105	102
6. Slightly skilled	98	97
7. Day labourers	96	95

Source: Tyler (1965, p. 341).

children's intelligence and economic status of 0·32, and Fleming (1943, p. 82) found 0·3. Others have found similar results. Since we have reason to believe that most of measured intelligence is genetically determined, it is unlikely that all of this correlation is the reflection of environmental influence.[1] If, then, measured intelligence is some function of genetic ability and environment, of which the former is normally distributed and the latter is positively skew, and the two factors are positively correlated, then we have reason to expect that measured intelligence will be somewhat skew and possibly leptokurtic.

The fact that distributions of measured intelligence are generally approximately normal is no refutation of this hypothesis.[2] The most common method of measuring intelligence is by means of the 'Intelligence Quotient' or I.Q. The assumption on which such tests are constructed is that there exist some crucial types of problem which are only just soluble by most

[1] Some writers have tended to suggest this (see Floud and Halsey, 1958), but it is doubtful whether they would maintain it rigidly. Tyler (1965, p. 70) quotes conclusions from researches in California, reported by Bayley, which showed that a child from a well-educated family is more likely to increase than to decrease in I.Q. as time passes. But this does not imply, of course, that all of I.Q. is environmentally determined.

[2] Burt claims that even the existing distributions are slightly leptokurtic (1961, p. 10).

children of a given age. In other words, the level of difficulty of a test is determined by the existing distribution of ability amongst children of a given age. The results of tests given to a particular child are used to identify him with a particular 'mental age', i.e. the age at which a representative group of children could solve the problems which he was able to solve. His I.Q. is then defined as his mental age expressed as a percentage of his chronological age.

The distribution of I.Q.s is generally approximately normal. But this result depends on a crucial assumption implicit in the process of computing an I.Q. The assumption is that 'intelligence' is a linear function of mental age. Thus, if a child of 10 scores a mental age of 8 its I.Q. is 80, and this is assumed to be *as far below the mean* as the I.Q. of another child with a mental age of 12 is above the mean. But suppose, as seems quite possible, that, at least over a substantial part of childhood, intelligence grows exponentially with mental age. If this were so, a normal distribution of mental ages for a given age-group would imply a lognormal distribution of intelligence.[1]

In point of fact, therefore, the shape of the distribution of intelligence is largely conventional. Tyler (1965, p. 27) writes in this connection:

It is quite possible to change a skewed distribution into a normal one simply by making the test on which it is based a little harder or a little easier, depending on the direction of the skewness. A test that produces a skewed distribution when given to a representative group of ten-year-olds may give a normal distribution for twelve-year-olds. A test that gives a skewed distribution on a population of college students may give a normal distribution for new recruits at an induction center. We know now that test scores can be manipulated to give us any sort of distribution that we want. Because there are definite mathematical advantages to be obtained from normal

---

[1] Let m = mental age, c = chronological age, and q = I.Q. = m/c. It is given that q is normally distributed. Let x = 'true' intelligence. Now the usual assumption is that $x = am$ ($a > 0$), so that, for a given value of c, x is also normally distributed. But if, for example, $x = ke^{rm}$ ($k > 0$, $r > 0$), then

$$\ln x = \ln k + rcq$$

and it follows that x is lognormally distributed.

distributions, one of the aims of present-day test-builders is the construction of tests that will *give* normal distributions for the types of population in which they are to be used.

Hence 'it is impossible to determine whether or not mental traits are actually distributed normally in the population'.[1]

We must, therefore, conclude that the distribution of intelligence, if it could be measured, might easily be skew (positively or negatively, but more probably the former). Certainly, there are examples of performance tests, which seem quite reasonable

TABLE 4.3

Scores of 186 Students on Gottschaldt Test B

Score (number of designs per minute)	Number of students
0·4–0·7	5
0·8–1·1	6
1·2–1·5	14
1·6–1·9	24
2·0–2·3	33
2·4–2·7	28
2·8–3·1	16
3·2–3·5	21
3·6–3·9	14
4·0–4·3	5
4·4–4·7	7
4·8–5·1	7
5·2–5·5	2
5·6–5·9	1
6·0 and over	3
Total	186

Source: Tyler (1965, p. 217), derived from a study by Thurstone.

tests of general ability and which yield skew distributions. An example is given in Table 4.3. This shows the results of a perceptual test (the Gottschaldt Test B) on 186 students. The test

[1] McNemar (1942, p. 15) wrote: 'It is our contention . . . that nothing can be inferred from the distribution of measured psychological traits with regard to the shape of the distribution which would result if we ever found a psychometric of truly equal units.'

'requires the subject to locate in a complex configuration a simple figure that he has been shown' (Tyler, 1965, p. 217). In this particular test the number of designs marked by the students was divided by the number of minutes taken, so that both perceptual ability and speed are involved. It is clear from inspection of the table that the distribution is skew; and a graphic test (on logarithmic probability paper) suggests that it is close to lognormal above the tenth percentile (from the bottom). Perhaps it can be argued that the explicit introduction of time in this test, with the conversion of the scores into rates per minute, is partly or wholly responsible for the skewness. This may be so; but time is of the essence in economic performance, and we cannot properly exclude it from any rational test of ability.

Up to this point we have been concerned, in principle, with the development of intelligence under the influence of genetic inheritance and home (and social) environment. In addition, we must take into account the influence of schooling on measured intelligence, on which there is a good deal of evidence. In one of the earliest studies, Gordon (1923) found that amongst families of canal-boat children, who received little or no schooling, the level of I.Q. fell off with age, the youngest member of a family having the highest I.Q. and the oldest the lowest. De Groot (1951) quotes the results of measurements of intelligence of applicants aged 13–14 to Philips Industrial Training School at Eindhoven in the Netherlands, which showed that average I.Q. fell from about 100 in pre-war years to 98 in 1944 and 95–6 in 1945–7. In 1948 it rose again to 98 and in 1949–50 it was back to 100. He attributes this temporary fall in average I.Q. to the deterioration of school conditions in Eindhoven during the German occupation of 1941–4. Tuddenham (1948) compared the results of Army Alpha tests on 768 enlisted men, representative of all white enlisted soldiers in the Second World War, with results of the same test in the First World War. The median score was 104, compared with a median of only 62 in the First World War. He suggests that this very great increase in average intelligence may be attributed to a small extent to the effects of greater practice in taking intelligence tests,[1] but that a large proportion is 'a consequence of more and better education for more people' (p. 56).

Husén (1951) compared the I.Q. scores of 722 young men in Malmö in 1938 and 1948, and found that those who had completed only seven years of primary school were 1·2 points below the over-all average, whilst the average scores of those with longer periods at school increased with the number of years of schooling. His conclusion was that 'schooling up to the stage of junior secondary school with leaving certificate, or higher, raises the I.Q. by 5–7 units' (p. 87). Lee (1951) used tests of Negroes in Philadelphia schools to compare the average performance of those born in Philadelphia with the performance of those who had migrated from the South. The results showed that the Southern-born Negroes, who started at a lower level, improved their average performance as the period of schooling increased. By the ninth grade the average of the two groups was almost identical (p. 231). His results do not show that the average I.Q. of all children increases with the length of schooling, but rather that those who suffer from some initial handicap can be brought up to the general level by suitable education. Tyler (1965, p. 473), after reviewing the evidence, concludes that 'there is abundant evidence that improved education leads to higher intelligence.'[2]

Since the distribution of education in many poorer countries is highly skew, with large numbers not attending school at all, or dropping out after one or two years, it would be natural to expect that the distribution of measured intelligence of a representative sample of the population aged, say, 13 in these countries would also be skewed, with a larger group below the mean than above it. And even in some of the more advanced countries

---

[1] But see some results quoted by Anastasi (1958, p. 196), which show substantial increases in average score in successive trials on tests given to college students.

[2] Cf. Burt's comment (1958, p. 9) that 'the cultural amenities of the home and the educational opportunities provided by the school can undoubtedly affect a child's performance in intelligence tests of the ordinary type, since so often they demand an acquired facility with abstract and verbal modes of expression'.

there are small groups of children who fail to complete elementary education, especially in the agricultural districts, and these will tend to swell the number of adults with lower than average I.Q.

The Distribution of School Achievement

While poor or inadequate schooling may depress measured intelligence, the positive effects of schooling are clearly predominant in affecting the level of scholastic attainment, or achievement. It is obvious that 'better' schools help children to reach higher levels of scholastic attainment than 'worse' schools. For example, schools with smaller classes, with better-qualified and more inspired teachers, and in which the average I.Q. of the children is higher to start with, will achieve better scholastic results than those in which the opposite situations exist. This is part of the explanation for the efforts made by middle-class people to get their children into private schools in England, or to live in good school neighbourhoods in America.

But it is during school years that the influence of home environment becomes particularly important. A remarkable study by Fraser (1959) amongst children in Aberdeen revealed that, while home environment and I.Q. are positively correlated, the correlation between home environment and scholastic achievement is even greater (p. 71). Similar conclusions can be drawn from the various studies of unrelated children reared together, such as those by Burt and Conway, summarized in Table 4.1 above. Fraser made separate correlations of ten aspects of home environment with I.Q. and achievement and found that three of these 'stand out as being mainly responsible for the higher correlation with school progress. These are in order: Abnormal background, income, parents' attitudes to the education and future occupation of the child' (p. 71). Her conclusion is: 'There would appear to be a common thread linking (these three items) together: a normal home background, emotional stability, freedom from tension and from economic insecurity, and consistent encouragement from parents are

G

necessary for a child if his school work is to reach the level allowed by his intelligence' (p. 72).

Kemp (1955) made a study of fifty junior mixed schools in London, and intercorrelated sixteen variables representing assessments of the school characteristics. He commented on his results as follows:

When schools are considered as units, rather than individual children, it is still found that the greatest single factor determining level of attainment is intelligence. More than half the variance in attainment in reading, problem arithmetic and general information is accounted for by this factor. However, it must be noted that socio-economic status is correlated very significantly with both intelligence (0·52) and this kind of attainment (0·56). When the former is partialled out the correlation drops to 0·62 [from 0·73]. If intelligence is held constant, the correlation between socio-economic status and attainment drops to 0·30 [p. 72].

On the basis of Kemp's results, Wiseman (1964) calculated that, if 25 per cent of measured intelligence is due to environmental factors, then just over half of the total variance of attainment could be attributed to these factors (p. 72). Similar conclusions can be drawn from Burt and Conway's studies of twins and of unrelated children reared together (shown in Table 4.1), if we follow the simplified approach described in Appendix 3.

But, while it seems reasonable to attribute the variation in measured intelligence to only two factors—genetic ability and 'environment'—there is evidence that achievement depends also on other personality traits, such as 'cooperativeness, agreeableness, persistence, and willingness to work' (Tyler, 1956, p. 115). Not much progress has so far been made in identifying the sources of these personality characteristics. Tyler believes that they

are not those that personality theorists, with their background in the clinic and the hospital, tend to think of first. They are not differences in basic drives but in *learned habits of work*. They are not differences in the degree to which negative qualities like anxiety and neurotic traits are present but rather the degree to which strong and well organized positive qualities such as interests, commitment, or enthusiasm about some line of endeavour characterize an individual [p. 119].

De Wolff and Härnqvist (1961, p. 140) write: 'Ability for a given type of education is not effectively measured with the help of one variable such as I.Q. A whole complex of personality traits (perseverance, motivation, interest) is required.' Burt (1959, p. 26), in discussing reasons why children from the 'lower social classes' fail to get into the grammar school or university, wrote:

But intelligence is by no means the sole characteristic of social importance: the presence or absence of certain motivational traits must also count. For the child to succeed, *both* high intelligence *and* high qualities of character are requisite ; but *either* lack of intelligence *or* lack of those character-qualities may be sufficient to ensure failure. This is evident from the case-studies we have carried out among pupils who have failed: those who showed high intelligence have commonly proved lacking either in certain moral traits (industry, perseverance, ambition, and the like) or in temperamental characteristics (readiness to undertake sedentary work with books and paper as contrasted with more active and practical work with people and things): all three are needed for an academic career.

The important point is that these personality traits seem to be closely associated with home background and are correlated with socio-economic class. Tyler's conclusion, quoted above, that what matters is *learned habits of work* suggests that children from disorganized homes and social environments will be at a disadvantage, and that those who come from families in which the chief earner is himself an office worker, or at least a skilled worker, will be more likely to succeed. To quote Burt again (1959, p. 26): 'The development of moral qualities even more than the development of intellectual qualities is largely dependent on environmental conditions.' Why, he asks, do some of the intelligent working class children in England fail to go to grammar school? Not, in his opinion, primarily because intelligence tests are biased.

This seems to me to be the least important of the causes. Rather more important are the differences in temperament and character. . . . By far the commonest reason is the child's poor performance in the formal tests of arithmetic and English: in the English test more especially children of 'unskilled labourers' are undoubtedly penalized, whereas children from the 'professional' classes derive a definite advantage from the intellectual background of the cultured home [pp. 29–30].[1]

Not only is school achievement dependent on both genetic and environmental influences (with the latter playing a large role) but these two factors are mutually correlated. Floud, Halsey, and Martin (1956) found, from their studies of children in Middlesborough and south-west Hertfordshire, that 'children at a given level of ability above the average are more or less likely to undertake advanced courses and go on to full-time further education according to their social origins' (p. 126). Further, within each social class the level of education of the parents is also correlated with the degree of success (in the grammar-school extrance examination) of their children. The 'better educated parents of successful children . . . were to a marked degree more interested in and ambitious for their educational future than were the parents of unsuccessful children' (p. 88). It seems that parental encouragement and stimulation is one of the crucial ways in which environment interacts with ability to produce school success.[2]

Since school achievement is dependent both on intelligence and on home environment (not to mention the quality of school education itself), and since home environment is largely a reflection of socio-economic class, which in most countries is highly

[1] But most psychologists would agree that lack of verbal ability is a substantial drawback to success in intelligence tests themselves. For example, Miner (1957) shows that the median correlation between tests of vocabulary and tests of general intelligence in a large group of studies was 0·83. This is partly because most intelligence tests contain a heavy loading of tests of verbal ability. But it is also because of the great importance of verbal ability for success in our culture. 'As society becomes more complex, there is an increasing demand for verbal skill. . . . Industrialization and scientific advancement are greatly facilitated when people can adequately communicate their experiences to others in verbal terms' (p. 32). Verbal skills are closely associated with class background, and are indispensable to school success, especially at the earlier stages. Children who are deficient in verbal skill tend to drop out early (p. 34).

[2] Cf. Fraser's conclusions quoted above. Burt (1958, p. 9) also observed that 'quite apart from what the child may learn, the constant presence of an intellectual background may stimulate (or seem to stimulate) his latent powers by inculcating a keener motivation, a stronger interest in intellectual things, and a habit of accurate, speedy, and diligent work'. See also the Robbins report on *Higher Education* (1963, App. 1, pp. 47–8).

skew, we have every reason to expect that 'educated ability' at the end of elementary education will be skew. This skewness will be further accentuated if intelligence itself, as we have suggested above, is slightly skew, and also, since intelligence and environment are correlated, if—as seems quite possible—intelligence and environment interact multiplicatively.

Unfortunately, it is difficult to test this hypothesis, since the grading of children by school results is largely a process of ranking on an ordinal scale. Marks in examinations may be either skew or symmetrical, depending on the degree of difficulty of the test; and in any case they are subject to a maximum of 100 per cent. However, 'grade-norm' scores, which have been used fairly widely in the United States, show that there is considerable dispersion in school achievement. Tyler (1965, p. 101) quotes some results of such tests which show very wide ranges of variation; for example, the age norms of a group of children who had spent three and a half years in school ranged from 6 to 15. 'The lowest in the group knew no more than the average child just beginning school, whereas the highest was already at the level of high-school students.' Other results cited by Tyler show that the inter-quartile range on an English achievement test for eighth-grade children was nearly equal to three years of age. For reading comprehension this range varies from one and a half years for third-graders to two and a half for fifth-graders. 'In general, the higher up the educational ladder we go, the greater this spread becomes, at least until we reach the level at which compulsory school laws no longer apply and selection cuts off the bottom portion of the distribution.' Similar results were found with tests of arithmetic.

But these results are indicative only of increasing *dispersion* of ability with age, not of increasing *skewness*. One study cited by Tyler, however, seems to throw some light on the latter aspect. Between 1928 and 1936 Learned and Wood carried out a number of tests in high schools and colleges of the state of Pennsylvania. These tests were designed 'to evaluate the educational system of the state in terms of what students who came through it actually knew. . . . The tests were highly reliable and gave high

enough correlations with college grades to make it clear that
they were measuring what teachers think students should know'
(Tyler, 1965, pp. 103–4). Some results of the 'general culture'
test—which included questions on fine arts, history, and social
studies, world literature, and natural science—are given in
Table 4.4.

TABLE 4.4

*Scores of Pennsylvania Students in a General Culture Test,
1928–34, at Given Percentiles*

Percentile	High-school seniors[1]	College sophomores[2]	College seniors[3]
90	314	381	473
75	243	316	393
50	179	254	314
25	126	196	244
10	90	147	188
Number of students	1,503	5,747	3,720
$(P_{75}-P_{25})/P_{50}$	0·65	0·47	0·47
$(P_{75}-P_{50})/(P_{50}-P_{25})$	1·21	1·07	1·13
$(P_{90}-P_{50})/(P_{50}-P_{10})$	1·52	1·19	1·26

[1] Last year at high school.
[2] Second year of college.
[3] Fourth year of college.

Source: Tyler (1965, p. 105), based on data published by Learned and Wood.
The 'score' is the number of questions answered correctly out of a total of
more than 1,200.

An important attribute of this test was that it contained a very
large number of questions—more than 1,200—and that no
student came anywhere near achieving full marks. The highest
score (number of questions answered correctly) amongst the
high-school seniors was 615, amongst the college sophomores
755, and amongst the college seniors 805. Hence, there was no
tendency to 'squeeze in' the upper tail of the distribution. At the
same time, the fact that the questions were regarded as reasonable for students of these age-groups suggests that the lower tail
was equally unrestricted. In practice, the lowest scores were 25,
25, and 45 for the three groups respectively.

If, then, we can regard this as a fair test of achievement amongst students of these ages, it is interesting to examine the shapes of the distributions which emerge. A convenient measure of relative dispersion for data of this kind is the relative inter-quartile range, $(P_{75} - P_{25})/P_{50}$. The table shows that the relative dispersion of high-school seniors was greater than for either college group. This is perhaps not surprising, since the college group would exclude a good many of the less able high-school graduates. What is more interesting is that each of the three distributions is positively skew. This is shown by the two measures $(P_{75}-P_{50})/(P_{50}-P_{25})$ and $(P_{90}-P_{50})/(P_{50}-P_{10})$. Once more, and for the same reason, the high-school group is more skew than either of the college groups; but the senior college group is distinctly more positively skew than the sophomores. These results, although they do not refer to students leaving elementary school, seem to provide some confirmation of our hypothesis that the distribution of general educated ability at this age is likely to be positively skew.

Burt (1943, p. 95) argues that, although individual ability 'conceivably may' follow the normal curve, individual *output* does not. The fallacy, in his opinion, lies in identifying 'capacity for work' with mental 'energy', and mental 'energy' with 'general intelligence', as measured by the usual tests.

If I take a large number of my students, I find that, with intelligence-tests, or academic examinations, the marks measuring their 'ability' conform pretty closely with the normal curve. Yet, when I collect records of their output as psychologists in later life, I find that the frequency-curve is not even approximately normal, but *J*-shaped; and this holds good in many other fields of human output for which detailed data are available.

The reason for this discrepancy, he suggests, is that the many capacities (or causes) which underlie output combine together, not additively but multiplicatively. 'If, for example, one of the "factors" is speed, industry, or retentiveness, the deviations must tend to augment those due to mere intelligent insight, by a process more akin to multiplication than addition' (p. 97). A similar point was made by Roy (1950a), as mentioned earlier in Chapter 2. What Burt seems to be saying is that there is a distinction between 'ability' and 'application'. Some people, in everyday terms, have ability, but they are slow or lazy, so that their output is not as high as one would expect on the basis of their ability alone. Those, however, who are both able and energetic are extremely productive. The two factors multiply.

This seems a plausible view, and it may well be the explanation for the skewness of the results in the perceptual test shown in Table 4.3, where the 'output' of recognized designs was expressed as a rate per minute. If there are two independent factors—'ability' and 'energy', or 'speed of response'—which are each distributed quasi-normally, and they combine multiplicatively in the production of 'output', then the distribution of output will be skew.[1] But it is not possible at present to say precisely in what form 'general ability' at the end of elementary schooling is distributed. For the reasons given above I believe that the *a priori* probability is that 'general educated ability' is skew. If, in addition, ability is combined with energy or with speed of response in order to produce output per unit of time, then there are even stronger reasons for expecting the output of persons without specialized training to be distributed asymmetrically, with a substantial positive skewness.

3. The Choice of Occupations

When children leave elementary school (but in some countries before that date and in others later) they are forced to decide what sort of occupation they intend to follow. From this point onwards, therefore, the distribution of abilities ceases to be a

---

[1] Boissevain put the same view in a paper in 1939. Most human accomplishments, he believed, depend on at least two factors, often more. 'It is necessary to have both intelligence and energy to excel in any profession. A man of great intelligence, but at the same time extremely lazy is unlikely to accomplish anything worth while, and the same is true of the man of great energy but of low intelligence' (p. 50). The important assumption which Boissevain made is that the distribution of output is the *product* of the distributions of the two or more factors. He went on to show that, if each of the factors is distributed binomially, their product will be increasingly skew as the number of factors increases.

single vector and becomes a matrix composed of a large number of independent vectors. We pass out of the realm of psychology, and economics begins to play an important role.

If all occupations required the same period of specialized training, and if the tuition costs were also the same, then we could expect that average earnings in all occupations would be approximately the same, except in so far as other net advantages existed. Let us set aside net non-pecuniary advantages for the time being, since their influence can always be allowed for at the end. In practice, occupations require varying periods of special education and training, ranging from zero for unskilled labour to ten years or more for some professions. Now, if all abilities were equal, if there were perfect knowledge about the relative earnings to be expected in each occupation, if there were no hindrances to entering courses leading to particular occupations, and if a perfect capital market existed, so that any student could borrow sufficient to cover the costs of his education at a fixed rate of interest, then we should expect to find that average earnings in each occupation would be a function of the costs of training for that occupation.[1] These costs consist of foregone earnings (opportunity costs) and tuition costs. Each of these is a function of the length of time required for training, and, in general, we could expect that differences in earnings would reflect differences in training periods.

Mincer (1958) has constructed a simple model along these lines, which offers a convenient starting-point for a discussion of occupational differentials. He assumes that abilities are identical and that there is complete freedom to enter any occupation. The only obstacle is that different occupations require different periods of training. On the assumptions that the only cost of a year's training is the foregoing of a year's earnings, that earnings in each occupation are constant over working life, and that a

---

[1] This assumes implicitly that there are no differences in risk between occupations. Such differences would affect earnings differentials in the same way as non-pecuniary net advantages, and we can provisionally leave them on one side. It is also implicitly assumed that the market would reach an equilibrium, at which point there would be no incentive for the proportions of students training for the different occupations to be altered.

year's extra training reduces working life by a corresponding period, he is able to show that, if each person makes the present value of expected earnings in each occupation equal, the ratio of earnings in an occupation requiring n years of training, a_n, to the earnings in an occupation requiring $(n-d)$ years, a_{n-d}, is a function of the continuous rate of discount, r, the maximum length of working life, l, and d. That is

$$\frac{a_n}{a_{n-d}} = \frac{e^{r(l+d-n)}-1}{e^{r(l-n)}-1}.$$

This ratio is greater than unity, a positive function of r, and a negative function of l.

In other words, as would be expected, (a) people with more training command higher annual pay; (b) the difference between earnings of persons differing by d years of training is larger, the higher the rate at which future income is discounted, that is, the greater the sacrifice involved in the act of income postponement; (c) the difference is larger, the shorter the general span of working life, since the costs of training must be recouped over a *relatively* shorter period [p. 285].

Mincer also suggests that changes in the ratio a_n/a_{n-d} for changes in n are negligible (at least when r and l are in the neighbourhood of 0·04 and 50 respectively), so that a_n/a_{n-d} can 'for all practical purposes' be treated as a constant, k. In that case, it follows that the equilibrium distribution of mean occupational earnings will be one that satisfies the equation

$$a_n = k^n a_0$$

or
$$\ln a_n = n \ln k + \ln a_0.$$

Hence, if, for example, the distribution of n were normal, the distribution of a_n would be lognormal.[1]

---

[1] An alternative model has been suggested by Becker (1964). He assumes that, for any individual, $y = x + rc$, where y = actual earnings, x = earnings if no 'investment in human capital', i.e. occupational training, had occurred, c = investment in human capital, and r = average rate of return on this investment. Provisionally ignoring x, he argues that r measures ability, so that y depends on ability (r) and training (c), which are multiplied. Hence, if r and c are random variables, y will be positively skew even if r and c are symmetrical (pp. 62–4). Even if x is symmetrical, y will be skew because of the influence of rc, which will be greater in some occupational and age groups than in others. Becker perhaps places too much emphasis on the influence of vocational train-

Mincer's conclusion is not upset if costs of tuition are allowed for, provided that tuition costs are a constant proportion of foregone earnings. But the relaxation of a number of his other assumptions would make some difference to his conclusions. First, there is a group of assumptions whose relaxation tends to increase the skewness; and, secondly, a smaller group whose relaxation tends in the opposite direction. In the first group we have: (1) the value of a_n/a_{n-d} is not in fact constant but increases with n; (2) the value of r is not the same for everyone but is probably greater for poorer people, and increases for everyone with n; (3) abilities are not equal but are positively correlated with n, and may well be multiplicative in their effect; (4) years of training—beyond the compulsory school age—are probably not normally distributed but positively skew; (5) earnings are not constant throughout working life but, as Mincer shows, they tend to increase with age up to a certain point; and they increase more and for a longer period of time in the more highly educated jobs. The longer it takes to attain the peak level of earnings, the higher must be the average level of earnings in a cross-section group of workers to be equivalent to a given present value.

On the other side, there seem to be two factors tending to reduce skewness of earnings: (6) people entering the more highly skilled occupations may expect to have a somewhat later age of retirement, i.e. a greater value of n (although Mincer cites some statistics which show that the less highly skilled have, on the average, more years of *working* life); (7) risks may be smaller and non-pecuniary benefits greater in the more highly skilled occupations.

A dominant factor seems likely to be the distribution of occupations according to the length of the training period. What prior expectation can one form about this? This is a difficult question to answer, and a number of different problems seem to be involved. First, there is the question of what defines a separate

ing and too little on the distribution of 'general educated ability' as a factor determining the dispersion and skewness of earnings. See also Becker and Chiswick (1966).

'occupation'. In practice, as government statisticians know well, there is a substantial conventional element in any definition of an occupation and in the degree to which occupations are divided. Why, for example, in the United States Census classification for 1960, are painters separated from paperhangers, while all accountants, or all physicians and surgeons, are in a single category? The answer is probably, in part, that it depends on the number of people involved. For practical statistical and administrative purposes it is usually a nuisance to have either very large categories or very small ones. Hence, I suspect, there is a tendency to define occupations in such a way as to arrive at a rough equality of numbers in each category.[1]

If we assume that the classification of occupations has been carried out on this sort of principle, what kind of distribution of occupations by period of training can we expect? For any given occupation, the period of training required is mainly determined by collective bodies, many of which, in Europe at least, are descended from the medieval guilds. More specifically, in modern times, we find the influence of governments, employers, trade unions, professional organizations, and educational institutions. The period and quality of training required for a particular occupation is often the result of conflicting pressures from these bodies. But, underlying this, we must presume that there are some more fundamental determinants. Although the trade unions and professional organizations often try to restrict entry by unnecessary prolongation of the required training period, in general we can expect that the period will be fixed roughly at a point at which the additional cost of an extra year of training is not quite covered by the increase in the present value of expected earnings.[2] It seems likely, however, that a careful review

[1] But only a very rough one. In the United States classification there are only 244 professors and instructors of statistics (which must surely be an underestimate) and, at the other extreme, 939,727 book-keepers (US 3, Table 1).

[2] The exact criteria for a 'profit-maximizing' decision would be difficult to specify, since they would depend on the degree of monopoly, legal and otherwise, expected to exist throughout the future working life of the current generation of trainees, forecasts of consumer income and tastes, and of technology, all of which affect relative demands for services of various types, the effects of the decision on the incomes of existing members of the trade or profession, as well as on future members, and so forth.

of existing training periods in many occupations would reveal a general bias towards requirements which are excessive from a social point of view.

Fortunately, perhaps, the dominant factor in determining training periods is the technical consideration that, beyond a certain point, in most occupations, the extra value of an extra year of training rapidly diminishes. The distribution of occupations by period of training is, I think, largely a reflection of this technical consideration. It is difficult to find any theoretical explanation for this; but in practice it seems that most occupations at present require only a few years of training, while a much smaller number require lengthy periods, as in the professions.

Some evidence about the distribution of education and training requirements for different occupations has been presented by Scoville (1966). He took the ordinal measures of requirements for 'general education development' (GED) and 'special vocational preparation (SVP) given in *Estimates of Worker Traits Requirements for 4000 Jobs* (U.S. Department of Labor, 1956) and converted them into estimated years of schooling or training. He then averaged these measures for all jobs falling within a census occupation. Frequency distributions prepared from his published estimates of mean GED and mean SVP for 204 census occupations are given in Figs. 4.1a and 4.1b. They show that GED has two modes and that (GED+SVP) is positively skew. As Scoville makes clear, the underlying data are not entirely satisfactory; but there seems no doubt that, broadly, the shapes of the two frequency distributions are of the right sort. It follows, then, that, if we truncate the distributions at the end of the eighth year (which represents the end of elementary education) the remaining parts of both distributions will be highly skew.[1]

The Mincer model, then, after adjustment for the effects of relaxing his special assumptions, would predispose us to expect

[1] In a few occupations, mainly in the professions, the length of training above a specified minimum is left to the individual to decide, e.g. specialization by medical practitioners or post-doctoral research by scientists. One must presume that maximization of personal net benefit over cost plays some part in determining these decisions.

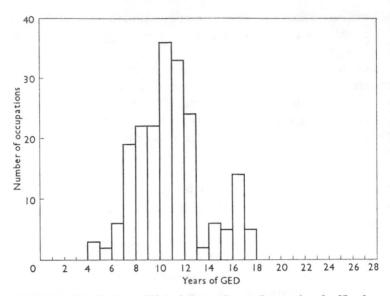

Fig. 4.1a. Distribution of United States Census Occupations by Number of Years of General Educational Development Required.

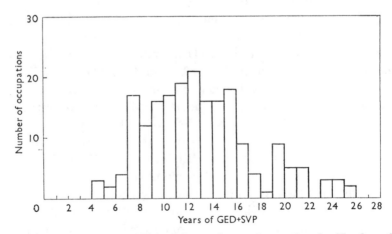

Fig. 4.1b. Distribution of United States Census Occupations by Number of Years of General Educational Development and Specific Vocational Preparation Required.

Source: Scoville (1966, pp. 388–90).

that the distribution of mean earnings of occupations would be positively skew, and, if training periods are as skew as Scoville's data suggest, more skew than a lognormal distribution. Two sorts of empirical data can be used to test this hypothesis. One consists of data on the relation between mean earnings and number of years of education; and the other of actual distributions of occupations by mean earnings.

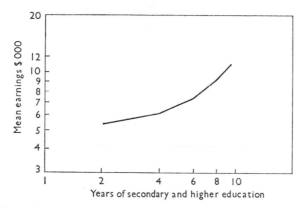

FIG. 4.2. United States, 1959: Mean Earnings of Males Aged 25–64 in the Civilian Labour Force by Years of Secondary and Higher Education Completed.

Source: Table 4.5.

According to Mincer's simple model, and on the assumption that training periods are normally distributed, we could expect that the regression of mean earnings of employees with different periods of education on the period of education (beyond elementary) would be approximately linear in the logarithms. From Fig. 4.2, which is based on United States data for males aged 25 to 64 in 1959, it will be seen that the relation between the logarithm of mean earnings and the logarithm of number of years of secondary and higher education is not linear but concave upwards. The data are not, of course, strictly appropriate for the test, for several reasons: the earnings measured are those found in a cross-section study, not the actual earnings over lifetime of men with different periods of education; the education variable includes only formal full-time education and excludes on-the-job training; the data relate to all men with earnings, whether they are employees or self-employed, and the earnings of the latter include significant amounts representing returns of investment in non-human capital. But, in spite of these qualifications, it seems difficult to believe that reality is as predicted in Mincer's simple model. In other words, on the basis of Fig. 4.2, we could expect the distribution of mean earnings to be more-than-lognormal skew. This conclusion is, of course, consistent with the prediction which we made after relaxing the special assumptions of Mincer's simple model.[1]

TABLE 4.5

United States, 1959, Mean Earnings of Males Aged 25 to 64 in the Civilian Labour Force with some Earnings in 1959, by Years of School Completed*

Years of school completed	Assumed mean total number of years	Mean earnings $
(1)	(2)	(3)
Elementary: 0–7	4	3,659
8	8	4,725
High school: 1–3	10	5,379
4	12	6,132
College: 1–3	14	7,401
4	16	9,255
5 or more	$17\frac{1}{2}$	11,136

* Earnings include wages, salaries, and income from self-employment.
Source: Columns (1) and (3) from US 4, p. 2.

Distributions of occupational earnings are available for only a few countries, and they vary in the degree of detailed breakdown of occupations and in the measure of earnings. For the United States the Censuses of Population of 1940, 1950, and

[1] It should be noted that the evidence of Fig. 4.2 seems, at least superficially, to be inconsistent with Becker's (1964) finding that the rate of return on high-school education (in 1949) was much higher than the rate of return on college education. I have not attempted to discover the reasons for this apparent inconsistency. Becker's results, of course, are based on actual calculations of costs and benefits, not on Mincer's model, and they refer to a different year. See also Houthakker (1959), whose results appear to be more consistent with those shown above.

1960 contain estimates of median wages and salaries in the preceding years for a fairly large number of occupations, and Miller
(1955 and 1966) has published estimates of mean earnings for a
more limited number of census occupations for each of the same
three years. The distribution of 1959 medians for male wage and
salary workers in 533 occupations is given in Table 4.6. It is a

TABLE 4.6

*United States, 1959, Distribution of Occupations by Median Wage
and Salary Earnings of Male Wage and Salary Workers in
the Experienced Civilian Labour Force*

Median earnings ($000)	Number of occupations
Under 1·0	9
1·0–	22
2·0–	13
2·5–	26
3·0–	41
3·5–	72
4·0–	77
4·5–	69
5·0–	60
5·5–	40
6·0–	24
6·5–	18
7·0–	28
7·5–	13
8·0–	9
8·5–	9
9·0–	3
Total	533

Source: US 3, Table 27.

fairly smooth distribution which, from inspection, can be seen
to be essentially unimodal and positively skew. When plotted on
logarithmic probability paper the points fall reasonably close to
a straight line over the range from the twentieth percentile from
the bottom of the distribution up to the ninety-eighth percentile.
The curvature at the two ends of the income scale suggests that
the upper tail is shorter and the lower tail is longer (or thicker)

than in a strictly lognormal distribution. The distribution of the 1949 medians of male earnings in 387 occupations is similar.

Miller's estimates (1966) of mean wage and salary earnings in 116 occupations, of all males and of males working 50–2 weeks, in 1939, 1949, and 1959, yield coefficients of skewness and kurtosis which are shown in Table 4.7.

TABLE 4.7

Coefficients of Skewness and Kurtosis of Distributions of Mean Male Occupational Wage and Salary Earnings, United States, 1939, 1949, and 1959

Variable		Skewness (g_1)		Kurtosis (g_2)	
		All males	Males working 50–2 weeks	All males	Males working 50–2 weeks
Actual income:	1939	1·393	1·287	1·905	1·716
	1949	1·156	1·001	2·250	1·884
	1959	0·979	0·925	1·874	2·074
Logarithm of income:	1939	0·262	0·142	−0·338	−0·084
	1949	−0·616	−0·787	3·069	4·164
	1959	−0·904	−1·187	3·332	5·959

Source of basic data Miller (1966), Tables C–6 and C–7.

These results suggest that, while the 1939 distribution is not significantly different from a lognormal distribution, the 1949 and 1959 distributions are positively skew in relation to a normal distribution, but negatively skew in relation to a lognormal distribution. They are leptokurtic in relation to both types of distribution. All the distributions are both skew and leptokurtic in relation to a normal distribution.[1]

Distributions of mean earnings of occupations are also available for Canada and Yugoslavia. Mean male earnings in 334 occupations in Canada in 1960–1 (taken from CA 1, Table 21) are distributed rather like those for the United States in Table 4.6, that is, they are clearly skew and leptokurtic in relation to a normal distribution, while in comparison to a lognormal dis-

[1] The standard error of g_1^2 in a sample of this size drawn from a normal population is 0·227; and the standard error of g_2 is 0·454.

tribution there are rather too many low values and too few high values. For Yugoslavia there are estimates of mean earnings (irrespective of sex) in ninety-five occupations in 1963.[1] These are very markedly skew and a lognormal distribution would be a more likely fit than a normal distribution, although the correspondence with a lognormal distribution is still not very clear.

From Australia there is abundant material on award rates—fixed under the compulsory arbitration system—for several hundred occupations. An example of the distribution of rates for males in 500 occupations in New South Wales in 1963 is given in Table 4.8. In spite of a few irregularities this distribution is again of the characteristic type. When plotted on logarithmic probability paper the bottom 40 per cent of the distribution falls almost exactly on one straight line and the top 60 per cent on another, with a slight kink at the point where the lines join. In several other years for which tests have been made the approximation to a lognormal distribution is even better.

Estimates of skewness (g_1) and kurtosis (g_2) have been made for 445 occupations for which Australian data are available in 36 out of the 39 years in the period 1914 to 1952. The skewness coefficients of the actual wage rates are distributed around a modal value of about 0·8, with 20 out of the 36 years lying between 0·7 and 0·9, and none less than 0·4. The standard error of g_1^2 in a sample of this size drawn from a normal population is less than 0·12. A few of the skewness coefficients of the logarithms of wage rates are negative. Their modal value is 0·4, and 20 out of 36 lie in the range 0·3 to 0·5. Most of these are not significantly different from zero. All the kurtosis coefficients, for both the natural wage rate and its logarithm, are positive. Of the kurtosis coefficients for the natural wage, all except four exceed three times the standard error (of 0·23); and of the coefficients for the logarithm of the wage rate all except three are above this level.

The Australian data are, of course, not exactly what is needed, since they refer to minimum rates, not earnings. Earnings would be higher and more widely dispersed, and the logarithm of earnings might well be more leptokurtic than the logarithm of rates.

[1] The source is YU 1, Table 121–13.

The Australian data are also limited for the most part to manual occupations, so that we are unable to say exactly how the distribution of all occupations would look; but there seems every reason to believe that the inclusion of non-manual occupations would not change the essential character of the distribution, although it might well increase the extent of the upper tail.

TABLE 4.8

Australia, 1963, Distribution of Occupations by Award Rates for Males in New South Wales

Weekly rate (shillings)	Number of occupations
Under 300	1
300–	13
320–	76
340–	110
360–	69
380–	60
400–	65
420–	28
440–	25
460–	12
480–	19
500–	6
520–	8
540–	8
Total	500

Source: AL 3.

These empirical distributions of occupational earnings are not inconsistent with what may be called the 'relaxed' Mincer hypothesis, although one might perhaps have expected rather more skewness. The use of medians in place of means, of course, tends to reduce skewness, and the use of minimum award rates (for manual occupations only) in the Australian case biases the distribution in the same direction. Moreover, the degree of dispersion and skewness probably depends fairly heavily on the fineness of the division of occupations. Even the 533 United States census occupations used in Table 4.6 constitute a very rough classification in comparison with, for example, the U.S. Department of Labor's *Dictionary of Occupational Titles* (1949).

If it were possible to obtain earnings data for a very detailed list of occupations, the distribution would certainly be more dispersed and probably more skew. Support for this view comes from the fact that, when certain census occupations are broken down by educational level, it is found that there are appreciable differences within occupations for mean earnings by education. Some examples are given in Table 4.9. It is interesting to note, from

TABLE 4.9

United States, 1959, Mean Annual Earnings of Males Aged 25 to 64 by Education Level within Selected Occupations ($)

Occupation	Educational level: years completed		
	Eight years of elementary school	Four years of high school	Four years of college
Accountants and auditors	7,156	7,270	8,341
Clergymen	3,509	4,032	4,488
Civil engineers	6,295	7,138	9,301
Electrical and electronic technicians	6,309	6,522	6,863
Buyers and department heads, store	6,942	8,220	10,287
Book-keepers	4,870	5,165	5,508
Insurance agents, brokers, and underwriters	6,828	7,387	9,444
Carpenters	4,387	5,325	5,791
Compositors and typesetters	5,993	6,312	6,915
Electricians	6,083	6,407	6,679
Automobile mechanics and repairmen	4,588	5,150	—
Plumbers and pipefitters	5,580	6,357	7,217
Bus drivers	4,294	5,020	—
Truck and tractor drivers	4,771	5,340	5,585
Barbers	4,409	4,737	—
Farm labourers, wage workers	2,169	2,957	4,135

Source: US 4, Table 1.

this table, that mean earnings for a given number of years of schooling vary quite considerably between occupations. Since the table includes self-employed, part of this could be a reflection of differences in the amounts of non-human capital employed, especially as between professional and manual occupations.

Part, also, could be the result of differences in risk and non-pecuniary benefits; and, in the case of farm labourers, differences of race. Then again, the market may not be in equilibrium or there may be monopolistic or monopsonistic factors at work in some occupations.

So far as these tests go, they seem to give broad support to Mincer's theory, although not to his simple model. Apart from this, the results of the tests enable us to suggest one more piece for the puzzle. We found earlier that the distribution of general educated ability, irrespective of occupation, was likely to be lognormal leptokurtic. Now we have found theoretical and empirical reasons for believing that the distribution of mean earnings *between* occupations is also roughly lognormal leptokurtic. The next problem is to see how we can fit these two parts of the puzzle together.

4. Relation of Distributions Between and Within Occupations

Since there is generally a positive correlation between ability and the length of time spent in education, we could expect to find some correlation between the average ability of the members of an occupation and their mean earnings. If this correlation were perfect, there would be no dispersion of ability within occupations and, apart from the influence of factors other than ability (such as hours worked and health), we could expect that there would be no dispersion of earnings within occupations. In this situation the whole of the dispersion of wages and salaries would be accounted for by the dispersion between occupations. This dispersion, however, would not only reflect differences in the period of education but would include the effect of the dispersion of general ability.

In practice, despite the fact that there is a positive correlation between occupation and ability, the dispersion of ability within occupations is extremely large. Figures published by Harrell and Harrell (see Tyler, 1965, pp. 338–9) help to throw some light on the problem. They analysed results of an Army General Classification Test given in the Second World War to men enlisting in the U.S. Army Air Force. The data relate to 18,782 white enlisted men, classified into seventy-four occupations, ranging from accountant, lawyer, and engineer down to farmhand, miner, and teamster. As with other general ability tests, the scores have been standardized, so that the dispersion within occupations is purely notional. But we can still compare the dispersion within and between occupations, and thereby gain some impression of the relative importance of the two components. From the tabulated data it appears that a typical standard deviation within occupations would be about 15 points (as is usual in these tests), or a variance of 225 points. The variance of the weighted means of occupations, on the other hand, is only 85 points; so that the proportion of the total variance attributable to the variance *between* occupations is only about a quarter.

It is likely that this estimate is biased downwards, because, as Harrell and Harrell point out (1945), many of the men from professional occupations would not have been included in their sample—since they would have become officers—while at the other extreme many of the less-able people in the lower occupations would not have attempted to enlist for the Air Force. Even so, it seems unlikely that more than about 30 per cent of the total variance of ability is accounted for by the variance between occupations.

Similar conclusions can be drawn if we analyse the variance of *earnings* into its 'between occupation' and 'within occupation' components. Some results of such an analysis for the United States in 1959 are given in Table 4.10. The 'between occupation' component in this case is the weighted variance of *medians* of occupations about the mean of all the medians in each group; and it is likely to be an underestimate of the variance of means, since the difference between the mean and median is greater in the higher occupations than in the lower.[1] From these calculations

---

[1] In estimating the variance between persons (the over-all variance) it was necessary to make assumptions about the position of the means of income classes, and, especially important, to estimate the appropriate figure to include for the upper open-ended group. The means of the closed classes were taken at their mid-points. For the open-ended class, $15,000 and over, an estimate

we can conclude that not more than about 25 per cent of the total variance of earnings is attributable to the variance between occupations. For particular groups of occupations, however, there are some cases where the 'between occupation' component is a good deal larger, especially in the 'household, service, and farm' group, which—as its name implies—is a rather heterogeneous group.

TABLE 4.10

United States, 1959, Percentage of Total Variance of Male Wages and Salaries Represented by the Variance between Occupation Medians[1]

Occupation group	All workers	Working 50–2 weeks
All occupations (except not stated)	22·1	16·6
Professional, technical, and managerial	5·2	4·9
Clerical and sales	13·1	8·7
Craftsmen, foremen, etc.	16·0	14·1
Operatives	14·6	13·0
Household, service, and farm	39·3	37·3
Labourers, excluding farm and mine	28·4	18·6

[1] Medians weighted by number of workers in the group.
Source of basic data: US 3, Tables 27 and 28.

The important conclusion which emerges from this discussion is that, at least in the United States, the proportion of total variance of either ability or earnings which is attributable to the between occupation variance is remarkably small. It is true that a finer division of occupations would increase this, as also a

was made of the Pareto coefficient (α) by plotting the last four points available from the data. The mean of the open-ended class was then estimated from the formula $\bar{X}_0 = \frac{\alpha}{\alpha-1} X_0$, where $\bar{X}_0$ = the mean of the open-ended class and X_0 = the lower limit of the class (\$15,000). Similarly, the assumed 'mean' used for computing the variance was set at $\bar{X}_0 = \sqrt{\left(\frac{\alpha}{\alpha-2}\right)} X_0$.

The method of estimating the variance of a distribution with a substantial open-ended group is of very great importance, since so much of the variance is contributed by this class. No perfect method exists; but the method described above, which is based on the assumption that the Pareto law applies to the upper tail, seemed to be reasonably appropriate in this case.

division within so-called single occupations between persons with more or less education. Nevertheless, even in the manual occupations, such as 'craftsmen, foremen, etc.', where differences in education are not very important, we find, according to Table 4.10, that only a very small part of the total variance is attributable to the between occupation component.[1] This suggests that factors other than occupation are more important. Amongst these factors we can identify 'general educated ability', which we have suggested is likely to be fairly widely dispersed and skew; but there are almost certainly other important factors such as personality traits, health, and pure luck. At the present stage it is impossible to give any estimate of the relative importance of these various components.

Since the correlation between occupation and ability is far from perfect, it seems a reasonable assumption—supported by Harrell and Harrell's data—that the distribution of ability within occupations is likely to be similar in shape to the over-all distribution of ability, i.e. lognormal leptokurtic. If this is so, we have a position where the distributions both within occupations and between occupations are of the same form. Now Aitchison and Brown (1954) have shown that, if the distributions of a variate both within occupations and between (many) occupations are lognormal, if the number of persons in each occupation is constant, and also the variance within each occupation, then the over-all distribution of the variate will be lognormal. So it seems reasonable to expect that, if the distributions between and within occupations were lognormal leptokurtic, the over-all distribution would be of the same form. In practice, the variance of income within occupations is not constant, nor are the numbers of persons. Some indication of the variation of the variance within occupations can be obtained from Miller's (1966) tabulation of quartiles of 1959 male 50–2 week wage and salary income for over a hundred occupations (his Appendix C, Table C–3). The difference between Q_3 and Q_1 ranges from over $4,000 for

---

[1] Mincer, also, was unable to account for more than a small part of the total dispersion of income of employees by taking into account differences in period of education (1958, pp. 293–4).

some of the professional occupations to about $500 for news-boys. This is a further factor tending to produce kurtosis in the over-all distribution, since the aggregation of distributions which have different variances tend to produce this effect.

5. Factors influencing the Allocation of Persons to Occupations

Although we have concluded that the variance of earnings between occupations explains only a minor part of the over-all inequality of income, it is still of great importance. The decision about which occupation a boy shall enter is still one of the most decisive for his future economic status, although perhaps not so important as the decision about which school or college he goes to. Let us then consider what factors influence the choice of occupation.

We are not here concerned with the choice of detailed occupations, but with the major choices between groups of occupations involving different periods and qualities of post-elementary education, and leading to different socio-economic status levels. Thus, our main interest is in the factors determining the amount of education which children receive, and, in particular, whether they leave school at the end of elementary school, or after secondary education, or only after completing a college (or university) education. The factors of major importance seem to be (1) the ability and other traits of the child, (2) the socio-economic class and educational level of the parents, and (3) regional and other locational factors. We shall discuss these in turn.

In most educational systems ability is of some importance in determining how far each child shall go. As Lipset and Bendix (1959) say: 'It may be expected that educational achievement will vary with intelligence, and that continuation in the educational system will depend, therefore, upon "above average" intelligence, especially when the student has a low-status background' (p. 227).[1] But the correlation between education and ability (as measured by intelligence tests) is far from perfect,

----

[1] See also the evidence in Wolfle (1954, pp. 148–54).

except perhaps in the United Kingdom, where the 'eleven plus' tests for grammar-school entrance have resulted in a very thorough sifting out of those who do well at intelligence tests.[1] Boalt (1954, p. 68) quotes a figure for the correlation between education and I.Q. in Sweden of 0·82. His study of the 1949 social class of Stockholm children who left the fourth form of the primary schools in 1936 also shows a significant positive correlation between I.Q. and subsequent social class. But the variation of I.Q. within social classes is still very large (p. 69). Lipset and Bendix quote results of a study by Kahl (1953) amongst Boston high-school boys, which showed a strong positive association between I.Q. and desire to go to college. But they also refer to some Cleveland data which suggest that social class is much more important than intelligence in deciding who *actually* goes to college (Lipset and Bendix, 1959, p. 231). This latter finding is supported by the interesting study of Wolfle and Smith (1956) amongst over 8,000 good-quality male high-school graduates in Illinois, Minnesota, and Rochester (New York). Relating the students' current occupations to their I.Q. and high-school class rank approximately twenty years earlier, Wolfle and Smith found that high-school ranking was of some importance (independently of length of education) in determining whether a student entered a professional occupation, but that I.Q. score was of little or no importance. On the other hand, there was a high correlation between father's occupation and percentage of sons attending college.

Against this, mention should be made of the view expressed by Anderson (1961, p. 569) that 'from two-thirds to three-fourths of the mobility in the United States [is] congruent with "intelligence" differentials', and his conclusion from studies of data for Britain, Sweden, and the United States, that 'ability, whether hereditary or not, and associated motivation, varying independently of schooling, plays a powerful role in generating mobility'. Possibly, he allows, education may have more influence in the

[1] But this applies only amongst part of the school population, since children attending private preparatory and 'public' schools are much less carefully sifted—in some hardly at all.

United States than in the other two countries. But Anderson's brief discussion is not based directly on an analysis of the distribution of ability within social classes. Burt (1961), discussing distributions of I.Q. within social classes in Britain, showed that, while there is some correlation between I.Q. and social class, there is also a wide variation of I.Q. within social classes. He estimates that if people were to be allocated to social class entirely on the basis of intelligence it would be necessary for 23 per cent of the British adult population to move down in class and for 22 per cent to move up (p. 12). This does not resolve the question whether ability or education is more important in determining subsequent occupation (and hence social class), but it suggests that factors other than ability are still very important.

There is a great deal of information from many countries to support the obvious fact that social class of parents is correlated with the education and occupation of their children. We showed earlier that ability itself is partly determined by social class, and school achievement even more so. In addition, the children of higher-class parents are usually more strongly motivated to proceed with higher education; their parents can give them better advice about the advantages of so doing; the financial obstacles to further education are much smaller; and they are more willingly borne by parents who know more about the benefits that will accrue to their children. For these, and other, reasons the children of the higher socio-economic classes in almost all countries fill far more than their proportionate share of places in the better high schools, and in colleges and universities. Lipset and Bendix (1954, p. 43) quote results from a study by Roper showing that, in a national sample in the United States in 1947, 67 per cent of white high-school seniors whose fathers were in the professional and executive category had been admitted to college, compared with 16 per cent of students whose fathers were 'factory and other workers'.[1] Similar results are given for Sweden by Boalt (1954, p. 68). Halsey (1961, p. 32) quotes the following estimates of the percentage of university

[1] See also Wolfle (1954, p. 162).

students coming from manual-worker families: Britain (1956), 26; Denmark (1959), 9; Germany, 6; Switzerland, 6.[1]

Floud, Halsey, and Martin (1956, p. 82) give figures for two areas in Britain which show that parents in the higher social classes have higher social aspirations for their children's education. In south-west Hertfordshire, for example, 82 per cent of professional and business parents wanted their child to have a grammar-school education, against only 48 per cent for skilled workers and 43 per cent for unskilled workers. There is abundant evidence, also, that children of the same measured ability, but of lower social class, tend to drop out earlier than those of higher social class (cf. Husén, in Halsey, 1961). Moreover, even where, as in the United States, high-school education has become widely available to children from all social classes, the children who drop out earlier are those whose parents have themselves had a lower education. For example, in the very large sample of American high-school students surveyed in *Project Talent*, it was found that the parents of twelfth-grade children were distributed by occupation in much the same way as employed males aged 35–39 in 1960; but 44 per cent of the fathers of twelfth-graders had completed some college and 55 per cent of mothers, as compared with only 9 per cent of persons in the 35–59 year age-group (Flanagan and others, 1964, pp. 5–47 and 5–50).[2]

Perhaps the most impressive evidence of the association between the class, or educational, level of parents and the education of their children is that which was collected in the Canadian Census of 1961, and which is summarized in Table 4.11. It will be seen that there is an absolutely consistent relation between income of family head (for employees only) and the proportion of children still at school at ages 15–18 and 19–24; and a strong, and perhaps even more striking, relation between education of

[1] Some figures showing the class composition of students in pre-revolutionary Russia are given by Kahan in Anderson and Bowman (1965). See also Anderson in Anderson and Bowman (1965, pp. 325–6) for additional data for a number of countries; and JA 4, p. 52. Also *Higher Education* (1963, p. 50).

[2] Anderson, in Anderson and Bowman (1965, p. 329), quotes from the report of the 1851 Census in Britain the comment that 'in general a parent, in whatever station, takes himself and his own social status as the standard up to which he purposes to educate his offspring'.

TABLE 4.11

Canada, 1961, Relation between Social Class of Parent and Education of Children

	Percentage of children at school in these age-groups	
	15–18	19–24
Income of head of family (employees only)		
Under $3,000	60·9	12·0
$3,000–4,999	72·3	18·4
$5,000–6,999	81·7	29·4
$7,000 and over	90·7	50·0
Total	72·5	21·3
Schooling of family head (all families)		
None	45·5	6·9
Elementary 1–4 years	51·8	8·5
Elementary 5–	66·3	14·6
Secondary 1–2	76·4	21·5
Secondary 3	82·4	28·9
Secondary 4–5	84·6	34·6
Some University	88·2	45·5
University degree	93·8	63·7
Total	70·6	20·0
Occupation of head of family (selected occupations only)		
Managerial	84·3	37·8
Professional Engineers	91·9	57·0
School teachers	92·6	57·9
Physicians and surgeons	94·9	73·6
Accountants and auditors	90·7	46·0
Clerical	77·8	23·9
Farmers and stockraisers	66·7	15·2
Carpenters	68·0	15·5
Non-farm labourers	58·7	9·8

Source: CA 5, pp. 10–18 and 10–19.

head (all families) and education of children.[1] These correlations are reflected also in the differences between different occupations, as shown in the third section of the table.

[1] Similar data from the United States are cited by Denison (1962, p. 79), who also shows that, although father's education and family income are inter-correlated, they are each to some extent independently associated with the education of the son. See also *Higher Education* (1963, App. 1, pp. 54–61) for evidence on the situation in Britain.

FACTORS INFLUENCING ALLOCATION 111

Similar problems seem to have arisen in the communist countries. In 1938 in the Soviet Union, for example, 'children of the intelligentsia and employees constituted 47 per cent of the student body although the group made up only some 17 per cent of the total population' (Inkeles, 1966, p. 526). Since that year no statistics of the social composition of students have been published. But a few years ago Krushchev was complaining that children of workers and collective farmers made up only 30 to 40 per cent of the enrolment in Moscow's higher schools (Feldmesser, 1966, p. 530). Some commentators have suggested that the Red Guard movement in China is, at least in part, a reflection of the same sort of problem.[1]

The gross correlation between social class of parents and the education of their children is so great that, even if allowance is made for the higher average I.Q. of children of upper-class parents, there can be little doubt that the independent influence of social class is, in most countries, of far greater importance than that of I.Q.[2] And, since I.Q. itself is partly environmentally determined, the relative importance of class and 'native ability' is even more preponderantly weighted on the side of the former.

[1] In *Doctor Zhivago*, when Zhivago's brother, Evgraf, now a General in the Red Army, discovers that Tania, the regimental laundry girl, is really his niece, he says to her: 'That's extraordinary, really extraordinary. I'll tell you what. I haven't got time now. But I'll find you again, you can be sure of that. I'll find you and send for you again. I never thought I'd hear a thing like that. I won't leave you this way, I've just got to take care of a few things. And then, who can tell, I might put myself down as your uncle, you'll be promoted to being General's niece. And I'll send you to a university' (Pasternak, 1958, p. 511).

[2] But if the mean I.Q. of children of parents of different occupational groups in Canada varied in the same way as it does in the United States, as indicated in Table 4.2, then the pattern of occupational variation in the proportion of children aged 19–24 still at school, shown in Table 4.11, could largely be explained on the assumption that the selection of children to stay on at school was entirely determined by their I.Q. Thus, in order to absorb the top 21·3 per cent of children, it would be necessary to take all children with an I.Q. of 112 and above (assuming a normal distribution with a standard deviation of 15). Then, on the basis of the Terman–Merrill estimates in Table 4.2, the proportion of professional children selected would be 60 per cent; of semi-professional and managerial 50 per cent; of clerical, skilled trades, and retail 37 per cent; of rural owners and farmers 13 per cent; of semi-skilled and minor clerical 32 per cent; of slightly skilled 18 per cent; and of day labourers 14 per cent.

Finally, we should note that children from country areas usually proceed far less in their education than those from the cities. Wolfle, for example (in Halsey, 1961, p. 53), points out that in Sweden 'the probability of successfully completing the "studentexamen" is from 20 to 40 times as great for young men and women living in Stockholm as for those living in remote rural areas'. And Ferrez (Halsey, 1961, p. 77) notes a wide variation in the proportions of children attending secondary school and university in different *départements* in France, and shows that these proportions are correlated with the degree of industrialization and degree of dispersion of the population within the *département*.[1]

From this brief survey of the factors influencing the allocation of young people to occupations, it is clear that simple models, such as those of Mincer or Becker, which assume that everyone has an equal opportunity—within the limits of his ability—of training for any occupation, are far from the truth. Hence, relative earnings in different occupations in 'class' societies are likely to be more widely dispersed than they would be if the assumptions of these models were valid. We can expect, therefore, that, as barriers to free entry to education are reduced, earnings differentials between different occupations will decline. This hypothesis will be further examined and tested in later chapters, when we come to examine differences in the degree of dispersion of earnings between countries, and changes within countries over time.

6. Variation of Earnings with Age

We have traced, so far, the factors influencing the distribution of general abilities up to the time at which young people finish elementary education; and, secondly, the factors which determine the amount of education and training which they receive for specialized occupations. This carries us up to the stage at

[1] He also reports that the chances of children of parents who are in liberal professions, civil servants and the like, going to the university in France are one hundred times as great as for the children of industrial workers, and fifty times as great as for the children of farmers and farm workers.

which young people enter the work force (at which, of course, their ages vary, depending on how long they have spent in full-time education). And we have advanced reasons for expecting that the distribution of full-time earnings of young men, let us say in the age-group 25–29, will be lognormal leptokurtic. Now it is necessary to consider the effects of age on earnings, where by 'age' we mean all those factors which change with time for the individual.

When young people enter the work force they are more or less equipped to undertake a particular type of occupation. They are, if we care to use the analogy, 'semi-finished' products, available for use in a number of different ways. In a broad sense they are capable, at this stage, of earning a particular income, depending on their general level of ability, their education, and their vocational qualifications (and depending also, of course, on the general state of demand for labour and on any specific conditions affecting the demand for labour of a particular type). But, as time passes, several changes take place. First, there are changes in effective abilities, resulting from biological changes and the effects of experience. Secondly, there are changes in health and strength, and in personality characteristics, such as ambition, which again are the result of biological and environmental influences. And, thirdly, there are changes of status, resulting from promotion or other shifts in position within the hierarchy of employees within organizations. We should also add a fourth category, of miscellaneous factors as yet unidentified, which go under the heading of 'chance'.

Changes in Ability

Psychologists believe that problem-solving ability usually increases with age up to some point in adolescence and, on the average, begins to decline from the age of 20–25. This pattern emerges very clearly in cross-section studies of persons of different ages. A well-known study is that by Foulds and Raven (1948), in which nearly 2,000 male employees of two organizations in Scotland were given two types of test. The first was the

Progressive Matrices (1938) Test, which is described by the authors as

a non-verbal test of a person's capacity at the time of the test to form comparisons, reason by analogy, and develop a logical method of thinking regardless of previously acquired information. In other words, it is a test of a person's capacity to understand and apply a fresh method of thinking. It is in no sense a test of any specific ability or aptitude, but it has repeatedly proved to be a valuable test of a person's normal capacity to learn any particular knowledge or technical skill he may desire to acquire [pp. 136–7].

The results of this test, when applied to different age-groups in the general population, are summarized in Fig. 4.3a.[1]

In the words of Foulds and Raven, this figure shows that 'the capacity to form comparisons and reason by analogy increases rapidly during childhood, appears to reach its maximum somewhere about the age of 14, after which it remains relatively constant until from about the age of 25 onwards it slowly declines' (p. 141). It should also be noted that the dispersion of ability—on this test—tends to increase with age, both absolutely and relatively.

Although all the available evidence from cross-section studies supports the conclusion that problem-solving ability declines in the sort of way depicted in Fig. 4.3a, some longitudinal studies (based on retests of the same individuals at different ages) have shown no consistent decline in ability with age (Tyler, 1965, p. 285). It is possible that differences in early education and other experiences of people who are currently in different age-groups may partly or wholly account for the apparent change in measured abilities with age. Until further work has been undertaken, however, I think that we must assume that a decline in this type of ability commences some time in the twenties or early thirties.[2]

---

[1] Similar results were obtained by Wechsler in cross-section studies using the Wechsler–Bellevue Test. See, for example, the diagram on p. 31 of Wechsler (1958).

[2] It has been suggested that some of the apparent improvement in ability in longitudinal tests is the result of conditioning; but the whole question is a matter of continuing debate amongst psychologists.

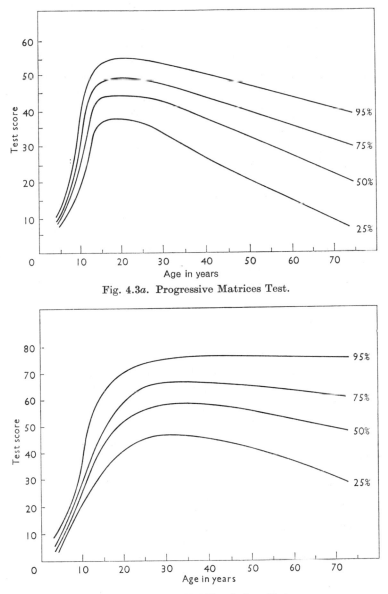

Fig. 4.3*a*. Progressive Matrices Test.

FIG. 4.3*b*. Mill Hill Vocabulary Test.

Source: Foulds and Raven (1948, p. 139).

As age advances there are changes not only in people's abilities but also in their accumulated *experience*. Experience is a factor which, by its nature, increases with age, at least so long as the loss of experience through failing memory is more than offset by the growth of new experience. Experience adds to effective ability by giving people an increasing repertoire of 'ready-made means of dealing with a situation' (Welford, 1958, p. 10). When confronted with a new problem, a man can either solve it from first principles or he can draw on his previous experience of dealing with similar problems. The older man, on average, may be less able to solve from first principles, but he has a wider experience of analogous cases to draw upon. Thus effective ability in the economic sphere (and probably elsewhere) will not decline exactly as depicted in Fig. 4.3a (even if we accept that as a correct picture of the changes in problem-solving ability with age). The value of experience can be represented by a line which slopes upwards with age, possibly resembling a logistic, with an upper ceiling. When this element is added to the pure problem-solving element, our measure of effective ability is likely to reach a maximum at a later age and to decline more slowly than in Fig. 4.3a. This is perhaps the explanation for the shape of the curves in Fig. 4.3b, which depict the results of a vocabulary test. This figure, which also comes from Foulds and Raven, is based on the Mill Hill Vocabulary Scale which, in their words, is a 'test of the general fund of information a person has acquired as a result of intellectual activity in the past' (p. 137). The figure shows that

the average person's ability to recall information normally increases up to the age of at least 25, and from about the age of 30 onwards remains relatively constant for about 25 years, after which it apparently declines a little. For people above the average, ability to recall information apparently continues to increase slowly even up to the age of 60. For people below the average the opposite appears to be the case. What ability they acquire in youth appears to decline fairly early in life [p. 141].[1]

[1] See also Bayley (1955, p. 817) on the tendency for intelligence measured by verbal concepts and abstractions to continue to grow amongst groups of 'superior' adults.

On the basis of these psychological studies it seems reasonable to predict that effective economic ability will tend to follow a path something like Fig. 4.3b, or perhaps something between 4.3a and 4.3b. But before we translate this prediction in terms of earnings we must allow for other factors. Actual earnings per unit of time depend not only on ability, as measured by these sorts of tests, but also on such factors as speed of response, health and strength, and ambition or willingness to work hard. It is well known, and indeed obvious from common observation, that, on the average, all of these decline beyond a certain age. Tyler (1965) summarizes evidence from a number of studies in these words (p. 290):

1. A gradual decline in all types of measurable ability sets in after thirty but does not become marked until well after fifty.

2. Sensory and perceptual abilities decline most and also earliest.

3. Motor abilities hold up well until late middle age, but there is a change in the methods by which tasks are done.

4. Performance in various kinds of learning experiments declines with age, but it is not clear whether actual ability to learn is impaired.

5. With regard to all these things there are wide individual differences, so that in any group there will be some persons superior to the average for groups much younger.[1]

When these factors are added, it seems that the most probable profile of earnings will be one which rises with ability, strength, and ambition during the first two decades of employment, reaches a maximum somewhere in middle age, and then begins to decline. The decline will be slow at first, but will gather speed from the late fifties or early sixties, when almost all factors are working towards reducing effective earning capacity. To this, however, there may be one exception, namely the effect of promotion within the managerial hierarchy. This one factor may result in a continued increase in status, and in accompanying earnings, for a few people right up to or beyond normal retirement age. But this is a factor which partly operates independently of ability, and it will be dealt with separately in the next section when we develop a theory for the 'Pareto tail'.

[1] See also Welford (1958).

Let us, then, compare our expectations about the typical age
profile of earnings with some actual observations. Table 4.12 and
Fig. 4.4 present estimates of medians, quartiles, and interquartile ranges for male wage and salary earners in Canada in
1960–1. Unfortunately, it is not possible to obtain similar data
for full-time males; but the general picture might not be much

TABLE 4.12

*Canada, 1960–1, Medians and Interquartile Ranges of Earnings
of Male Wage and Salary Earners aged 15 and over, by Age*

Age-group	Median	IQR	IQR/Median
	($)	($)	(%)
15–	1,142	1,345	118
20–	2,542	1,982	78
25–	3,845	2,178	57
35–	4,366	2,437	56
45–	4,274	2,532	59
55–	3,897	2,437	63
65–	2,890	2,421	84
All	3,679	2,328	63

Source: CA 1, Table 15.
Estimates based on those reporting earnings only.

altered if we could do so, except perhaps to reduce the slope of
the curves at each end of the age range. In general, the picture
presented is one which corresponds with expectations. An interesting feature is that the absolute degree of dispersion, as
measured by the interquartile range (which is most probably not
influenced by the 'hierarchy' effect) increases up to the 35–44
year age-group but remains fairly constant thereafter. This
result, which is generally confirmed by data from Sweden and
the United States, runs contrary to what might be expected
from the evidence about changes in abilities (see Figs. 4.3a and
4.3b) and is superficially in conflict with many inferences about
changes in degree of inequality of income with age made by
various economists.[1] In almost all cases, however, these inferences have been about *relative* income dispersion, as measured
by the coefficient of variation, the standard deviation of the

[1] See, for example, Mincer (1958), Kravis (1962), and Morgan (1962).

logarithm of income, or the Lorenz measure of inequality. And most of these studies have been based on data relating to families or spending units, or to income of individuals from all sources.

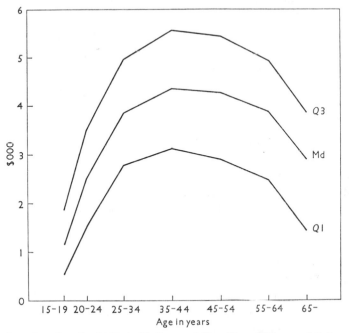

FIG. 4.4. Canada, 1960–1: Median and Quartiles of Wage and Salary Earnings by Age.
Source: CA 1, Table 15.

As can be seen from Table 4.12, there is no conflict here with the conclusion that *relative* income dispersion increases with age, at least beyond middle age.[1]

[1] This conclusion is, as we have said, broadly supported by data from Sweden and the United States. Unfortunately, it does not seem to be possible to analyse distributions of wages and salaries by age-groups for these two countries in the same manner as for Canada; but for Sweden a distribution of 1960 incomes from all sources of 'active' men shows no appreciable increase in the interquartile range from age-group 40–44 to 60–66; and in the United States a study of earnings from all sources in particular occupations gives much the same result, except for occupations containing a large proportion of managers or self-employed professions, such as accountants. Indeed, in many manual occupations even the *relative* dispersion of earnings seems to be very stable. These results, like the Canadian ones, are based on cross-section data, and might be upset if longitudinal data were available.

There is some evidence that age affects people in different occupations differently. Welford (1958, p. 53) mentions that 'several researches have shown that declines of performance with age are less among people of high educational or occupational level'. Where the difference is greatest is in 'fairly high-grade intellectual activity, judgement or the use of verbal or other symbols. With more straightforward sensori-motor tasks, differences of performance with educational and occupational level are usually small'. Some studies of earnings have also suggested the same conclusion, namely that those with higher education, or in more skilled occupations, reach a maximum somewhat later than others.[1] But the Canadian data, presented in Table 4.13, exhibit no tendency for *median* earnings to reach a maximum later for the more highly educated. It is possible that *mean* earnings would move somewhat differently, since there is some growth in dispersion within education groups, and probably also of skewness, as age increases. But it is also possible that some of the previous studies have been misleading, either because incomes other than wages and salaries have been included (e.g. profits of the self-employed), or because the conclusions have been based on cross-section material. In 1951, for example, median earnings of United States male labourers (except mine workers) were shown by Miller (1955, p. 54) to be at their maximum in the age-group 25–34, while according to the 1960 Census the median for male labourers (except farm and mine) did not reach its maximum until the age-group 35–44, the same as for many skilled occupations (US 3, Table 31).

One important conclusion to be drawn from Table 4.13 is that there is much greater absolute variation in earnings between age-groups amongst the more highly educated than amongst those with less education. University-educated men, for obvious reasons, take longer to reach their maximum earning capacity than others; but the maximum is much higher. The fall in their earnings in the final age-group is also much greater, both absolutely and proportionately. This last phenomenon, however, may be mainly a reflection of changes during the past generation

[1] See, for example, Lydall (1955), Miller (1955 and 1966), and Mincer (1958).

TABLE 4.13

Canada, 1960–1, Medians and Interquartile Ranges of Earnings of Male Wage and Salary Earners aged 15 and over, by Age and Education

Age-group	Elementary[1]			Secondary			University[2]		
	Median	IQR	IQR/Median	Median	IQR	IQR/Median	Median	IQR	IQR/Median
	($)	($)	(%)	($)	($)	(%)	($)	($)	(%)
15	1,010	1,307	129	984	1,464	149	678	728	107
20	2,191	1,857	85	2,914	1,732	59	1,883	2,806	149
25	3,163	1,999	63	4,223	1,897	45	5,530	2,938	53
35	3,421	1,862	54	4,635	2,153	47	7,014	4,199	60
45	3,363	1,947	58	4,599	2,433	53	7,007	5,177	74
55	3,246	2,017	62	4,313	2,600	60	6,505	5,747	89
65	2,298	2,174	95	3,103	2,644	85	4,251	5,004	118
All	3,089	2,207	71	3,961	2,403	61	5,575	4,699	84

[1] Includes some with no schooling and kindergarten only.
[2] Includes those with some university experience as well as those who graduated.

Source: CA 1, Table 17.

Estimates based on those reporting earnings only.

in the quality of university-trained men, or, at any rate, of the failure of older men to keep up in the rapid increases in salaries which have occurred during the past twenty-five years.

It is also interesting to note that, whereas we found that the absolute dispersion of all wage and salary earners showed no strong tendency to increase between age-groups, there is more evidence of such a tendency when the population is divided by educational level, especially amongst the university-educated. The rapid growth in the interquartile range of this latter group with age is most striking, and I suspect that it reflects the 'hierarchy' effect, which is concentrated heavily on this relatively small group.

The Role of Chance

From what has been said so far, it seems to be possible to account for observed changes in average earnings with age fairly adequately by regarding them as reflections of psychological and biological changes in ability, health, strength, and ambition. Does this imply that there is no room left for chance ? Of course, chance has never really been excluded, since all the variables we have been discussing have been probability variables. In any attempt to explain the behaviour of individuals there must always be a stochastic element, since no person exactly conforms to identified laws. There remains, in other words, a penumbra of ignorance; and it is to this that we give the label 'chance'.

But a more specific issue arises. As we saw in Chapter 2, some theories of income distribution have attempted to explain the shape of the distribution as being the outcome of an indefinitely repeated stochastic *process*. This is a different proposition. It is not merely the assertion that for example

$$Y = f(X) + \epsilon \tag{4.1}$$

where Y = earnings, X = 'ability', and ϵ is a random term; but that, for example,

$$Y_t = Y_{t-1} + \epsilon_t. \tag{4.2}$$

In the former case most of the explanatory power rests on 'ability', which may be regarded as representing all the identified independent factors. In the latter case, where the stochastic process is indefinitely repeated, virtually all of the characteristics of the income distribution are reflections of the probability distribution of ϵ_t, and nothing depends on changes in identifiable independent factors.

In so far as we have been able to discover independent factors which explain much or all of the variation of income with age we have, *ipso facto*, reduced the necessity for and relevance of a stochastic process theory of income distribution. We cannot exclude the possibility that there is some Markov chain component, that is, a dependence of current income on previous period income plus a random term; but there does not seem to be much need for it. A *sufficient* hypothesis to explain observed changes in earnings with age would be equation (4.1), where 'ability' is itself a function of age of the form discussed above. Each individual, in this case, would have an expected level of earnings, depending on his original general abilities, his education, and his age. His actual earnings would be his expected earnings plus the random term reflecting 'chance'.[1] The difference between an individual's earnings in year t and year $(t+1)$ would then depend partly on changes in his 'ability', induced by the change in his age, and partly on the difference between the two error terms.

It could be argued that, although income itself is not subject to a stochastic process, the factors which determine 'permanent' income are subject to such a process. We may have the equation

$$X_t = X_{t-1} + U_t \qquad (4.3)$$

where X = 'ability' and U_t is a random term. But we have already shown that average ability has a characteristic movement with age, which cannot be expressed adequately in terms of (4.3). Moreover, even in the case of the ability of individuals, it would be difficult to justify the assumption that the distribution of ability at or near the end of working life is mainly a consequence of a stochastic process. The correlation between initial and final abilities is likely to be large, which means that most of the final

[1] Cf. Friedman's (1957) distinction between 'permanent' and 'transitory' income.

variance depends on the initial variance, and relatively little on the stochastic process.[1]

In Chapter 2 we argued, on wider grounds, that stochastic process theories, such as Champernowne's, must be rejected as being unrealistic both in their assumptions and in their predictions. But it seemed that Rutherford's theory, which assumed a stochastic process to operate within each cohort, might be more realistic in both respects. The evidence presented in this section, however, is not easily reconcilable with Rutherford's theory, at least if it is to be applied to the distribution of employment incomes separately. In the first place, Rutherford's theory must clearly be modified to incorporate the parabolic movement of mean earnings over working life. But, secondly, Rutherford's theory implies that the variance of earnings in each cohort is growing over time. We have seen that there is some doubt whether this is true; and, even if it were true, it does not seem to be very important, except for a relatively small group of highly educated people. The increase in dispersion amongst these people can be explained on non-stochastic grounds, as will be seen in the final section of this chapter. Thus, although the data are not entirely inconsistent with Rutherford's assumption that there is a stochastic process within cohorts, they do not give strong support to his theory, or at least to the practical importance of his theory in explaining the distribution of earnings from employment.[2]

Implications of the Variation of Earnings with Age

The parabolic movement in the whole structure of earnings over working life, as reflected in, for example, the positions of the median and quartiles in Fig. 4.4, has certain implications for our theory of income distribution. We suggested that the distribution of earnings near the beginning of working life could be

---

[1] Of course, if individuals were eternal, and provided that the expected level of ability did not decline with age, the situation might be different.

[2] Since the absolute and relative importance of property ownership increases with age, and since a stochastic process theory of property income seems to be more plausible, Rutherford's theory in the form in which he advanced it, namely to apply to total income, is not directly contradicted by the facts presented here.

expected to be lognormal leptokurtic. If this shape were to be exactly retained over the span of working life, but the position of the distribution were to shift in some roughly parabolic fashion, and if the number of persons in each age-group were approximately the same, then the distribution of all employees —irrespective of age—would be more positively skew than the distribution within any single age-group. The overlapping of distributions at both younger and older ages would give double weight to the lower income classes in the aggregate distribution, while the number in the upper tail of the distribution would be largely composed of persons in a single age-group in the middle of the life-span. This may well be the explanation for the rather fat lower tail, which is a typical feature of most earnings distributions, even for full-time employees. The upper tail will be *relatively elongated*, but not sufficient to yield a Pareto distribution.

If, in addition, there is a tendency for the variance of earnings to increase with age, as there is in the Canadian case at least up to the 35–44 age-group, the result of aggregating distributions of different age-groups will be to accentuate the kurtosis of the distribution. We can, therefore, expect that an aggregate distribution of employees, of all ages and all occupations, will be more skew and more leptokurtic in the logarithm of income than a distribution of employees in a single age- or occupation-group.

7. The Upper Tail of the Distribution

It now remains to find a theoretical explanation for the Pareto upper tail. As mentioned earlier, this phenomenon does not occur in all distributions of employees but it seems to be typical of most. The principal exceptions are certain distributions from the communist countries of eastern Europe. Our theory will provide an explanation of this difference also.

Up to this point it has been assumed that employees' full-time earnings are mainly determined—in the long run—firstly, by the differential average cost of training for different occupations and, secondly, by the distribution of general ability within occupations. But not all jobs are paid on this basis. A dominant feature of modern industry is the rise of large organizations; and within large organizations there develops—inevitably—a hierarchic structure. The management 'chart' of a large organization is like a family tree, with one man at the top, and increasing numbers in each grade as we pass downwards to the bottom. In general, the function of each employee, apart from those in the lowest grade, is to supervise those in the grade immediately below him and, indirectly, those in all succeeding grades below that, who lie within his sphere of control. People occupy, as it is said, different positions of responsibility, and what they are paid depends on the degree of their responsibility. They are 'responsible' for the actions of all those below them, and in particular for those in the grade immediately below them; and, since each employee is assumed to be productive, or at least is costing the firm his salary, the amount of output for which each supervisor is responsible can be measured approximately by the total salaries of the people whom he controls.[1] It can be expected, therefore, that the reward for taking responsibility will be related in some way to the total salaries of the people for whom the employee concerned is responsible.

It should be noted that this criterion of payment is, in principle, quite separate from the criterion of ability. It is, of course, true that when a firm is selecting staff for promotion it will generally look for the most able (although people are often promoted on other grounds also, such as seniority or nepotism). But it is not the level of ability which determines the salary. The salary is determined mainly by the *post*, i.e. by the position in the hierarchy, which, as we have said, is an indicator of the number of people supervised, directly and indirectly.[2] And it is a universal rule that a higher post commands a higher salary.

[1] It could be argued that it is the gross value of output (including both labour and materials) falling under the control of the supervisor which is relevant, rather than the cost of labour alone. This may be so; but in practice the two hypotheses seem to amount to much the same thing over large sections of the economy.

[2] Cf. Patton (1961, p. 7) who writes that there is 'an apparently irresistible tendency in the business community—from the president to the office boy—to impute values to an executive *position*'. And he points out that even quite

Why this should be so may not be immediately obvious, when we consider the non-pecuniary advantages which men in higher positions often enjoy in comparison with those occupying more routine or more menial positions. Perhaps, as Marris (1964, pp. 92–3) has suggested, this is a sociological rather than an economic question, and the salary may be more an indicator of status than a reward for work done. In any case, as Marris remarks, the salaries of subordinates are decided by their seniors, who are unlikely to pay them more than themselves. 'Therefore, the world over, Presidents are paid more than Vice-Presidents, Commissars more than Deputy-Commissars, . . . and middle managers more than junior managers.' I think, however, that there is more in it than this. A man who accepts a higher post accepts responsibility for the work of all those in the grade below him. He has more 'worry' than any of his subordinates, and 'worry' is a cost for which he expects to be remunerated. I think there is little doubt that, if posts of higher responsibility were not paid more highly, there would be a marked shortage of people willing to take them.[1]

A Model of Hierarchical Earnings

As mentioned in Chapter 2, some years ago I suggested a simple model, based on the hierarchical principle, to account for incompetent people are still paid according to their status in the organization.

Patton recounts a story about Alfred P. Sloan, Jr., who was president of General Motors for twenty-three years. When he was once asked, 'What does it take to be a top executive in G.M. ?' he replied: 'Naturally such a man has superior talents, drive, and is ready to work hard. But, more importantly, he must be willing to pay the price of being a top executive, by putting company interests ahead of everything else, including a comfortable home life' (p. 26).

Klein and Haworth, in an article in the London *Observer*, 4 December 1966, wrote that in British industry 'despite all the emphasis on the need for technological and scientific expertise, the highest rewards tend to go to those with general managerial responsibilities. A technologist or scientist going into industry is only likely to get to the top, financially, if he abandons his special subject and moves into management.' Thus managerial *responsibility* is something separate from technical or other *ability*.

[1] Berliner (1966, p. 158) writes, in connection with the Czech economy, which 'is reported to have achieved the most equalitarian income distribution in Eastern Europe', that 'not only are the rewards for managerial excellence small, but the loss of income from demotion to the rank of engineer is so small that some managers regard demotion as a welcome relief from responsibility'.

the Pareto distribution of higher salaries (Lydall, 1959). A similar model had, in fact, already been put forward by Simon (1957). In this section I propose to explain my model in somewhat greater detail, and also to show how certain predictions of the model are consistent with observed phenomena.

The assumption is made that employees are arranged within a firm, hierarchically, in grades. To begin with, we shall assume that, in a given firm, there are k clearly defined discrete grades. G_i is the ith grade, where $i = 1, 2,..., k$, and the grades are numbered from the lowest upwards.

Now let x_i be the standard wage or salary in G_i and y_i the number of employees in that grade. Two crucial assumptions are now made:

$$y_i/y_{i+1} = n, \quad \text{where } n \text{ is constant for all } i \text{ and} > 1 \quad (4.4)$$

$$x_{i+1}/nx_i = p, \quad \text{where } p \text{ is constant for all } i \text{ and} < 1. \quad (4.5)$$

In words, we are assuming, firstly, that on the average managers in a given grade supervise a constant number of people in the grade below them, this 'grading constant' applying throughout the hierarchy; and, secondly, that the salary of managers in a given grade is a constant proportion of the aggregate salaries of the people whom they directly supervise.[1]

It is further assumed, for the reasons mentioned above, that $x_{i+1}/x_i > 1$, i.e. that $np > 1$.

Now, if there is only one man—the managing director or president—in G_k, the number in G_{k-1} will be n, in G_{k-2}, n^2, and so forth. Hence

$$y_i = n^{k-i}. \quad (4.6)$$

If we write Y_i for the total number of employees in all grades $\geqslant G_i$, then

$$Y_i = 1+n+n^2+...+n^{k-i} = \frac{n^{k-i+1}-1}{n-1}.$$

Let Q_i be the proportion of all employees in the firm who are in the grades down to and including G_i.

---

[1] A recent study which throws some light on this hypothesis is that of Thorelli (1965). His results are far from conclusive, but he believes that his tests do show 'a substantial degree of association . . . between the relative salaries of line executives and their salary spans of control (p. 301).

So
$$Q_i = \frac{Y_i}{Y_1} = \frac{n^{k-i+1}-1}{n^k-1} \approx n^{1-i}, \tag{4.7}$$

for reasonably large n or k.

We also have, from (4.5),
$$x_i = (np)^{l-1}x_1, \tag{4.8}$$

whence
$$i-1 = \frac{\ln x_i - \ln x_1}{\ln np},$$

After substituting for $(i-1)$ in (4.7), we obtain
$$\ln Q_i \approx \lambda \ln x_1 - \lambda \ln x_i \tag{4.9}$$

where $\lambda = \dfrac{\ln n}{\ln np} > 1$ (since $p < 1$ and $np > 1$).

Thus, for given values of x_1, n, and p, the relation between Q_i and x_i is approximately linear in the logarithms. Since we have assumed discrete grades, this is not a continuous function, as in the Pareto case, but we may call it a 'quasi-Pareto' distribution.

If, however, we now assume that i varies continuously, and that the relations (4.6) and (4.8) remain true within the range $1 \leqslant i \leqslant k$, then it is easy to show that expression (4.9) is true in the full Pareto sense, i.e. as a continuous function. Further, if all firms have the same values of x_1, n, and p, and, in all, the relations (4.6) and (4.8) apply continuously over the range $1 \leqslant i \leqslant k$ for various values of k, and provided that either n or k is reasonably large, then the expression (4.9) will be true of all employees in all firms combined.[1]

Finally, if we assume—more realistically—that the minimum wage is not constant in all firms but varies over a range, which is limited in comparison with the range of all earnings, it can be shown that, for all levels of income above the upper limit of the minimum wage, the expression (4.9) is still true.[2]

Some Empirical Tests of the Model

The prediction of the model is that the upper tail of the distribution of employee salaries will, in general, follow the Pareto law.

---

[1] See Appendix 4, section 1.   [2] See ibid., section 2.

We already knew, of course, that this was so. An interesting problem arises, however, in trying to account for the failure of some distributions to follow the Pareto law. On the basis of our theory we can predict that, in countries in which managers are not paid on the basis of responsibility, but on an 'ability' criterion, the upper tail of the distribution will not follow the Pareto law but is more likely to resemble the upper tail of a lognormal leptokurtic distribution. Interestingly enough, the countries in which the upper tail most consistently deviates from the Pareto law are those of communist eastern Europe. The distributions for Hungary, Czechoslovakia, and Yugoslavia all show curvature in the logarithmic relation between income level and the proportion of higher paid employees exceeding each level, and there is some evidence of the same phenomenon occurring in Poland in recent years. Hitherto, it has been the official policy of these countries to pay salaries according to 'ability' rather than responsibility;[1] and, in fact, communist managers have been given much less responsibility than managers in capitalist countries, since the task of a manager has been to carry out the plan laid down for him. In such a situation there is less reason for paying a manager a higher salary because he controls more men or materials, since there is less scope for him to exercise his initiative. The introduction of the new economic reforms in eastern Europe, however, will place much greater responsibility for the success or failure of an enterprise on its managerial staff, and it seems probable that, if the reforms are pursued vigorously, within a few years the distribution of salaries in eastern Europe will begin to follow the Pareto law.[2]

[1] The formula for income payments in the 'first phase' of communism, as originally laid down by Marx (*Critique of the Gotha Programme*), was that labour should be paid according to its quality and quantity.

[2] McAuley (1966) writes in relation to the wages system in Czechoslovakia: 'The first criticism directed against it is that wage differentials for production workers are too narrow; that they provide little incentive for the worker to raise his qualification. Also, present methods of payment give the worker little incentive to increase his productivity—the premia system is ineffective. Secondly, it is argued that differentials as a whole (i.e. between production workers and administrative workers, doctors, teachers, etc.) are too small; that there is little incentive to move into the higher professions' (p. 179). In the spring of 1964 the Czech government decided that wage equalization was

A second prediction of the model is that the salary of the managing director will be a function of the total number of people employed in the firm. If W is the salary of the managing director in a firm which employs N persons, then, on the assumptions of the model, it can be shown that

$$W \approx aN^{1/\lambda} \quad \text{where} \quad a = (\ln n)^{1/\lambda}x_1 \qquad (4.10)$$

and λ is as defined previously.[1] In practice, there is usually a high correlation between total sales and persons employed, so that the managing director's salary should, on our hypothesis, be related to sales as well as to the number employed. For example, if sales are proportionate to number employed

$$W \approx AS^{1/\lambda} \qquad (4.11)$$

where $S = $ sales and A is a constant; and, if the logarithm of sales is proportionate to the logarithm of number employed,

$$W \approx aS^{1/\beta\lambda} \qquad (4.12)$$

where β is the elasticity of sales with respect to number employed.

In recent years a good deal of information has been collected about the relation between managing director's salary and size of firm. Baumol (1959, p. 46) was, so far as I know, the first economist to suggest that 'executive salaries appear to be far more closely correlated with the scale of operations of the firm than with its profitability'; but he gave no data to support this view. Roberts (1959) analysed a sample of seventy-seven large United States corporations and found that both sales and profits were positively correlated with managing director's compensation (salary, bonuses, and deferred payments); but, since sales and profits were highly intercorrelated, it was difficult to determine which of them was more influential. On the basis of a number of different tests, however, Roberts concluded that sales was

partly responsible for the slowness of the rise in productivity and asked enterprises 'to widen differentials whenever possible' (p. 180). But the results of these changes are likely to be much less dramatic than those of the new economic reform, which, by placing a much greater responsibility for the success or failure of an enterprise on its management, will inevitably result in a considerable widening of managerial incomes.

[1] Proofs of this and succeeding propositions are given in Appendix 4, section 3.

a more important variable than profits ;[1] and when he discussed
this idea with businessmen he found that they generally felt that
it was right (pp. 105–8). From a regression of the logarithm of
managing director's compensation (C) on the logarithm of sales
(S) he estimated that the elasticity of C with respect to S was
0·37.

Patton (1961, p. 46) quotes some results from the McKinsey
survey of executive compensation in twenty-four industries in
the United States in 1959, which imply an average elasticity of
chief executive's compensation with respect to sales of 0·275. A
recent report by McKinsey and Company, Inc. (1965, p. 7) states
that on the average in the United States there is a 24 per cent
increase in the chief executive's compensation for each doubling
of sales. This implies an elasticity of 0·31. In Britain, France,
and Germany the elasticity appears—from the same source—to
be about 0·25. In each of these latter countries the correlation
between chief executive's compensation and sales is about
0·75–0·80. The correlation of chief executive's compensation
with number of employees is lower in Britain, but higher in
France and Germany.[2]

If our theory is true, if the minimum wage is the same in all
firms, and if sales are proportionate to the number of persons
employed, the coefficient λ, which is the same as Pareto's α, will
be the reciprocal of η, the elasticity of managing director's
salary with respect to sales. Thus, a further test of our theory is
to compare the reciprocal of the value of η, derived from cross-
section studies, with the value of α, derived from size distributions of employment incomes. Such a comparison is made in
Table 4.14 for a few countries. In all cases except the 1964 figure

---

[1] Roberts's conclusions are supported by those of McGuire and others (1962)
from an analysis of forty-five of the hundred largest corporations in the United
States, for which data were available for each year from 1953 to 1959. They
found a correlation of chief executive's salary with sales of 0·61, and with
profits of 0·55. The partial correlation of salary with sales, after removing the
effect of profits, was 0·25. They concluded that the evidence 'would seem to
support the likelihood that there is a valid relationship between sales and
executive incomes as Baumol assumed, but not between profits and executive
incomes (p. 760).

[2] Similar data are also given for a number of other countries, but the samples
of companies are so small that the results are of doubtful significance.

TABLE 4.14

Test of Hierarchic Model

Country and year	η	$1/\eta$	α
United States, 1959	0·275	3·64	3 25[1]
United States, 1964	0·31	3·23	—
Britain, 1964	0·25	4	2·8–3·5[2]
France, 1964	0·25	4	2·27[3]
Germany, 1964	0·25	4	3·4[4]

[1] Males working 50–2 weeks.
[2] All males, 1961–2. The slope varies.
[3] Males paid for the whole year in private and semi-public sectors, 1963.
[4] Males and females, full-year working, 1957.

for the United States, the estimate of η from the cross-section studies is lower than would be expected from the observed value of α. This inconsistency could be reconciled if the relation between managing director's salary and sales were of the form (4.12) with $\beta < 1$; which would imply that sales per employee were lower in larger firms than in smaller ones. But this seems rather improbable. Of course, the cross-section estimates for the European countries, especially those for France and Germany, are based on much smaller samples than in the United States, so that the discrepancies may be the result of sampling errors and biases. When due allowance is made for the limitations of the data, the results of this test are not, I think, unsatisfactory.

8. General Conclusions

At the beginning of this chapter we set out to answer the problem: How is it that children whose original genetic endowments are not very different should, by middle age or later, have spread out so widely that their earnings from employment have a range of as much as fifty to one? And how do we account, in particular, for the shape of the Standard Distribution, which is lognormal leptokurtic with, in most cases, a Pareto upper tail?

Our answer runs along the following lines. The dispersion of genetic intelligence is moderate, and, as far as we can tell, approximately normal. Measured intelligence, however, already incorporates some environmental influence, which may account for as much as 25 per cent of its total variance. Since environment and genetic ability are correlated, and possibly interact multiplicatively to some extent, and since the environmental factor in most countries is highly skew, we should expect the distribution of measured intelligence to be somewhat skew and leptokurtic. But it is difficult to verify this hypothesis, because the scaling of intelligence tests is largely arbitrary.

During the early school years, up to the end of elementary education, the environmental influences on the development of a child's abilities are very great. Achievement in school tests reflects these influences, as well as personality traits which are themselves partly genetic and partly environmentally determined. Once more, the environmental factor is skew, there is a positive correlation between it and the other factors, and there may be some multiplicative interactions. Hence, we can expect the distribution of achievement to be more widely dispersed than measured intelligence, and to be lognormal leptokurtic.

Preparation for specific occupations involves further periods of education and training. If children, or their parents, balanced the costs of this against the expected mean earnings in different occupations, and if there was a perfect market, we could expect the distribution of mean earnings of occupations to reflect (predominantly) differences in the periods of training. On special assumptions, if the distribution of required periods of training were normal, the distribution of mean earnings of occupations would be lognormal. In fact, the distribution of periods of training is skew, so that we can reasonably expect the distribution of mean earnings of occupations to be more skew than the lognormal. There is some evidence from a few countries that this is so.

If, within occupations, the distribution of ability is similar to the over-all distribution of 'general educated ability', and the distribution of mean earnings between occupations is lognormal leptokurtic, then the over-all distribution of full-time male earnings in the early years of work can be expected to be lognormal leptokurtic. But the variation of abilities and other traits with age results in a roughly parabolic movement of mean earnings over working life; and this factor tends to increase the skewness and kurtosis of the combined distribution of earnings of all employees, irrespective of age.

Finally, we have advanced a special theory, based on the hierarchic principle of management in large organizations, and the payment of managers according to their responsibility rather than their ability, which accounts for the existence of the Pareto upper tail. Some predictions from this theory have been tested and found, in general, to give it support.

If we go back, then, to the newly born child and consider what factors are likely to influence its ultimate position in the employment income structure, we can identify the following: first, its inherited qualities, of intelligence and other personality traits; secondly, and most important, the socio-economic class into which it is born and in which it grows up; thirdly, the type of school attended and the period of formal education; fourthly, the changes which occur in adult abilities, health, strength, and personality characteristics during the first twenty or thirty years in employment; fifthly, the individual's willingness and opportunity to take a managerial position at some stage in his career, and hence to move from the 'ability' criterion of payment to the 'responsibility' criterion; and, finally, at all stages, an element of luck, some of which may be purely temporary, and some more permanent in its influence on the subsequent career.

An infinite variety of combinations of these many factors is possible, and the ultimate distribution of individual earnings reflects both the variances of the component factors and the manner in which they interact. But, while any result is possible, the expected outcome for any individual is heavily influenced by the class into which he is born. At every stage, socio-economic class exercises a bias towards improving the chances of the upper-class child. His genetic endowment, on the average, is higher; his environment is better ordered and gives greater stimulus and opportunity to his development; his schooling is of better quality and more prolonged; he is encouraged to prepare for a superior profession or occupation, and the financial obstacles are less; and his opportunities of appointment and promotion are often favourably influenced by personal and family connections. While pure chance factors are important, the position within a given generation, in all countries, is that a child's career and its life earnings, are largely determined by the class into which it is born.

5

THE INTERNATIONAL COMPARISON

THE purpose of this chapter is to present the data which have been collected on the distribution of employment income in about thirty countries. A systematic search has been made for information from all countries, and it is believed that virtually all available sources have been covered. Each distribution has been classified according to our code (see Appendix 6); and the degree of dispersion of the distribution has been measured by techniques which will be explained below. On the basis of this preliminary processing it has proved possible to make approximate estimates of the degree of dispersion of the Standard Distribution in most of the countries. The countries have then been arranged in rank order of this degree of dispersion, and some preliminary comments are made on the results. Further analysis of the underlying causes of the differences between countries, with particular reference to the theoretical considerations outlined in the previous chapter, is deferred until Chapter 7, when we shall also be able to draw upon the data on changes in income dispersion within countries over time, which will be presented in Chapter 6.

1. Method of Measuring Dispersion

Many different methods of measuring dispersion—or inequality—have been proposed by different authors. Pareto's α coefficient is probably the first; but it measures only the shape of the upper tail. Gini's coefficient of mean difference and the Lorenz measure of concentration are two closely related alternatives. Their values, unlike Pareto's α, are influenced by the shape of the distribution over its whole range. But, as has frequently been pointed out, they are not unambiguous indicators of the degree of inequality, since distributions of various shapes may have the same concentration coefficient. If the distribution is exactly lognormal, of course, this problem does not exist; and we can measure the degree of relative dispersion either by the coefficient of concentration, or by the standard deviation of the logarithm of income, or by several other coefficients.[1] Other measures which have been used at one time or another are the coefficient of variation, the relative interquartile range and the relative inter-decile range. Recently some Hungarian statisticians have argued the merits of three new coefficients, derived from paired relations between the mean, the mean of all cases below the mean, and the mean of all cases equal to or greater than the mean.[2]

Doubtless, all of these coefficients have their uses, and some of them, such as the Lorenz coefficient of concentration, are especially popular. But the strength of a single coefficient—namely its ability to summarize a whole distribution in a single figure—is also its weakness. Since, as we have seen, distributions of income vary greatly in their shape, depending on how they are defined and on other circumstances, a single measure of dispersion—while convenient for some purposes—can also be misleading. The trouble is that a single coefficient summarizes too thoroughly. It leaves out too much of the detail which may be important in judging the character of the distribution. The use of a single index of inequality is, therefore, not an ideal arrangement, except where one can be fairly confident that the essential shape of the distribution, i.e. its functional form, is constant. And in those circumstances it does not matter much which of the many alternative indexes or coefficients are used.

Apart from this consideration, there is a very practical reason why, in this study, no attempt has been made to calculate Lorenz coefficients. In order to compute the Lorenz coefficient one needs *both* the number of persons in each income class *and* the amount of income received. If the latter piece of information is lacking, it is, of course, possible to estimate it for the closed income classes (by, for example, assuming that the mean of each class lies at its

[1] See Table A-1 in Aitchison and Brown (1957, pp. 154-5) for several examples of monotonically related coefficients of the lognormal distribution.

[2] See Éltető (1965) and his reference to the unpublished dissertation by Frigyes.

midpoint, or by some more sophisticated variant of this assumption), but the estimation of the mean of the upper open-ended class is not so easy. The best solution seems to be to assume that the upper tail follows the Pareto law (an assumption which can be roughly tested so far as the classes below the top class are concerned) and, after estimating the value of α from the last few known points, to extrapolate this value to cover the whole of the open-ended class. In that case the mean of the open-ended class, $\bar{X}_0$, is related to the lower limit of that class, X_0, by the formula

$$\bar{X}_0 = \frac{\alpha}{\alpha-1} X_0.$$

But there must always be a vestige of doubt about the validity of this assumption and, since the proportion of income received by the open-ended class is often quite substantial, any error in this assumption can have a significant effect on the estimate of the concentration coefficient. In the majority of cases the available distributions of employment income do not give the amounts of income received by each income class and, for the above reasons, I think it is preferable not to try to estimate them if alternative methods of measuring income dispersion are at hand.

An alternative method, which seems to me to be preferable, both on the ground that we need to study the shape of the distribution in its various parts, and on the ground that the data on aggregate income are often not available, is as follows. From the published frequency distributions we estimate, by graphic or other methods, the values of specified quantiles, and we relate these to one another. The particular technique which I have found to be both convenient and informative is to estimate the following percentiles, measured from the *top* of the distribution: $p_1, p_2, p_5, p_{10}, p_{20}, p_{50}, p_{75}, p_{85}, p_{95}$. Each of these is then expressed as a percentage of p_{50} (the median). If we use the notation

$$P_i = \frac{100 p_i}{p_{50}}$$

then P_1, P_2, P_5, P_{10}, and P_{20} tell us about the relative dispersion of the upper tail of the distribution, and P_{75}, P_{85}, and P_{95} tell us about the relative dispersion of the lower tail. When we are dealing with distributions which have essentially the same shape, e.g. lognormal distributions, all of these indicators of dispersion tell the same story (indeed, this is a useful empirical method of testing whether two distributions are essentially of the same form); but, when the distributions differ in shape, the indicators may move in different directions, and this helps us to understand what forces are at work.

In practice, in this study, estimates of the selected percentiles have been made by graphic interpolation of the cumulated frequencies (using natural, semi-logarithmic, and double-logarithmic paper, depending on the shape of the distribution and the portion being estimated). Experiments were also made in the use of an electronic computer to fit a logistic to a linear weighted sum of income and the logarithm of income; but the results were not generally found to be as reliable as those from the graphic process. Our estimates of the P_i for each distribution are given in detail in the Country Tables in Appendix 7. Each table contains the coding of its distributions and brief additional notes, where necessary, about special definitions or difficulties. The source of each distribution is given and the list of source references will be found in Appendix 8.

In studying these tables it is very important to pay attention to the definitions, as summarized in the code and notes. The position of the median of a distribution, in relation to the mean or mode, depends on the shape of the distribution and hence on its definition. A distribution of full-period males will be unimodal with a rapidly declining lower tail. Hence the median will be near the mode and the value of P_{95} will be 30 or more (see, for example, table FR–1, or table US–4). But a distribution of all male employees, irrespective of 'intensity' of work, will have a thicker lower tail, and the values of both p_{50} and p_{95} will be depressed, but especially p_{95}, so that P_{95} will be substantially lower than in the full-period distribution (see US–1). The effect of including part-period workers on the female distribution is usually even more dramatic, as can be seen by comparing tables US–2 and US–5.

Moreover, a change of definition effects not only the estimates of P_{75}, P_{85}, and P_{95} but also those of the upper percentiles. Usually the inclusion of all employees increases P_1, P_5, etc., compared with the full-period case (see table AU–1, where the effect is small, or tables GE–3 and US–1 and US–4, where the effect is somewhat greater). In some cases the distributions are truncated at the lower end, as where the data are drawn from tax assessments. This tends to raise the value of P_{95}, as can be seen in table AL–3, and it may well affect the upper percentiles also. It is not easy to compare truncated distributions with others, nor can one be sure how their parameters are affected when money incomes increase and the truncation point (for example, the tax exemption limit) is held constant. Such distributions must, therefore, be used with special caution.

2. A Summary of Results from the Between-Country Comparison

The variety of definitions used in the different countries is such that we can make a comparison only by bringing together data on a number of different definitions and trying to find some consistent relationships. Although, as we saw in Chapter 3, a very large number of different definitions are possible, of which a good many are in fact in use, the majority of actual distributions are included if we confine ourselves to eight main types. These are listed in the column headings of Tables 5.1, 5.2, and 5.3 (pp. 142–4).

The most frequently available distribution in non-communist countries is one which is often a by-product of income taxation —for all employees, in all industries, working with all intensities —as shown in Col. (1). In the communist countries, however, where data are not usually derived from income-tax sources, the commonest type of distribution is that which is shown in Col. (5), covering non-farm employees working full-period. There is a tendency, also, in all countries, for data on the earnings of manual workers to be collected on a full-period basis (see Col. (8)). In some countries no information (or very little) is available

[Cont. on p. 147.]

TABLE 5.1

Fifth Percentile of Selected Distributions by Country

		All employees — All industries			Non-farm			Manual workers, non-farm W and S	
		W and S		Total income	W and S		Total income		
Country and year	Sex	All (1)	F/P (2)	All (3)	All (4)	F/P (5)	All (6)	All (7)	F/P (8)
Argentina, 1961	T	246			231			201(m)	
Australia, 1959–60	M	190(p)							
	F	178(p)							
	T	200(p)							
Austria, 1957	M	223	220						
	F	247	237						
	T	234	227						
Belgium, 1964	M					(206)			150
	F					187			144
	T					(205)			158
Brazil, 1953	M					389			
	F					334			
	T					386			
Canada, 1960–1	M	214	203		212			177	
	F	221	195		218			192	
	T	230	214		225			185	
Ceylon, 1963	T								
Chile, 1964	M					(378)		349	
	F							278	
	T							362	
Czechoslovakia, 1964	T				170				
Denmark, 1956	T			218(p)					
Finland, 1960	M			273(p)					
	F			272(p)					
	T			286(p)					
France, 1963	M					282			190
	F					226			178
	T					274			200
Germany (F.R.), 1957	M	211							148(a)
	F	242							143(a)
	T	225	213						154(a)
Hungary, 1962	M					181		163	
	F					163		151	
	T					190		173	
India, 1958–9	M								
	F								
	T							297	263
Japan, 1955	M					270			
	F					235			
	T					303			
Mexico, 1960	T	599			506(m)				
Netherlands, 1959						223(p)	231(p) (f)		162(p)
New Zealand, 1960–1	M			183			180		
	F			194			191		
	T			191			187		
Poland, 1960	M								195
	F								175
	T				210				204
Spain, 1964	F				239				
Sweden, 1959	M			212(p)			197(b)	158(t)(b)	
	F			259(p)			188(b)	160(t)(b)	
	T			232(p)					
United Kingdom, 1960–1	M	199(p)	199(a)						161(a)
	F	218(p)	208(a)						153(a)
	T	214(p)	200(a)						169(a)
United States, 1959	M	214	206		212	206		183	169
	F	237	182		235	183		228	183
	T	238	215		235			207	178
Yugoslavia, 1963	T						207		

(a) Adults only.
(b) Manufacturing, mining, and building.
(f) Full-period.

(m) Manufacturing only.
(p) Persons assessed for tax.
(t) Total income from all sources.

TABLE 5.2

Tenth Percentile of Selected Distributions by Country

		All employees			Non-farm			Manual workers non-farm, W and S	
		All Industries							
		W and S		Total income	W and S		Total income		
Country and year	Sex	All (1)	F/P (2)	All (3)	All (4)	F/P (5)	All (6)	All (7)	F/P (8)
Argentina, 1961	T	194			184			171(m)	
Australia, 1959–60	M	161(p)							
	F	159(p)							
	T	172(p)							
Austria, 1957	M	177	174						
	F	197	190						
	T	187	180						
Belgium, 1964	M				164				135
	F				158				132
	T				165				142
Brazil, 1953	M				252				
	F				207				
	T				242				
Canada, 1960–1	M	176	167		173			158	
	F	188	168		188			171	
	T	189	176		187			163	
Ceylon, 1963	T				273				
Chile, 1964	M							277	
	F							228	
	T							279	
Czechoslovakia, 1964	T				150				
Denmark, 1956	T			185(p)					
Finland, 1960	M			211(p)					
	F			218(p)					
	T			227(p)					
France, 1963	M				205				163
	F				185				155
	T				203				169
Germany (F.R.), 1957	M	170							185(a)
	F	199							132(a)
	T	181	173						140(a)
Hungary, 1962	M				156			144	
	F				144			136	
	T				162			153	
India, 1958–9	M								
	F								
	T							240	212
Japan, 1955	M				211				
	F				193				
	T				237				
Mexico, 1960	T	349			299(m)				
Netherlands, 1959	T					177(p)	180(p)(f)		146(p)
New Zealand, 1960–1	M			152			150		
	F			167			166		
	T			161			159		
Poland, 1960	M							167	
	F							157	
	T				176			174	
Spain, 1964	T				196				
Sweden, 1959	M			169(p)			161(b)	142(t)(b)	
	F			214(p)			160(b)	147(t)(b)	
	T			186(p)					
United Kingdom, 1960–1	M	162(p)	161(a)						145(a)
	F	176(p)	166(a)						138(a)
	T	176(p)	164(a)						152(a)
United States, 1959	M	176	168		174	167		162	149
	F	204	161		203	161		197	162
	T	197	176		195			182	157
Yugoslavia, 1963	T				174				

(a) Adults only.
(b) Manufacturing, mining, and building.
(f) Full-period.

(m) Manufacturing only.
(p) Persons assessed for tax.
(t) Total income from all sources.

TABLE 5.3

Seventy-fifth Percentile of Selected Distributions by Country

| | | All industries | | | Non-farm | | | Manual workers, non-farm, W and S | |
| | | W and S | | Total income | W and S | | Total income | W and S | |
Country and year	Sex	All (1)	F/P (2)	All (3)	All (4)	F/P (5)	All (6)	All (7)	F/P (8)
Argentina, 1961	T	69			73			73(m)	
Australia, 1959–60	M	79(p)							
	F	62(p)							
	T	63(p)							
Austria, 1957	M	73	77						
	F	63	69						
	T	64	69						
Belgium, 1964	M				84				86
	F				82				83
	T				78				77
Brazil, 1953	M				..				
	F				..				
	T				..				
Canada, 1960–1	M	64	77		67			66	
	F	50	69		51			59	
	T	56	70		58			62	
Ceylon, 1963	T					71			
Chile, 1964	M							53	
	F							59	
	T							53	
Czechoslovakia, 1964	T				79				
Denmark, 1956	T			65(p)					
Finland, 1960	M			53(p)					
	F			44(p)					
	T			51(p)					
France, 1963	M				73				75
	F				75				79
	T				71				73
Germany (F.R.), 1957	M	74							86(a)
	F	59							86(a)
	T	58	67						80(a)
Hungary, 1962	M				81			82	
	F				82			82	
	T				78			79	
India, 1958–9	M								
	F								
	T							54	70
Japan, 1955	M					64			
	F					76			
	T					61			
Mexico, 1960	T	57			66(m)				
Netherlands, 1959	T				54(p)	54(f)(p)			55(p)
New Zealand, 1960–1	M			79			82		
				70			71		
				65			65		
Poland, 1960	M								75
	F								63
	T				75				74
Spain, 1964	T				72				
Sweden, 1959	M			69(p)			79(b)	79(t)(b)	
	F			51(p)			70(b)	70(t)(b)	
	T			52(p)					
United Kingdom, 1960–1	M	75(p)	85(a)						83(a)
	F	78(p)	75(a)						85(a)
	T	66(p)	74(a)						77(a)
United States, 1959	M	61	74		63	75		62	74
	F	42	70		43	70		50	72
	T	50	68		52			54	69
Yugoslavia, 1963	T					76			

(a) Adults only.
(b) Manufacturing, mining, and building.
(f) Full-period.
(m) Manufacturing only.
(p) Persons assessed for tax.
(t) Total income from all sources.

Notes on Tables 5.1, 5.2, and 5.3

Argentina: Wage and salaries from main employment only. Sources: Col. (1), table AR–1; Col. (4), table AR–2; Col. (7), table AR–3.

Australia: Persons assessed for tax, with income of £105 or more. Sources: tables AL–4, 5, and 6.

Austria: Wage-tax data, including pensioners. Exclusion of pensioners from combined M and F reduces 1st, 5th and 10th percentiles from 379 to 376, 234 to 228, and 187 to 181. Full-period means employed for 335 days or more. Sources: tables AU–1, 2, and 3.

Belgium: Social-security tax data, excluding mines, government, and (probably) agriculture. Earnings per day expressed as monthly rate. Higher incomes extrapolated from 1947 (for non-manual) and 1955 (for manual). Sources: Col. (5), table BE–1; Col. (8), table BE–2.

Brazil: Federal government employees. Nearly 180,000 persons covered. Estimates rough. Source: table BR–1.

Canada: Census data. Full-period is 40–52 weeks. Manual excludes personal services as well as farm. Sources: Col. (1), tables CA–1, 2, and 3; Col. (2), tables CA–10, 11, and 12; Col. (4), tables CA–4, 5, and 6; Col. (7), tables CA–7, 8, and 9.

Ceylon: Central government employees. Over 280,000 persons covered. Estimates rough. Source: table CN–1.

Chile: Based on claims for unemployment benefit by nearly 100,000 workers out of 1,340,000 covered by social security. Source: table CH–2.

Czechoslovakia: Employees in socialized industry (almost entirely non-farm) who worked at least 180 h in May (or 160 h in certain industries), Source: table CZ–1.

Denmark: Estimated from post-tax data by applying average tax rates at each percentile level. Source: table DK–1.

Finland: Income-tax data, but exemption limit is very low. Only persons whose major source of income was wage or salary covered. Source: table FN–1.

France: Excludes agriculture, household service, and government administration. Average monthly earnings expressed as an annual rate. Sources: Col. (5), table FR–13; Col. (8), table FR–14.

Germany: All employees based on wage-tax statistics. A few high and low earners may be excluded. Full-period means working eleven months or more. Manual data based on a survey; excludes apprentices and agriculture, transport and government, and limited to establishments employing 10 or more. Sources: Cols. (1) and (2), tables GE–2 and 3; Col. (8), tables GE–4, 5, and 6.

Hungary: Includes a small number of state farm employees. Sources: Col. (4), table HU–1; Col. (7), table HU–2.

146   THE INTERNATIONAL COMPARISON

India: Survey data. Urban workers in crafts and production processes, including self-employed artisans (hence not strictly wage and salary income). Full-period means working 43–56 h in the week. Estimates rough. Source: table IN–1.

Japan: Special survey by tax authorities. Excludes workers in firms where no person is subject to tax, and employees of government and public enterprises. Source: table JA–2.

Mexico: Census data. Covers all reporting income from employment in May 1960. Source: table ME–1.

Netherlands: Income-tax data, in which married couples are counted as single units. Part-period workers counted at equivalent annual rate. Wage and salary income is for persons for whom this is their main source of income. Sources: Col. (4), table NL–4; Col. (6), table NL–2; Col. (7), table NL–5.

New Zealand: Census data. Sources: Col. (3), tables NZ–1, 2, and 3; Col. (6), tables NZ–4, 5, and 6.

Poland: Employees in the socialized sector, including a few state farm employees. Covers only full-time workers who worked throughout the month of September. Manual M and F data are for 1961, although combined data are for 1960. Sources: Col. (5), table PO–1; Col. (8), tables PO–3, 5, and 6.

Spain: Excludes government employees and establishments employing less than ten manual workers. Wages and salaries include family allowances. Source: table SP–1.

Sweden: Col. (3) from income-tax assessments. Exemption limit Kr. 1,200. Non-farm data are from Census and relate to 1960; limited to manufacturing, mining, and building. Sources: Col. (3), tables SW–11, 12, and 13; Col. (6) tables SW–4, 5, and 6; Col. (7), tables SW–8 and 9.

United Kingdom: Col. (1) based on income-tax assessments under Schedule E (wages, salaries, pensions, and miscellaneous fees). Excludes secondary sources of earnings. Exemption limit £190. Col. (2) based on sample survey in 1953–4, since when dispersion has grown slightly according to tax data. Refers to persons working 48 or more weeks in the year. Manual data are for males 21 or over and females 18 or over, in most industries except agriculture, coal mining, docks, railways, commerce, and personal services. Limited to those normally working 30 or more hours in the week. Earnings are for a week in October when establishment was working normally. Sources: Col. (1), tables UK–1, 2, and 3; Col. (2), table UK–9; Col. (8), table UK–7.

United States: Census data. Covers all in the experienced civilian labour force on date of Census, who had $1 or more of wage or salary in 1959. Full-period means working 50 or more weeks in the year. Sources: Col. (1), tables US–1, 2, and 3; Col. (2), tables US–4, 5, and 6; Col. (4), tables US–7, 8, and 9; Col. (5), tables US–10, 11, and 12; Col. (7), tables US–13, 14, and 15; Col. (8), tables US–16, 17, and 18.

Yugoslavia: Sample survey data. Some farm employees (in state farms) probably covered. Income is *net of taxes* (but these are not very progressive). Limited to 'permanent' employees—presumably those at work in each month of the year. Source: table YU–1.

---

about the distribution of employment income as such, but tabulations have been made—usually from income-tax sources —of the total income of employees. This is the main type of information available for Denmark, Finland, and Sweden, as shown in Cols. (3) and (6). The greatest variety of information is usually available for those countries which have collected income data in their population censuses, especially the United States and Canada, and to some extent New Zealand and Sweden. Mexico, also, collected income data in its most recent census, but the tabulations are rather limited.

For some countries the only source of information about the distribution of income of employees is on a household basis. This is true in a number of the poorer countries, where income data have been collected in the course of household budget surveys. It is difficult to know how to interpret these household income distributions in relation to our normal distributions of employees; the available material is summarized in Table 5.8, and we shall discuss it briefly when we come to that point.

The purpose of Tables 5.1, 5.2, and 5.3 is to bring together estimates of P_5, P_{10}, and P_{75} for all available distributions of the eight types listed in the column headings, and on this basis to enable us to draw some conclusions about the degree of dispersion of employment income in each country. What we intend to do is to estimate the values of P_5, P_{10}, and P_{75} for the Standard Distribution in each country (or rather for a slightly modified version which includes non-adult males). The Standard Distribution is represented (in its modified form) by figures for males in Col. (5). As will be seen, this precise distribution is available for only Belgium, Brazil (for government employees only), France, Japan, and the United States. The problem is, therefore, to find a way of estimating the percentiles of the Standard Distribution for the remaining countries, with the help of the estimated percentiles of other variants of income. It had originally been hoped that there would have been a reasonable number of cases in which data were available from the same country on two or more definitions, so that the effects of changing definitions could be judged on the basis of a sample of at least five or six cases. But it turns out that this is not always possible. The largest number of cases in which percentiles are available for two alternative definitions occurs in the comparison of Cols. (1) and (2), and (5) and (8). In Cols. (1) and (2) there are four countries —Austria, Canada, Germany, and the United States—with published distributions for the same year on both a full-period and an all-period basis, and one—the United Kingdom—for which there are estimates of the two distributions from different sources and for different years. Cols. (1) and (4) occur together in four countries, of which one—Mexico—is probably not very reliable; and Cols. (4) and (7) also occur together four times. Cols. (5) and (8) are available for five countries, of which one—the United States—already appears in the previous combination. Cols. (4) and (5) occur together only once; and Cols. (7) and (8) twice, of which one consists of some rather shaky data for India. The greatest difficulty, however, is in moving from Cols. (3) and (6) to Cols. (1) or (2) and (4) or (5). The Netherlands seems to be the only country which prepares distributions on both a total income and an employment income basis for the same group of people; and there are certain features of its tabulations which are not exactly in line with our requirements.[1]

Some further difficulties also arise. In some countries there are no separate tabulations for males and females, so that the male percentiles must be estimated from the percentiles for males and females combined. A few distributions, mainly amongst workers, are for adults only. Some of the non-farm distributions, also, are confined to manufacturing only, or to manufacturing, mining, and building. The distributions of full-period employees sometimes include part-time workers and

---

[1] In particular, the inclusion of married women's income with the income of their husbands.

sometimes, explicitly or implicitly, exclude them. And the period of measurement varies—from a year to a day.

As if all this were not enough, a fundamental problem sometimes occurs in deciding who should be counted as an 'employee'. In the case of distributions of wage and salary income, in principle everyone with any income at all from this source should be included, unless there are explicit exclusions of, for example, part-period workers. But in the United States and Canadian censuses the persons who are included (in most tabulations) are those who were members of the employee work force at the date of the census. Thus part-period workers who ceased to work before the date of the census are excluded, whilst those who happened to be at work (or looking for work) at that date are included. Again, where the distribution measures total income from all sources, there is room for many different definitions of an employee. The most common one is that employees are those whose main source of income in the period of measurement (usually a year) was wages or salary. But an alternative is to include those who 'normally' spend most of their working time in employment, or—as in the New Zealand census—those who gave their occupation as employee at the date of the census. In a special Australian definition the people included in 'Occupation 1' are those who received less than a small amount (£100 in recent years) from non-employment sources.

It is obvious that it is impossible to take account of all these complications in a statistically respectable manner with such a limited sample of countries (and with an even more limited number of observations of particular definitions). Hence, the method followed in estimating the percentiles of the Standard Distribution for each country has essentially been to use 'considered judgement'. From inspection of Tables 5.1, 5.2, and 5.3 we can draw the following tentative conclusions.[1]

1. The dispersion of full-period workers is always less than the dispersion of all-period workers. The difference for males is of the same order in Canada and the United States, but somewhat

---

[1] Compare our discussion of the effects of differences of definition on the degree of dispersion in Chapter 3.

less in Austria and, possibly, in the United Kingdom. In the United States, which is the only country for which we have both full-period and all-period data for manual workers as well as for all employees, the difference in dispersion is actually greater for manual workers—both absolutely and relatively—than for all employees. This is presumably because most part-period employment is concentrated on manual workers. Amongst females, moreover, the difference in dispersion between full-period and all-period employees is much greater than amongst males, because there is more part-period work amongst females; and a consequence of this is that distributions of both sexes combined differ more than purely male distributions.

2. Total income is more widely dispersed than income from wage and salary only. But, as we have said, the only data we have to go on came from the Netherlands; and the difference is not very large.

3. Non-farm employees are less dispersed than those in all industries, mainly because farm workers generally receive lower wages than non-farm workers. The difference is very large in Mexico (although this is partly because the non-farm distribution is limited to manufacturing), but surprisingly small in Canada, New Zealand, and the United States. Argentina, the Netherlands, and Sweden are in an intermediate position in this respect.

4. Manual workers are, of course, less dispersed than all employees; but the relative difference varies quite considerably between countries. Table 5.4 summarizes what I have called the 'class differential', which is defined as the ratio of (P_A-100) to (P_M-100), where P_A is the percentile value for all male employees and P_M is the corresponding percentile value for manual workers (each percentile being first expressed as a percentage of its own median). These figures suggest that class differentials are fairly small in the communist countries, and in the more developed countries of recent settlement, such as Argentina, Canada, and the United States, but wider in Europe. Within Europe there is perhaps a tendency for differentials to grow as one moves south-eastward, although the basis for this conclusion

TABLE 5.4

Class Differentials in Certain Countries, in Approximate Rank Order

	Differential coefficient[1]	
	P_5	P_{10}
Poland[2]	1·1	1·0
Argentina	1·3	1·2
Hungary	1·3	1·3
Canada[2]	1·5	1·3
United States	1·5	1·4
United Kingdom	1·6	1·4
Sweden[3]	1·7	1·5
France	2·0	1·7
Belgium	2·0	1·8
Netherlands[2]	2·2	1·9

[1] $(P_A-100)/(P_M-100)$, where P_A = percentile for all male employees and P_M = percentile for male manual workers. Only comparable distributions are used for each country, except Sweden (see below), but the type of distribution used is not the same for all countries.

[2] Based on males and females combined.

[3] Manual percentiles in manufacturing, mining, and building only, while all employees include all non-farm. Hence differential coefficients may be upward biased.

is very limited. It must be remembered that this particular concept of class differential is not the same thing as over-all degree of dispersion. The class differential will be small where dispersion is high amongst both manual and all employees—as it is in Argentina—and large where the dispersion of manual workers is very low, as in Belgium or the United Kingdom, but the dispersion of all employees is average.

5. The dispersion of females is sometimes greater than the dispersion of males, and sometimes less. Where all employees (in all industries, working at all intensities) are covered, female dispersion is generally greater, mainly because of the greater proportion of part-period female employees. Amongst full-period employees, however, the dispersion of females is more often less than the dispersion of males; and amongst manual workers almost universally so (except, strangely, in the United States in 1959).

6. The dispersion of both sexes combined is generally wider than the dispersion of males, but it is sometimes less than the dispersion of females. It is difficult to find any consistent pattern here.

3. The Percentiles of the Standard Distribution

With the help of these—and other—observations an attempt has been made to estimate *approximately* the values of P_5, P_{10}, and P_{75} for the modified Standard Distribution in each country represented in Tables 5.1, 5.2, and 5.3. These estimates were then used to rank countries in order of degree of dispersion (of full-period non-farm males), and the results are given in Table 5.5. *It should be emphasized that these estimates are based on personal judgement of the data given earlier, in Tables 5.1, 5.2, and 5.3.*

For only four countries—Belgium, France, Japan, and the United States—are direct estimates available on the required definition; and the Belgian data are not very good, for the reasons given in the notes to Tables 5.1, 5.2, and 5.3. For a few more countries the difference between the desired definition and the actual definitions available are not great, e.g. Canada (where the exclusion of farm workers seems to make little difference to the all-employee distribution), Hungary (for which the original data may already be virtually on a full-period basis), and the United Kingdom (in which farm workers are a very small section of the population, who do not differ greatly from the others). The estimates for Czechoslovakia, Germany, New Zealand, Poland, and Yugoslavia are more uncertain, but they are probably not far wrong. The most difficult countries to estimate are: Argentina, where we need to move from 'all' to 'full-period', and also from 'T' to 'M'; Australia, where we need to move from 'all' to 'full-period', and also to 'non-farm' (which may not involve a very great adjustment);[1] Austria, where the move to 'non-farm' may be important; Brazil, where the available data cover only federal government employees; Chile, where the basis of the estimate is some (unsatisfactory) data for manual workers only; Denmark, Finland, and Sweden, where we have

[1] Some help is given by table AL–8, although not above P_{10}.

TABLE 5.5

Approximate Rank Order of Countries by Degree of Dispersion

Country and year	Percentiles of Standard Distribution[1]			Skill differential: bricklayers[4]
	P_5	P_{10}	P_{75}	
Czechoslovakia, 1964	165	145	85	..
New Zealand, 1960–1	178	150	83	89
Hungary, 1964	180	155	83	75
Australia, 1959–60	185	157	84	91
Denmark, 1956	200	160	82	82
United Kingdom, 1960–1	200	162	80	87
Sweden, 1959	200	165	78	94
Yugoslavia, 1963	200	166	80	..
Poland, 1960	200	170	76	..
Germany (F.R.), 1957	205	165	77	76
Canada, 1960–1	205	166	79	63
Belgium, 1964	206	164	82	90
United States, 1959	206	167	75	72
Austria, 1957	210	170	80	82
Netherlands, 1959[2]	215	175	70	75
Argentina, 1961	215	175	75	74
Spain, 1964	220	180	75	75
Finland, 1960	250	200	73	88
France, 1963	280	205	73	..
Japan, 1955	270	211	64	65
Brazil, 1953	380	250	..	..
India, 1958–9[3]	400	300	65	..
Ceylon, 1963	400	300	..	83
Chile, 1964[3]	400	300	..	..
Mexico, 1960	450	280	65	68

[1] This is the 'modified' Standard Distribution, including non-adult males.
[2] Married couples in this distribution are treated as single units.
[3] Very rough estimates based on data for manual workers only.
[4] Hourly wage rates in 1964 for adult labourers in building expressed as percentage of rates for bricklayers. Some of the rates are 'prevailing', some 'average', some 'standard', and some 'minimum'. The data for Denmark, Hungary, and Japan are earnings, not rates. Where a range of rates is given the mid-point has been taken. The United States figure is the median of six cities, the United Kingdom figure is the median of four cities, the Swedish figure is the median of three cities, the Belgian figure is the average of Brussels and the provinces, and the Australian figure is the average of Melbourne and Sydney. Source: ZA 12, 86–116.

only distributions of total income; Ceylon and India, where the underlying data are extremely limited;[1] Mexico, where the census results are not too reliable, and in any case need to be adjusted to a full-period basis; Netherlands, where the original data refer to tax assessments, in which married couples are counted as single units, and where separate distributions for male employees are not published; and Spain, where we have to move from 'T' to 'M', and where the original data on wages include family allowances.

In spite of all the difficulties, I believe that the *general* picture presented in Table 5.5 is reasonably correct. In detail, however, I have felt considerable uncertainty about where to put the Netherlands and—to a lesser extent—Spain and Argentina. I have also been somewhat surprised by the results for France. On all normal criteria one would have expected France to occupy a position in the rank order at least in the region of Spain and Argentina, if not higher. But the French statistics seem to leave no room for doubt about the accuracy of the result shown, which is consistent with the degree of dispersion found in France since at least 1959 (see table FR–4). The estimates for Brazil, India, Ceylon, Chile, and Mexico are obviously very rough; yet they are probably of the right order.

In the next chapter we shall be making some use of the 'skill differential' as a measure of the degree of dispersion. We shall there point out some of the weaknesses of this indicator and the unsatisfactory nature of many of the quoted figures for skill differentials. But the skill differential is *some* sort of indicator of wage dispersion, at least within the manual worker group. In a spirit of curiosity I decided to estimate skill differentials for as many as possible of the countries listed in Table 5.5, to see how they would compare with my own—quite independent—estimates of dispersion. The most easily available skill differential— and one which seems to mean approximately the same thing in different countries—is the ratio of the building labourer's rate to the bricklayer's rate. In its regular survey of wage rates in a

---

[1] Note that the estimates derived from a survey in Bombay City (table IN–2) suggest a less wide dispersion than those used here.

large number of countries, the International Labour Organization obtained rates in 1964 for bricklayers and building labourers in eighteen of our twenty-five countries, and the skill differentials computed from these are given in the final column of Table 5.5 (see the note to the table for further details). The most relevant comparison seems to be between these differentials and

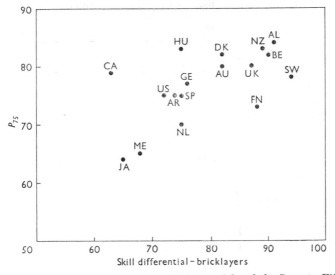

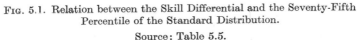

FIG. 5.1. Relation between the Skill Differential and the Seventy-Fifth Percentile of the Standard Distribution.

Source: Table 5.5.

P_{75}; and a scatter diagram of these two columns is shown in Fig. 5.1. The result suggests that there is a positive relation between the two measures, although not a very close one (the value of r is 0·59). It also suggests that skill differentials vary more widely than P_{75} and that, approximately, the value of P_{75} changes by two-fifths of the change in the skill differential. Of course, other measures of the skill differential might well give different results; but there are no satisfactory standardized measures of skill differentials for a wide range of countries. It must be remembered, also, that our estimates of P_{75} are subject to error, in fact probably subject to more error than the estimates of the percentiles above the median.

In view of the roughness of our estimates, it may be desirable to arrange countries in class intervals of relative dispersion. This is done in Table 5.6. Although it would be rash to make

TABLE 5.6

Groups of Countries in Rank Order of Dispersion

	Percentiles of Standard Distribution[1]		
	P_5	P_{10}	P_{75}
Czechoslovakia New Zealand Hungary Australia	165–85	145–57	85–83
Denmark United Kingdom Sweden Yugoslavia Poland Germany (F.R.) Canada Belgium United States Austria	200–10	160–70	82–75
Netherlands[2] Argentina Spain	215–20	175–80	75–70
Finland France Japan	250–80	200–15	73–64
Brazil Chile[3] India[3] Ceylon Mexico	380–450	250–300	65

[1], [2], [3]: See corresponding notes to Table 5.5.

categorical statements, it does seem that our twenty-five countries fall into five groups. The most equally distributed countries (in terms of employment income only) are two communist countries—Czechoslovakia and Hungary—and the two countries of Australasia. For this group, P_5 lies between 165 and 185, P_{10} between 145 and 157, and P_{75} between 85 and 83. The next group, which seems to be very homogeneous in terms of dispersion, consists of eight countries from western Europe and North

America, plus Yugoslavia and Poland. Here P_5 lies between 200 and 210, P_{10} between 160 and 170, and P_{75} between 82 and 75. Next we have three countries—Netherlands, Argentina, and Spain—with P_5 in the range 215–20, P_{10} in the range 175–80, and P_{75} in the range 75–70. The fourth group also contains only three countries—Finland, France, and Japan—but it has a wider range of dispersion: P_5 is between 250 and 280, P_{10} between 200 and 215, and P_{75} between 73 and 64. Finally, we have five countries from Asia and Latin America with the greatest degree of dispersion: P_5 is in the region of 400, P_{10} between 250 and 300, and P_{75} at 65 (for the two countries for which estimates of P_{75} are available).

The broad picture seems, then, to be that, amongst non-communist countries, the degree of dispersion of pre-tax employment income is related roughly to the degree of economic development, although Australia and New Zealand are exceptionally equal on this criterion, and France is exceptionally unequal. The communist countries are, in relation to level of economic development, all more equal than the non-communist countries, but amongst them the more highly industrialized seem to be more equal than the others. The widest dispersion occurs amongst the very poor and industrially backward countries of Asia and Latin America.

Of course, if taxes, transfers, and fringe benefits could be taken into account the picture might be rather different. The structure of direct taxes is much more progressive in the advanced capitalist countries than in the communist countries. If we made an adjustment for this factor only, the countries of western Europe and North America would rise in the rank order compared with those of eastern Europe.[1] If, further, we allowed for family allowances, France, and perhaps Belgium, would improve their position somewhat compared with the other developed capitalist countries. But we have, at present, no means of estimating the effects of private fringe benefits on the degree of inequality of effective employment income. If the

---

[1] The Yugoslav percentiles are, in fact, already based on a post-tax distribution.

figures cited in Appendix 1 are at all typical of the position in
the non-communist countries, then private fringe benefits may
offset a large part of the equalizing effects of progressive income
taxes.[1] Even if all the appropriate adjustments could be made,
it seems likely that the dispersion of net real employment incomes in Australia and New Zealand would be smaller than in
other non-communist countries; France would still remain
exceptionally unequal; and the poor countries of Asia and Latin
America would stay at the bottom of the list.

TABLE 5.7

*Approximate Rank Order of Countries by Dispersion of Manual
Workers' Earnings*

Country and year	Percentiles of Standard Distribution[1]		
	P_5	P_{10}	P_{75}
Belgium, 1964	150	135	86
Germany (F.R.), 1957	150	137	85
Netherlands, 1959	153	140	70
Sweden, 1959	155	140	80
Hungary, 1962	162	143	83
United Kingdom, 1960–1	162	146	82
Canada, 1960–1	165	145	78
United States, 1959	169	149	74
France, 1963	190	163	75
Argentina, 1961	190	165	75
Poland, 1960	195	167	75
India, 1958–9	250	190	75
Chile, 1964	300	250	60

[1] In principle this refers to male manual workers, non-farm and non-service,
of all ages, working full-time and full-period.

Two further tables may help to shed a little more light on the
differences between countries. The first is Table 5.7, which shows
an approximate rank order of countries (for which data are
available) in terms of dispersion of *manual* workers' earnings
only. The ordering of the countries in this table is broadly similar
to that of the same countries in Table 5.5; but there are a few
interesting differences. The communist countries—Hungary and

[1] No information is available about the incidence of fringe benefits in communist countries, but a number of isolated facts suggest that there too they
may be progressive.

Poland—have fallen in the rank order, and Belgium, Germany, and France have risen. This suggests, as we have already seen in Table 5.4, that 'class differences' between manual workers and managers are greater in the latter three countries and smaller in eastern Europe.

TABLE 5.8

Approximate Rank Order of Certain Countries by Dispersion of Household Income: (1) *All Employees, Urban or Non-farm*

Country and year	Percentiles of household income					Source table
	P_5	P_{10}	P_{20}	P_{75}	P_{95}	
Hungary, 1962	190	165	140	72	40	HU–3
United Kingdom, 1964	..	180	144	75	48	UK–10
Israel, 1959–60	..	192	150	76	(35)	IS–3
Japan, 1963	..	196	152	74	39	JA–2
Yugoslavia, 1963[1]	..	..	153	72	42	YU–1
Ivory Coast, 1956[2]	246	214	171	71	43	IC–1
Korea (Rep.), 1963	(296)	224	169	69	33	KO–1
Guatemala, 1952–3	327	263	194	64	(29)	GA–1
Philippines, 1961	..	293	205	64	27	PH–1

(2) *Manual Workers, Urban or Non-farm*

Country and year	P_5	P_{10}	P_{20}	P_{75}	P_{95}	Source table
Hungary, 1962	181	159	136	73	41	HU–4
Italy, 1953–4[2]	192	162	136	79	52	IT–1
United Kingdom, 1964	..	167	142	77	50	UK–10
France, 1956	207	172	143	73	45	FR–15
El Salvador, 1954[3]	216	183	150	80	(39)	ES–1
Puerto Rico, 1953	..	188	150	70	(39)	PR–1
Indonesia, 1957[4]	226	196	153	77	47	ID–1

[1] Income after tax.   [3] Three towns only.
[2] Total expenditure, not income.   [4] Djakarta only.

Table 5.8 contains data on the dispersion of *household* income of employee households in a few countries for which such figures could be obtained. In the top half of the table the distributions relate to all households headed by employees, while the bottom half contains only those in which the head is a manual worker.

As in previous tables, the least developed countries are, generally speaking, more widely dispersed than the more developed. It is perhaps surprising to find that the dispersion of household income in Israel is about as great as in Japan, especially in view of the number of complaints which have been made in Israel about excessive equalization. Perhaps it is the complaints which have helped to establish the present differentials, which, as can be seen in table IS–3 in the appendix, seem to have widened considerably in recent years.[1] It is interesting also to find that dispersion in Yugoslavia is about the same as in Japan. There are not enough countries in the table to permit us to draw very strong conclusions, and in any case it is difficult to know how to interpret distributions of household income or to relate them to distributions of individual earners. But the evidence from this table is consistent with previous evidence on individual dispersion, and it tends to confirm the impression that inequality is greatest in Asia, Africa, and Latin America.

Finally, there are three countries for which some scraps of information have been collected. For Greece, we have in tables GR–1 and GR–2 data on a limited group of families and persons who were assessed for income tax. These figures suggest, as we should expect, that the dispersion of earnings is fairly wide in Greece; but exactly how it compares with other countries is impossible to say.

For Norway there are two estimates. The first is a distribution of manual workers in manufacturing and mining in 1960 by hourly earnings, roughly adjusted to remove the effect of overtime premiums (see table NO–1). The dispersion is very low—as is to be expected when the effects of variations in hours are eliminated—but is similar to the dispersion of hourly earnings of

---

[1] Irving Sobel, writing in Galenson (1962), says that wage differentials in Israel 'are undoubtedly among the narrowest in the world'; and that the range of pay between the lowest paid Israeli workers and the highest paid technical or professional groups 'is perhaps the narrowest in the world' (p. 243). These comments do not seem to be supported by the data in tables IS–1 and IS–2, or by the figures for household income quoted above. It may be that the situation has changed since the period to which Sobel refers; or it may be that people misjudge the degree of inequality in their midst by relying too heavily on quoted figures of nominal rates, rather than on actual earnings.

manual workers in industry, trade, and services in Germany in 1962 (table GE–7). Allowing for the fact that the German distribution covers a more heterogeneous group of industries, and that no adjustment has been made to the German figures for overtime premiums, one might conclude that there is little to choose between the two distributions. On this basis we might decide to place Norway somewhere near Germany in the rank order of over-all dispersion in Table 5.5. But a discrepant note is struck by the estimates in table NO–2, which suggest a rather wide dispersion of household income in Norway, especially for households below the median. Unfortunately, these data are not strictly for households in the normal sense; they are probably more like the tax data for persons in the Netherlands, which include the incomes of married women with their husbands. In fact, the dispersion shown in table NO–2 is fairly close to the 1959 dispersion of Netherlands income shown in table NL–2, except in the extreme upper tail. On this argument, then, we might be inclined to rank Norway near the Netherlands in Table 5.5. Until better data are available from Norway it will be impossible to resolve this problem.

Finally there is the great enigma of the U.S.S.R. Distributions of employment income in Russia for 1914, 1928, and 1934 have been studied and discussed by Bergson (1944). We have analysed these distributions by our standard technique in tables UR–1 and UR–2; but these figures are now only of historical interest and we shall postpone comment on them until Chapter 6. Since 1934 no distributions of any kind have been published for the Soviet Union. Goldman (1965, p. 368) quotes Figurnov for the statement that in 1959 the average earnings of Soviet employees in the top 10 per cent of the distribution was 5·8 times the average of the bottom 10 per cent. This measure of dispersion is not a particularly robust one, since its value depends heavily on the estimated total earnings of workers in the bottom tenth of the distribution. If the distribution includes young people, females, part-time workers, or people who have not worked the whole year, the size of this coefficient of dispersion will be substantially increased, as can be seen if one compares the value of P_{95} in various tables in the appendix.[1] We do not know exactly how the Soviet distribution is defined. In most cases, the published eastern European distributions relate to full-time, full-period workers in the socialist sector, including both men and women. Apprentices are included in some countries (e.g. Hungary) but excluded in others (e.g. Poland). If we assume that the Soviet data refer to full-time, full-period employees of all ages and both sexes, then we have the following approximate corresponding figures for some other countries: Canada, 1960–1, about 7; France, 1963, about 10; Poland, 1964, and Hungary, 1962, less than 5.

Another set of data is quoted by Yanowitch (1963, p. 686), in the form of interdecile and interquartile ratios, for wage earners only. In 1959 these were stated, in the Soviet source, to be 3·28 and 1·84 respectively. The corresponding figures for non-farm manual workers in the United States in 1959 were about 6·9 and 2·7 for all workers and 3·5 and 1·9 for those working 50–2 weeks in the year; in Hungary in 1952, for non-farm manual workers, probably working full-period, they were 3·5 and 1·6; and in the United Kingdom in 1960, 2·6 and 1·6 respectively. On the basis of these few straws we may guess that the dispersion of all employee incomes in the Soviet Union is somewhat greater than in Hungary and less—on a pre-tax basis—than in the United States or most of western Europe; but the dispersion of manual workers' earnings may well be greater than in western Europe.

This completes our discussion of between-country differences in employment income dispersion. In the next chapter we turn to consider the evidence on changes in dispersion over time. After that we shall be ready to discuss all our data in the light of the theory suggested in Chapter 4; and to submit the theory to some empirical tests.

---

[1] P_{95} is the median of the bottom tenth of the distribution and it usually overestimates the mean; but it is sufficiently close to the mean to give some indication of the effects mentioned in the text.

6

CHANGES IN DISPERSION OVER TIME

A SATISFACTORY theory of employment income distribution
should be able to explain both differences in dispersion between
countries and changes in dispersion within countries over time.
For this reason we have collected empirical data on distributions
of employment income not only for as many countries as possible but also for as many years as possible in each country.
Each distribution has been analysed according to our standard
technique, and the relative percentile values are given in the
Country Tables in Appendix 7. But in our discussion of changes
in wage dispersion over time we can also draw on another source
of information, namely, the skill differentials. Until recently,
most discussions of changes in wage structure depended almost
entirely on estimates of the skill differentials; and a large
literature has grown up around them. Before we can proceed,
therefore, it is necessary to consider what is meant by a skill
differential and how these differentials have been estimated.

1. The Meaning of a Skill Differential

A skill differential may be defined in various ways; but all
definitions have one basic component, namely, the ratio of the
wage in a skilled occupation in a particular industry to the wage
of unskilled labour in the same industry. Very frequently, also,
use is made of the reciprocal of this ratio. Skill differentials are
usually estimated only for adult males, but there is no reason, in
principle, why they should not be computed also for females. In
addition to the simple case of the differential between 'fully
skilled' and 'fully unskilled' wages, estimates can be made of
the ratio of unskilled to semi-skilled rates, or of semi-skilled to
skilled; but this becomes more difficult to control because of
greater uncertainty in the definition of semi-skilled occupations.

So far we have not specified what is meant by the 'wage' of a skilled or unskilled worker. A wide range of possibilities exists. It can mean the collectively agreed standard rate of pay for a time-worker working the standard week; or an observed rate for a standard week; or an average or 'typical' rate for a standard week. Alternatively, it can mean the actual average earnings of a group of workers for an actual week (including both time- and piece-workers); or average *hourly* earnings in an actual week; or 'straight time' hourly earnings, exclusive of overtime premiums. And many other definitions could be employed.

Unfortunately, the definition of the wage used in computing particular skill differentials is often described in very vague terms. Many authors refer, without further specification, to 'wage rates', which leaves open a wide range of different inter-pretations. If all workers in a given occupation were paid the standard rate (and of course they would all have to be time-workers for this), and if all worked the same number of hours, the term 'wage rate' would be unambiguous. In practice, nominal rates of pay vary considerably for the same class of workers, even sometimes within the same firm, and hours of work also vary; so that actual weekly earnings—even of time-workers in a narrowly specified occupation—have an appreciable disper-sion. Moreover, there is no guarantee that the average of actual earnings will be related in any consistent way—between indus-tries and over time—to nominal standard rates.

The use of skill differentials to indicate changes in relative wages of different occupations has been largely a pragmatic matter, and I know of no clear statement of the theory under-lying it. What can be inferred from the discussions which have taken place is that the authors concerned have been searching for a measure of the *relative price of labour* of different qualities. What is implicitly assumed is that labour of a given quality is a clearly definable category, and that there is *one* price of such labour in a given market. This latter assumption implies the existence of a perfect market, or of some form of enforced wage-fixing. But, in fact, it is extremely difficult to define precisely what is meant by a particular quality of labour service; and the price of labour, even of a carefully defined quality, seems to vary greatly between firms and between industries, even in a single market area. Which, of course, suggests that the labour market is very imperfect.

For example, Reynolds (1951, p. 190) found wide variations in New Haven in the starting rates of twenty-eight manufacturing firms for the same type of labour, the ratio of the highest paying plant to the lowest paying being more than 1·7, both in 1940 and in 1948. Lester (1952, p. 488) studied a large number of manufacturing plants in Trenton, New Jersey, during 1951 and found that, while 'the two or three top-paying firms in the area clearly had a work force of higher quality than the two or three lowest-paying firms', it was difficult to discover any close relationship between quality of labour and starting rates in intermediate firms.

For example, firms with starting rates of around $1.00 an hour and average hourly earnings of $1.50 to $1.70 an hour often seemed to have a work force and a pace of operations that compared favourably with firms in the same sort of operations or industry which were paying starting rates of around $1.30 and had average hourly earnings from $1.85 to $2.10.

Slichter (1950, p. 80) found that hiring rates for common labour in eighty-five plants in Cleveland in 1947 varied from 50 cents to over 100 cents an hour.

Hill and Knowles (1956) published some interesting figures on average earnings during a specified week in May 1952 of time-working fitters and labourers in engineering firms in Britain. Weekly earnings of fitters ranged from under 130 shillings to over 320 shillings, with an interquartile range of 46·1 shillings; and even hourly earnings ranged from under 3 shillings to 6 shillings and over (p. 101). For labourers, hourly earnings ranged from less than 2·6 shillings to 5·4 shillings, although over half of the firms were within the range 2·8–3·2 shillings (p. 118). These figures, of course, include firms in various parts of the country, so that regional differences are responsible for part of the dispersion; but inter-firm differences within a small market area are still considerable.

Hourly rates for various occupations in Jamaica are given in the Jamaican *Annual Abstract of Statistics*. In September 1963 the rate for a motor mechanic in the mining industry ranged from 7s. 2d. to 10s. 4d.; and unskilled male labourers in the same industry could get from 5s. 3d. to 7s. 9d. Similar, or even wider, differences are quoted for other industries. In the Philippines in 1937 the ratio of the maximum to the minimum daily rate for skilled workers was as much as five in some industries, and for unskilled workers more than four (PH 2, p. 728).

Even within a single firm there is often a wide variation in the earnings of workers of a defined level of skill. Ostry, Cole, and Knowles (1958) analysed the earnings in a normal week of skilled, semi-skilled, and unskilled workers in a large British steel firm, and found that there was a considerable overlap between the distributions. They drew the following important conclusions:

But even if skill could be rigorously defined and every worker accurately graded, the complexity of modern industrial processes is such that the administrative need for retaining a two- or three-fold skill classification (appropriate enough to more primitive methods of production) itself introduces complications. As each broad category will comprise workers of very different degrees of skill, the range of skills within each category may well include differences almost as great as that between the average levels of skill of the different categories. In practice, of course, the grading of workers by skill can rarely be defended as accurate. In any case skill is only one of the recognized elements of doing a job; other elements—responsibility for men or materials, intensity of physical or mental effort, hazards or other unpleasantness—are also eligible for reward. Some of these elements may on occasion be rewarded by specific payments above the wage rate, or they may be taken into account—though perhaps not explicitly—when the level of the rate itself is fixed. Practice in these respects may differ even within a single department of a single firm; thus a straight comparison of the wages of workers in different skill categories may tell one little about even the imputed relative skills of these workers. That overall differences in workers' wages, regardless of their composition, should continue to be loosely referred to as 'skill differentials' results from a persistence in classifying jobs only by skill; and it implies an essential tidiness and rationality which is belied by the haphazard development of many wage structures [p. 221].

It is clear, therefore, that the skill differential is a difficult concept to define unambiguously, and even more difficult to measure accurately. This does not mean that the skill differential is useless as a measure of wage dispersion, but rather that it should bo used with care, and with special attention to the way in which it has been computed.

Let us reconsider what it is that we are trying to measure. Unless we have a reason for wanting to study the earnings of a particular occupation, it is to be presumed that we wish to measure the over-all degree of dispersion of earnings, either for all employees, or for manual workers taken separately. There arc good arguments, as we have said earlier, for limiting the coverage of the distribution to adult males working full-time and full-period. The question is then: How much information about the dispersion of this Standard Distribution can we expect to get from a study of skill differentials ? Now the over-all distribution of earnings can be broken down into two components— the dispersion between occupations and the dispersion within occupations—and it is only the former component that can be measured by the skill differential. As we saw earlier, the dispersion between occupations is generally only a minor proportion of the total: for example, in the United States in 1959 the variance between occupations accounted for less than a quarter of the total variance of earnings of males working 50–2 weeks. Thus, at the best, the skill differential can help to explain only a part of the over-all dispersion of earnings.[1]

But this is not all. Even as a measure of occupational dispersion the skill differential suffers from two weaknesses. First, it will usually be either upward or downward biased; and, secondly, it is subject to sampling error. As is shown in Appendix 5,

[1] An example of the way in which the use of skill differentials may suggest quite misleading conclusions is the following quotation from the editorial introduction to Galenson (1962, p. 8): 'For one reason or another, narrow rather than wide differentials seem to prevail in underdeveloped countries. In Pakistan, the skilled–unskilled ratio is about two to one, roughly the United States ratio a quarter of a century ago. The premium for skill in Indonesia is only about 50 per cent, while Israel has one of the most compressed wage and salary structures in the world.' Compare these comments with our estimates of dispersion in Tables 5.5 and 5.8 (using India as an approximation for Pakistan).

under conditions where the expected value of the change in all skill differentials is zero, the actual dispersion of occupational earnings is likely to be increasing; so that the skill differential indicator will be downward biased.[1] More generally, when dispersion is changing, skill differentials which are small in the initial situation will tend to underestimate both upward and downward movements, while differentials which are large in the initial situation will tend to overestimate changes in either direction.[2] At the same time, since the practice is to use only a few skill differentials to estimate changes in dispersion, there is clearly an element of sampling error in any such estimates.

The most serious problem which arises in the use of skill differentials is, however, to ensure that the wage definition used in the calculation is both clear and relevant. Differentials based on wage *rates* are almost always suspect and can often show movements quite different from those based on *earnings*. This is particularly likely to be the case where rates are being controlled—as part of a deliberate policy of equalization—but earnings are effectively out of control. It is probable that a good deal of the 'wage drift' which has appeared in certain countries is a reflection of this fact. As a recent report by O.E.C.D. remarked (1965, p. 33), the available figures on occupational wages 'rarely represent the level of earnings in a given occupation adequately, and to the extent that wage drift compensates for the failure of basic rates to move in line with earnings, they may also be poor indicators of the movement of earnings over time'.

In spite of all these difficulties, however, skill differentials are sometimes the only information we have about changes in dispersion; and they are often the only series which is published annually. We shall, therefore, refer to the available figures on

---

[1] As an illustration of this bias, consider the case where in year 1 the work force is divided into two equal groups, one receiving $2 an hour and the other $4 an hour. Now assume that over the next n years there is an equal chance of each person increasing or decreasing his rate by $1. Then the expected mean differential in year $(n+1)$ is the same as in year 1, i.e. 2. But the standard deviation of wage rates will increase from $1 in year 1 to $1.414 in year $(n+1)$.

[2] For a further discussion of the problem of bias see Bahral (1962).

skill differentials in our discussion below and attempt to use them so far as they can be trusted.

We shall now consider the evidence on changes in dispersion in particular countries. Since by far the greatest volume of data is available for the United States, we shall start with that country and proceed via Canada to western Europe and Australasia. The evidence for other countries, except Japan, is very limited; and we shall leave them until the last.

2. Changes in Dispersion in the United States

For the United States we have the following principal data: (1) annual estimates of skill differentials in building from 1907, and estimates of skill differentials in manufacturing for selected years since the same date; (2) more general estimates of changes in the dispersion of occupations for a few individual years; (3) estimates of percentiles of all employees in considerable detail for the census years 1939, 1949, and 1959, and for a few industries in the 1890s. We shall start by considering the evidence on long-period changes over the past half-century or more, and then examine the more abundant evidence on the changes in dispersion since 1939.

Long-Period Changes

The only long continuous annual series indicative of wage dispersion is the series for skill differentials in the building industry, first published by Ober (1948) and later extended to 1952 by Douty (1953).[1] This series shows the percentage ratio of union hourly wage rates for journeymen to the rates for labourers and helpers, based on data collected by the Bureau of Labor Statistics. The series is depicted in Fig. 6.1 (which also contains, for comparison, similar data for the United Kingdom). Over the whole period the change has been very large: a differential of 185 in 1907 had fallen to 138 in 1952 (and, according to O.E.C.D., to 127 in 1959–61). Even so, the level reached in the 1940s was still above the typical level in the United Kingdom in the 1930s. Within the period, there have been very substantial

[1] The O.E.C.D. report (1965) adds a further figure for 1959–61.

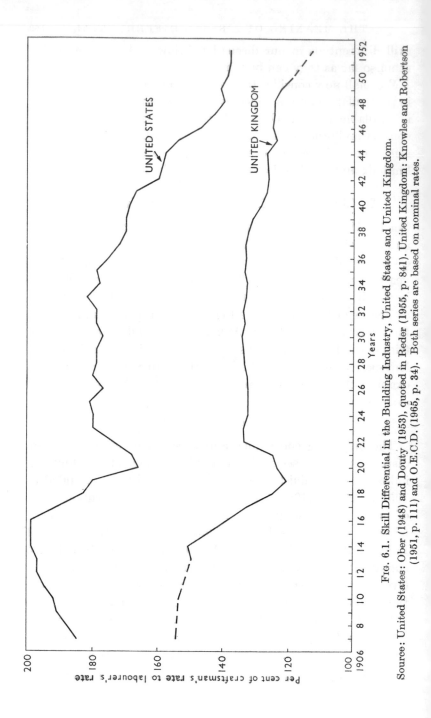

Fig. 6.1. Skill Differential in the Building Industry, United States and United Kingdom.

Source: United States: Ober (1948) and Douty (1953), quoted in Reder (1955, p. 841). United Kingdom: Knowles and Robertson (1951, p. 111) and O.E.C.D. (1965, p. 34). Both series are based on nominal rates.

fluctuations in both the direction and the rate of change of the differential. In the years before the First World War the building differential was increasing, and by 1916 it had reached nearly 200; but from 1916 to 1920 it fell precipitately back to 166. From 1920 to 1923 it made a sharp recovery, but only to a level around 180; and this level was maintained, more or less, for the next ten years. In 1933 the differential began a long downward slide, which, with only brief interruptions, it seems to have maintained until at least 1960. The most notable features of this series seem to be: first, the sharp effects of the First World War, and its aftermath; secondly, the period of unusual stability from 1923 to 1933; and, thirdly, the steady decline since 1933. We may also note in passing that the broad picture is very like that observed in the United Kingdom—except that it is magnified.

Various attempts have been made to explain the movements in this skill differential. The factors most commonly suggested have been prices, employment, immigration, education, and trade-union activity. It is not part of our purpose to enter seriously into this debate, since it would require a major research effort to arrive at a well-founded view; and, in any case, we cannot be sure that the building skill differential is a reliable indicator of changes in wage dispersion generally. But it seems fairly obvious from inspection of Fig. 6.1 that the differential does not correlate closely with the business cycle. The correlation with prices is considerably better, especially from 1916 to 1922 and from 1940 onwards; but prices fell substantially from 1929 to 1933, and there is not much evidence that the skill differential increased. The question whether the slump of 1929–33 had any appreciable effect on skill differentials is one which has been much debated; but no firm conclusion seems to have been reached, or probably could be reached without a great deal more research effort. On balance, it seems doubtful whether differentials increased very much, if at all, during this period.[1]

---

[1] Dunlop (1939) studied movements in the quartiles of hourly earnings of wage-earners in 14 industries and 179 occupations and found that from 1928 to 1932 there was some tendency for the relative interquartile range to widen for males, but not for females. From 1933 to 1937, on the other hand, in 76 out of 96 cases the range narrowed. Hence he concluded that dispersion tends

Two of the other factors which have been suggested, namely immigration and education, are by their nature unlikely to influence year-to-year fluctuations in differentials. Both immigration and education affect the qualitative composition of the stock of labour, but we should hardly expect to notice an immediate response to changes in the composition of the current flow of new members of the labour force. The influence of these factors, however, may well be of profound importance over the long run. In Chapter 7 we shall consider these, along with other factors influencing the dispersion of educated abilities in the labour force; and we shall try to assess the extent to which they explain both the differences in dispersion between countries and the changes within countries over time.

The influence of trade unions on wage dispersion is a difficult problem to analyse satisfactorily. Much has been written on this; but little conclusive evidence has been produced. There was a rapid growth of trade-union membership in the United States from 1933 onwards, when the position of the unions was greatly strengthened under the law, and this may partly explain the fall in the skill differential from 1933 to 1941. The policy of the unions may also be responsible for the continued fall in the 1940s. But some economists would argue that, at the most, trade-union policy may have affected nominal rates, while earnings would reflect underlying market forces of supply and demand.[1] My own view is that the main effective influence of the trade unions in this field is probably to strengthen the forces of the market rather than to run counter to them. When there are weak trade unions there are usually considerable market

to widen in depression and close again during recovery. Bell (1951) studied changes in hourly earnings and wage rates in over 600 occupations and found no clear evidence of widening of differentials in the period 1928–32; but his method of analysis is faulty (it is an example of the regression fallacy) and it gives his results a downward bias. Even so, if there had been any substantial widening of differentials in these years I think that Bell's method would have detected it. Reder (1957) also made a careful study of the evidence and concluded that 'there is no clear cyclical pattern of occupational wage rate differentials' (p. 372). 'The wage advantage of the skilled increased during the 1920–1921 depression but not in that of 1929–1932' (p. 373).

[1] See Reder (1957, p. 375) who argues against the views expressed by Turner (1952).

imperfections, which the growth of trade unions tends to sweep away. Thus, a once-for-all strengthening of trade unions may appear to have a large effect, although it is really only a means of bringing the market closer to its underlying equilibrium position.

So far, we have considered movements in only one set of skill differentials. Additional, although less complete, information is available for differentials in United States manufacturing, and this is given in Table 6.1. The estimates, which come in the main

TABLE 6.1.

Skill Differentials in the United States

	Building[1]	Manufacturing[2]
1907	185	205
1918–19	182	175
1931–2	179	180
1937–40	170	165
1945–7	148	155
1952–3	137[3]	137
1959–61	127	138[4]

[1] Union wage scale for journeymen as a percentage of the wage scale for labourers and helpers in the building trades.

[2] Median of average straight time hourly earnings of skilled occupations as a percentage of earnings of unskilled in a large number of manufacturing industries.

[3] 1951–3.

[4] 1955–6.

Sources: Ober (1948), extended for years subsequent to 1947 by data in O.E.C.D. (1965, p. 34) and in Miller (1966, p. 79).

from Ober's pioneering article (1948), are unfortunately only for a few years; but for these years, as the table shows, they move very similarly to the building differential. Whether they would also move in the same way in the intervening years is unknown, but it seems more than likely.[1] In any case, the long-term trend of the two series is the same; and it seems safe to conclude that in the half-century from 1907 to 1960 the relative margin

[1] Perlman (1958) argues that the 1952–3 figure was underestimated by Kanninen (1953) and that, to be comparable with Ober's series, it should be at least 145 and probably higher. See also Miller (1966, p. 79) for a cautionary comment on the estimate for 1955–6. It is important to note that the manufacturing differential is based on hourly *earnings* while the building differential is based on union *rates*.

between skilled and unskilled labour in the United States—in terms of either rates or hourly earnings—fell very substantially.[1]

This conclusion is supported in a general way by two additional pieces of evidence. First, Keat (1960), who analysed wage rates in 141 occupations in seventeen industries (including railways, building, and various manufacturing industries) found that from 1903 to 1956—which were both years of high activity—the unweighted coefficient of variation of the whole sample of occupations fell from 0·496 to 0·326, or by about a third. When the occupations were weighted by the numbers of persons employed, the coefficients were different, but the general trend was the same; and broadly similar results emerged when he analysed average *earnings* in all available production occupations in 1903 and 1946. For example, the unweighted coefficient of variation of male earnings in 326 occupations in 1903 was 0·428, and 0·388 when weighted. In 1946 the corresponding coefficients—for 1,918 occupations—were 0·263 and 0·289. Thus the unweighted figures show a fall of 40 per cent and the weighted figures a fall of 26 per cent.[2] Keat also quotes a number of figures for teaching occupations—in both universities and schools—which suggest that from 1904 to 1953 there was an enormous decline in the ratio of earnings in these occupations to average wage earnings in manufacturing. High-school teachers' salaries (in cities of over half a million population) fell from 288 per cent of the manufacturing wage in 1904 to 136 per cent in 1953, and similarly for many other categories. This, of course, could be a rather special case. The relative supply of persons qualified and willing to

[1] It is difficult to reconcile this with Ozanne's conclusion (1962), from his study of differentials in the McCormick works of the International Harvester Company in Chicago from 1858 to 1959, that there has been no long-term downward trend in differentials. Ozanne's data seem to contradict every other series and every hypothesis. For example, 'Contrary to current theory, the 100-year McCormick Works' evidence clearly indicates that prosperity widens and depression narrows occupational differentials' (p. 299). If his data are reliable, one can only assume that this is an example of the well-known difficulty of drawing conclusions about social phenomena from observations of a single member of the population.

[2] These results may well underestimate the decline in relative dispersion between occupations, since the use of a larger sample of more detailed occupations in the later year would tend to increase apparent dispersion.

teach may have grown much more rapidly than in other professional or managerial occupations; and the trend may have been reversed somewhat since 1953.

Secondly, a rough indication of changes in relative dispersion of earnings of male manual workers in non-service occupations can be obtained from a comparison of table US–23 with tables US–16, 17, and 18. From this comparison a very remarkable result emerges. If the figures for the 1890s can be trusted, it seems that there was scarcely any significant change in the dispersion of earnings of full-period manual workers in American industry between that decade and 1939. For males the value of P_5 in the 1890s was about 194 and in 1939 the same; the value of P_{10} in the 1890s was 165 in railways and 169 in manufacturing, while in 1939 in non-farm non-service industries it was 167; and so on. For females in Massachusetts manufacturing in 1899 P_5 was 169 and P_{10} 148, compared with 177 and 154 in United States industry in 1939; and for males and females combined the corresponding figures were 201 and 176 in 1899 and 200 and 174 in 1939. There are, of course, some differences of definition and coverage; but the coincidence is such that it is difficult to avoid the conclusion that no fundamental change in relative dispersion of manual workers' earnings took place over this forty-year period.

How can this conclusion be reconciled with the previous evidence about the decline in skill differentials between 1907 and 1937–40? I think the answer may be, firstly, that skill differentials are, at best, a very uncertain indicator of changes in the over-all degree of dispersion of earnings. As we have seen, the proportion of the total variance of earnings contributed by the variance between occupations is small. But, secondly, we have also seen that in some circumstances the skill differential may be downward biased. If we follow the assumptions of Case 2 in Appendix 5 we can make approximate estimates of the extent of this bias. We shall assume that the distribution of wage rates is lognormal, so that we can use Keat's (1960) estimates of the coefficient of variation of wage rates to estimate the standard deviation of the natural logarithm of wage rates. Using Table A–1 in Aitchison and Brown (1957) to make this transformation we obtain $\sigma_{03} \approx 0\cdot47$ and $\sigma_{56} \approx 0\cdot32$. Also from Keat we have $r_{03\cdot56} \approx 0\cdot8$, and from Table 6.1 we have for manufacturing $d_{03}^{(ij)} \approx 0\cdot72$ (assuming no change in the differential from 1903 to 1907). Then it follows from Appendix 5 that the estimate of $d_{56}^{(ij)}$ will be $0\cdot39$, which is a fall of 46 per cent. This compares with the fall in the logarithmic standard deviation of 32 per cent. Similarly, if we assume that from 1903 to 1939 there was no change in σ and that $r_{03\cdot39} \approx 0\cdot83$, then the differential would show a fall from 205 per cent to 172 per cent, which is very similar to the actual figure shown in Table 6.1.[1]

There is, therefore, no necessary contradiction between the evidence from tables US–16 and 23 and the evidence from the skill differentials. In the following ten years, however, as we shall see in the next section, both sorts of evidence point in the same direction. Hence, there can be no doubt that there was a definite change between 1907 and the 1950s; but the interesting conclusion emerges that all—or almost all—of this change took place between 1939 and 1949.[2]

Changes between 1939 and 1959

The evidence from the building skill differential suggests a fairly rapid decline in dispersion from 1941 to 1948, and a levelling off for at least a few years after that. If the O.E.C.D. figure for 1959–61 is correct, however, there must have been a new fall in the differential from 1952 to the end of the fifties. The manufacturing skill differential also shows a substantial fall from 1937–40 to 1952–3, followed by a period of stability to 1955–6. But the skill differentials are no longer our principal source of information. From 1939 onwards we have a vast amount of material on income distribution from the decennial censuses

---

[1] By the same reasoning the skill differential in building would show a fall from 185 to 156, compared with the actual fall from 185 to 170.

[2] A further small piece of confirmatory evidence on this is that the coefficient of variation of full-time male mean earnings in 116 occupations in 1939 was $0\cdot449$ (see Table 6.2, below), which is not very different from Keat's estimate of the coefficient of variation of male earnings in 326 occupations in 1903 of $0\cdot428$.

and, in the post-war years, from various sample surveys. We shall base our discussion entirely on the census data, which by their nature are much more comprehensive than those from other sources.[1]

From a study of tables US–1 to 18 and 20–2 it is clear that there was a substantial fall in dispersion of employee earnings in the United States from 1939 to 1949. This is true for males and females, for both full-period and all-period workers, and for manual workers as well as for all employees. The closest approximation to the Standard Distribution is table US–10, which shows—for the period 1939 to 1949—a fall in P_5 from 264 to 199, of P_{10} from 197 to 166, and of P_{20} from 153 to 135. At the same time the lower percentiles rose. These figures probably underestimate the decline in dispersion, since the 1939 data are for full-time equivalent earnings, while the 1949 data refer to *full-period* employees, whether or not they were working full-time. We could expect this bias to be more important in the case of the females.[2]

The fall in dispersion was proportionately greater for all employees than for manual workers separately. For all males (table US–10) the value of $(P_{20}-P_{75})$ fell from 83 to 59, or by 29 per cent, while for male manual workers it fell from 68 to 53 (table US–16), or by only 22 per cent. For females the corresponding movements were a fall from 90 to 63, equal to 30 per cent, and from 50 to 50, or no change. The latter values, however, are probably misleading, since the 1939 figures are upward biased for the reasons mentioned above. As a result of these changes the 'class differential' in the United States, which is the name given earlier to the ratio $(P_A-100)/(P_M-100)$, where P_A and

---

[1] Very useful studies, using the same source material, have been made by Miller (1955 and 1966).

[2] It should also be noted that there is a slight bias in the all-period 1939 data, resulting from the exclusion of employees earning less than $100. This exclusion was necessary in order to avoid including a large number of persons who, although reported as 'employees', received zero income in 1939. It has the effect of raising the level of P_{95}, and possibly of other percentiles, although the effect above the median is probably small. No such exclusion needs to be made in 1949 and 1959, because persons with zero income are already excluded; and in any case the proportion of unemployed was much lower in these years.

P_M are corresponding percentiles for all employees and manual workers respectively, fell considerably over this period. At the P_5 level the male class differential fell from 1·74 in 1939 to 1·39 in 1949, and for females it fell from 1·70 in 1939 to 1·28 in 1949.

When we turn to the period 1949 to 1959, we find a quite different picture. The general impression is one of stability, with a slight tendency towards widening dispersion, especially amongst females. The male full-period non-farm distribution (table US–10) shows very little change, but the female distribution (table US–11) seems to have become significantly more dispersed, at least from P_2 downwards. For manual workers separately, the same conclusion emerges, except that the evidence for growing dispersion amongst females is even more pronounced. For males and females combined the over-all change is not very great for either group, although there is some evidence of a growth in the proportion of lower paid workers.

With the help of the census data we can separate the two components of the over-all change in dispersion of earnings: the changes in dispersion between occupations and the changes in dispersion within occupations. From Miller's (1966) estimates of mean wages and salaries for 116 male occupations in 1939, 1949, and 1959 I have computed two measures of inter-occupational dispersion which are shown in Table 6.2. It will be seen that both measures tell approximately the same story, namely, that there

TABLE 6.2.

Dispersion of Mean Male Earnings in 116 Occupations in the United States, 1939, 1949, and 1959

	1939	1949	1959
Coefficient of variation			
All males	0·520	0·364	0·373
Males working 50–2 weeks[1]	0·449	0·321	0·319
Standard deviation of logarithms			
All males	0·477	0·368	0·396
Males working 50–2 weeks[1]	0·421	0·330	0·341

Source: Miller (1966), Tables C–6 and C–7.

[1] In 1939, full-time as well as full-period.

was a substantial fall in inter-occupational dispersion from 1939 to 1949, but some tendency towards an increase in the following decade.

Changes in dispersion within occupations cannot satisfactorily be measured by standard deviations—either of the original data or of the logarithms—because of uncertainty about the distribution of earnings in the open-ended classes, especially in the upper one. A more reliable measure is one based on quantiles; and fortunately Miller has published estimates of relative inter-quartile ranges for full-period males in the same 116 occupations. These show that, in the period 1939 to 1949, there was a decrease in dispersion in 105 of these occupations; while in 1949 to 1959 there was an *increase* in seventy-two of them.[1] It is interesting to note, also, that the proportion of occupations showing increases in dispersion is much greater amongst the less skilled than at higher levels. For example, out of 53 occupations in the groups covering operatives, service workers, and labourers, all but 9 had an increase in dispersion between 1949 and 1959; while amongst the other occupations—covering professional and managerial workers, clerical, sales, and craftsmen—only 28 out of 63 showed an increase. These results suggest widening dispersion amongst the less highly skilled and no change, on balance, elsewhere. Possible explanations seem to be a greater influx of Negro labour from farming, or a growing employment of part-time male workers in less skilled occupations.

It is reassuring to find that all these indicators move in much the same way. What they show is that from 1939 to 1949 there was a very great fall in dispersion, both between occupations and within occupations, even when only full-period workers are taken into account; while from 1949 to 1959 there was a slight tendency towards an increase in dispersion, which again occurred both between and within occupations. Until 1939 the dispersion of employee earnings in the United States was relatively wide. In terms of Table 5.5 above, the United States would have appeared well below the position now occupied by all developed countries except France and Japan; while in

[1] See Miller (1966), table C–7.

terms of Table 5.7 (for manual workers only) it would have been approximately in line with modern Poland. The big change occurred during, and perhaps immediately after, the Second World War.

3. Canada

A number of different skill differentials in Canada have been quoted by different authors. The O.E.C.D. report (1965, p. 34) cites two differentials, one for building and the other for motor vehicle parts, which each rose slightly from 1923-9 to 1930-3 and fell considerably from 1930-3 to 1951-3. During the 1950s the building differential continued to fall, while the motor vehicle parts differential widened. Reynolds and Taft (1956) suggest that differentials in most Canadian industries fell from 1930 to 1939, and also between 1943 and 1952, but with more exceptions in the latter period. Günter (1964, p. 142) cites a fall in the bricklayer's rate differential from 200 in 1938 to 161 in 1962, and a fall in the electrical fitter's rate differential—in the electric light and power industry—from 185 to 149 in the same period.

But the most comprehensive published data on Canadian skill differentials are those given by Woods and Ostry (1962). Their Table xLVIII (pp. 432-3) contains fifteen skill differentials based on hourly rates in selected years from 1923 to 1958. The sizes of these differentials are widely varied (in 1923-9, for example, they range from 229 down to 112, and in 1958 from 200 down to 117) and the best way to summarize them seems to be to take the median of each year. The results are given in Table 6.3. Because of the wide dispersion of the differentials, no great reliance can be placed on these figures, and a slight change in the rank order can cause a substantial shift in the median. For example, the sharp fall in the median in 1950 does not represent the typical change in that year. Most of the fifteen differentials in 1950 were not very different from their 1949 level and six were even larger. The median *change* in differential was only −1·8. Nevertheless, the figures in the table may give us a rough guide to changes in the skill differentials over longer periods.

Table 6.3

Skill Differentials in Canada[1]

	Median of 15 differentials
1923–9	176
1930–3	188
1943–6	164
1947	160
1948	155
1949	160
1950	144
1951	143
1952	140
1953	141
1954	139
1955	142
1956	142
1957	144
1958	142

[1] Skilled hourly rate as percentage of unskilled hourly rate in selected occupations in ten industries.

Source: Woods and Ostry (1962, pp. 432–3).

The results are broadly consistent with the conclusions reached by other investigators, namely, that differentials widened somewhat in the depression and fell considerably between 1930–3 and the early 1950s, after which they remained—on average—fairly steady. But, as has been emphasized previously, nothing definite can be concluded from these changes in differentials about the over-all change in the dispersion of individual earnings.

For information about actual earnings from 1930–1 onwards we can draw on the rich material collected in the Canadian censuses. These form the basis of appendix tables CA–1 to 12. Unfortunately, we cannot separate full-period workers from the others before 1950–1; so we must try to use the data for all workers before that. Table CA–1 shows an appreciable fall in dispersion of males above the median from 1930–1 to 1940–1, but some increase below the median. The latter phenomenon may be the result of a change in effective coverage of low-wage workers in the two censuses, or of inaccuracy in the process of interpolation, which is based on a very few income classes in 1940–1. For females, on the other hand, there appears to have been virtually no change in dispersion above the median in this period (table CA–2). The dramatic change, which affected both males and females, occurred in the following decade, when P_5 for males fell from 271 to 193, and for females from 283 to 203. Similar—but slightly smaller—movements occurred amongst non-farm employees (tables CA–4 and 5), and amongst manual workers (tables CA–7 and 8), where the changes were particularly large for males. From 1950–1 to 1960–1 this movement was partially reversed, both for males and for females, and amongst manual workers as well as amongst all employees. Over this last period we have estimates for full-period workers separately (tables CA–10, 11, and 12); and these also show a significant widening of dispersion.

The over-all picture for Canada seems, therefore, to have been as follows: probably not much change in the 1920s; an appreciable fall in dispersion for males in the 1930s, but little or no change for females; a rapid fall in dispersion for all categories in the 1940s; and a partial reversal of this movement in the 1950s. Unfortunately, we cannot determine, from the available evidence, how much of the fall in dispersion in the 1940s occurred during the war years and how much afterwards.

4. United Kingdom

According to Knowles and Robertson's (1951) series for skill differentials in the building industry, part of which is shown in Fig. 6.1 on page 170, there was a sharp decline in this differential during the First World War, after a long period of relative stability since 1880. In the early 1920s, however, as in the United States, the war-time fall in the differential was partly made good. From 1922 to 1937 there was great stability; and from 1937 to 1941 some decline. This was followed by another period of approximate stability until 1948, after which the series fell rapidly for a few years and, according to the O.E.C.D. estimate, must have continued to fall until 1959–61. Other skill differentials computed by Knowles and Robertson followed a

broadly similar path. If we allow for the probable downward
bias in movements of the skill differential, we could, I think,
conclude that inter-occupational wage dispersion did not decline
significantly from the 1880s—or even from the 1900s—to the
1930s, but that there might well have been a decline from the
1930s to the 1950s.[1] Unfortunately, there is no direct evidence
on inter-occupational dispersion by which to check this conclusion.

The only reasonably reliable source of information for long-
period changes in dispersion in the United Kingdom is the data
collected by the Board of Trade and the Ministry of Labour
about the earnings of manual workers in British industry in
1906, 1938, and 1960. These figures are analysed in appendix
tables UK–6, 7, and 8. The first of these tables shows a moderate
decline in dispersion of male earnings from 1906 to 1938, but
an *increase* in dispersion of full-time male earnings—at least
above the median—from 1938 to 1960. These results could be
regarded as consistent with the evidence from the skill differentials for the earlier period; but it is impossible to reconcile
them with the trend in the skill differentials over the later period,
unless we assume that from 1938 to 1960 dispersion between
occupations was moving in the opposite direction from dispersion within occupations. This latter assumption cannot be
completely rejected as a possibility; but it seems rather unlikely. My own inclination would be to doubt the reliability of
changes in the skill differentials based on nominal rates as indicators of changes in average earnings differentials, especially
in the past two decades.[2]

[1] If $r_{01.37} \approx 0.8$ and the true dispersion of occupations was constant over
this period, we could expect, on the assumptions of Case 2 in Appendix 5, that
a differential of 150 in 1901 would fall to 138 in 1937; and if $r_{37.52} \approx 0.85$ we
could expect a differential of 133 in 1937 to fall to 127 in 1952. The building
skill differential in 1901 was about 150, in 1937, 133 and in 1952, 116.

[2] Some support for this view is given by the estimates made by Routh
(1965, p. 104) of average annual earnings of male skilled and unskilled workers
in various years. His estimates imply a fall in the earnings differential (of all
skilled in relation to all unskilled) from 157 in 1913–14 to 141 in 1922–4;
a recovery to 151 in 1935–6; a fall to 143 in 1955–6; and a further recovery
to 149 in 1960. This series shows remarkable stability, but the directions of its
movements are not inconsistent with the view that over-all wage dispersion

When we turn to consider changes in the dispersion of all employees, the information available is even more limited. For recent years the Inland Revenue has published distributions of employees classified according to ranges of Schedule E earnings, which is approximately what is needed, although it includes pensions and excludes earnings from secondary sources and below the tax-exemption limit. Routh (1965, p. 52) has made a heroic attempt to construct a distribution of annual earnings for all employees in 1911–12, using income-tax data for a small minority of high incomes (less than half a million out of a total of more than 16 million) and other scraps of information for the remainder. His figures are analysed in appendix table UK–4, which can be compared with table UK–5, which is based on Routh's similar—but more reliable—estimates for 1958–9. The result shows some decline in dispersion for males—but in rather an irregular fashion—and an *increase* in dispersion for females. The pattern for males is broadly consistent with that revealed by the data for manual workers, and it seems fair to conclude that there was some decline in over-all dispersion in the United Kingdom over this period, but not a dramatic one, as in North America. Of course, the United States and Canada started with a much higher level of dispersion. By 1960, if we judge on the basis of our estimates for the Standard Distribution in Table 5.5, all three countries had converged towards a rather similar position, with the United States still a little more widely dispersed, particularly below the median.

Finally, for the years since 1954–5 we can study the movements in the Inland Revenue's distribution of Schedule E incomes. Selected years from 1954–5 to 1961–2 are shown in appendix tables UK–1, 2, and 3. They suggest a slight widening of dispersion amongst males and a somewhat greater widening amongst females. Part of this, however, could be the result of

fell somewhat from before the First World War to the inter-war period, fell again during the Second World War, but increased during the 1950s.

Routh also produces some interesting evidence to show that in the engineering industry from 1940 to 1959, while the rate differential for fitters had fallen considerably, the earnings differential remained practically constant (pp. 153–4). The balance, of course, appears as 'wage drift'. See also Knowles and Robertson (1951) for similar data for the period 1926 to 1948.

changes in the relative position of the tax-exemption limit, since, when money incomes are rising, a fixed exemption limit is falling in relative value and leads to the inclusion of a larger proportion of very low incomes. Nevertheless, I doubt whether the whole of the change can be explained away on this ground,

5. Sweden

For Sweden there is abundant material on income distribution in the census reports, as well as for recent years in the tax reports. The census income data are not collected by direct questioning, as in the North American and New Zealand censuses, but by matching persons covered in the census with their corresponding tax returns. This may improve the reliability of the data in one sense, but it has the offsetting disadvantage that persons whose incomes fall below the tax limit are not covered. Moreover, there are probably some errors in the matching process. In each year there is a fairly substantial group for whom no income information is available, and it is not possible to know what proportion of these belong in the lowest income class and what proportion are the results of mis-matching of returns. In our analysis the 'no income' group have been excluded, which probably gives a downward bias to our estimates of dispersion in Sweden. Two further difficulties are that, except in 1951, the Swedish tabulations are all made on total income from all sources; and that there are no separate distributions of full-period employees.

With these qualifications in mind, let us look at the Swedish results in the appendix tables. First, for the period 1920 to 1930 we have tables SW–4, 5, and 6. These show a substantial increase in dispersion for males, and a smaller one for females. From 1930 to 1945 there was a decline for both sexes, which brought the male distribution (below P_{20}) back to approximately where it was in 1920, and the female distribution back at the upper end of the scale. The 1951 distribution seems to behave in a rather odd way, especially for females, and it is likely that the change in the technique of matching returns in that year may have been responsible for a change in coverage.[1] The male distribution shows a substantial fall in dispersion above the median, while the female distribution shows a large increase in dispersion at all levels. If we ignore this year, and proceed direct to 1960, we find that dispersion for both males and females fell from 1945 to 1960, except perhaps for females below the median. The interesting result which emerges is that, over the whole period 1920 to 1960, relative dispersion for both sexes changed very little.

For the period from 1930 onwards, almost all the Swedish tables tell much the same story—a decline in dispersion from 1930 to 1945, and a further decline in the next fifteen years. The major exception is the behaviour of female manual workers, whose dispersion seems to have changed little after 1945. The fall in the dispersion of male manual workers over the whole period was really dramatic. For example, P_5 for male manual workers in manufacturing, mining, and building, fell from 217 in 1930 to 158 in 1960, and other percentiles showed corresponding movements (table SW–10). Even so, the dispersion of male manual earnings in Sweden in 1960 was not exceptionally low by north-western European standards.

The distributions based on the Swedish tax reports for 1954 to 1964 add little to the general picture (tables SW–13, 14, and 15). They suggest some growth in dispersion for males over this period but little change for females.

6. Norway

We have no distributions for Norway in earlier years but there are some estimates of skill differentials. Soltow (1965, p. 133) quotes wage-rate differentials for skilled machine shop employees, which fell from 130 in 1914 to 117 in 1920, 120 in 1930, 121 in 1938, 111 in 1950, and 112 in 1957. Proportionately, some of these are significant changes, but they tell us little about the

---

[1] In the other censuses the people selected for the income study—a subsample of the whole population—were matched with their tax returns for the preceding year; but in 1951 they were matched with their returns for the *succeeding* year. This may have affected the proportion of people for whom no tax return could be found.

over-all dispersion of earnings. Leiserson (1959, p. 139) gives a series of index numbers of average *earnings* of skilled and unskilled workers in the metal trades, which shows a slight decline in the differential from 1938 to 1952, and a slight recovery in the next three years. So far as they go, these data tend to suggest that wage dispersion has changed little in Norway over the past thirty years.

7. Germany (F.R.)

Two estimates of dispersion of German manual workers' daily wages near the beginning of the century are given in table GE–8. As is to be expected, the dispersion for miners is greater than for municipal workers; but there is little difference between the two distributions over the range from P_5 to the median. Over this range, also, the figures are remarkably similar to the corresponding figures in table GE–7, which relate to *hourly* earnings of manual workers in a wide range of industries in 1962. In fact, the whole set of percentiles for municipal workers in thirty-three cities in 1907 is hardly distinguishable from the set for all industries in 1962, except at the P_2 level (and possibly above). The dispersion of monthly earnings in 1962 is, naturally, somewhat wider (table GE–4); but the evidence, so far as it goes, does not suggest that there has been any substantial change in dispersion amongst full-time manual workers in Germany over the past half-century.

For more recent years, changes in differentials between technical and production employees in Germany, cited by O.E.C.D. (1965, p. 37), suggest that dispersion was narrowing from 1950 to 1957; but distributions of all employees (analysed in table GE–1) lead to the opposite conclusion. I am unable to explain this discrepancy. Both series suggest that dispersion was fairly constant after 1957.

8. Austria

Distributions of manual workers' earnings in trade-union firms in Vienna (tables AU–4, 5, and 6) show, from 1926 to 1947, a slight fall in dispersion of males below the median and a general fall in dispersion for males and females combined. From 1947 to 1960 there seems to have been a slight widening of dispersion for males above the median, and a similar movement for males and females combined. On the whole, there has been remarkably little change over a third of a century.

9. Netherlands

The Netherlands tax distributions show great stability from 1949 to 1959 for all employees (tables NL–1 and 2), but some decline in dispersion amongst manual workers from 1952 to 1959 (table NL–3). It was official policy to maintain constant differentials over this period, and average earnings in manufacturing rose at the same rate for both skilled and unskilled workers from 1954 to 1960 (O.E.C.D. 1965, p. 37). But the evidence of our distributions suggest that over-all dispersion amongst manual workers declined, especially from 1952 to 1954.

10. Belgium

The industrial census of 1896 collected data on daily earnings of manual workers. The dispersion of these can be compared with the estimated dispersion of manual workers—also effectively on a daily rate basis—in 1964 (tables BE–2 and 3). It will be seen that dispersion has fallen appreciably, especially for females above the median. The decline for males is roughly in line with the decline in the United Kingdom from 1906 to 1960.

11. France

From 1951 onwards very comprehensive and detailed studies of wage and salary distributions in France have been made by I.N.S.E.E. (Institut National de la Statistique et des Études Économiques), using returns made by employers in connection with the social security administration. But evidence on changes before that is very limited. For the 1890s we have three distributions of manual workers' earnings: for males and females in the tobacco industry, and for men employed on the railways.[1] These

---

[1] Some distributions for wage-earners in Paris in the 1860s were made by the Paris Chamber of Commerce, but the definitions used are doubtful and the results seem unreliable. The data are given in ZA 1, pp. 196–7.

are analysed in table FR–16. When they are compared with corresponding data for French manual workers in 1963 (table FR–14), the distribution of male tobacco workers is seen to be much less dispersed, but the distribution of female tobacco workers is very similar to the 1963 distribution for all non-farm female wage-earners, and the distribution of male railway workers is also fairly similar to the distribution of all male wage-earners, except below the median where the modern distribution is more dispersed. The results for males are contradictory, and the evidence as a whole is insufficient to justify any strong conclusion; but the impression it gives is that there has not been much change over the past seventy years.

A variety of figures on French skill differentials have been cited by different authors, and sometimes used to develop arguments about world-wide trends in wage dispersion. But many of the figures seem to be inconsistent with one another; and even more inconsistent with such evidence as exists about the dispersion of actual earnings. I suspect that in France there is often an even wider discrepancy between official rates and actual earnings than in other countries.[1] The evidence from our own analysis of employment income dispersion—based on the I.N.S.E.E. tabulations—suggests that from 1951 to 1961 there was a fairly steady increase in dispersion for all employees—both male and female—but little change for manual workers, except perhaps for some widening amongst females (tables

---

[1] Dunlop and Rothbaum (1955) quote figures for the French skill differential in 1937–40 and 1952–3 of 130 and 123 respectively, the net change being the result of a fall during the war, a widening immediately afterwards, and then a further fall. Reynolds and Taft (1956, pp. 206–25) state that differentials fell considerably during the war, and also between 1945 and 1949. From 1949 to 1951 they were almost stable, in 1952–3 they widened, and in 1954 and 1955 there was a further narrowing. But they point out that these figures are based on official rates and that earnings may have moved quite differently. Günter (1964), using rates of pay 'actually applied' in Paris, finds no evidence for a change in the male skill differential from 1948 to 1962, and a widening for females. The O.E.C.D. report (1965, p. 34) presents two series, one of which—for masons in the Paris region—shows a large fall from 1900 to 1928–30, and an increase thereafter, including an increase from 107 to 117 between 1937–40 and 1945–7. The other series—for time-working fitters in the Paris metal industries (also based on rates)—shows a slight fall from 1928–30 to 1938–40, a recovery to approximately the 1928–30 level in 1945–7, and an increase between 1951–3 and 1960–1.

FR–1 to 12).[1] From 1961 to 1963 there seems to have been a fall in dispersion at the top of the income distribution but a widening of inequality at the bottom. This last phenomenon may be the result, as I.N.S.E.E. suggests, of the influx into the work force of a large number of young people born in the early post-war years. As we noted in Chapter 5, the dispersion of French employment earnings is exceptionally wide in comparison with other advanced countries. Of course, as the O.E.C.D. report (1965, p. 38) points out, French family allowances are higher than in most other countries, and, since the same absolute amounts are paid irrespective of income level, the relative dispersion of total income, including family allowances, must be less than for earnings alone.

12. Australia

The Australian tax reports give distributions of incomes from wages, salaries, and pensions—for males and females separately —from 1952–3 onwards. But these distributions are confined to persons who received less than £100 from other sources— so-called 'Occupation 1'. They are a useful guide to changes in dispersion from year to year, but cannot be used directly for comparisons with other distributions covering all employees. I have made estimates of the dispersion of all wages and salaries for two years—1953–4 and 1959–60—which are analysed in tables AL–4, 5, and 6; and we can compare these with the results of a survey of earnings made in New South Wales in 1938 (table AL–7). The results show a fall in dispersion for males from 1938 to 1953–4, but a recovery by 1959–60 to a level almost identical with the pre-war position. For females there was also a substantial fall (above the median) from 1938 to 1953–4, but a smaller increase in the next six years. From P_{10} upwards female dispersion in 1959–60 remained less than before the war.

From the 'Occupation 1' distributions (tables AL–1, 2, and 3) it seems that dispersion of both males and females was growing steadily from 1952–3 to 1962–3. Unfortunately, we do not know

---

[1] Note that the inclusion of apprentices after 1952 creates a discontinuity in the series

whether this was mainly a reaction to a period of compression of differentials during the early post-war years or was indicative of some more fundamental changes. As we shall see below, there was a compression of inter-occupational wage rates between 1948 and 1952, and this was followed by a widening of the wage rate structure to 1963. We have also seen, in Chapter 5, that in 1959–60 the dispersion of earnings in Australia was still significantly less than in other advanced capitalist countries, except New Zealand.

As a by-product of the Australian system of compulsory arbitration, statistics of official award rates are published each year for a large number of occupations. For the period 1914 to 1952 it was possible to study the behaviour of male rates in a constant sample of 445 occupations in New South Wales. The sample is 'constant' in the sense that the occupations have the same name throughout the period; but there is no guarantee that the content of each occupation remained unchanged. Nevertheless, the dispersion of rates in such a sample is a suggestive indicator of the degree of dispersion between occupations. Fig. 6.2 shows the movements in the coefficient of variation of this sample in each year during the period, except the three years 1941, 1942, and 1945 when no data were published.

It should first be noted that the coefficient of variation of the wage rates fluctuates around a very low level, never exceeding 0·17. This contrasts sharply with the coefficient of variation of United States wage rates which, as we saw earlier, fell from around 0·5 in the 1900s to around 0·3 in the 1950s. In relation to itself, however, the Australian coefficient fluctuated quite considerably. From a level approaching 0·17 in 1914 it declined throughout the First World War, and in 1920 reached a figure of about 0·11. This level was maintained approximately until 1925, when there began a slight upward trend to 1930. In January 1931 Australia devalued, and this was followed by a national plan involving a sharp cut in all wage and interest rates. The adjustments to wage rates were apparently such as to increase their coefficient of variation: average rates fell by 7·5 per cent in 1931 but the standard deviation of rates was

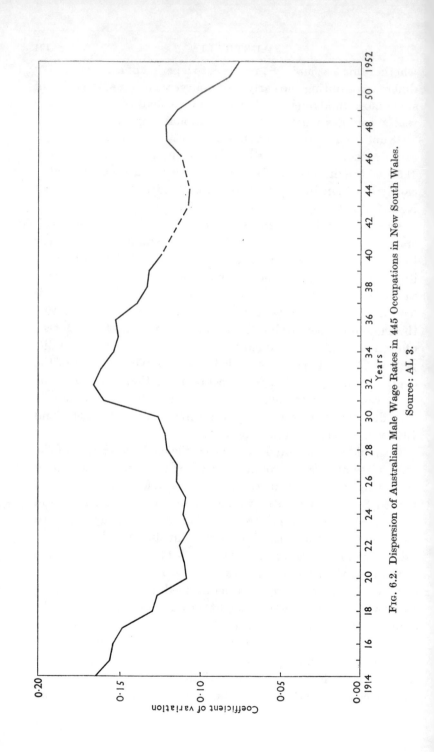

FIG. 6.2. Dispersion of Australian Male Wage Rates in 445 Occupations in New South Wales.

Source: AL 3.

slightly increased. Hence there was a sharp upward movement
in the coefficient of variation. During the remainder of the 1930s,
however, the coefficient of variation gradually fell, until, by the
beginning of the war, it was nearly back to the 1930 level.
During the war years the dispersion of rates fell further, and the
coefficient of variation reached a low point of 0·11 in 1944. By
1947, however, it was back once more close to the pre-war level.
In 1948 there began a new decline to an unprecedently low figure
of 0·075. At this point—because of a reclassification of occupations—our continuous series ends. But in 1956 the coefficient of
variation of over 400 wage rates published for that year was
0·11, and in 1963—for 500 rates   0·14.

We do not know how far changes in the inter-occupational
dispersion of wage rates are reflected in changes in the dispersion
of earnings of individuals. Wage drift has been significant in
Australia in the post-war period, and has fluctuated with the
general level of activity. It has also been found that wage drift
in the 1950s was closely correlated with changes in dispersion of
employment income (Lydall, 1965). It may well be that at least
part of the fluctuation in wage-rate dispersion was offset by
wage drift, so that changes in the dispersion of earnings were
less than those suggested in Fig. 6.2. It seems probable, however,
that there was some fall in dispersion of earnings during the
First World War, some increase in 1931, and a decline, followed
by a recovery, between 1948 and 1963.

13. New Zealand

In each of the New Zealand censuses from 1926 onwards information was collected about the total income of individuals. The
results, for persons classified as employees at the date of the
census, are analysed in tables NZ–1 to 6. Tables NZ–7, 8, and 9
are based on data published in the tax reports.

From tables NZ–4, 5, and 6 it appears that dispersion—for
both males and females—grew considerably between 1925–6 and
1935. In the latter year New Zealand was still suffering from
the effects of the world depression and many employees were
working less than a full year. By 1944–5, however, distributions

for both sexes had returned to approximately their 1925–6 shape. In 1950–1 there was a further decline in dispersion, but this was largely—although not entirely—offset by 1960–1. Similar, but less pronounced, movements can be seen in the tax distributions for the period from 1945–6 to 1956–7.[1]

The New Zealand distributions cover all employees, whether full-year working or not, and they are therefore likely to be more sensitive to changes in economic conditions. But they give some support to the view that the dispersion of earnings is significantly increased during a slump, and falls—at least temporarily—during a rapid inflation (as in the Korean War boom). From a long-term point of view, however, the New Zealand distributions are remarkably stable, showing little change over the thirty-five years from 1925–6 to 1960–1, except for some reduction in the proportion of very low incomes.

14. Japan

Skill differentials, based on daily wage rates in the building industry, have been estimated by Taira (1961, pp. 228–9) for the period 1883 to 1956. The series fluctuated within the range of 145 to 154 from 1883 to 1901.[2] Then it slowly rose to a new level of around 163, which was maintained from 1907 to 1914. During the First World War the differential fell fairly sharply, reaching a minimum of 140 in 1919, but it recovered again during the next thirteen years, reaching a new peak of 169 in 1932. There was little change from 1932 to 1936, but a sharp decline in the next three years to 149. No figures are available for the remaining years of the Second World War; but in 1948 the differential reappears at approximately its pre-war level, and, with the exception of 1951, it remains in the region of 145 until the end of the series in 1956.

The most remarkable thing about this skill differential is its extraordinary stability: over a period of more than seventy years it fluctuated within a range of 140–70. There is no evidence

---

[1] The female tax distribution for 1945–6 seems to be unusually dispersed above the median.

[2] Up to 1939 these are based on five-year moving averages of the original series.

to suggest a long-term downward trend, as in some of the other
countries, and the only periods of fairly rapid change were during the First World War and between 1936 and 1939 (which
were also war years in Japan). If we allow for the fact that a
constant skill differential normally implies an increasing over-all
dispersion of occupations, it would not be surprising to find that
dispersion was growing in Japan during this period. Taira has
also made some estimates of the relative dispersion of individual
wage earnings in manufacturing in certain years, and these suggest that dispersion for males rose considerably from 1924 to
1933, fell again to 1939, and rose back to approximately the
1933 level in 1958. Unfortunately, not all of these distributions
are defined in the same way, and in particular those for the
years 1924 and 1933 are based on daily earnings while those for
1948 and 1958 are based on monthly earnings. Moreover, the
1958 distribution includes workers in small establishments
(5–29 workers) while the earlier distributions for the most part
exclude these.[1] But there is no evidence here to contradict the
view that dispersion of wage earnings was at least no smaller in
1958 than in 1924.

Our own dispersion estimates are based on distributions of
wages and salaries in private firms, published by the National
Taxation Board, for the years from 1951 onwards. These distributions exclude employees of firms in which no person was liable
for taxation—mostly very small firms; and also daily workers,
paid on a daily or hourly basis for casual employment. In 1965,
out of nearly 47·5 million persons employed in total, less than
21 million were covered by the published distributions; and, of
these, only 17·2 million were employed for the whole year. The
distributions analysed in tables JA–1, 2, and 3 are based on
these full-year employees only.

Separate distributions for males and females are available
only for 1953, 1954, and 1955, and, as will be seen from table

---

[1] Changes in female dispersion are generally in the same direction as for
males—with the exception of 1958, when female dispersion was less than in
1948—but their relative fluctuations are greater. Over the whole period 1924–
58 female dispersion was unchanged, and when males and females are combined
there is little difference between the beginning and end years.

JA–2, the dispersion of males is greater than for females. Hence, changes in the combined distribution may reflect changes in the relative position and importance of females in the total work force. Over the period 1951 to 1965 the dispersion of this combined distribution fluctuated to an exceptional degree, widening appreciably (above the median) from 1953 to 1960 and narrowing fairly rapidly thereafter. By 1965 the over-all degree of dispersion was significantly less than in 1951.

For the years from 1956 onwards the published tables include a breakdown of employees according to the size of establishment in which they were employed, and these help to throw some light on the reasons for the fluctuations in over-all dispersion after that date. A summary of estimates derived from these tables is given in Table 6.4, from which it will be seen that the dispersion of earnings has varied considerably between different sizes of establishment. It is well known that Japan has for many years had a stratified labour market, with very large differences between average earnings in establishments of different sizes. Our data reflect this tendency, as can be seen from the section of the table which shows the relative median earnings in each size of establishment. In 1956, for example, median earnings in establishments employing 1–29 persons were only half the median in the largest establishments.

Over the period covered by the table, there has been a considerable evening up of average earnings in different sizes of establishment. From 1956 to 1959 (or 1960) there was little change; but after 1960 the changes were dramatic. By 1965 median earnings in the group of small establishments were only 15 per cent below those in the 100–499 employee establishments, and the median in the largest size class was only 18 per cent above the median in the 100–499 class.

When we turn to the estimates of dispersion within the different size classes we find a similar trend. From 1956 to 1959 there was a widening of dispersion in every size class; but thereafter, although dispersion within the largest size continued to grow for a while, dispersion in the small and medium-sized establishments was falling; and the same trend developed after 1961 also in the

Not listed
Last checked
3-6-9( ) OK

4 left needs
mending

Establishment, Japan,

...ear, of both sexes)

	1960	1961	1963	1965
	324	312	317	291
	345	330	299	293
	332	306	292	275
	270	274	265	254
	333	318	296	280
	250	241	223	223
	246	238	217	218
	245	227	225	210
	212	216	212	201
	252	241	229	217
	180	178	163	165
	179	174	170	162
	181	175	172	161
	167	167	164	160
	187	181	171	165
	73	75	83	85
	89	88	98	94
	137	128	121	118

Per cent of all employees in each size class				1960	1961	1963	1965
1–29	34	34	33	30	30	29	30
30–99	21	21	23	22	22	22	22
100–499	21	21	21	23	23	23	24
500 and over	24	24	24	25	25	26	24

Source: Based on data in JA–2 for the relevant years.

largest establishments. (Estimates of the percentiles below the median show similar tendencies, although the changes were not so dramatic.) By 1965 the degree of dispersion within each size class was much more alike than it had been in 1956, although there was still some tendency for the higher percentiles to be relatively further from the median in the smaller establishments.

Thus, it seems that the recent decline in the dispersion of earnings in Japan can be largely interpreted as a movement towards a more unified labour market. The evidence suggests that after 1959 or 1960 forces were at work in Japan which were breaking down the old isolation between different labour markets and making for more homogeneous conditions of employment. There was a levelling up of average wages in establishments of different size and a levelling down of the previous very wide dispersion within the smaller establishments towards the pattern already existing in the largest establishments. Since we do not have separate distributions for males and females, we cannot say precisely what effect these movements had on the dispersion of the Standard Distribution; but it is almost inevitable that the dispersion of the Standard Distribution declined after 1960, thus bringing Japan's 1965 position in Table 5.5 closer to that of Finland, and probably above that of France.

15. Argentina

Distributions for 1953, 1959, and 1961 are analysed in tables AR–1, 2, and 3. They suggest a slight increase in over-all dispersion from 1953 to 1961; but for manual workers in manufacture there was little net change. It is interesting to note that such relative stability of dispersion was maintained despite a very rapid growth of money earnings. Median earnings rose in money value more than sevenfold in eight years.

16. Poland

Tables PO–1 to 6 suggest that Polish dispersion—of manual workers as well as of all employees—declined significantly from 1957 to 1960, after which there was little change.

17. U.S.S.R.

No distributions have been published for the U.S.S.R. since 1934; but the earlier distributions, from 1914 to 1934, are analysed in tables UR–1 and 2. They show that dispersion in manufacturing fell considerably from 1914 to 1928, but increased a little for manual workers—and a good deal more for all employees—in the next six years. This was the period of the First Five-Year Plan, during which earlier egalitarian tendencies

TABLE 6.4

Variation in Percentiles by Size of Establishment, Japan, 1956 to 1965

(All employees employed for the whole year, of both sexes)

Percentiles and size of establishment	1956	1957	1959	1960	1961	1963	1965
P_5							
1–29 employees	315	307	324	324	312	317	291
30–99	325	338	337	345	330	299	293
100–499	303	323	319	332	306	292	275
500 and over	249	248	262	270	274	265	254
All	308	316	321	333	318	296	280
P_{10}							
1–29 employees	240	240	252	250	241	223	223
30–99	239	251	248	246	238	217	218
100–499	233	239	244	245	227	225	210
500 and over	200	196	207	212	216	212	201
All	238	246	249	252	241	229	217
P_{20}							
1–29 employees	182	181	183	180	178	163	165
30–99	176	181	182	179	174	170	162
100–499	172	176	183	181	175	172	161
500 and over	157	156	162	167	167	164	160
All	179	185	187	187	181	171	165
Median as per cent of median of 100–499							
1–29	69	68	72	73	75	83	85
30–99	87	83	88	89	88	98	94
500 and over	135	142	139	137	128	121	118
Per cent of all employees in each size class							
1–29	34	34	33	30	30	29	30
30–99	21	21	23	22	22	22	22
100–499	21	21	21	23	23	23	24
500 and over	24	24	24	25	25	26	24

Source: Based on data in JA–2 for the relevant years.

largest establishments. (Estimates of the percentiles below the median show similar tendencies, although the changes were not so dramatic.) By 1965 the degree of dispersion within each size class was much more alike than it had been in 1956, although there was still some tendency for the higher percentiles to be relatively further from the median in the smaller establishments.

Thus, it seems that the recent decline in the dispersion of earnings in Japan can be largely interpreted as a movement towards a more unified labour market. The evidence suggests that after 1959 or 1960 forces were at work in Japan which were breaking down the old isolation between different labour markets and making for more homogeneous conditions of employment. There was a levelling up of average wages in establishments of different size and a levelling down of the previous very wide dispersion within the smaller establishments towards the pattern already existing in the largest establishments. Since we do not have separate distributions for males and females, we cannot say precisely what effect these movements had on the dispersion of the Standard Distribution; but it is almost inevitable that the dispersion of the Standard Distribution declined after 1960, thus bringing Japan's 1965 position in Table 5.5 closer to that of Finland, and probably above that of France.

15. Argentina

Distributions for 1953, 1959, and 1961 are analysed in tables AR–1, 2, and 3. They suggest a slight increase in over-all dispersion from 1953 to 1961; but for manual workers in manufacture there was little net change. It is interesting to note that such relative stability of dispersion was maintained despite a very rapid growth of money earnings. Median earnings rose in money value more than sevenfold in eight years.

16. Poland

Tables PO–1 to 6 suggest that Polish dispersion—of manual workers as well as of all employees—declined significantly from 1957 to 1960, after which there was little change.

17. U.S.S.R.

No distributions have been published for the U.S.S.R. since 1934; but the earlier distributions, from 1914 to 1934, are analysed in tables UR–1 and 2. They show that dispersion in manufacturing fell considerably from 1914 to 1928, but increased a little for manual workers—and a good deal more for all employees—in the next six years. This was the period of the First Five-Year Plan, during which earlier egalitarian tendencies were reversed and incentives were deliberately increased. It is probable that dispersion has fallen considerably over the past twenty-five years, but no hard figures are available.[1]

These are all the countries for which time series of distributions could be found. They are obviously of very uneven quality and extent. Nevertheless, I think that they add something to our background knowledge of the ways in which employment income distributions behave. In the next chapter we shall put together the empirical facts reviewed in this chapter and in Chapter 5, examine them from the point of view of the theory outlined in Chapter 4, and derive some subsidiary hypotheses which can be tested statistically.

---

[1] See Nove (1966) for a comment on some recently published statistics of wages in the U.S.S.R., which, however, give little clue to the changes in dispersion.

7

EXPLAINING THE DIFFERENCES

1. Introduction

In Chapter 4 we developed a theory to explain the shape of the Standard Distribution of employment income; in Chapter 5 we reviewed available evidence on the differences in dispersion between countries; and in Chapter 6 we examined the changes in dispersion which have taken place in certain countries over the past one or two generations. We shall now attempt to bring the theory and the facts into relation to one another; and, in particular, we shall consider how far the theory can be used to make valid predictions about differences in dispersion, both between countries and over time.

But first let us briefly recapitulate the conclusions of Chapters 5 and 6. In Chapter 5 we found that, when countries are ranked according to the degree of dispersion of the Standard Distribution, the most equal are two countries of eastern Europe, together with Australia and New Zealand. Then follows a large cluster containing most of the countries of western Europe, the United States, and Canada, and two other eastern European countries. Below this level there are, first, a few remaining countries of western Europe—Netherlands, Spain, Finland, and France—together with Argentina and Japan; and finally, at a much greater distance, five representatives of the very poor countries of Asia and Latin America. Supplementary data on the distribution of household income of employee families give the same general picture, and in particular they confirm that the poor countries are at the bottom of the list.

A summary of the results of Chapter 6 might run as follows. Over the long period from the beginning of the century until about 1960 practically the only available evidence relates to the dispersion of wages. Of the five countries for which such figures exist—namely, Belgium, France, Germany, the United Kingdom, and the United States—the only country in which a dramatic change took place was the United States. In Belgium there was some fall in dispersion from 1896 to 1964, but not a great deal; in France the evidence is contradictory and does not suggest any major change; in Germany, also, there seems to have been little change from 1907 to 1962; in the United Kingdom there was a moderate fall in dispersion from 1906 to 1960, as in Belgium; but in the United States there was a very substantial fall in male wage dispersion from 1899 to 1959, almost all of which occurred between 1939 and 1949.

While this rather limited evidence suggests that wage dispersion (in terms of individual earnings, not of occupational rates) has changed little in the industrialized countries of western Europe during the past half-century, there are scraps of evidence which suggest that the dispersion of all employee earnings declined more appreciably. But we do not have adequate information to judge this accurately; and, in any case, the transformation of many firms during this period from management by the entrepreneur towards management by paid employees would tend to obscure the picture.

If we now consider individual sub-periods, we find some evidence (from New Zealand and Sweden) for a substantial widening of dispersion between 1920 and 1930, which was almost certainly the result of the world depression. A similar trend occurred in the U.S.S.R. between 1928 and 1934, but for different reasons. For the period 1930 to 1940 there are no figures from any country except Canada; but from 1930 to 1950 —or thereabouts—there was a substantial decline in dispersion in several. These included the United States, Canada, New Zealand, and Sweden. In the case of the latter two countries this movement was largely a reversal of the tendency for dispersion to widen in the 1920s; but in the United States and Canada there seems to have been a fundamental shift in the pattern of income dispersion, especially between 1940 and 1950. Finally, there is evidence from a number of countries that during the 1950s there was a trend towards widening dispersion.

The countries which show this trend are Australia, Argentina, Canada, France, Germany, Israel, Japan (where the trend of the 1960s is, however, quite the opposite), New Zealand, Sweden, the United Kingdom, and the United States. The only country which showed a declining trend in dispersion in this period was Poland—from 1957 to 1960.

These are, then, the facts which we must try to explain.

2. Predictions of the Theory

In the theory which we developed in Chapter 4 it was suggested that the main influences determining the shape of the Standard Distribution are genetic inheritance, family class background, formal education and training, age (representing changes in experience and ability during adult years), and the hierarchic structure of organizations. How are these factors likely to vary between countries? There is no reason to expect that the relative distribution of genetic ability varies substantially between different peoples. A small minority of scientists—not usually geneticists—believe that mean genetic ability may vary between peoples; but even they do not suggest that the *dispersion* of genetic ability within each national group is likely to be very different. We can, I think, safely ignore this factor in our discussion of differences between countries, and within countries over time.

Family class background, as we have seen, is a most important influence on the child's—and hence the adult's—general level of ability. This influence would combine with such inter-class genetic differences as may exist to create a strong bias towards higher effective ability for the upper-class child. We should expect to find, therefore, that the distribution of ability in one generation is to a considerable extent a reflection of class inequalities in the previous one.[1] Hence, except where there is

---

[1] Burt (1961, p. 15) has suggested that, if there were no social mobility—as in a strict caste system—inter-class differences in intelligence would eventually disappear (because of regression of the genetic characteristic towards the population mean). But this leaves out of account the important influence of social class on the early education of the child, as well as on other aspects of its personality, and the inequalities of formal education which normally accompany class differences.

some radical structural change in society, we can predict that earnings distributions will exhibit a large element of continuity within each country. This, of course, is not a very strong prediction, since many other factors besides class structure tend to perpetuate themselves. But the facts, as we have seen, are at least not inconsistent with this prediction. Some people, indeed, may be surprised at the degree of stability of earnings dispersion over one or two generations which the available data reveal.

But class background is only one of the factors determining the dispersion of abilities. The principal exogenous factor is formal education. Of course, education also may be a monopoly of the upper classes—as it has been in most societies. But it is not merely the association between education and social class which perpetuates income differences. Even in a society which concentrated most of its educational resources on those with the greatest 'ability' (and even if, for the moment, we assumed that ability is not pre-determined to any degree by class background), the distribution of earnings would be highly dispersed—in fact, possibly more dispersed than in a class-dominated educational system. What matters is the *inequality* of education, as well as its association with other factors generating differences in ability. We can, therefore, predict that societies in which education is more unequally distributed will exhibit a wider dispersion of earnings than those in which it is more equally distributed. The lowest degree of dispersion would occur in societies in which there was a *negative* association between education and ability, for example, in countries where the children from poorer class backgrounds received more (or better) education than those from higher class backgrounds. There is some tendency in this direction in the communist countries (in as much as children of workers get preference), and this may be part of the explanation for the fact that the dispersion of earnings in these countries is lower than would be expected on other grounds. But even in these countries there is inevitably an opposite tendency for education to be concentrated on those with the greatest ability, especially at the higher levels.

Apart from the influences of family class background and of

204   EXPLAINING THE DIFFERENCES

formal education on effective abilities there is, I believe, another
environmental factor of very great importance. There is abundant evidence to suggest that children who grow up in agricultural districts—and especially farm children—are, in almost all
countries, significantly handicapped in finding employment in
non-farm industries. Prima facie plausibility for this view is
based on the almost universal tendency for agricultural wage
incomes to be lower than wages in non-agricultural employment. For example, Lee and others (1957, pp. 755–6) show that
service income (wages, salaries, and proprietors' income, including imputed rent of farm buildings) in United States agriculture
was less than half the level of service income in other industries
in 1880 and 1900. In 1919–21 it was just over half, and in 1949–
51 it was about 70 per cent. In Australia average wage and salary
earnings for men in agriculture were between 57 per cent and 70
per cent of earnings in manufacturing over the period 1947–8 to
1962–3, with a rising trend.[1] In Sweden the average income of
male wage earners in agriculture, forestry, etc. in 1960 was 63
per cent of the income of wage earners in manufacturing.[2] In
Mexico, in 1960, this ratio—for men and women combined—
was less than 50 per cent.[3] In Hungary, in 1962, average regular
monthly earnings of male agricultural wage earners were less
than 75 per cent of earnings of male wage earners outside agriculture. Data for a large number of countries on wages in agriculture and in manufacturing (in ZA 9), although not entirely
comparable, make it clear that wages in agriculture are invariably lower, ranging from less than one-third in some of the
poor countries of Asia and Latin America to about one-half to
two-thirds in the developed capitalist countries. In the four
countries of eastern Europe covered in our analysis the percent-
ages are generally higher, ranging from 72–3 per cent for Poland
and Yugoslavia to 85–6 per cent for Hungary and Czechoslovakia.[4]

Apart from this indirect evidence of differences in effective

[1] See Keating (1967).   [2] SW 5, Table 21.   [3] ME 1, Table 1.
[4] See also Bellerby (1956, p. 270) and ZA 10 (p. 120) for further evidence
on the ratio of agricultural to non-agricultural income per head.

ability of agricultural and non-agricultural workers, there is
also a good deal of direct information on the relative levels of
intelligence in the two groups. McNemar (1942, p. 37) found
that the mean I.Q. of rural children aged 6 and over was about
95, compared with 105 or more for children living in urban or
suburban areas. It is interesting to note that this difference was
greater amongst the older children than amongst the younger.
Anastasi (1958, p. 526) refers to an Iowa study which showed
the same tendency for the I.Q. difference between urban and
rural children to widen with age, the rural children being particularly at a disadvantage in verbal tests and tests involving
speed. Differences between urban and rural I.Q. have also
been found in several other countries (pp. 526–7). Anastasi
suggests that the reasons for these differences include poorer
educational facilities in rural areas (one-room schools, fewer
books, worse equipment, poorer teachers, shorter terms),
the lack of other cultural institutions (libraries, museums, etc.)
and the lack of stimulus from the varied experiences of urban
life (p. 528).[1] Of course, it might be objected that I.Q. tests are
biased towards the abilities which are mainly useful in urban
activities. As tests of 'pure' intelligence they are unsatisfactory
in this, as in other, respects. But this objection merely serves
to support our argument: that rural children are not well qualified to earn a living in an urban environment.[2]

Finally, it is easy to find evidence, from almost any country,
that both the quality and the quantity of education in rural
areas are lower than in urban areas. In the United States, for
example, where the differences are by no means extreme, Bogue

[1] Farm people are usually thought of as slow of thought and speech.
Sir Francis Chichester, on his arrival in Plymouth after a four months' solitary
voyage from Sydney, apologized for the slowness of his reactions to journalists'
questions. 'When you are alone', he said, 'you think more slowly week by
week.'

[2] In a survey made by the French National Statistical Institute it was found
that, out of just over 2 million men working in agriculture in 1959, 11 per cent
had left the industry five years later. Of those who moved, 30 per cent went
into unskilled work, nearly 20 per cent into construction, and 13 per cent into
transport driving. Less than 10 per cent became office workers and only about
5 per cent machine operators, engineers, and technicians (*The Economist*, 17
December 1966, p. 1276).

(1959, p. 333) shows that in 1950, at all ages above 5, school attendance rates were higher in urban than in rural areas; and educational retardation was much greater in rural areas, especially in rural-farm areas (p. 534).[1] In 1950 in the United States the median of years of schooling for farm labourers and foremen was 8·0, for farmers and farm managers 8·3, and for all males aged 14 and over in the civilian labour force 9·7. In 1960 the corresponding figures were 8·2, 8·7, and 11·1.[2] Some of these differences may be the result of migration of better-educated farm boys to the towns; but certainly not all. It is wrong to assume that only the better-educated migrate. Data on school attendance rates and levels of education in Japan in 1950, in agricultural and non-agricultural prefectures, given by Taeuber (1958, pp. 67–8), show similar differences. In Canada, in 1961, 15 per cent of males aged fifteen and over in agriculture, forestry, fishing, and trapping had completed less than five years of schooling, compared with 6 per cent in other industries (CA 8, Table 17). Finally, in every country in which illiteracy rates are computed, the rate is higher in the rural areas, the absolute difference being sometimes as much as 20–30 per cent (ZA 6, Table 4).

Thus a great deal of statistical material supports the common-sense view that farm people are generally at a disadvantage in an urban environment.[3] Of course, if farm boys all worked on

---

[1] Similar data on school attendance rates in Canada in 1961 are given in CA 5, p. 10–10.

[2] These figures come from US 2, Table 10, and US 3, Table 9 respectively.

[3] Johnson (1953) made a study of the difference between mean earnings in 1940 of United States male rural–urban migrants and other urban male wage and salary earners. After allowing for differences in age he found a difference of only 11 per cent; but his method is very approximate, assuming, in particular, no difference between earnings of migrants and others within broad occupational groups.

Adam Smith wrote: 'The policy of Europe considers the labour of all mechanics, artificers, and manufacturers, as skilled labour; and that of all country labourers as common labour' (1947, i. 90).

In an essay on Mrs. Hannah More, E. M. Forster describes her efforts, in nineteenth-century England, to educate the rural poor of Somerset. 'Around her house for a radius of many miles the faint glimmer of education spread— samplers and alphabets, the sparks of our present conflagration. The farmers, wiser than she, foresaw that in time it would be impossible to find a "boy to plough or a wench to dress a shoulder of mutton", and that the evil old days

farms the difference in their educational and environmental background would not directly influence the distribution of non-farm earnings. In practice, however, there has been—in almost all countries and in almost all recent periods—a net movement of population from the farms to the towns. Hence the deficiencies of a farm upbringing—from an urban point of view—must have had an important influence on the distribution of earnings of urban employees.

The strength of this influence will clearly depend on the extent of net migration from agriculture. Unfortunately, we do not have a great deal of information about the industrial or occupational background of urban employees, although some estimates of rural–urban migration are available. But we can plausibly assume that—on the average— the higher the proportion of agricultural workers in the total labour force, the greater the pressure of migration towards the towns, and the greater the proportion of urban employees who are of farm origin. We can, therefore, make the prediction that in countries with a higher proportion of farm workers the dispersion of non-farm earnings will be greater; and also that in a country in which the proportion of farm workers in the labour force is falling the dispersion of non-farm earnings will also have a tendency to decline.

These are the main predictions which we shall attempt to verify. But, for completeness, we should also consider possible differences in the effects of age and of the hierarchic structure on the dispersion of earnings in different countries and at different times. We know relatively little about differences between age effects between countries. Most of the information we have comes from a few of the more advanced countries. We know, from these countries, that changes with age tend to be greater for the more highly educated than for the unskilled. It may perhaps be guessed that in countries with relatively few educated people the total effect on earnings of age variation will be less than in more highly developed countries. To that extent

might come back when the monks had preached Christianity from the top of Glastonbury Tor' (1967, pp. 264–5).

we might expect dispersion to be less in the poorer countries. But this factor is probably of minor importance compared with others which tend to accentuate dispersion in the poorer countries.

About the hierarchy effect we can perhaps be a little more definite in our predictions. On the assumptions of the model which we have proposed, the value of Pareto's α will depend on n, the number of persons directly controlled by each supervisor, and p, the ratio which the earnings of the employees in any grade bear to aggregate earnings of those whom they directly supervise in the grade below. Now, it is to be expected that, in countries where education is very unequally distributed, which are also for the most part the countries with a high proportion of agricultural workers in the labour force, there will be a marked shortage of people willing and able to take managerial positions.[1] In these countries, therefore, we can probably expect both n and p to be larger than in countries where education is more widespread and the proportion of farm workers is lower. If this is so —and unfortunately I know of no direct method of verifying the assumption—then the hierarchy effect will work in the same direction as the education and environment effects previously discussed.

It seems, then, that we can reasonably concentrate our attention on the two basic predictions: that dispersion will vary with the distribution of education; and that it will vary with the proportion of agricultural workers in the total male labour force. We shall consider the inter-country evidence on the first of these predictions in section 3, and on the second in section 4. In section 5 we shall discuss possible reasons for the changes in dispersion in the United States and Canada, especially the marked shift during the 1940s; in section 6 we shall consider the changes in Japan; and in section 7 the changes in other countries.

---

[1] This shortage may be partly met by the importation of foreign managers, as frequently happens with foreign-owned companies. But there is a limit to how far managerial differentials can be reduced in this way, since foreign managers expect much higher earnings than local employees; and, in fact, because of 'imperfections', the differentials within foreign-controlled firms may remain wider than they need to on pure market considerations.

3. The Distribution of Education

The appropriate data for testing our first prediction would be a distribution of the 'quantity' of education (and training) amongst non-farm employees in the countries in our sample. Although such data do not exist at present for many of the countries, the situation is much better than it was a few years ago, as a consequence of the inclusion of questions on educational level in a considerable number of the population censuses held around the year 1960. Most of the figures used in this analysis are taken from the summaries of these census results published in the United Nations' *Demographic Yearbooks* for 1963 and 1964 (ZA 4 and ZA 5). These give distributions of males and females separately by age and educational level, but only for the whole population, not for employees. Separate information for employees may exist in some cases in the original sources; but it has not been possible to check on this. In any case, the general distribution of education is probably a reasonable guide to the situation amongst employees separately.

Educational systems differ in different countries; and the methods used in collecting information about educational levels also vary. We have attempted to standardize the data so as to represent in each case the number of years of schooling completed; and for each range of years of schooling we have estimated a mean value. This mean number of years has then been converted into an estimated mean 'quantity' of education by assuming the following increments of 'quantity' for each year: years 1–4, 0·75 units; years 5–8, 1 unit; years 9–12, 1·5 units; years 13–16, 2 units; and years 17–20, 2·5 units. The principle underlying this conversion scale is that each extra year of education costs the child, or his parents, at least a year's loss of income, and that this cost varies with age (or the number of years of previous education). As a very rough approximation we can assume that the value of an extra year's education will correspond with this opportunity cost; and data from the United States and one or two other countries suggest that the scale chosen may not be too far wrong.[1]

The application of these estimated mean 'quantity' values to the frequency distributions of males aged 25–64 (or the nearest available equivalent age range) permits us to estimate the total 'quantity' of education in each group, classified by number of years of schooling; and from these data it is then possible to plot Lorenz curves of the distribution of education. Where there are sufficient points to justify placing some reliance on the shape of these curves, we have proceeded to estimate Lorenz coefficients of concentration of education. The results of these estimates are given in Tables 7.1, 7.2, 7.3, and 7.4. Since, as will be seen, Lorenz coefficients are not available for all the countries, they have been supplemented by an alternative—less satisfactory— indicator of educational inequality, which is available for a slighter wider range of countries, namely, the percentage of males aged 25–64 with less than about five years of education (but sometimes more or less than this where the statistics dictate a different cutting point).

In Table 7.1 we compare our indexes of educational inequality with our earlier estimates of dispersion of the Standard Distri- bution (from Table 5.5). Unfortunately, educational inequality indexes are available for only fifteen out of the twenty-five countries, and for some of these the indexes are not very satis- factory. In the table we have separated out the communist countries, since the dispersion of earnings is lower in all of these than would be expected on any of our criteria. Within each of the two groups it will be seen that there is a reasonably good positive relation between inequality of education and inequality

---

[1] In O.E.C.D. (1964, pp. 26–7) Denison uses a similar approach to estimate the contribution of education to improvement of labour quality; but he rightly discounts the age differences in earnings in order to make an allowance for the influence of ability. This is not relevant to our calculation, however, which is based on the simple assumption that the addition to the 'quantity' of education from one extra year can be roughly imputed from the cost of that year. Estimates of differences in earnings at different levels of education in Hydera- bad (India) are quoted by Harberger in Anderson and Bowman (1966, p. 19). They are broadly in line with those from the United States and Canada, although the relative differences are greater.

THE DISTRIBUTION OF EDUCATION 211

TABLE 7.1

*Inequality of Education and Dispersion of the
Standard Distribution*

Country and year of education data	5th percentile of Standard Distribution	Males aged 25–64		
		Lorenz coefficient of education ($\times 1,000$)	Per cent with education for less than X years	X
United Kingdom, 1951	200	176[1]	2[1]	8
Canada, 1961	205	300	9	5
United States, 1960	206	285	7	5
Argentina, 1947	215	445[2]	38[2]	4
Finland, 1950	250	..	31[3]	4
France, 1954	280	218[4] [5]	5[4] [5]	6
Japan, 1960	270	241[5]	0·6[5]	1
Brazil, 1950	380	780[6]	78[6]	4
India, 1961	400	..	85[6]	6
Chile, 1960	400	538[5]	54[5]	5
Mexico, 1960	450	680[7]	80[7]	5
Czechoslovakia, 1961	165	..	0·5	8
Hungary, 1960	180	325	17	5
Yugoslavia, 1961	200	..	23[8]	4
Poland, 1960	200	..	45[6]	7

[1] All males and females in the work force.
[2] Males aged 20 and over.
[3] Males aged 7 and over.
[4] French-born only.
[5] Males aged 25 and over.
[6] Males aged 25–59.
[7] Males aged 30 and over.
[8] Males aged 10 and over.

Sources: Percentiles from Table 5.5. Education data: United Kingdom and France from O.E.C.D. (1964); Argentina and Brazil from ZA 11; Finland and Yugoslavia from ZA 7, Table 60; Japan from JA 6, Table 52; others from ZA 4 and ZA 5.

of earnings, with the exceptions of France, Japan, and—possibly —Chile. We have already had reason to comment on the unusually wide dispersion of earnings in France. It may be that the French earnings data are in some respects inappropriate;[1] and

[1] We know that they are based on earnings net of social security contributions; but it is unlikely that this could account for more than a small part of the difference in dispersion.

the French education data are not official figures but estimates by Malinvaud (O.E.C.D., 1964, p. 60) which relate only to French-born citizens. The substantial numbers of foreign workers in France are certainly distributed around a much lower average educational level, and, if they were included, the education inequality indexes for France would be significantly increased. But the position of France remains a puzzle.

So far as Japan is concerned, the degree of dispersion of earnings has already fallen since 1955, and it may well continue to fall over the next few years. One of the striking facts about Japan is the remarkable development of its educational system and the very high standard (in terms of number of years) already achieved there. In this respect Japan is already ahead of many of the countries of western Europe, and its pattern of income distribution seems likely to move steadily towards the western European or North American pattern.

Our earnings data for Chile, as noted in Chapter 5, are not at all satisfactory; and they may well exaggerate the degree of dispersion in that country. Even so, the inequality of education in Chile is very great. Blitz, in Harbison and Myers (1965, p. 98), states that in 1952 nearly 57 per cent of children aged 7–14 in Chile were not attending school; 9 per cent never attend school at all and 30 per cent drop out in the first two years. The position is much worse in rural areas than in the cities; but, even in the cities of Santiago and Valparaiso, Blitz estimated that the average number of years of schooling of male manual workers was only 4·8 (p. 104).[1]

In Tables 7.2 and 7.3 we compare indexes of educational inequality with the dispersion of household income in certain countries, for all employees and manual workers respectively. The results are generally in line with those already discussed,

[1] The tendency to drop out of school is very high in Argentina also, despite the fact that education is free and fairly well developed. Horowitz, in Harbison and Myers (1965, pp. 19–20), reproduces an educational pyramid for Argentina in 1959, which shows that 'out of every 1,000 students who enter the first grade, only 733 enter the second grade; and it is estimated that only about 35 per cent of the children who enter primary school complete the sixth grade. This school-desertion rate ranges from 38 per cent in the highly industrialized Buenos Aires region to 86 per cent in the rural northeast region.'

and they give further empirical support to the prediction that inequality of education and dispersion of earnings are positively associated.

TABLE 7.2

Inequality of Education and Dispersion of Household Income: All Employees

Country and year of education data	10th percentile of household income	Lorenz coefficient of education ($\times 1,000$)	Per cent with education for less than X years	X
		Males aged 25–64		
Hungary, 1960	165	325	17	5
United Kingdom, 1951	180	176[1]	2[1]	8
Israel, 1961	192	370	20	5
Japan, 1960	196	241[2]	0·6[2]	1
Yugoslavia, 1961	198[3]	..	23[4]	4
Korea, 1960	224	570[5]	40[5]	5
Guatemala, 1950	263	800	91	5
Philippines, 1960	293	570[2]	60[2]	5

[1] Males and females in the work force.
[2] Males aged 25 and over.
[3] Extrapolated from estimate of P_{20} by comparison with Japan.
[4] Males aged 10 and over.
[5] Males aged 25–60.

Sources: Percentiles from Table 5.8. Education data from ZA 4 and ZA 5, except United Kingdom, Japan, and Yugoslavia, as shown in Table 7.1, and Guatemala from ZA 11.

Table 7.4 contains estimates of inequality of education for five other poor countries of Africa, Asia, and Latin America. Unfortunately, no estimates of earnings inequality are available for these countries; but it would not surprise us to learn that the dispersion of earnings in these countries was wide.

The results of these tests are generally consistent with our prediction; their tendency is certainly in the right direction. Regrettably, there are not really enough countries in the crucial table (Table 7.1) to give a satisfactory test of the theory; but at least it can be said that the data are not such as to make us abandon it.

TABLE 7.3

Inequality of Income and Dispersion of Household Income: Manual Workers

Country and year of education data	10th percentile of household income	Males aged 25–64		
		Lorenz coefficient of education ($\times 1,000$)	Per cent with education for less than X years	X
Hungary, 1960	159	325	17	5
Italy, 1961	162[1]	258	15	8
United Kingdom, 1951	167	176[2]	2[2]	8
France, 1954	172	220[3][4]	5[3][4]	6
El Salvador, 1961	183[5]	744[4]	56[4]	1
Puerto Rico, 1960	188	490	46	5
Indonesia, 1961	196[6]	660	84	5

[1] Total expenditure, not income.
[2] Males and females in the work force.
[3] French-born only.
[4] Males aged 25 and over.
[5] Three towns only.
[6] Djakarta only.

Sources: Percentiles from Table 5.8. Education data from ZA 4 and ZA 5, except United Kingdom and France from O.E.C.D. (1964).

TABLE 7.4

Inequality of Education in Some Other Poor Countries

Country and year of education data	Males aged 25–64		
	Lorenz coefficient of education ($\times 1,000$)	Per cent with education for less than X years	X
Panama, 1960	540	56	5
Malaya, 1957	600	54	4
Honduras, 1961[1]	760	89	5
Pakistan, 1961[1]	870	88	5
Ghana, 1960[2]	860	84	4

[1] Males aged 25 and over.
[2] Males aged 25–54.

Sources: ZA 4 and ZA 5.

4. Proportion of Agricultural Workers in the Labour Force

Our second prediction is that there will be a positive association between the dispersion of earnings and the proportion of agricultural workers in the labour force. Data are readily available on this latter characteristic for most countries; and in Table 7.5 we compare our estimates of dispersion of the Standard Distribution with the percentage of occupied males in agriculture, forestry, hunting, and fishing. The figures for the non-communist countries are plotted on a scatter diagram in Fig. 7.1, and the results can be seen to be broadly consistent with the prediction. Once again, Chile seems to be exceptionally dispersed, while Spain and Finland deviate substantially in the opposite direction. The earnings data for Spain are not satisfactory, since they include family allowances, which will tend to reduce the degree of dispersion. In this comparison Japan is no longer exceptional but lies close to the regression line that could be fitted to the data; and the position of France, although unusually high in comparison with other countries where the proportion of the work force in agriculture is the same as hers, is less remarkable than it appeared previously.

The principal weakness of the relation is that there is a large cluster of countries with a dispersion index in the region of 200 which show a wide variation in the percentage of males in agriculture, ranging from 6 to 23. It seems that, except in France, when the proportion in agriculture falls below about 25 per cent, this factor ceases to be of dominant importance.[1] An obvious reason for this is that, once the proportion in agriculture reaches a moderate level, the supply of agricultural workers to industry will tend to be much reduced. In addition, countries in which the proportion in agriculture falls below 25 per cent are invariably fairly rich countries (by world standards) and they can afford to spend more on raising educational and other amenities in the rural districts. This hypothesis receives

---

[1] In France the proportion of males in agriculture was in excess of 25 per cent until about 1957.

TABLE 7.5

Percentage of Occupied Males Engaged in Agriculture and Dispersion of the Standard Distribution

Country and year of dispersion estimate	5th percentile of Standard Distribution	Per cent of males in agriculture (c. 1960)[1]	Per capita G.D.P. at factor cost, 1958[2]
			(US $)
New Zealand, 1960–1	178	18	1,687
Australia, 1959–60	185	13	1,399
Denmark, 1956	200	23	1,177
United Kingdom, 1960–1	200	6	1,238
Sweden, 1959	200	18	1,507
Germany (F.R.), 1957	205	10	1,222
Canada, 1960–1	205	16	1,692
Belgium, 1964	206	7	1,043
United States, 1959	206	9	2,324
Austria, 1957	210	18	746
Netherlands, 1959	215	13	1,038
Argentina, 1961	215	23	573
Spain, 1964	220	46	355
Finland, 1960	250	38	576
France, 1963	280	20	1,168
Japan, 1961	270	26	339
Brazil, 1953	380	54	130
India, 1958–9	400	65	70
Ceylon, 1963	400	50	123
Chile, 1964	400	34	398
Mexico, 1960	450	59	335
Czechoslovakia, 1964	165	20	680
Hungary, 1964	180	37	490
Yugoslavia, 1963	200	50	265
Poland, 1960	200	39	475

[1] Economically active males in agriculture, forestry, hunting, and fishing as percentage of all economically active males.

[2] Currencies converted to U.S. dollar at 'parity rate'. For notes on method used see ZA 8.

Sources: Percentiles from Table 5.5. Per cent in agriculture from ZA 5, Table 9, supplemented by special estimates for United Kingdom, Belgium, Brazil, Ceylon, and Czechoslovakia. G.D.P. *per capita* from ZA 8, except communist countries from Harbison and Myers (1964, pp. 45–8).

some support from Fig. 7.2. This diagram shows, first, that, in general, *per capita* G.D.P. is not a good predictor of earnings dispersion, although there is some (negative) association. But, for the countries which were in the south-west cluster of Fig. 7.1, the introduction of *per capita* G.D.P. helps quite considerably to explain the differences in dispersion. The principal remaining deviants are the United States and Canada. In their case dispersion is greater than would be expected from the combined effects of proportion of males in agriculture and *per capita*

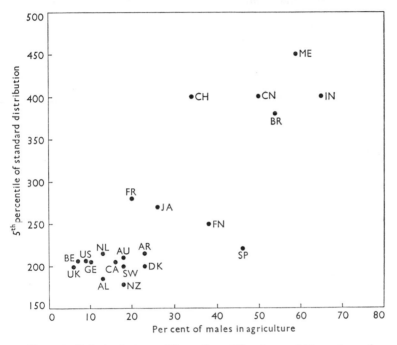

FIG. 7.1. Relation between Dispersion of Earnings and Percentage of Males in Agriculture.

Source: Table 7.5.

G.D.P. Here perhaps it is worth remarking that both of these countries are very large in area and that the inequality of education in both is probably greater than in most of the countries of western Europe and Australasia.[1] Although the hypothesis cannot at present be tested statistically, it seems

[1] Appendix tables US–20 to 22 and CA–4 to 9 show that regional differences in the United States and Canada contribute significantly to over-all dispersion.

plausible to suggest that, amongst countries with less than 25 per cent of males in agriculture, the combined influence of *per capita* G.D.P. and inequality of education can explain most of the differences in the dispersion of earnings.

The additional data in Tables 7.6 and 7.7, and also the data for the communist countries at the bottom of Table 7.5, give

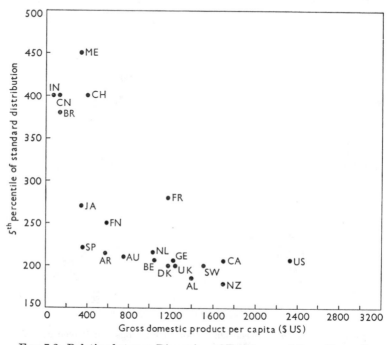

FIG. 7.2. Relation between Dispersion of Earnings and Gross Domestic Product per Capita.

Source: Table 7.5.

further support to our theory. Yugoslavia is perhaps less dispersed than might be expected, and Puerto Rico more so. One can think of special factors in the Puerto Rican case, especially the heavy emigration of labour to the United States; but there is no obvious reason—other than government policy—why the dispersion of earnings in Yugoslavia is not greater than in Poland.

TABLE 7.6

Percentage of Occupied Males Engaged in Agriculture and Dispersion of Household Income: All Employees

Country and year of dispersion estimate	10th percentile of household income	Per cent of males in agriculture (c. 1960)
Hungary, 1962	165	37
United Kingdom, 1964	180	6
Israel, 1959–60	192	12[1]
Japan, 1963	196	26
Yugoslavia, 1963	198	50
Korea, 1963	224	60
Guatemala, 1952–3	263	71[2]
Philippines, 1961	293	69

[1] Jewish only.
[2] Per cent of total population.

Sources: Percentiles from Table 5.8. Per cent in agriculture from ZA 5, Table 9, supplemented by special estimates for the United Kingdom and Guatemala. The latter comes from Harbison and Myers (1964, p. 46).

TABLE 7.7

Percentage of Occupied Males Engaged in Agriculture and Dispersion of Household Income: Manual Workers

Country and year of dispersion estimate	10th percentile of household income	Per cent of males in agriculture (c. 1960)
Hungary, 1962	159	37
Italy, 1953–4	162[1]	28
United Kingdom, 1964	167	6
France, 1956	172	20
El Salvador, 1954	183[2]	71
Puerto Rico, 1953	188	30
Indonesia, 1957	196[3]	69

[1] Total expenditure, not income.
[2] Three towns only.
[3] Djakarta only.

Sources: Percentiles from Table 5.8. Per cent in agriculture from ZA 5, Table 9, supplemented by a special estimate for the United Kingdom.

5. Changes in Dispersion in the United States and Canada

(a) United States

We concluded earlier that there had probably been little net change in the dispersion of earnings in the United States (at least amongst manual workers) between the beginning of the century and 1939. To judge by the skill differentials, there may have been a fall in dispersion during the First World War, but, if so, this was at least partly redressed in the years immediately following the war. There has been much argument about the character of the changes in skill differentials during the slump of 1929–33, but there is no convincing evidence that the average differential moved significantly in either direction. Although we do not have direct evidence on changes in the dispersion of earnings in this period, it may well be that there was some growth of dispersion during the depression and a decline during the recovery. The evidence from Sweden and New Zealand is very suggestive in this respect, even though it relates to all employees, not to full-period workers. But even amongst full-period workers it may be expected that a sharp recession will tend to increase the dispersion of earnings, even if only because piece-work earnings—which are both high and widely dispersed in boom periods—are more affected by a fall in activity than time-work earnings. Some evidence from Australia for recent years shows that changes in dispersion tend to be associated with the level of economic activity (Lydall, 1965), although these figures also do not strictly relate to full-period workers.

But we are not particularly concerned with short-term fluctuations in dispersion. Our main interest is to explain long-run changes, that is, changes in the level of dispersion which occur between years of comparable degrees of unemployment. For the United States, then, the essential problem is to explain, first, the relative stability of dispersion from 1900 to 1939, and, second, the radical fall in dispersion between 1939 and 1949. Our basic hypothesis is that changes in dispersion are affected by (1) changes in the distribution of education, and (2) changes in the proportion of farm workers in the male labour force. But in the case of the United States we must take notice of a further —and unusual—feature of its labour supply, namely, that for most of its history a substantial part of the net addition to the labour force came from foreign immigration. Most of these immigrants until the 1920s were workers and peasants, poorly educated and handicapped by an inadequate knowledge of English. Thus the supply to non-farm industry of workers of less than average effective ability, which is generated in all countries by the migration of farm workers to the towns, was greatly augmented in the United States by the influx of European workers and peasants. In our analysis of factors causing changes in the dispersion of earnings in the United States, therefore, we must pay attention not only to changes in the distribution of education and in the percentage of agricultural workers in the labour force, but also to changes in the contribution of immigration to the total labour supply.

Indicators of the movements in these three factors over the period 1910 to 1960 are presented in Table 7.8. The Lorenz coefficients for education are based on estimates of education

TABLE 7.8

Possible Influences on Earnings Dispersion in the United States

Year	Lorenz coefficient of education[1] ($\times 1,000$)	Per cent of farm workers in male labour force	Per cent of foreign-born workers in male labour force[2]
1910	390	34·7	21·9
1920	373	30·4	20·0
1930	358	24·8	16·4
1940	335	21·7	11·8
1950	317	14·9	8·3
1960	303	8·1	6·6

[1] Males aged 25 and over.
[2] Foreign-born whites only until 1950. Labour force excludes unemployed in 1940 and 1960.

Sources: Lorenz coefficients based on data in O.E.C.D. (1964, p. 25). Per cent of farm workers from US 6, Table 2, except 1960, which is from US 3, Table 1. Per cent foreign-born from United States Census reports.

distributions made by Denison. They are subject to measurement error on this account, and also because a certain amount of judgement is involved in drawing a Lorenz curve through a limited number of points. Nevertheless, the coefficients are interesting, because they show that inequality of education was declining throughout the period. In each decade the coefficient fell by at least 15 points; but the largest fall, both absolutely and relatively, occurred between 1930 and 1940. From the second column of the table it appears that the proportion of males in agriculture was also falling throughout this period, and especially fast between 1940 and 1950. In section 4 we noticed that in countries in which less than about 25 per cent of male workers are engaged in agriculture there is generally a fairly low level of dispersion of earnings, and that below this point the percentage of males engaged in agriculture has little further effect on the degree of dispersion. If this was true also in the United States, we could argue that somewhere around 1930 the United States passed over this watershed and entered the phase in which the proportion of workers in agriculture is no longer an important influence on the dispersion of non-farm earnings.

The third column of the table shows that the widening influence of the presence of poorly educated foreign-born workers in the labour force was weakening throughout this period, and especially after 1930. Until 1920 the absolute number of foreign-born workers in the labour force was growing; but, after that, deaths and retirements exceeded net immigration, so that in the decade 1930–40 there was a substantial fall in the absolute number of foreign-born workers in the labour force. Account should also be taken of the occupational composition of the foreign-born section of the labour force. Throughout the nineteenth century, when the United States population was being swollen by a large influx of European immigrants, most of the immigrant workers took employment in the towns. Since they were less well-educated—on the average—than the native workers, and suffered from other disabilities, they mainly filled the lower-paid occupations. In 1910, for example, 26 per cent of all economically active persons were recorded as labourers, but

59 per cent of immigrants in the previous ten years had been so described.[1] If all immigrants who came in as labourers had remained in that position, 36 per cent of all non-mine labourers in 1910 would have immigrated in the previous ten years. Lebergott (1064, p. 28) has estimated that in 1870 60 per cent of miners were immigrants and 40 per cent of unskilled workers. In 1900 the corresponding figures were 44 and 28. According to Thomas (1954, p. 146), while about one-tenth of all male workers in 1900 were general labourers, amongst immigrant Italians the percentage was 33, amongst Poles 29, and amongst Irish and Hungarians 22 each. In 1910 nearly 40 per cent of all non-farm white male labourers were foreign-born, which was almost twice the proportion in the whole labour force (Thomas, 1954, Table 42).

Immigration continued to be heavily weighted with unskilled workers up to 1930, although less so in the 1920s than earlier. In 1930, 20 per cent of all economically active persons were recorded as labourers, but 34 per cent of immigrants in the previous ten years had been so described. After 1930 the picture changed radically. In 1940 the corresponding figures were 16 and 17; and in 1950, 11 and 7.[1] Whereas immigrant labourers in 1900–9 represented 36 per cent of labourers recorded in 1910, in the following decade the figure was down to 25 per cent. In the decade ending 1930 it was only 9 per cent, and in the following two decades less than one per cent.

While 1930 was probably the underlying turning-point in the forces making for a wide dispersion of earnings in the United States, the change may well have been obscured for several years by the special circumstances of the Great Depression. But when recovery had begun in the second half of the 1930s, and especially after the outbreak of the Second World War, the United States was ripe for a major change in income differentials. This change took place during the decade of the 1940s. During this period several developments occurred which could be expected to have substantial effects on income dispersion. First, there was a very low influx of migrants throughout the decade, and especially during the war years 1942–5; secondly,

[1] Source: US 7, pp. 60 and 74.

there was a rapid decline in the percentage of the male work force in agriculture; and, thirdly, associated with the decline in agriculture, there was an enormous mobilization of manpower into the armed forces and into war industry. This third event was probably decisive, since it swept up the surplus of unskilled labour from every corner of the economy. In many cases it gave ill-educated workers, both from farms and urban areas, an opportunity to obtain a basic training and to overcome their earlier disabilities, so that when their time for demobilization arrived, they were ready to take better jobs than they could have hoped for before the war. Some evidence for this effect is given in Ginzberg (1943). He found that a large proportion of a group of soldiers being discharged in 1941 were looking for better jobs than they had had before their service in the army. Many of the unskilled men had had opportunities of vocational training previously denied to them, as well as completely new experiences which had shaken them out of old habits.

Thus, since the decade of the 1940s the United States has become a much more homogeneous society than it was at any time in the previous 150 years. In the 1960s the proportions of farm workers and of foreign-born workers are both down to insignificantly low levels, and the average standard of education of both groups is higher than ever before. The one remaining major source of heterogeneity is the difference in education, environment, and effective ability of Negroes and whites; but this also will doubtless be overcome as time passes.[1]

The above interpretation of the changes in earnings dispersion in the United States is not, of course, entirely original. Many of the economists who have discussed the changes in skill differentials in America have suggested that rising standards and greater homogeneity of education, the fall in immigration, and the decline in the supply of agricultural workers have been important factors in causing differentials to diminish. We may refer in particular to the observations of Muntz (1955, pp. 578–82), Reder (1957, pp. 373–4), and Keat (1960). The following

---

[1] Even in 1959, to judge by table US–19, racial differences contributed only a very small amount to the total dispersion of earnings.

quotations from Reynolds (1959, pp. 489–90) are also very apposite:

Why did unskilled wage rates not rise faster before 1914? Why did they not rise fast enough to close the large gap existing between laborers and craftsmen? The answer may be mainly that the supply of unskilled labor was swollen before 1914 from two sources which are now much less important—American farm boys and European immigrants.

The latter came mainly from rural areas and 'entered American industry at the unskilled level'. Since 1914 both immigration and rural labour supply have been much reduced; but 'perhaps most important of all has been the diffusion of educational opportunities throughout the population'.[1]

(b) Canada

No attempt will be made to analyse Canadian experience in the same detail as that of the United States. We saw earlier that the trends of dispersion in Canada have been similar to those of the United States. This, of course, is only to be expected in view of the close association between the two labour markets; since the United States market is so much the larger of the two, it is reasonable to infer that the influence of the United States on Canada has been greater than the influence in the opposite direction. Nevertheless, it is of some interest to see whether Canada experienced the same sort of changes in the underlying factors as those which we have found in the United States. The relevant figures are brought together in Table 7.9.

Estimates of the distribution of education are not available for Canada before 1941. The Lorenz coefficient shows a small decline from 1941 to 1951, but no significant change in the next decade. Throughout this period the Canadian coefficient of inequality was lower than the coefficient for the United States, but the gap was closing, especially after 1950. On this basis we could expect that the dispersion of earnings in Canada would be smaller than in the United States in each period, but with a

---

[1] See also Kuznets (1966, pp. 273–5) for similar conclusions, although not related solely to the United States.

TABLE 7.9

Possible Influences on Earnings Dispersion in Canada

Year	Lorenz coefficient of education[1] (× 1,000)	Per cent of male labour force aged 15 and over in agriculture	Per cent of male labour force born outside Canada[2]
1911	..	39·0	33·2
1921	..	37·9	34·3
1931	..	33·7	34·7
1941	294	31·5	26·5
1951	284	19·3	20·5
1961	286	12·2	21·7

[1] For males aged 14 and over, or 15 and over, in the labour force.

[2] Males aged 10 and over in 1911–31, 14 and over in 1941–51, and 15 and over in 1961. 1941 figures exclude men on active service.

Sources: Lorenz coefficient based on data in CA 6 Table 18, CA 7 Table 19, and CA 8 Table 17. Per cent in agriculture from CA 8 Table 3. Per cent born outside Canada from censuses (supplied by the Dominion Bureau of Statistics).

diminishing difference; and if we refer to appendix tables CA–4 and US–1 (or CA–10 and US–4 for the latter two years) we find that Canadian dispersion was in fact significantly narrower than in the United States in 1940 and 1950. By 1960 dispersion in the two countries was nearly the same, except that it was somewhat wider in the United States in the lower part of the distribution. Thus, broadly, our hypothesis is sustained.[1]

The Canadian indicators of work-force composition show that a radical shift took place between 1941 and 1951. The proportion of males in agriculture, which had never previously been less than 30 per cent, fell precipitately to less than 20 per cent; and by 1961 it was down to just over 12 per cent. At the same time, the proportion of male workers who were born outside Canada fell from 26·5 per cent in 1941 to 20·7 per cent in 1951. In 1961 this percentage was slightly greater; but the social composition

[1] The Lorenz coefficients for Canada relate to all males in the work force, while the coefficients for the United States relate to all males aged 25 and over, irrespective of whether they were members of the work force. The difference of definition might be responsible for the residual gap between the coefficients in 1960 (or 1961). The estimated coefficient for males aged 25–64 in Canada in 1961 is 300, almost identical with the United States coefficient for males of 25 years and over in 1960.

of the immigrants of the 1950s was very different from what it had been in the years before the Second World War. Thus all the evidence from Canada is essentially consistent with our theory.

6. Changes in Dispersion in Japan

We saw in the last chapter that Japanese skill differentials fluctuated to some degree over the period 1883 to 1956, but showed no marked upward or downward trend. Lockwood (1954, p. 497), who studied the movements of Japanese skill differentials over the period 1885 to 1935, came to a similar conclusion. In the 1950s, however, our estimates of earnings dispersion show an increase up to 1959 or 1960, and a rather rapid decline during the next five years.

The history of Japan is a classic example of a country which was transformed from a backward, predominantly agricultural, economy into an advanced industrialized economy within the space of a hundred years. At the time of the Meiji Restoration in 1868 the proportion of the Japanese work force engaged in agriculture may have been as high as four-fifths;[1] and the standard of education of the mass of the population was certainly very low. Even in 1895, according to official estimates, less than one person in six in the productive age-groups had completed six years of elementary education, and less than 1 in 300 had completed secondary schooling. Hence, there is every reason to expect that in the second half of the nineteenth century the dispersion of non-farm earnings in Japan must have been very wide. And there is an abundance of fragmentary evidence that this was so. Lockwood, for example, draws attention to the relative labour-intensity of Japanese technique and its reliance on 'masses of unskilled and semi-skilled labor. Close economy has had to be practised in the use of land, machinery, and the more advanced technical and managerial skills. This tendency appears in the hand cultivation of crops, in human transport, in

[1] Lockwood (1954, p. 462) quotes Hijikata's estimate that in 1880 81 per cent of the work force were in agriculture, fishing, and mining; but he believes that this figure is exaggerated. However, at the turn of the century, according to official reports, three out of every five families in Japan were engaged in farming (p. 463).

"overstaffing" of factories and government offices, in the cheapness of unskilled personal services of all kinds' (p. 470). 'The early success of the Japanese textile industries in the face of long established Western competition owed much to the abundance of low-wage labor of the requisite skills' (p. 471). Hence, even although a large proportion of the factory labour force in the early days consisted of women and children, the dispersion of male earnings must also have been very wide.

One of the crucial decisions taken within the first few years of the Meiji Era was the establishment of a new system of education, embracing elementary, secondary, and higher levels. Compulsory four-year elementary education was promulgated in 1886, and was achieved in practice for males by the end of the century. In 1907 the compulsory period of elementary education was extended to six years;[1] and further extensive reforms at the end of the Second World War included a further rise in the compulsory period of education to nine years. At the same time both secondary and higher education were also being rapidly developed.

The results of this major educational effort can be seen in the estimates in Table 7.10 of the proportions of the 'productive-age' population who had attained various levels of education in

TABLE 7.10

Distribution of Education in Japan

(Per cent of 'productive-age' males and females combined)[1]

Year	Level of education completed			
	None[2]	Elementary	Secondary	Higher
1895	84·1	15·6	0·2	0·1
1905	57·3	41·6	0·9	0·2
1925	20·0	74·3	4·9	0·8
1935	7·1	82·1	9·2	1·6
1950	2·3	78·5	15·8	3·4
1960	0·5	63·9	30·1	5·5

[1] Productive-age population means 15–54 years before 1935 and 15–59 from 1935 onwards.

[2] This is the residual. They may not all have had no education at all.

Source: JA 4, 56–7.

[1] For the history of the development of Japanese education see the useful government publication (in English) JA 4.

selected years. In the forty years from 1895 to 1935 Japan was transformed from a country in which 84 per cent of the productive-age population had not even completed six years of elementary school to one in which 93 per cent had completed elementary education, and nearly 11 per cent secondary. A further rapid advance in the years after the Second World War brought Japan by 1960 to a point where more than a third of the productive-age population had completed secondary education, a higher figure than in any western European country, and exceeded only by the United States and Israel.[1] It is difficult to make reliable estimates of the Lorenz coefficient for education in Japan from the limited number of educational levels shown in Table 7.10; but there is no doubt that the coefficient fell dramatically from a figure of about 900 in 1895 to about 350 in 1925. And estimates for 1950 and 1960, based on the more detailed figures collected in the censuses, yield coefficients for males aged 25 and over of 320 and 240, respectively.

While this process of equalizing educational opportunities was going on, there was also a large-scale proportionate movement of the Japanese work force out of agriculture. Table 7.11 gives the relevant figures, beginning in 1920 when the first census was taken. By that year the proportion of active males engaged in agriculture, forestry, and fishing had already fallen to less than half; and this declining trend has continued since, with the exception of a sharp upward jump at the end of the Second World War, when several million Japanese citizens were repatriated from the ex-colonies and demobilized from the armed forces. On the basis of our theory, we should expect that both the equalizing of education and the fall in the proportion of workers in agriculture would have had an equalizing influence on the dispersion of Japanese earnings. But the very limited evidence at our disposal does not confirm this prediction. It may be that the evidence should be disregarded; but it is also possible to suggest an explanation for the apparent contradiction.

One of the special features of the Japanese labour market is the very wide differences which have existed between earnings

[1] See Layard and Saigal (1966, Table 7).

TABLE 7.11

Percentage of Active Males in Agriculture, Forestry, and Fishing in Japan

Year	Per cent
1920	48·2
1930	43·1
1940	35·7
1950	40·2
1955	33·8
1956	32·8
1957	30·9
1958	29·5
1959	27·4
1960	26·6
1961	25·3
1962	24·1
1963	22·5
1964	21·1
1965	20·1

Sources: 1920–55: Taeuber (1958, Table 28). Data relate to area of Japan in 1950. 1956–65: JA 7, based on Labour Force Survey.

in different sizes of firm. To some extent such differences occur in all under-developed countries;[1] but the size of the differences in Japan have probably been exceptional. According to Allen (1965, p. 216) these wage disparities are a comparatively recent phenomenon. 'At the beginning of the century—at a time when large-scale enterprises were few—they were very small and it was only after the First World War that they became at all conspicuous.' Why did these inter-firm differentials come into existence? Allen's explanation is that 'when the development of large-scale manufacturing industries began, firms were faced with a shortage of adequately trained labour, for workers in the existing small-scale industries were not necessarily of the type required and there was still some reluctance to enter factory employment' (p. 217). So large employers decided that the most effective means of overcoming this shortage was

to offer employment on good conditions to school leavers who would submit to training and to factory discipline. They not only paid

[1] See Turner (1965, p. 16) for a reference to a similar position in Egypt.

relatively high wages but they also provided many fringe benefits and gave an informal undertaking that the job, once secured, would be permanent. This was the origin of what came to be known as the 'life-long engagement' system under which workers received an implied guarantee against dismissal, and wages rose with seniority and length of employment [p. 217].

Allen argues that this system was not primarily the result of an ancient Japanese social tradition, as some have suggested, but that it arose to meet the labour requirements of large-scale industries.

The important feature of this system, from our point of view, is that it seems to have represented a response to a defect in the general system of education. Intensive on-the-job training was needed in order to raise the skill of workers to the level required by modern industry; and, since this involved the firms concerned in substantial costs, they developed a hiring and wages system which encouraged workers to stay with them permanently, thus ensuring that the effects of the training would remain internal to the firms concerned. But, if this was so, then estimates of inequality of education which are derived from data on the distribution of workers by levels of *formal* education are misleading, since they fail to take account of the extra years of on-the-job training. I know of no empirical evidence on the distribution of periods of on-the-job training in Japan, nor of its evolution over the past half-century. What can be said, however, is that the growth of on-the-job training, which developed significantly, according to Allen, only after the First World War, could be responsible for maintaining a fairly constant degree of dispersion of earnings, even though the other forces—of inequality of formal education and proportion of workers in agriculture—were tending to bring about a reduction in differentials. This interpretation of the changes (or lack of changes) in earnings dispersion in Japan in the years up to 1960 is also consistent with the explanation which we shall offer of the sudden drop in dispersion during the 1960s.

As we saw in the last chapter, there was a rise in dispersion within each size class of establishment in Japan from 1956 to

1959 or 1960. Our figures also showed (Table 6.4) a rise in dispersion *between* the medians of size classes from 1956 to 1957. This was, in fact, the tail end of an upward movement in dispersion between size classes of establishment which began in 1950, and which, according to Allen (1965, p. 216) probably brought the differences to a higher point than they had ever reached before. But an opposite movement set in very quickly. After 1957 the dispersion of medians of size classes of establishment fell steadily, and by 1965 it was of quite modest proportions. But dispersion of earnings *within* size classes continued to grow for two or three more years. Thereafter the fall in this component also was quite decisive, especially in the small- and medium-size classes, and by 1965 the dispersion within all size classes was at least back to the 1956 level, and amongst the small and medium firms it was much lower.

It is clear that these wide fluctuations in earnings dispersion in Japan over a period of fifteen years were essentially short-term. No one would suggested that they reflected some dramatic rise and fall in the underlying dispersion of Japanese effective abilities. The probable explanation is rather that by the 1950s the structure of the Japanese work force was moving rapidly towards a level of advanced homogeneity, comparable with that already existing in western Europe and North America. Inevitably, the structure of earnings had sooner or later to adapt itself to these new conditions. But temporarily some other forces prevented this movement, and even reversed it. Allen (1965, p. 218) has suggested that the widening of dispersion in the first half of the 1950s was associated with a change in the structure of industry and a growth in the demand for new types of skill, so that 'employers in large-scale industries were forced to strengthen the inducements needed to attract school-leavers of ability and to retain the workers once they had been trained'. While this may explain the widening gap between average earnings in large and small firms, it is difficult to see why it should have caused an increase in dispersion *within* each size class of firm. If large firms were offering better rates to new entrants one would expect to find a decrease in dispersion within large firms; but this does not occur until after 1961, when it was already happening in the smaller size classes also.

Although I have not been able to make a thorough study of this problem, I am inclined to believe that the temporary growth in dispersion of earnings in Japan in the 1950s was a result of a lack of adaptation of industry to a fundamental change in the structure of abilities in the work force. The supply of unskilled, poorly educated, culturally backward workers from the country areas was drying up, and the supply of well-educated school-leavers from urban areas was increasing. The larger firms recognized the change in the labour-supply situation fairly quickly and raised their initial hiring rates for school-leavers. But the small firms continued to expect to be able to obtain an unlimited supply of cheap labour from the countryside. So, temporarily, the smaller firms lagged behind, and perhaps in a desperate effort to retain their better quality and more senior workers, who were now attracted by the much better prospects in the larger firms, they even widened their differential payments. In this way they might hope to hold on to their existing labour force without making a fundamental upward revision of their rates for the lowest paid workers. But the situation could not last. Sooner or later the small firms had to raise their hiring rates for new entrants or lose the chance of employing any of the well-educated young people coming into the labour market. Once they accepted this unpleasant necessity, the dispersion of earnings within small firms rapidly shrank back and the average level of earnings in smaller firms moved up much closer to the level in the larger firms. And all of this happened quite suddenly, because the tension which had developed between the underlying supply of labour and the institutional structure of the market had become unbearable.[1]

[1] Both Allen (1965) and Yamamura (1966) draw attention to the fall in the supply of workers from agriculture in recent years and they attribute much or all of the change in differentials since 1956 to this 'dwindling surplus of labor in traditional sources of supply', as Yamamura puts it. But they do not give a very convincing account of why this factor, which has been operating for quite a long time, should have had such a dramatic, and delayed, impact after 1956. Much emphasis has been placed by these writers, and by Lockwood (1954, p. 494), on the fact that in earlier periods 'industrial wage rates remained tied . . . ultimately to the plane of living of the peasant'. But this does not

The changes in dispersion in Japan do not, perhaps, provide very much positive support for our theory, primarily because, while the theory relates essentially to longer period changes, there are no satisfactory Japanese statistics on changes in dispersion prior to 1951. What the theory does suggest, however, is that the underlying forces in Japan were changing over quite a long period in such a way as to cause a decline in the dispersion of earnings. Whether such a decline took place in the inter-war years we do not know. There were a number of short-term factors, such as the world depression, which may have prevented it. And then there were ten years of war, followed by another period of 'disequilibrium' during the first few years of the Occupation. Thus, it was only in the 1950s that a clear avenue opened for the underlying forces to show their effects on the dispersion of earnings. But the puzzling feature of what happened was that during the first part of the decade the movement was in the opposite direction to that which could have been expected; and that this was followed by a 'whiplash' in the next few years.

7. Changes in Dispersion in Other Countries

The other countries for which figures are available on long-term changes in dispersion are all in western Europe or Australasia. Results from these countries, as we have seen, tend to suggest that there was not very much change in over-all dispersion between the 1920s and the 1960s, and that even between 1900 and 1960 there was only a moderate decline in the dispersion of wage earnings. A comparison between the 1920s and the 1960s can be made for Sweden, Austria, and New Zealand. Each of these countries was already in the 1920s an advanced, well-educated country, in which educational inequality was probably not much different from what it is now. But in each case the proportion of men in agriculture (and related industries) was higher than the figure obtaining in the 1960s. In Sweden, for

explain the dispersion of earnings, only their average level. In order to explain dispersion—at least in the long run—we have argued that it is the *differences* between the abilities of the reasonably educated urban worker and those of the ill-educated peasant-worker that are relevant.

example, the percentage in agriculture, forestry, and fishing fell
from 40 in 1930 to 18 in 1960; in Austria it fell from 31 in 1934
to 18 in 1961; and in New Zealand it fell from 33 in 1936 to 18
in 1961. According to our theory, we could expect to find some
reflection of these changes in the dispersion of earnings. Unfortunately, however, we do not have estimates of the dispersion
of full-period earnings in the earlier years in any of these three
countries. The available figure (for all-period workers) suggest
that there was some fall in dispersion (at least in the central
part of the distribution) in Sweden, and also in New Zealand;
but that in Vienna the only significant decline in dispersion was
below the median.

So far as they go, these movements are in the right direction,
although, on general grounds, we might have expected them to
have been somewhat greater. It is possible to think of particular
circumstances which would have restricted the changes in
Sweden and New Zealand. The dispersion of earnings in New
Zealand was already extremely narrow in the 1920s, probably
because the standard of education in New Zealand farm areas was
already very high. New Zealand farm workers were never comparable with the ill-educated and culturally backward peasants
of Europe, nor with the poor whites of the United States. Thus
the dispersion of earnings in New Zealand in the 1920s was probably close to the limit of what is practicable in a typical modern
capitalist society. In the case of Sweden, also, the degree of dispersion in 1920 was not large, and despite the high proportion of
male workers still in agriculture in Sweden at that time, there
must have been sufficient homogeneity of education to offset
this influence. In addition, there was always the possibility of
emigration to America, which reduced the supply of farm
workers to the Swedish towns.

For four western European countries—Belgium, France, Germany, and the United Kingdom—we have some evidence on the
changes in the dispersion of wage earnings between about 1900
and 1960. In the cases of Belgium and the United Kingdom the
figures show a definite decrease in dispersion, while in France
and Germany there is no clear trend. But the French and

German data for the early period are very limited, and it would be unwise to draw any firm conclusion from them. So far as Belgium and the United Kingdom are concerned, neither country has had a large proportion of workers in agriculture at any time in this century. In 1930 the proportion of males engaged in agriculture, forestry, and fishing in Belgium was 18 per cent, and in 1900—to judge by Clark's (1951, p. 411) figures—the proportion cannot have been more than about 21 per cent. In Great Britain the proportion of the total occupied population in agriculture, forestry, and fishing in 1901 was 9 per cent; even if Ireland is included, the proportion in the United Kingdom was still only 13 per cent (Clark, 1951, pp. 408–9). By 1963 the percentage of males in agriculture, forestry, hunting, and fishing in Belgium had fallen to 7·1; and in the United Kingdom (in its present boundaries) to about 6. Thus the changes in agriculture, although they were in the right direction, were not such as to have a marked effect on the dispersion of earnings. What seems more probable is that the gradual strengthening of the educational systems of these two countries during the present century tended to reduce educational inequality, and hence to lay the basis for some reduction in earnings dispersion.[1] No reliable figures are available about the distribution of education in these countries at the beginning of the century; but in Great Britain already in 1887 16 per cent of the total population were enrolled in schools, and in Belgium 11 per cent. In 1954 the British figure was approximately the same but the Belgian percentage had risen to 15.[2]

---

[1] Comparing the situation in England in the 1870s with conditions seventy years later, Phelps Brown (1949, p. 4) wrote: 'Since that time one social gulf has been bridged—that between the unskilled wage-earners and the skilled. A glance at a street scene of seventy years ago, in the pages, say, of *Punch*, will point the contrast: the respectable tradesman, heir to "the gentleman millwright in his top hat"; and the unskilled labourer, a Caliban, ragged, misshapen, illiterate, drunken.' He concluded that 'save where there is immigrant peasant labour, the extension of education goes with a higher ratio of unskilled earnings to skilled'.

[2] These, and other, figures for a large number of countries are given by Easterlin in Anderson and Bowman (1966). They are, of course, only very rough indicators, even of current educational inputs, since the proportion of children of school age in the population can vary quite widely at different times.

The only other country for which we have estimates of dispersion from before the Second World War is Australia. These are for New South Wales in 1938. If we compare the dispersion of male earnings with that obtaining in Australia generally in 1959–60 there is practically no change, except perhaps a small decrease at the very top of the distribution. This lack of movement can presumably be attributed to the homogeneity of education in Australia in both periods, and to the fact that even in 1938 only about 25 per cent of Australian males were engaged in agriculture, forestry, fishing, and trapping. As in New Zealand, the Australian farm worker has never been very much poorer than his opposite number in the towns—indeed he has sometimes been better off—and, although the standard of education and cultural amenity in the country areas has generally been lower than in the towns, the Australian farm worker has not been at a severe disadvantage in urban employment.

8. Conclusion

We have tried in this chapter to use our theory of employment income distribution to predict the manner in which earnings dispersion will vary between different countries and over time. We have suggested that the theory points to two major variables as likely to be important—namely, the degree of inequality of education and the proportion of male workers in agriculture. In addition, in the United States and Canada the proportion of foreign-born workers in the labour force is a relevant variable. We have tested these predictions with the data at our disposal and we have found that—with a few exceptions—the predictions are verified. The volume of statistical material available for making these tests is, unfortunately, limited; and it cannot be claimed that the tests give extremely strong support to our theory. Nevertheless, the lack of serious discrepancies between predicted behaviour and actual behaviour is at least reassuring.

8

SOME THOUGHTS ON POLICY

1. Recapitulation

THE principal purpose of this book is to make a contribution to
our understanding of the factors responsible for the inequality
of incomes. But the scope of our study has been limited to only
one part of the problem, namely, the dispersion of employment
earnings. In most countries a more important source of inequality
is inequality of ownership of property; and, where such inequality exists to any marked degree, it is often the cause of
much popular discontent. Even so, the dispersion of earnings is
itself a source of a good deal of inequality; it varies from one
country to another, and it has changed substantially in at least
some countries. Hence it is a subject which seems to justify
separate investigation.

After reviewing existing theories of income distribution, and
finding them to be unsatisfactory in various ways, we took a
closer look at the shape of the distribution of employment
income. We found that differences of definition and coverage
can have very large effects on the observed shape of the distribution, so that, if we wish to develop a coherent theory, which
will be applicable to various countries at varying periods of time,
we must choose a particular type of distribution on which to concentrate our analysis. The distribution which we selected—the
Standard Distribution—is the distribution of pre-tax wage and
salary earnings of adult male employees, working full-time and
for the full period, in all non-farm industries and in all areas
of the country. Examination of a number of examples of this
distribution from various countries showed that it has a characteristic shape: it is unimodal; positively skew; closer to a lognormal than to a normal distribution, but leptokurtic even in

the logarithm of income; and its upper tail, in almost all cases, approximates to the Pareto law.

In the development of a theory to explain this distribution we have abstracted from short-term fluctuations in market conditions, which temporarily raise or depress the earnings of particular individuals or occupational groups, and we have rejected the suggestion that everything can be explained by the indefinite repetition of a stochastic process. Our efforts have been devoted instead to discovering the factors underlying the supplies of workers of different abilities, or, in other words, the qualitative composition of the labour force. We have shown that the variation of abilities of male adults comes from three main sources: (1) variation of general abilities at the end of elementary education; (2) occupational differentiation; and (3) variation of abilities with age over working life. In addition, employees who enter the managerial hierarchy, though often selected on the basis of ability, are paid on a different criterion, namely, their degree of responsibility; and this organizational factor provides a plausible explanation of the existence of a Pareto distribution of the upper tail.

Having developed our theory, we next turned to examine empirical data on the dispersion of employment incomes in about thirty countries, and on changes in dispersion in a number of these countries during the past few decades. The inter-country comparison showed that the richer countries were generally less dispersed than the poorer, although the relation was by no means perfect. But the dispersion of earnings in the communist countries was found to be usually lower than in non-communist countries at comparable levels of development. The historical comparison showed that, wherever over the past half-century there have been significant long-term changes, the movement has been towards greater equality of earnings. Wars and major depressions may interrupt the trend, the former by reducing dispersion, the latter by widening it; but the long-term downward trend in dispersion stands out in a comparison of peace-time years of roughly comparable degrees of unemployment. In some of the countries of western Europe there seems to have been relatively little change in the dispersion of earnings of manual workers since the beginning of this century, although the data are inadequate to support a strong conclusion; but in at least two countries (Belgium and the United Kingdom) there appears to have been a significant decline. In North America there seems to have been little change in the over-all dispersion of earnings until 1939; but in the following ten years there was a dramatic shift in the structure, bringing the degree of dispersion down from a fairly high figure to a level similar to that existing in most of western Europe. In western Europe and Australasia, meantime, there seems to have been little change. For other countries, information is lacking about long-term trends, although abundant evidence exists for recent years from Japan, which reveals some unusual and interesting fluctuations.

Our next task was to apply our theory to the empirical data, developing for this purpose testable hypotheses to explain the differences between countries and the changes over time. Of the three principal components of differential ability identified in our theory, we found that the most important was the variation in general ability. Hence it could be expected that, as between different countries or in the comparison over time, the major source of differences in dispersion was likely to be found here. Following this line of reasoning we looked for factors which could account for differences in the dispersion of general abilities. The major components of the variation of general abilities had earlier been shown to be genetic ability, environment, and education. Since there is no reason to expect that the variation of genetic ability is very different in different countries, or that it is likely to change significantly over a period of half a century, we concentrated our analysis on differences in environment and education.

Now it is clear that there are wide differences in both environment and education between different countries, and that conditions in some countries have changed in these respects very greatly even in the past fifty years. But these are not simple variables to measure. In the case of education something can be done to introduce quantitative measurement by using statistics or illiteracy or—better still—of the distribution of the adult population by numbers of years of full-time education. From such data we estimated Lorenz coefficients of education in certain cases, and more limited indicators of educational inequality in others. Where such indicators are available they seem to be fairly well associated with the degree of dispersion of the Standard Distribution.

In the case of environment the choice of indicator was more difficult. The dominant environmental influence on the development of children's abilities seems to be 'socio-economic class'. Class differences exist in all countries, but in some they are more extreme than in others. In so far as differences in children's general abilities reflect the class status of their parents we have a mechanism for perpetuating class differences, and the differences between countries at one period of time can be said to be largely the reflection of differences existing earlier. This is true, but not very helpful. But there is one aspect of the environment which is of great importance and which has changed dramatically in many countries: namely, the proportion of the population living on farms. And this factor can easily be expressed in quantitative terms. The hypothesis which we have tested is that there is a positive association between the proportion of the male work force engaged in agriculture and the dispersion of non-farm male earnings. The results of the tests, both between countries and over time, give some support to the hypothesis, at least for those cases where the proportion in agriculture is greater than 25 per cent. Amongst countries with less than this proportion, however, there seems to be an association between dispersion and *per capita* income, which suggests that in the richer countries the quality and quantity of education provided in rural areas is much closer to the level attained in urban areas.

In the United States and Canada our two hypotheses are supplemented by a third, which takes account of the fact that, for a large part of their history, the supply of urban workers in these countries was augmented by an inflow of poor workers and peasants from Europe. Thus, we could expect that the dispersion of non-farm earnings in these countries would be positively associated with the percentage of foreign-born persons in the work force. This is found to be broadly the case; and the corollary is, of course, that, so long as there was large-scale emigration from Europe, the dispersion of earnings in the European countries from which the migrants came was likely to be less unequal than it would otherwise have been. This may partly explain the fact that dispersion in some parts of Europe seems to have declined relatively little in the past fifty years.

But now what of the future? What light does our study throw on the problem of achieving greater equality of earnings? We shall arrange our discussion of this question under two main headings. First, we shall consider a number of special circumstances, of an institutional or short-term nature, which may affect the dispersion of earnings; and, secondly, we shall discuss the problem of how to influence the fundamental, long-term, determinants of dispersion.

2. Institutional and Short-term Factors

The first point to note is that actual earnings distributions, for all employees, are not the same as the Standard Distribution. Actual distributions are generally more dispersed than the Standard Distribution because women's earnings are less than men's, and because the Standard Distribution excludes part-time and part-period workers.[1] Hence any factors which tend to reduce the differences between men and women, or to reduce the amount of part-time and part-period work, will reduce over-all inequality. For full-period workers, in the developed countries, the median earnings of women seem to be mostly between a half and two-thirds of the earnings of men; and the question which arises is whether this ratio is an accurate reflection of the difference of average effective abilities of men and women, or whether it is partly institutionally or sociologically determined. It is, of course, obvious that the careers of most women are interrupted for a number of years—and at a crucial period—while they are bearing and rearing children. The effect of this 'institutional'

[1] Strictly, it also excludes non-adults, but this is a smaller problem.

factor is to limit the opportunities of most women to rise to high positions in the professions or in the managerial hierarchy. But there is no obvious reason, on grounds of ability, why the average earnings of the average woman should be reduced so substantially. In most societies there is still a strong prejudice against giving equal opportunities to women; and this is expressed not only in actual inequalities of pay for the same job but—even more influentially—in *de facto* restrictions on the sorts of work for which women can be employed. This social atmosphere is reflected also in the attitudes and aspirations of women themselves. From the earliest age most of them are brought up to expect and accept a position of inferiority; and in some countries women themselves reject any suggestion that they should be the economic equal of men. The inferiority of women is often accentuated in the poorer countries by educational discrimination; but in the richest countries the average educational attainment of women is not far short of that of men. Yet their economic inferiority remains. Thus, there seem to be good reasons for believing that inequality of earnings of men and women is, at least in part, a result of social prejudice, and that this source of inequality could be reduced quite 'costlessly' by a change of social attitudes.

A similar situation exists in certain multiracial societies. The most fully documented case is that of the United States, where the earnings of Negroes are consistently lower than those of white workers, even when all such factors as age, sex, education, region, and size of city have been taken into account.[1] Of course, the environmental background of Negroes is, on the average, much less favourable than that of whites, and this depresses their effective abilities; but the earnings differentials are so large that there can be little doubt that racial discrimination also plays a part. Here again, a change in social attitude would immediately result in greater economic equality.[2]

[1] See Becker (1957) and, for more detailed and more recent figures, Fuchs (1967).

[2] The clearest example of racial discrimination producing artificial economic inequality is South Africa, where there are legal prohibitions against employing Africans in certain skilled occupations. The Australian Aborigine is not legally

Apart from sex and race discrimination, a further 'institutional' cause of inequality is the existence of short-time working and casual labour. Some of this may be the result of a deficiency of aggregate demand—which will be discussed separately below; but there are also industries which develop the habit of relying on casual labour for part or all of their labour force. Sometimes this is economically unnecessary and, by a suitable institutional change, the industry can revise its methods, give its labour force reasonably permanent tenure, and still make at least as good—or even better—profits than before. But the initiative for making this sort of change often has to come from outside the industry. Sometimes, also, it may be promoted by the successful action of trade unions in raising the wages or improving the conditions of casual labour.

Another cause of very low incomes is excessive turnover of labour. Generally, it is the less skilled workers who move most frequently and, because they fail to establish themselves in any firm, their low earnings level is perpetuated.[1] Moreover, since each time that they move they lose some employment, their annual earnings are even further depressed. There are probably many different reasons for high mobility. Some of it is a natural process of searching for the right job, and to that extent is justified. But there are other cases where the worker is maladjusted and unable to settle. Sympathetic guidance and an effort to give such workers an adequate training can partly eliminate this cause of poverty.

An important source of inequality in most countries is geographic immobility of labour. Wages are generally higher in large cities (although net advantages are not necessarily correspondingly favourable), and in almost every country there are backward or 'depressed' areas in which earnings are considerably

---

discriminated against, but he is generally very poor. It is difficult to know how much of his present poverty is the result of social neglect and how much the result of discrimination in employment. But there is certainly some discrimination.

[1] A table in FR 4, p. 52, shows that the proportion of workers in France on low rates of earnings who work for the same employer throughout the year is much less than the corresponding proportion of higher paid workers.

below the national average.[1] Improved mobility and greater perfection of the labour market would undoubtedly reduce differentials of this sort, although there is probably an irreducible residual which reflects non-pecuniary advantages of living in smaller cities or in rural areas. And, of course, part of the differences between earnings in different sizes of city may be the result of differing proportions of workers with an agricultural background.

Amongst the institutional factors possibly affecting dispersion of earnings must also be considered, first, the strength and policy of trade unions; and, secondly, the presence or absence of minimum wage legislation. The action of both these forces is rather similar, in as much as they represent attempts to compel employers to adjust differential wage payments by external pressure, whether collective or statutory. It is difficult to believe that very large changes in relative dispersion can be imposed on employers contrary to underlying market forces; but it may well be that pressures of this sort can help to reduce imperfections of the labour market which would otherwise exist. In a purely *laissez-faire* situation, quite irrational differences in wage rates can persist for long periods of time because of ignorance and immobility; and pockets of exploitation in particular areas or amongst particular groups of workers may be finally eliminated only through the action of trade unions or of a statutory authority. Examples where such pressure seems to have been effective are the 'sweated' trades of London in the 1890s and migrant workers in the United States in the 1960s. We do not know, of course, to what extent the forcible raising of 'sub-normal' rates leads to a reduction in employment; but there are reasons for believing that the fall in employment is usually not very great and that both employers and workers learn to adjust to the new situation in other ways.

But clearly there is a limit to what can be done in this way without adverse repercussions, either by reducing employment

---

[1] Fuchs (1967) gives some interesting data on variations of hourly earnings with city size in the United States, after adjustment for age, sex, education, and colour of worker.

opportunities for less able workers or by inducing a general increase in all wage and salary rates, and hence stimulating inflation. In principle, we can say that there is usually some scope for reducing dispersion, especially by raising very low earnings, in any country where hitherto there has been no intervention by trade unions or the government. But, beyond a certain point, attempts to squeeze differentials are likely to be offset by wage drift. We have referred earlier to two instances in Britain where changes in wage-rate differentials were partly or wholly offset by wage drift.[1] Data for Denmark in O.E.C.D. (1965, Table 37) show that wage drift over the period 1948–58 almost entirely compensated for the decline in rates differentials. Günter (1964, p. 151) cites similar examples of discrepancies between rates and earnings differentials in Stockholm in 1962. Leiserson (1959, p. 85) quotes the following comment of the Norwegian Central Bureau of Statistics on the changes in wage rates and earnings in Norwegian manufacturing industry in the first few years after the Second World War: 'the contractual wage increase has been largest for those groups which had the lowest average earnings at the end of the war, while the wage drift in large part has been strongest for the higher wage groups.' After discussing the evidence on the incidence of wage drift between industries in Norway, Leiserson concludes: 'In general, these variations seem to have been of a character to soften the impact on the wage structure of the equalizing tendencies involved in the "solidaristic" policy of the unions' (p. 90).

Although our knowledge of the effects of union policy and of minimum wage legislation is still very inadequate, the examples quoted above are consistent with the predictions of economic theory, that earnings differentials in the long run cannot deviate greatly from the equilibrium levels determined by supply and demand. Hence, I think we can conclude that, while intervention by collective and statutory bodies can have some effect on the dispersion of earnings, especially where it is directed towards eliminating pockets of monopoly or monopsony, there are limits to the power of either trade unions or statutory regulation to

[1] See p. 184 n. above.

compel the market to accept any particular set of arbitrarily determined wage differentials.

Short-term Influences on Dispersion

If we turn now from the institutional factors influencing dispersion to the 'short-term' factors, it is obvious that the principal short-term factor is the level of aggregate demand. When demand fluctuates, one of its first effects is to change the distribution of hours worked—a rise in demand causing an increase in overtime work and a reduction in short-time, and vice versa. Unfortunately, we do not know whether, on balance, the dispersion of hours is increased or diminished by such changes. Table 8.1 gives data on the number of hours usually worked by

TABLE 8.1

Canada, 1960–1, Wage and Salary Earners Aged 15 and over by Hours Usually Worked (Percentage distributions)

Hours usually worked	Male	Female	Total
1–19	1·82	7·85	3·59
20–9	0·99	6·07	2·49
30–4	1·10	4·39	2·07
35–9	6·36	14·81	8·86
40	49·24	43·21	47·46
41–4	10·40	8·43	9·82
45–9	12·06	7·51	10·72
50 and over	18·03	7·73	14·99
Total	100·00	100·00	100·00

Source: CA 1, Table 24. The data cover only those reporting their hours usually worked.

wage and salary earners in Canada in 1960–1. Both the male and the female distributions have the same mode of 40h; but the male distribution is positively skew and the female distribution negatively skew. 1960–1 was a year of substantial unemployment in Canada (about 7 per cent) and it may be that the dispersion of hours for both males and females was rather greater than it would be in a year of higher demand. We do not know exactly how dispersion of hours varies with the level of activity; but it seems probable that minimum dispersion of hours is achieved when demand is fairly high, but not so high as to result in large amounts of overtime working.[1]

But all of this ignores the effect of unemployment. When unemployment grows, the proportion of workers employed for less than, say, fifty weeks in the year increases; and, since there is an upper limit of 52 weeks, even in years of high demand, a recession inevitably increases the dispersion of weeks worked. This is probably the major factor responsible for the widening dispersion of all workers' earnings in the 1930s, which we found in Chapter 6 when we studied data from Sweden, Canada, and New Zealand. It is possible, also, that in a prolonged depression the level of standard rates for unskilled workers may decline more than that of skilled workers; but on this matter, as we have seen, there is no conclusive evidence.

The only other short-term factor, which has been suggested by some authors as a cause of changes in dispersion, is the rate of change of prices. The main argument is that the fall in skill differentials in various countries during and immediately after the two world wars was the consequence of inflation. Dunlop and Rothbaum (1955, pp. 357–8), on the basis of a study of changes in skill differentials in Italy, France, and the United States, concluded that 'the size of the skill differential in per- centage terms is closely related to the movement of the price level'. They also maintained that high employment levels do not have as large an influence on differentials as inflation (p. 362). But their whole analysis is based on rates, not earnings; and there is a good deal of doubt about the validity of the figures quoted, especially those for France and Italy. We have discussed in Chapter 6 the many difficulties in using skill differentials as

---

[1] Some indication of the relative importance of variation in hours worked in the total dispersion of earnings is given by German data on distribu- tions of hours worked, and of monthly and hourly earnings, of male manual workers in October 1962 (GE 4, p. 517). Each distribution is approximately lognormal, and from graphic estimates of the standard deviations of the logarithms it appears that about one-sixth of the variance of the logarithm of monthly earnings is attributable to the variance of the logarithm of hours worked.

indicators of earnings dispersion, and we have offered alternative hypotheses to account for the well-attested changes in dispersion in the United States between 1939 and 1949. While we cannot dismiss completely the possibility that price changes in themselves have some effect on the dispersion of earnings, it seems probable that these effects are not very large and, in any case, are only temporary. A striking example of a country which has had very fast inflation is Argentina; and yet, over the period 1953 to 1961, when median earnings increased sevenfold, the dispersion of earnings in Argentina remained remarkably stable (see appendix tables AR–1, 2, and 3). In fact, if anything, it seems to have been increasing.[1]

Our general conclusion from this review of institutional and short-term factors affecting dispersion is that dispersion can be reduced by (1) reducing discrimination on grounds of sex and race, (2) decasualization and the reduction of unnecessary turnover of labour, (3) greater geographic mobility of resources, and (4) maintaining a high and fairly stable level of demand. In addition, in some countries pockets of exploitation can be eliminated by trade-union action or minimum wage legislation; but it seems doubtful whether dispersion can be reduced for any appreciable period of time by these methods below the level appropriate to the underlying forces generating differences in effective abilities.

Recent Changes in Dispersion in a Number of Countries

Before we leave the question of short-term changes we ought to make some comment on the evidence which emerged in Chapter 6 that dispersion in a number of countries was widening during the 1950s. Table 8.2 summarizes results from eleven countries for which comparable data are available near the beginning and end of the decade. In ten cases there is some evidence of widening dispersion, and in only one—the

---

[1] Günter (1964, p. 149) analyses changes in differentials in a number of countries in recent years and comes to the conclusion that the figures do not support the Dunlop–Rothbaum thesis that inflation has a more important effect on narrowing differentials than full employment.

TABLE 8.2

Changes in Dispersion During the 1950s

Country	Type of distribution (sex and intensity)	Period From	To	P_s First Year	Second Year	Source table
Argentina	M+F, all	1953	1961	234	246	AR-1
Australia	M, all	1952–3	1962–3	157	185	AL-1
Canada	M, all	1950–1	1960–1	193	214	CA-1
Canada	M, F/P	1950–1	1960–1	184	203	CA-10
France	M, F/P F/T	1951	1963	253	293	FR-1 and 4
Germany	M+F, all	1950	1961	201	222	GE-1
Japan	M+F, F/P F/T	1951	1961	293	318	JA-1 and 3
Netherlands	M+F, F/P	1952	1959	232	231	NL-2
New Zealand	M, all	1950–1	1960–1	171	183	NZ-1
Sweden	M, all	1951	1960	211	222	SW-1
United Kingdom	M, all	1954–5	1961–2	195	203	UK-1
United States	M, all	1949	1959	211	214	US-1
United States	M, F/P	1949	1959	206	206	US-4

Netherlands—no change.[1] The figure for Japan, however, should probably be ignored, since Japanese dispersion fell considerably after 1961 bringing P_5 by 1965 down to 280. But the Japanese case is a very special one, and the general trend amongst a fairly wide sample of developed countries seems clearly to have been in the direction of widening dispersion. The table shows only one or two types of distribution for each country. Examination of the appendix tables will show that, where female distributions are given separately, the dispersion of female earnings generally grew more than the dispersion of male earnings. On the other hand, where distributions of manual workers are available separately, the dispersion of manual earnings sometimes failed to grow, or—in the case of the Netherlands—even declined. Thus, the evidence suggests that the widening tendency was mainly concentrated on non-manual employees, and especially on females.

What were the reasons for these changes? There are three which seem to me to be worth considering. First, it may be suggested that the inflation of the war, the immediate post-war years, and the period of the Korean boom was at least partly

[1] Although the second distribution for the United States shows no change, alternative measures, e.g. for non-farm employees or at other percentile levels, almost all testify to some widening of dispersion. The widening was generally greater for females than for males.

responsible for compressing earnings differentials; and that the slower pace of inflation in the 1950s permitted a gradual readjustment of differentials to their long-term equilibrium levels. This hypothesis is not inconsistent with the available evidence for most of the countries, and I think there may be a small element of truth in it. But, as has been said earlier, there is not much support in general for the hypothesis that inflation, as such, is a cause of lower differentials.

A second possible explanation is that during the 1950s there was an unusual growth in the demand for highly educated and specialized managerial, scientific, and technical personnel. This was a world-wide trend, but it was especially marked in the richer countries. It is well known that since the end of the Second World War the developed countries have been passing through a new phase of the industrial revolution, with increasing emphasis on engineering (especially electronics) and chemicals (especially synthetics). The demand for scientists and technologists has grown enormously, while, at the same time, radical changes in managerial techniques have led to a rapidly developing demand for highly educated and technically qualified managers and managerial specialists. And this growth of demand for qualified personnel has had an 'accelerator' effect within the educational system, requiring a rapid growth of secondary and higher education, which itself has added to the total demand for highly qualified people. It is not surprising, therefore, that the dispersion of non-manual earnings should have widened in this period of high demand and short supply of qualified people.[1]

Evidence from the United States and Canada gives support to the hypothesis that much of the recent widening of dispersion is the result of exceptional demands for highly educated personnel. Bristol (1958) reported the results of a reinterview study of over a thousand spending units in the years 1954–6. Unfortunately, a third of the initial sample fell out by the third year, but, if we accept the representative character of those remaining,

[1] An extreme example is the extraordinary opportunities which have opened for anyone with a knowledge of computer programming. Since this is not an inherently difficult skill to acquire, the earnings of computer programmers probably contain a large temporary element of rent.

there is clear evidence from the survey that, over these years, the incomes of people with low educational qualifications rose significantly less than the incomes of those with higher qualifications. Similar results were reported by Morgan and Lininger (1964) in a comparison of mean annual earnings of employee heads of spending units in 1956–7 and 1961–2. They found that, over this period, mean earnings of persons with less than nine grades of school increased by 7 per cent, while mean earnings of those with twelve grades increased by 13 per cent, and mean earnings of those with a college degree increased by 30 per cent. Data for Canada, reported in O.E.C.D. (1965, p. 127), show that from 1958 to 1962 the median earnings of engineers without a degree rose by 9·4 per cent, of those with a bachelor's degree by 13·8 per cent, and of those with a master's degree by 15·3 per cent. The increases for scientists over the same period were even greater, and showed a similar tendency for those with higher qualifications to receive larger increases.

It is impossible to predict with confidence what will happen to relative earnings of highly educated personnel in future. On the side of demand, there may well be some continued growth, although perhaps not as fast as in earlier years. A great deal will depend on the strength of military demand, which now absorbs a large proportion of engineers and scientists in many countries. On the supply side, however, it is likely that growth will accelerate, so that within a few years the balance may swing over towards excess supply, at least in certain fields. There is already some evidence that this is happening in physics and chemistry. But the demand for mathematicians and statisticians seems to be insatiable.

While this second explanation of the observed widening of dispersion in the 1950s seems to me to be the most important, there is a third hypothesis which may also be of some significance, especially for the poorer countries. This hypothesis is that the market for highly educated people is becoming increasingly international; that highly educated people are more mobile than others; and that the barriers to their entry into the richer countries are now lower than for the less skilled. When we add to this the fact that inter-country differences in average incomes are extremely wide, it becomes easy to show that the dispersion of earnings in the poorer countries must tend to grow. The phenomenon of the 'brain drain' is well known. Perkins (1966, p. 617) quotes a U.N.E.S.C.O. report that 43,000 scientists and engineers emigrated to the United States between 1949 and 1961, many of whom came from less developed countries. 'Of 11,000 immigrants from Argentina alone between 1951 and 1963, nearly half were technicians and professional people. . . . In 1964–65, 28 per cent of internships and 26 per cent of residencies in U.S. hospitals were filled by foreign graduates—nearly 11,000 in all—and 80 per cent of the foreign interns and 70 per cent of the foreign residents were from developing countries.' He reports also that it is estimated that over 90 per cent of Asian students who go to the United States to study never return home. Professor Sarc of Turkey said in a discussion at the International Economic Association in 1963 that, of fourteen people sent abroad by the Turkish Statistical Office in the previous decade, only one remained in the Office's employment.[1]

In a situation of this sort one might expect to find that dispersion of earnings in the countries losing qualified people would be increasing faster than in the United States. This prediction is broadly supported by the data in Table 8.2. Further evidence is given in an article in *The Economist* (27 August 1966, p. 829), which shows that between 1964 and 1966 salaries increased faster in six western European countries than in the United States. The article suggests that this trend had been going on for at least five years. The whole question, as it affects the poorer countries, is discussed at greater length by Seers (1966). Unfortunately, he, like others, is unable to offer any satisfactory solution to the problem. Perhaps the best hope is that the internal supply of highly qualified people will catch up with demand in the United States. This, like many other proposals vital to the future of humanity, would be greatly assisted if steps were taken to reduce military activities and military preparations in the leading industrialized countries.

[1] See Robinson and Vaizey (1966, p. 687).

3. The Fundamental and Long-term Determinants of Dispersion

Although we have noted a number of short-term influences on the dispersion of earnings, our theory suggests that, in the final analysis, the factors determining the degree of dispersion are (1) genetic differences, (2) environmental differences, (3) inequality of education, and (4) the hierarchic structure of organizations. We know little about the possibilities of altering the first and last of these factors, although it seems probable that some reduction in hierarchic differences would accompany a levelling up of general abilities. The two factors on which social policy can most clearly be brought to bear are environment and education. We shall start by considering the latter.

Education Policy

The attitudes of governments to popular education have changed dramatically in the past fifty years. With the exception of some of the new countries of European settlement—in effect, those in North America and Australasia—where an unusually democratic attitude developed at an early stage, the characteristic attitude of governments and of the upper classes has been that the lower classes should receive only as much education as was strictly necessary, and no more than was good for them. Tawney (1964, p. 129) describes the situation in England in the middle of the last century as follows:

In origin a discipline, half-redemptive, half-repressive, for the lower orders, elementary education has been, throughout its history, not an education, but a social, category. It had been designed for those for whom it was expedient to provide the rudiments of instruction, since, if wholly untaught, they were a danger to society, but inexpedient to provide more, since they were equally a danger, if taught too much. It was to be kept, the Committee of Council insisted in 1839, "in close relation with the condition of workmen and servants". A generation later Mr. Lowe, as Vice-President of the Committee, could still describe elementary education as "the education of the labouring poor", and repudiate with emphasis the impious suggestion that it might enable them 'to raise themselves above their station and business in life'.

These were, of course, the bleak years of British social policy, when everything was subjected to short-term commercial and industrial advantage. Indeed, England, which during the seventeenth and eighteenth centuries had probably been leading Europe in the spread of popular education, fell back during the industrial revolution and the first half of the nineteenth century. In late Elizabethan times about two-thirds of yeomen could write their own names, and in Cromwell's army perhaps as many as four-fifths.[1] At the accession of George III, Sargant estimated, 56 per cent of townspeople and 40 per cent of country people signed their names in marriage registers; but by the accession of Queen Victoria there was scarcely any improvement in the towns, although the percentage of signatures in the country had risen from 40 to 60. 'England, during those seventy-seven years, had become a great manufacturing country, and the towns had so far outgrown the means of instruction, that the educational efforts made had effected no improvement.'[2] As late as 1870, when the first comprehensive state school system was started, only two-fifths of children aged 6–10 were at school;[3] and even now the British educational system in some respects lags seriously behind systems in other advanced countries.

The first country in which de facto comprehensive primary education was established was the United States—but then only in the northern states. In 1833–5 a French traveller, Michael Chevalier, observed: 'Almost everywhere in the North all children go to the primary schools';[4] and even in the earliest times the standard of literacy in the American colonies had been

---

[1] Davies quoted by Anderson in Anderson and Bowman (1966, p. 348).

[2] Quoted by Anderson in Anderson and Bowman (1966, pp. 348–9). In 1833, according to the Education Returns collected in that year, only one in three of children of school age 'were receiving any kind of daily instruction, and the education they received was of very dubious value'. Deane (1965, p. 150).

[3] See Tawney (1964, p. 128).

[4] Quoted by Storr in Anderson and Bowman (1966, p. 134). As early as 1647 a Massachusetts statute had required 'each town of Masachusetts Bay to maintain an elementary teacher and, if the town was of a certain size, a grammar master as well' (p. 135).

exceptionally high. Over the period 1640–1700, for example, 95 per cent of petitions, addresses, and other documents in the Massachusetts and Connecticut archives were properly signed.[1]

In France the Revolution led to the elaboration of a plan of universal education; but in 1816–20 the median percentage of bridegrooms writing their signatures in marriage registers in 78 departments was only 46, compared with a median of 33 thirty years earlier. In 1854–5 the median reached 67 and in 1876–783, while the corresponding figure for brides rose from 23 in 1816–20 to 71 in 1876–7.[2]

One of the most striking examples of the rapid spread of education throughout a population is that of Japan. At the time of the Meiji Restoration in 1868, Japan had a traditional school system which, according to Passin, may have resulted in as much as 40 per cent literacy amongst males, although it was literacy of a relatively low order.[3] A modern school system was established in 1872, and four-year elementary education, made compulsory in 1886, was fully in effect by the end of the century. Thus was laid the foundation of Japan's enormous industrial advance over the past hundred years. Today the Japanese educational system is one of the most highly developed in the world, as can be seen from the fact that in 1960 38·5 per cent of children aged 15 to 19 were still at school, which was a higher enrolment ratio than in any European country except Iceland and the U.S.S.R.[4]

The communist countries, also, are notable for the size of their educational efforts. The Russian case, as Goldsmith commented, is 'of quite unusual interest because there had been, over forty years, one of the biggest increases in educational input and output, both in terms of increased literacy and in

---

[1] Quoted from a study by Shipton by Anderson in Anderson and Bowman (1966, p. 353).

[2] See Anderson in Anderson and Bowman (1966, p. 333).

[3] See Passin in Anderson and Bowman (1966, p. 419).

[4] JA 4, p. 220. The data for the European countries refer to slightly earlier years, but the Japanese enrolment ratio is growing faster than in Europe and by the middle 1960s was even further ahead. The figure quoted for 1960 may in fact be an underestimate, since the 1960 Census report (JA 6, p. 497) shows 45·4 per cent of children aged 15 to 19 still at school.

average content of a worker's education that the world had ever seen'.[1] In 1958 the U.S.S.R. had achieved an enrolment ratio amongst children aged 5 to 14 of 71·5 per cent, and amongst those aged 15 to 19 of 48·6 per cent.[2] In China also, even during the civil war, the communists 'made the campaign against illiteracy in their areas a major part of their activity' and 'for the first time brought large-scale educational programmes to the reach of the peasant masses'.[3] Since taking power the Chinese communists have devoted very large resources to education at all levels.[4]

These scattered facts and figures give some picture of what has been done to spread education in a few countries. But educational policy is in a more fluid state at the present time than it has ever been. Increasing desire, the world over, for economic growth; increasing awareness of the role of education in promoting economic growth; a high level of demand for qualified people in all countries; and, finally, in the poor countries, a rising conviction amongst the population that education is a birthright of every child; all these factors combine to make increased education a matter of the highest priority. But, up to the present, relatively little emphasis has been placed on the role of education as an equalizing force.

[1] Report of discussion at the 1963 conference of the International Economic Association, in Robinson and Vaizey (1966, p. 646).

[2] See Svennilson, Edding, and Elvin (1961, p. 96). Since compulsory education in the U.S.S.R. does not start until the age of 7, the enrolment ratio for children in the first group is biased downwards, and in the second group biased upwards, in comparison with countries in which compulsory education starts at an earlier age.

[3] Fitzgerald (1964, pp. 159–60).

[4] Orleans (1961, p. 5) writes: 'In less than 10 years the Communist regime managed to increase the enrolment in primary schools by some 60 million and in institutes of higher education by some 500 per cent.' China has also placed great emphasis on establishing additional schools in factories, public organizations, and streets, both for full-time and part-time study (p. 20). For a graphic description of educational activity in a Chinese village see Myrdal (1965). Harbison and Myers report that 'China, in fact, is the third largest producer of engineers in the world (after the U.S.S.R. and the U.S.A. in that order), with an annual output rate of 75 per cent of that of the United States. An even more remarkable fact is that 90 per cent of China's 250,000 scientists and engineers have been trained since the Communist take-over in 1949' (p. 88). For an account of a similar mass education campaign in Cuba see the chapters by Jolly in Seers (1964).

It is true that demands to provide universal primary or—later—secondary education are, in practice, demands for policies which promote equality. But the aim is rarely made explicit.

In the recent debates in England on how much public education to provide, and in what form, the aims of education policy have never been very precisely stated. The Crowther Report remarked that 'it is now considered to be the right of every boy and girl to be educated';[1] but it did not say what this meant. The Robbins Committee attempted to go further than this when it stated: 'Throughout our Report we have assumed as an axiom that courses of higher education should be available for all those who are qualified by ability and attainment to pursue them and wish to do so.'[2] The Committee added that 'The good society desires equality of opportunity for its citizens to become not merely good producers but also good men and women.' But it is not obvious why the application of these principles should imply, as the Robbins Committee presumably believed that they did, that only 15 per cent of each age-group should enjoy full-time higher education.[3]

A phrase which is frequently used to define the limits of educational provision is 'the capacity to profit'. For example, the chairman of the O.E.C.D. conference on ability and educational opportunity in 1960 expressed the opinion that 'The right to education must in practice be contingent, partly on the ability of the economy to sustain it, and partly on the capacity of the individual to profit from it.'[4] But how is 'capacity to profit' to be judged? The use of the word 'profit' is surely not meant to imply that only economic benefits should be taken into account; and no one has yet suggested a method of valuing the non-economic benefits of education. Nor has anyone suggested what minimum rate of profit, if we could measure it, would justify additional educational effort. The phrase, in other words, is ambiguous, perhaps deliberately so; but the practical effect of its use is to give policy-makers and administrators an apparent justification for deciding that certain groups of children do not

---

[1] *15 to 18* (1959, p. 34).   [2] *Higher Education* (1963, p. 8).
[3] Ibid. (1963, p. 71).   [4] Elvin in Halsey (1961, p. 11).

have a 'capacity to profit' from further education, and can therefore safely be allowed to drop out. The apt comment on this was made by Tawney when he remarked, in a different context, 'When the boys and girls of well-to-do parents attain the great age of thirteen to fourteen, no one asks whether—absurd phrase—they are "capable of profiting" by further education. They continue their education as a matter of course' (1964, p. 143).

Another criterion which has been suggested is that each child has the right 'to receive an education suited to its character and abilities'.[1] This, however, is equally ambiguous, unless precise definitions are given of the terms 'character' and 'ability', and unless a rule is specified which relates the amount of education to varying amounts of these two (or more) qualities. In practice, I suspect that 'character and abilities' means much the same as 'capacity to profit': it is an invitation to the decision-maker to use his own judgement about who is worthy of further education. And even if 'character' is set on one side, and the opportunity to proceed further is based solely on 'ability', this, as we have seen, means selection on the basis of qualities which are largely environmentally determined. Most children from poor homes and poor neighbourhoods are already educationally ruined by the time they reach the age of selection for secondary education. To select on the basis of 'character and abilities' may seem a morally comfortable principle; but it is merely putting the official stamp of approval on a process which is, in fact, socially discriminatory. This is not to deny that, when there is a shortage of places available, the 'natural' criterion for selection seems to be 'ability', as measured by an examination. But the fact that we may be forced to use this method of selection in practice does not make it a satisfactory principle on which to base educational policy.

Can the principle be reformulated so as to base educational opportunity on 'natural' ability? Some may be tempted to argue that justice requires that the amount of education a child receives should vary directly with his inherent ability. This

[1] Marshall in Halsey, Floud, and Anderson (1961, p. 149).

seems to be what Mrs. Floud had in mind when she suggested that the aim of educational policy should be 'to bring ability, educational opportunity and performance into something like perfect relationship'.[1] There is no doubt that this principle has a wide appeal. It is 'democratic'; it is opposed to class privilege; and it has the sanction of generations of teachers who have sought out the able boy, irrespective of background, and given him their attention and their encouragement. It is the principle of *la carrière ouverte aux talents*, the apparent antithesis of the odious caste system. But is it really acceptable?

The question is one whose answer clearly depends on personal value judgements. But in order to make an informed judgement we need to understand the implications of the alternatives. The principle of relating education to inherent ability (if it could be operated, which is very doubtful) would result in much greater social mobility than in most—perhaps all—existing societies. It would reduce (but not eliminate) inter-generation perpetuation of class monopoly. In each generation the most able, irrespective of class origin, would always come to the top. Hence, inequality over generations would be much reduced; but inequality within each generation would be increased. The application of the rule 'to him that hath shall be given' would ensure a perfect correlation between ability and education, so that effective abilities would be more dispersed than in an alternative system. We should have established meritocracy.[2]

An alternative rule might be to follow a deliberately *compensatory* policy. Children with poor backgrounds, or other handicaps, including lower measured 'ability' might be given *more* attention than others, at least in their earlier years. To some extent this happens already in special schools for mentally retarded children, or others with special handicaps. But the principle is not generally extended to all children. Recently there have been some tentative moves in this direction: for example,

---

[1] Halsey (1961, p. 94).
[2] This discussion leaves out the influence of inherited property on income and status. It is true that the meritocratic principle is a counterweight to the power of inherited wealth. But we are concerned with its justification in its own right.

the 'headstart' programme in the United States, designed to prepare Negro children from poor neighbourhoods for formal education by giving them a period of pre-school instruction; or the proposals of the Plowden Report to devote specially large resources to schools in poor areas in Britain.[1] The ultimate object of the compensatory rule would be to offset at least some of the influence of poor inheritance and, especially, of a retarding early environment. If something was achieved in this direction, the dispersion of earnings would be reduced. In the long run, I believe that this is the only morally defensible rule, and that it is the rule which humanity will eventually adopt. Some of the richer countries could and should already begin to move in this direction. They should certainly not be content with the narrow concept of correlating education with ability. Tawney's critique of this concept is still valid:

> So the doctrine which throws all its emphasis on the importance of opening avenues to individual advancement is partial and one-sided. It is right in insisting on the necessity of opening a free career to aspiring talent; it is wrong in suggesting that opportunities to rise, which can, of their very nature, be seized only by the few, are a substitute for a general diffusion of the means of civilization, which are needed by all men, whether they rise or not, and which those who cannot climb the economic ladder, and who sometimes, indeed, do not desire to climb it, may turn to as good account as those who can.[2]

But I would suggest that, in at least some cases, we need to go further and to give 'more' education to those who start life with less ability.[3]

But what rule can we offer to the poor countries of the world —the great majority? In their case it is obviously not possible to devote much of their very limited resources to the compensatory policy. Their problem is that their present educational

---

[1] *Children and their Primary Schools* (1967).

[2] *Equality*, new edition (1964, pp. 108–9).

[3] It is noteworthy that, in all the recent literature on the economic effects of education, practically no attention has been given to the distribution aspects of the question. While the explicit treatment of education as 'investment in man' is an important step forward, it is necessary to remember that 'man' consists of men; and that, in the final analysis, it is the welfare of the individual that should count.

structure is both backward and extremely unequal. In many, illiteracy is as high as 70 or 80 per cent. Enrolments at the 'first level' are in some cases less than 10 per cent of the children aged 5–14. Harbison and Myers (1964, p. 38) estimated that in 1959–60 the mean first level enrolment ratio in seventeen countries with the lowest index of 'human resource development' was 22 per cent; and in the next group of twenty-one countries it was only 42 per cent. These countries face agonizing choices in allocating their desperately scarce resources. There is strong popular pressure—quite understandably—for the extension of primary education to all; whilst the 'planners' are deeply conscious of the acute shortages of qualified manpower. Obviously, no universal prescription can be given to overcome these difficulties. In the final analysis the economic development of each country will depend on the efforts which its own people are willing to make. In the early stages of development these interlocking bottlenecks can be smashed only by heroic efforts by large sections of the population. But widespread popular enthusiasm for educational development is unlikely to be generated, still less to continue, unless the programme includes rapid expansion of education for all children at the primary level as well as more specialized education at secondary and higher levels. Cold calculations that, since only a limited volume of resources is available, then these should be devoted mainly to developing secondary education, while primary provision is largely frozen, ignore the political aspects of the problem and take a very limited view of the welfare aspects.

Changing the Environment

We have seen that in countries with more than about 25 per cent of the male work force engaged in agriculture the degree of dispersion of earnings is associated with this proportion; and we have argued that this is a reflection of the poor environmental conditions in which farm children grow up—from the point of view of developing their productive abilities. Of course, the fact that a high percentage of a country's work force is engaged in agriculture is itself an indicator of that country's poverty, since most services and many manufactured goods cannot be imported. But a high concentration of population in agriculture also generally means that the average size of farm is small, and that most of the farm population is illiterate and technically backward. For these reasons it almost inevitably follows that both the raising of average *per capita* income and the reduction of inequality of earnings necessitate a large-scale shift of manpower out of agriculture. This is not merely a response to the pressure of increasing population, although that is an additional reason for rapid development of industry. Even if population were constant in the poorer countries, their only avenue to progress would be through industrialization. For 'industrial man', as we have argued, is in general a productively superior being to 'agricultural man'; and only in the very rich countries, where conditions in farming areas can be brought up close to those existing in cities, can the average farmer be as well off as the average city dweller. Thus, the argument for industrialization is not merely an argument for economic growth in aggregate but it is also an argument for greater equality amongst men.

Of course, town life itself is not ideal, and in almost all countries there are hidden slums inhabited by the submerged groups of the population. Often it is poor migrants from the country—or from other lands—who occupy the worst of these slums. It is not sufficient, therefore, to stimulate industry and to absorb an increasing flow of agricultural migrants into the towns. Direct measures are also needed to improve urban housing, health, and education, especially in the slum areas.

4. Concluding Remarks

The task which we set ourselves at the beginning was, broadly speaking, to discover the factors responsible for human differences in effective abilities, and hence in earnings. What we have found is that men, although somewhat unequally endowed at birth, are so twisted and shaped by their environment and education that the differences between them are steadily widened, so that the spread of their earnings grows to great dimensions. The question is: How much do we care? Are we willing to accept such differences between men, within each country, and, on a wider canvas, between countries? A long tradition of the philosophy of the Enlightenment emphasizes the essential equality of man, both by nature and by right. This judgement, or perhaps act of faith, was well expressed by Hobbes:

Nature hath made men so equall, in the faculties of body, and mind; as that though there bee found one man sometimes manifestly stronger in body, or of quicker mind than another; yet when all is reckoned together, the difference between man, and man, is not so considerable, as that one man can thereupon claim to himselfe any benefit, to which another may not pretend, as well as he.[1]

Man is born everywhere more or less equal; it is by art, rather than by nature, that he has been made unequal. Do we want to reverse the influence of 'art'? It depends on our value judgements. If we follow Mill we shall agree that: 'Among the works of man, which human life is rightly employed in perfecting and beautifying, the first in importance is surely man himself.'[2]

The instruments at our disposal are education and economic development. Economic progress is essential to rescue man from poverty; but education is not merely a means to this end, although this is one of its purposes. Education is the key to development of the human personality, to making man human. As Wharton writes, in a very moving passage:

The typical peasant knows that he is illiterate, and it is a source of personal shame. The accomplishment of achieving literacy brings more than prestige or status. It brings with it a sense of personal accomplishment—the idea that he too is capable of perfecting himself through his own efforts and that he is not merely a lump of

---

[1] *Leviathan*, Everyman edition (1934, p. 63).
[2] *On Liberty*, Everyman edition (1936, p. 117). It is true that Mill also emphasized the importance of encouraging genius: 'these few are the salt of the earth; without them, human life would become a stagnant pool' (p. 122). But this was an argument for freedom, not for special favours.

humanity spending a few tortured years of suffering on earth without hope of improving his lot and that of his children.[1]

In his *Discourse on Political Economy* Rousseau followed a similar line of thought: 'It is therefore one of the important functions of government to prevent extreme inequality of fortunes; not by taking away wealth from its possessors, but by depriving all men of means to accumulate it; not by building hospitals for the poor, but by securing the citizens from becoming poor.' He discusses various ways of achieving this aim, and concludes:

But all these precautions will be inadequate, unless rulers go still more to the root of the matter. . . . There can be no patriotism without liberty, no liberty without virtue, no virtue without citizens; create citizens, and you have everything you need; without them, you will have nothing but debased slaves, from the rulers of the State downwards. To form citizens is not the work of a day; and in order to have men it is necessary to educate them when they are children.[2]

The tremendous scientific achievements of the past half century have lifted man's horizon. To some this seems to imply journeys to the moon, or further; to others it is the opportunity to acquire ever-increasing stocks of goods, and to drown human personality in a surfeit of matter. A third alternative is to use our new-found knowledge, and growing economic power, to realize the old dream of raising man—all men, everywhere—to his full stature. Many years ago Tawney set this target for his own country:

Every year a new race of some 600,000 souls slips quietly into the United Kingdom. . . . The purpose of the educationalist is to aid their growth. It should be easy to regard them, not as employers and workmen, or masters and servants, or rich and poor, but merely as human beings. . . . Here, if anywhere, it should be possible to forget the tedious vulgarities of income and social position, in a common affection for the qualities which belong, not to any class or profession of men, but to man himself, and in a common attempt to improve them by cultivation.[3]

---

[1] Anderson and Bowman (1966, p. 211).
[2] Everyman edition (1935, p. 267).   [3] Tawney (1964, p. 141).

This is surely the goal which, some day soon, all nations must choose, and which will eventually become an international responsibility. Only then can we say that the work of the economist—who is also a humanist—is beginning to bear its real fruit.

APPENDIX I

Fringe Benefits

FRINGE benefits may be defined as costs of employing labour, other than direct cash payments to employees, which create benefits for employees beyond what is strictly necessary for their productive efficiency. At the margin there may be considerable dispute about how much of particular costs are 'necessary' for production efficiency and how much are really fringe benefits. Are the costs of better furniture for managerial offices a necessary cost of production or a benefit? And what about business lunches, company cars, and overseas business trips? Even more difficult to decide may be the provision of free health services. But, if we set aside the most disputable cases, there are a great many labour costs which clearly fall in the category of salary-substitutes.

Perhaps the best way to illustrate the range and variety of fringe benefits now in use is to reproduce a table (with some rearrangement of items) from a recent survey of 120 large British organizations (covering both public and private corporations in industry and commerce, and some trade unions). This table (A1.1) gives the numbers of organizations who mentioned each type of benefit in response to the question: 'What are the most popular fringe benefits?' The report comments that 'the fringe benefits quoted were almost always the ones which companies were already offering'.[1] It should be noted that this list does not include normal holiday payments, nor compulsory social security contributions by the employer, which are very important standard fringe benefits in most countries.

Additional fringe benefits, mentioned by Patton (1961) with reference to the United States, include deferred contingent compensation (a tax-evading device), country clubs, and 'unreported expense accounts'. Patton estimated that in the United States the cost of fringe benefits (pension, vacation, sick leave, insurance, etc.) had approximately trebled in the previous twenty years. 'In the bellwether steel industry, for example, fringe costs soared from 8 per cent of payroll in 1940 to 26 per cent in 1958' (p. 18). Stock options have become of very great importance as a means of rewarding higher executives. According to Patton, one company arranged its stock option scheme so as roughly to offset the effect of taxation on salaries (p. 198).

An inquiry carried out in 1961 by the European Economic Community into the cost of labour in thirteen industries in the countries of the

[1] *Executive Salary Development*, report of a survey by Challoner Management Appointments Limited, London, July 1966 (restricted circulation).

TABLE A1.1. *Opinions by 120 British Organizations on the Most Popular Fringe Benefits*

Benefit	Number of votes
Pensions—various types	86
Insurances	
Life assurance	28
Widows and orphans pension	3
Accident	3
Medical	11
Privileges	
Company car	60
Buying privileges	3
Share options	4
Status symbols (office, etc.)	3
Savings scheme	1
Senior secretary	1
Extra payments	
Profit sharing and prosperity bonus	16
House purchase subsidy and company housing	13
Removal assistance	2
Educational subsidies for children	5
Car allowances, service, and repairs	4
Sickness and Welfare	
Free lunches, etc.	11
Sickness benefit pay	14
Holidays and the like	
Extra holidays and days off	16
Sabbatical leave	1
Management organization and conferences	3
Subsidized holidays	1

Common Market produced some interesting results.[1] Taking the median of the thirteen industries as a representative figure, we find that direct salary payments were approximately the following proportions of total cost of employing manual workers:

	Per cent
Germany	74
France	61
Italy	52
Netherlands	71
Belgium	70

Taken from a summary published in *Études et Conjoncture*, January 1965.

The balance of the cost was represented by compulsory social security contributions (especially large in France and Italy), special bonuses, holiday pay, and other smaller items.

Unfortunately, there is very little information about the relative importance of fringe benefits at different income levels; but the following figures have been estimated by a private agency for the United Kingdom.[1] The figures relate only to managerial staff.

Basic salary (£)	Fringe benefits as a percentage of basic salary (%)
1,050	11·2
1,600	14·8
2,200	14·5
2,850	16·5
3,500	18·7
4,200	21·3
6,250	28·1
7,000 and over	31·1

If these figures are typical of the situation in other countries, the effects of (mainly untaxed) fringe benefits must be such as largely to offset the progressiveness of income taxes.

[1] Privately circulated report by Hay-MSL, *United Kingdom Salary Guide for Management, 1966.*

APPENDIX 2

Distributions Based on Additive and Multiplicative Factors

ACCORDING to the Central Limit Theorem, if a random variable, y, is the sum of a number of random variables, which are mutually independent and of finite variance, then, except in special and unusual circumstances, the distribution of y approaches the normal distribution as the number of component variates increases, provided that no single component variate dominates the others. Thus, if $y = \sum_{i=1}^{i=n} x_i$, where the x_i are independent variates of finite variance, y approaches the normal distribution as $n \to \infty$ (Cramér, 1946, pp. 213–18).

A corollary of this theorem is that if $y = \prod_{i=1}^{i=n} x_i$ then, on the same assumptions, y will approach a lognormal distribution, i.e. $\log y$ will be normally distributed. A lognormal distribution is, of course, skew and leptokurtic in the usual sense, i.e. in relation to the normal distribution.

If the number of variates which combine in y (additively or multiplicatively) is small, then the distribution of y will depend on the shapes of the distributions of the component factors and on whether they are independent or not. We shall consider the following cases.

1. *Sum of n variates which are jointly normally distributed*

The distribution of the sum will be normally distributed in all cases, irrespective of the degree of correlation between the factors or of differences in their coefficients of variation.

2. *Product of n variates, each normally distributed*[1]

    (a) *Factors independent ($\rho_{ij} = 0$), coefficients of variation identical ($c_i = c_j$).*
    The product will be both skew and leptokurtic. Skewness and kurtosis will increase with both n and c.

    (b) *Factors independent ($\rho_{ij} = 0$), coefficients of variation differ ($c_i \neq c_j$).*
    The product will be more skew and leptokurtic than in (a), but the increase will not be great unless the coefficients of variation differ considerably.

    (c) *Factors positively correlated ($\rho_{ij} > 0$), coefficients of variation identical ($c_i = c_j$).*
    The product will be skew and leptokurtic. Skewness and kurtosis will increase with n, ρ_{ij}, and c.

          [1] For this group of cases see Haldane (1942).

(d) *Factors positively correlated* $(\rho_{ij} > 0)$, *coefficients of variation differ* $(c_i \neq c_j)$.

The product will be more skew and leptokurtic than in (c), depending on the degree of difference between the coefficients of variation.

3. *Product of n variates which are jointly lognormally distributed*

The distribution of the product will be lognormal in all cases, irrespective of the degree of correlation between the logarithms of the factors or of differences in their coefficients of variation.

4. If there is a limited number of components and they are *not* all normally or lognormally distributed, then the resulting distribution of their sum or product will depend very much on the shape of their individual distributions, and on the correlations between them. If, for example, one out of three components is very positively skew, then both the sum and product of the three factors will be positively skew. In such a case the resulting distribution could be leptokurtic in the logarithms.

Factors Contributing to the Variance of Intelligence and Scholastic Attainment

The Variance of Intelligence

LET y_1, y_2 be the measured intelligence of a pair of persons; x_1, x_2 some index of their genetic ability; z_1, z_2 some index of their environment; and m_1, m_2 the error in measuring y.

We make the heroic assumption that

$$y = x + z + m.$$

Measurement error

The correlation coefficient $r_{y_1 y_2}$ for identical twins reared together is given by Burt as 0·925 (see Table 4·1, p. 74, above).

In this case we have $x_1 = x_2$ (by definition) and $z_1 = z_2$. The latter equality may not be exact, however, since there may be some slight variation in the environmental influence.

Assuming both equalities to hold, we have

$$y_1 - y_2 = m_1 - m_2.$$

So

$$V(y_1) + V(y_2) - 2r_{y_1 y_2}\{V(y_1)V(y_2)\}^{\frac{1}{2}} = V(m_1) + V(m_2) - 2r_{m_1 m_2}\{V(m_1)V(m_2)\}^{\frac{1}{2}}.$$

It seems reasonable to assume that

$$V(y_1) = V(y_2), \quad V(m_1) = V(m_2) \quad \text{and} \quad r_{m_1 m_2} = 0.$$

Hence we obtain

$$r_{y_1 y_2} = 1 - \frac{V(m)}{V(y)},$$

or

$$\frac{V(m)}{V(y)} = 1 - r_{y_1 y_2}.$$

For the value of $r_{y_1 y_2} = 0·925$

$$V(m) = 0·075 V(y).$$

Since there may, in fact, be some slight variation in the environment, this is probably an overestimate of the measurement error. In round figures we might perhaps put it at about 5 per cent.

Genetic ability

Burt's estimate shows a value of $r_{y_1 y_2} = 0·269$ for unrelated children reared together.

In this case we have $z_1 = z_2$ but $x_1 \neq x_2$.

Thus
$$y_1 - y_2 = x_1 - x_2 + m_1 - m_2.$$

If we assume that $V(y_1) = V(y_2)$, $V(x_1) = V(x_2)$, $V(m_1) = V(m_2)$, and $r_{x_1x_2} = r_{m_1m_2} = r_{xm} = 0$, as seems plausible, then

$$V(x) = (1 - r_{y_1y_2})V(y) - V(m)$$

and, if we assume, as suggested above, that

$$V(m) = 0{\cdot}05V(y).$$

Then
$$V(x) = (0{\cdot}95 - r_{y_1y_2})V(y).$$

For the value of $r_{y_1y_2}$ estimated by Burt, at $0{\cdot}27$ approximately,

$$V(x) = 0{\cdot}68V(y).$$

It may, however, be wrong to assume that $r_{x_1x_2} = 0$, since children put out to foster parents may be put into homes which are more or less similar to the homes from which they came. Since there is a small correlation between measured intelligence of child and socio-economic class of parent, there may also be a small correlation (but smaller) between genetic ability and socio-economic class.

If $r_{x_1x_2} = 0{\cdot}1$ for unrelated children reared together, then since

$$V(x) = \frac{1}{1 - r_{x_1x_2}} \{(1 - r_{y_1y_2})V(y) - V(m)\}$$

and, again assuming that $V(m) = 0{\cdot}05V(y)$, we have

$$V(x) = \frac{0{\cdot}68}{0{\cdot}9} V(y) \approx 0{\cdot}75V(y)$$

for unrelated children.

Environment

If we could assume that for all children $r_{xz} = 0$, as well as $r_{xm} = r_{zm} = 0$, it would follow, on the same assumptions as previously, that

$$V(y) = V(x) + V(z) + V(m)$$

and if
$$V(x) = 0{\cdot}75V(y)$$

and
$$V(m) = 0{\cdot}05V(y)$$

$$V(z) = 0{\cdot}2V(y).$$

However, we have substantial reasons for believing that $r_{xz} > 0$. In that case,
$$V(y) = V(x) + V(z) + V(m) + 2r_{xz}\{V(x)V(z)\}^{\frac{1}{2}}.$$

Even so, we can still conclude that environment contributes, either on its own or in combination with genetic factors, something of the order of 20–30 per cent of measured intelligence.

T

The Variance of Scholastic Attainment

Following the same procedure as above, and using Burt's estimates of the correlations for 'general attainments', we can estimate approximately that

1. Measurement error contributes about 10 per cent (probably less) to the variance of attainment.
2. Genetic ability contributes about 40 per cent.
3. The remaining 50 per cent is attributable to environment, alone and in combination with genetic ability.

These conclusions again depend on special assumptions analogous to those made in the previous section.

APPENDIX 4

The Hierarchic Hypothesis

1. *The Continuous Case*

We assume that the relations

$$x_i = (np)^{i-1}x_1 \tag{A4.1}$$

$$y_i = n^{k-i} \tag{A4.2}$$

apply continuously in the range $1 \leqslant i \leqslant k$.

Now
$$Y_i = \int\limits_i^k y_t \, dt = \int\limits_i^k n^{k-t} \, dt = \frac{1}{\ln n}(n^{k-i}-1). \tag{A4.3}$$

Hence
$$Q_i = Y_i/Y_1 = \frac{n^{k-i}-1}{n^{k-1}-1},$$

or
$$n^{k-i} = (n^{k-1}-1)Q_i + 1$$

and
$$k-i = \frac{\ln\{(n^{k-1}-1)Q_i+1\}}{\ln n}. \tag{A4.4}$$

From (A4.1) we have
$$i - 1 = \frac{\ln x_i - \ln x_1}{\ln(np)},$$

and by substituting for i in (A4.4) and rearranging we obtain

$$Q_i = x_1^\lambda x_i^{-\lambda} - \frac{1}{n^{k-1}-1},$$

where
$$\lambda = \frac{\ln n}{\ln(np)}.$$

If n and k are reasonably large (e.g. $n > 3$, $k > 5$),

$$Q_i \approx x_1^\lambda x_i^{-\lambda}. \tag{A4.5}$$

2. *Aggregating over all Firms in the Economy*

In this section we write $Y_j(x)$ for the number of persons with a wage $\geqslant x$ in firm j, N_j for the total number of persons in firm j, w_j for the minimum wage in firm j. There are M firms in all.

Clearly $N_j = Y_j(w_j)$.

We consider two simplified cases.

(a) *If $w_j = w$ in all firms*

Here all firms have the same minimum wage but their sizes differ. From (A4.5) we have

$$Y_j(x) \approx N_j w^\lambda x^{-\lambda} \quad (x \geqslant w)$$

If $Y^T(x)$ is the total number of persons in the economy with wage $\geqslant x$

$$Y^T(x) = \sum_{j=1}^{M} Y_j(x) \approx w^\lambda x^{-\lambda} \sum_{j=1}^{M} N_j.$$

So the proportion of employees in the whole economy with a wage $\geqslant x$ is

$$Q^T(x) = \sum_{j=1}^{M} Y_j(x) \Big/ \sum_{j=1}^{M} N_j$$

$$\approx w^\lambda x^{-\lambda}.$$

(b) w_j varies between firms but $N_j = N$ for all firms

Let $f(w)$ be the density function of w but with the conditions that $w^* \leqslant w < w^{**}$, i.e. w^* is the minimum value of w and w^{**} is its maximum value.

Thus $\int_{w^*}^{w^{**}} f(w)\,dw = 1.$

For any specified wage level x, where $w^* < x < \infty$,

$$Y_j(x) \approx Nw_j^\lambda x^{-\lambda} \quad \text{when } x > w_j$$

and $\qquad\qquad Y_j(x) = N \quad \text{when } x \leqslant w_j.$

Now, keeping x constant and allowing w_j to vary over all firms, and integrating, we have

$$Y^T(x) \approx \int_w^x Nw^\lambda x^{-\lambda} f(w)\,dw + \int_x^{w^{**}} Nf(w)\,dw. \qquad (A4.6)$$

Since we are concerned only with the upper tail of the distribution of employees we can ignore values of $x < w^{**}$, so that the second term in (A4.6) disappears.

Hence

$$Y^T(x) \approx Nx^{-\lambda} \int_{w^*}^{w^{**}} w^\lambda f(w)\,dw \quad (x \geqslant w^{**})$$

$$\approx ANx^{-\lambda} \qquad (A4.7)$$

where $A = \int_{w^*}^{w^{**}} w^\lambda f(w)\,dw$, constant for all values of x.

Thus $Q^T(x) = Ax^{-\lambda}$ for $x \geqslant w^{**}$.

3. *Relation of Managing Director's Salary to Size of Firm*

We return here to the notation and assumptions used in section 1.

From (A4.1) the managing director's salary in a firm with k grades, and whose minimum wage is x_1, is

$$x_k = (np)^{k-1} x_1$$

or $\qquad\qquad k-1 = \dfrac{\ln x_k - \ln x_1}{\ln(np)}. \qquad (A4.8)$

From (A4.3) the total number employed in a k-grade firm is

$$Y_{1(k)} = \frac{1}{\ln n}(n^{k-1} - 1)$$

or

$$n^{k-1} = bN_k + 1,$$

where $b = \ln n$ and $Y_{1(k)} = N_k$. So

$$k - 1 = \frac{1}{\ln n}\ln(bN_k + 1). \tag{A4.9}$$

Combining (A4.8) and (A4.9) we have

$$\ln(bN_k + 1) = \lambda(\ln x_k - \ln x_1).$$

where

$$\lambda = \frac{\ln n}{\ln(np)}.$$

So

$$x_k^\lambda = x_1^\lambda(bN_k + 1) \approx x_1^\lambda bN_k, \quad \text{since } b > 1.$$

Hence

$$x_k \approx aN_k^{1/\lambda}, \quad \text{where } a = b^{1/\lambda}x_1.$$

Since this will be true for all values of k, we have, more generally, for all firms whose minimum wage is x_1,

$$W \approx aN^{1/\lambda}, \tag{A4.10}$$

where W = managing director's salary and N = number of persons employed.

If sales are proportional to the number employed

$$S = \gamma N,$$

and

$$W \approx a\gamma^{-1/\lambda}S^{1/\lambda} \tag{A4.11}$$

If sales vary with a power of N,

$$S = N^\beta,$$

and

$$W \approx aS^{1/\beta\lambda}. \tag{A4.12}$$

APPENDIX 5

Bias in Estimating Changes in Dispersion from Skill Differentials

LET $Y_t^{(i)}$ be the mean earnings of occupation i in period t.

We define the skill differential between occupations i and j in period as

$$D_t^{(ij)} = Y_t^{(i)}/Y_t^{(j)},$$

and the ratio of mean earnings of occupation i in period t to period $(t-1)$ as

$$U_t^{(i)} = Y_t^{(i)}/Y_{t-1}^{(i)}.$$

We also write $y_t = \ln Y_t$, $d_t = \ln D_t$, and $u_t = \ln U_t$.

We assume that the change in occupational dispersion can be measured in two alternative ways:

1. 'True' change in dispersion is $T_t = \sigma_{y_t} - \sigma_{y_{t-1}}$.
2. A measure based on skill differentials, namely,

$$\overline{C}_t = \frac{1}{n} \sum_{}^{n} C_t^{(ij)},$$

where $C_t^{(ij)} = d_t^{(ij)} - d_{t-1}^{(ij)}$, n is the number of skill differentials, and $d_{t-1}^{(ij)} > 0$.

In what follows, we shall assume that u_t is a random variable, and that $\sigma_{u_t}^2 > 0$.

Case 1. The $\{u_t\}$ are mutually independent and also independent of $\{y_{t-1}\}$, and $E(u_t) = 0$

In this case the expected value of $\overline{C}_t$, for any random sample of skill differentials, is zero.

$$C_t^{(ij)} = d_t^{(ij)} - d_{t-1}^{(ij)},$$

and

$$d_t^{(ij)} = y_t^{(i)} - y_t^{(j)}.$$

So

$$C_t^{(ij)} = y_t^{(i)} - y_t^{(j)} - y_{t-1}^{(i)} + y_{t-1}^{(j)} = u_t^{(i)} - u_t^{(j)}. \tag{A5.1}$$

Hence

$$E[C_t^{(ij)}] = E[u_t^{(i)}] - E[u_t^{(j)}]$$

$$= 0, \text{ for all values of } i \text{ and } j.$$

But the value of T_t is positive.

Since $y_t = y_{t-1} + u_t$ and $r_{y_{t-1}u_t} = 0$,

$$\sigma_{y_t}^2 = \sigma_{y_{t-1}}^2 + \sigma_{u_t}^2;$$

and, since $\sigma_{u_t}^2 > 0$,

$$\sigma_{y_t} > \sigma_{y_{t-1}} \quad \text{and} \quad T_t > 0.$$

Thus the estimate from the differentials is biased downward.

The extent of this bias depends on the importance of $\sigma_{u_t}^2$ in relation to $\sigma_{y_{t-1}}^2$. The bias can be estimated if we know the value of $r_{y_t y_{t-1}}$.

Since
$$\sigma_{u_t}^2 = \sigma_{y_t}^2 + \sigma_{y_{t-1}}^2 - 2r_{y_t y_{t-1}} \sigma_{y_t} \sigma_{y_{t-1}},$$
it is easy to show that
$$\sigma_{y_t} = \sigma_{y_{t-1}}/r_{y_t y_{t-1}}.$$
Let the estimate of σ_{y_t} from the skill differentials be E_1 and the measured figure be E_2. Then $E_1 = \sigma_{y_{t-1}}$ and $E_2 = \sigma_{y_{t-1}}/r_{y_t y_{t-1}}$. The proportional bias in E_1 is, therefore,
$$B = \frac{E_1 - E_2}{E_2} = r_{y_t y_{t-1}} - 1$$

Case 2. The $\{u_t\}$ are mutually independent, but $E(u_t)$ is a linear function of y_{t-1}.

Here we assume that
$$E(u_t) = \alpha + \beta y_{t-1}, \tag{A5.2}$$
and, of course, $r_{y_{t-1} u_t} \neq 0$. Since
$$\sigma_{y_t}^2 = \sigma_{y_{t-1}}^2 + \sigma_{u_t}^2 + 2r_{y_{t-1} u_t} \sigma_{y_{t-1}} \sigma_u$$
and
$$\sigma_{u_t}^2 = \sigma_{y_t}^2 + \sigma_{y_{t-1}}^2 - 2r_{y_t y_{t-1}} \sigma_{y_t} \sigma_{y_{t-1}},$$
it can be shown that
$$r_{y_{t-1} u_t} = \frac{r_{y_t y_{t-1}} \sigma_{y_t} - \sigma_{y_{t-1}}}{\sigma_{u_t}}.$$
So
$$\beta = \frac{r_{y_t y_{t-1}} \sigma_{y_t} - \sigma_{y_{t-1}}}{\sigma_{y_{t-1}}}. \tag{A5.3}$$
From (A5.1) we have
$$E[C_t^{(ij)}] = E[u_t^{(i)}] - E[u_t^{(j)}],$$
and, substituting from (A5.2),
$$E[C_t^{(ij)}] = \alpha + \beta y_{t-1}^{(i)} - \alpha - \beta y_{t-1}^{(j)}$$
$$= \beta d_{t-1}^{(ij)}$$
$$= \left(\frac{r_{y_t y_{t-1}} \sigma_{y_t} - \sigma_{y_{t-1}}}{\sigma_{y_{t-1}}}\right) d_{t-1}^{(ij)}, \text{ from (A5.3)}.$$

How does this compare with $T_t = \sigma_{y_t} - \sigma_{y_{t-1}}$? The answer will depend on:

1. The relation between σ_{y_t} and $\sigma_{y_{t-1}}$.
2. The size of $r_{y_t y_{t-1}}$.
3. The relation between $d_t^{(ij)}$ and $\sigma_{y_{t-1}}$.

For example, if $\sigma_{y_t} > \sigma_{y_{t-1}}$ by sufficient to make $r_{y_t y_{t-1}} \sigma_{y_t} > \sigma_{y_{t-1}}$,
$$E(C_t^{(ij)}) \gtrless T_t$$
as
$$d_{t-1}^{(ij)} \gtrless \left\{\frac{\sigma_{y_t} - \sigma_{y_{t-1}}}{r_{y_t y_{t-1}} \sigma_{y_t} - \sigma_{y_{t-1}}}\right\} \sigma_{y_{t-1}}.$$

Broadly, when dispersion is widening, a large initial skill differential will overestimate the increase, while a narrow initial differential will underestimate it.

Similarly, when dispersion is falling, a large initial skill differential will overestimate the fall and a narrow one underestimate it.

In the special case where $\sigma_{y_t} = \sigma_{y_{t+1}}$, the average estimate of the proportional change in dispersion from any randomly selected skill differential will be

$$E[C_t^{(ij)}]/d_{t-1}^{(ij)} = r_{y_t y_{t-1}} - 1$$

which is biased downwards, except in the unlikely case that $r_{y_t y_{t-1}} = 1$. The proportional downward bias is the same as in Case 1, namely $(r_{y_t y_{t-1}} - 1)$.

Case 3. Some other relation between u_t and y_{t-1}.

Here the outcome will depend on the relation between u_t and y_{t-1}. For example, if dispersion is changing rapidly at the upper end of the distribution but not changing much in the middle, estimates of over-all dispersion which are based on skill differentials drawn from the middle of the distribution will clearly underestimate the extent of the over-all change.

APPENDIX 6

Distribution Classification Code

Area

Whole country (more or less)	1
One region or large area	2
Urban areas only	3
One town or a group of towns	4

Industries

All industries (more or less)	1
Non-farm	2
Non-farm, non-personal service	3
Manufacturing (or manufacturing and mining)	4
Manufacturing, mining, and building	5
Government	6
Private	7
MMB, transport and local authorities	8
Other specialized groups	9

Age

All (including 15 or 16 and over)	1
Adults only (or excluding apprentices)	2

Sex

Male	1
Female	2
Both combined	3

Occupation group

All	1
Manual	2
Skilled manual	3
Unskilled manual	4
Non-manual	5

Source of income

Employment only[1]	1
All sources	2
Household income	3

Intensity of work

All	1
Full-period only	2
Full-period and full-time only	3

[1] Including a small amount of non-employment income

Income period

Year	1
Month	2
Week	3
Day	4
Hour	5

Special limitations

None	0
One race only	1
Taxpayers only	2
Union firms only	3
Other	4

APPENDIX 7

Country Tables

AUSTRALIA: TABLE AL–1

Per-centiles	1952–3	1955–6	1958–9	1962–3		
1	221	238	244	264	Area: Australia	1
2	188	205	212	230	Industry: All	1
5	157	172	176	185	Ages: All	1
10	140	150	151	158	Sex: M	1
20	123	128	127	133	Occupation: All	1
75	81	80	81	78	Income: W & S	1
85	61	61	62	59	Intensity: All	1
95	34	32	31	28	Period: Year	1
					Limits: Taxpayers	2
Median £	770	903	990	1,148		
Source	AL 1	AL 1	AL 1	AL 1		

Notes:

Includes only taxpayers in 'Occupation 1', i.e. with less than £100 of non-W & S income. Exemption limit £105, but only taxpayers above that included. Occupational pensions included in W & S. Data based on 'main' tabulations only.

Intermediate years also available. M & F not available separately before 1952–3.

AUSTRALIA: Table AL–2

Percentiles	1952–3	1955–6	1958–9	1962–3		
1	216	235	238	259	Area: Australia	1
2	193	208	209	224	Industry: All	1
5	167	175	176	185	Ages: All	1
10	151	154	155	161	Sex: F	2
20	133	135	134	138	Occupation: All	1
75	67	66	65	63	Income: W & S	1
85	51	49	49	46	Intensity: All	1
95	(33)	(31)	(29)	(27)	Period: Year	1
					Limits: Taxpayers	2
Median £	430	480	530	598		
Source	AL 1	AL 1	AL 1	AL 1		

Notes:

See Table AL–1.

AUSTRALIA: Table AL–3

Percentiles	1949–50	1952–3	1958–9	1962–3		
1	238	231	262	289	Area: Australia	1
2	216	200	226	247	Industry: All	1
5	179	169	188	202	Ages: All	1
10	155	149	162	173	Sex: M & F	3
20	135	130	136	143	Occupation: All	1
75	66	66	64	63	Income: W & S	1
85	51	49	47	44	Intensity: All	1
95	(34)	28	25	23	Period: Year	1
					Limits: Taxpayers	2
Median £	426	689	859	971		
Source	AL 1	AL 1	AL 1	AL 1		

Notes:

See Table AL–1.

Occupation 1 in 1949–50 includes only those with less than £50 of non-employment income.

AUSTRALIA: TABLE AL–4

Percentiles	1953–4	1959–60		
1	260	290	Area: Australia	1
2	212	241	Industry: All	1
5	170	190	Ages: All	1
10	146	161	Sex: M	1
20	128	134	Occupation: All	1
75	81	79	Income: W & S	1
85	63	60	Intensity: All	1
95	34	30	Period: Year	1
			Limits: Taxpayers	2
Median				
£	790	1,045		
Source	AL 1	AL 1		

Notes:

Estimated distribution of *all* taxpayers in receipt of wages or salaries. For method of estimation see Lydall (1965).

AUSTRALIA: TABLE AL–5

Percentiles	1953–4	1959–60		
1	216	246	Area: Australia	1
2	193	214	Industry: All	1
5	171	178	Ages: All	1
10	153	159	Sex: F	2
20	132	137	Occupation: All	1
75	66	62	Income: W & S	1
85	50	45	Intensity: All	1
95	32	28	Period: Year	1
			Limits: Taxpayers	2
Median				
£	445	565		
Source	AL 1	AL 1		

Notes:

See Table AL–4.

AUSTRALIA: TABLE AL–6

Percentiles	1953–4	1959–60		
1	257	298	Area: Australia	1
2	214	248	Industry: All	1
5	179	200	Ages: All	1
10	153	172	Sex: M & F	3
20	134	141	Occupation: All	1
75	66	63	Income: W & S	1
85	48	45	Intensity: All	1
95	27	23	Period: Year	1
			Limits: Taxpayers	2

Median		
£	708	910

Source	AL 1	AL 1

Notes:

See Table AL–4.

AUSTRALIA: TABLE AL–7

Per-centiles	1938				
	M	F	M & F		
1	307	349	306	Area: New South Wales	2
2	248	280	249	Industry: All	1
5	195	211	194	Ages: All	1
10	160	170	162	Sex: M, F, M & F	1, 2, 3
20	132	136	132	Occupation: All	1
75	78	66	61	Income: W & S	1
85	..	49	..	Intensity: All	1
95	..	25	..	Period: Week	3
				Limits:	0

Median			
£	4·88	2·35	4·58

Source	AL 2	AL 2	AL 2

Notes:

Special inquiry amongst all employees in New South Wales requesting earnings before tax (including bonuses, etc.) in week 15–21 May 1938, or weekly average for longer periods ending in the specified week, or in the immediately following week.

Excludes pensioners and those on unemployment relief works.

ARGENTINA: Table AR–1

Per-centiles	1953	1959	1961		
1	413	413	425	Area: Argentina	1
2	318	317	336	Industry: All	1
5	234	234	246	Ages: All	1
10	186	190	194	Sex: M & F	3
20	151	152	154	Occupation: All	1
75	71	74	69	Income: W & S	1
85	57	62	53	Intensity: All	1
95	33	30	38	Period: Year	1
				Limits:	0
Median Pesos	8,950	39,450	64,300		
Source	AR 1	AR 1	AR 1		

Notes:

Data derived from social security records.
W & S from main employment only.

ARGENTINA: Table AR–2

Per-centiles	1953	1959	1961		
1	398	408	408	Area: Argentina	1
2	306	304	316	Industry: Non-farm	2
5	221	223	231	Ages: All	1
10	175	181	184	Sex: M & F	3
20	142	146	146	Occupation: All	1
75	74	74	73	Income: W & S	1
85	60	60	59	Intensity: All	1
95	37	37	33	Period: Year	1
				Limits:	0
Median Pesos	10,540	44,800	74,000		
Source	AR 1	AR 1	AR 1		

Notes:

See Table AR–1.
Excludes employees in farming and fishing, and in domestic service.

ARGENTINA: TABLE AR-3

Per-centiles	1953	1959	1961		
1	273	264	284	Area: Argentina	1
2	241	235	246	Industry: Manufacture	4
5	197	197	201	Ages: All	1
10	170	166	171	Sex: M & F	3
20	143	138	142	Occupation: Manual	2
75	72	75	73	Income: W & S	1
85	57	60	58	Intensity: All	1
95	37	(32)	31	Period: Year	1
				Limits:	0
Median Pesos	9,280	40,600	72,600		
Source	AR 1	AR 1	AR 1		

Notes:

See Table AR–1.
Covers 'obreros industriales'.

AUSTRIA: TABLE AU-1

	1957			
Percentiles	All	Full year		
1	366	364	Area: Austria	1
2	296	292	Industry: All	1
5	223	220	Ages: All	1
10	177	174	Sex: M	1
20	140	138	Occupation: All	1
75	73	77	Income: W & S	1
85	55	65	Intensity: All & F/Y	1, 2
95	22	30	Period: Year	1
			Limits:	0
Median Schillings	24,980	26,400		
Source	AU 2	AU 2		

Notes:

Based on wage-tax statistics. Each person included only once.
Covers wages, salaries, and pensions.
Full year means employed for 335 days or more in 1957.

AUSTRIA: TABLE AU–2

Percentiles	1957 All	Full year		
1	364	344	Area: All	1
2	315	299	Industry: All	1
5	247	237	Ages: All	1
10	197	190	Sex: F	2
20	155	151	Occupation: All	1
75	63	69	Income: W & S	1
85	45	52	Intensity: All & F/Y	1, 2
95	(18)	26	Period: Year	1
			Limits:	0
Median Schillings	14,850	16,180		
Source	AU 2	AU 2		

Notes:
See Table AU–1.

AUSTRIA: TABLE AU–3

Per- centiles	1957 All	Full year	All excluding pensioners		
1	379	366	376	Area: Austria	1
2	309	300	303	Industry: All	1
5	234	227	228	Ages: All	1
10	187	180	181	Sex: M & F	3
20	149	144	146	Occupation: All	1
75	64	69	67	Income: W & S	1
85	45	52	48	Intensity: All & F/Y	1, 2
95	19	24	18	Period: Year	1
				Limits:	0
Median Schillings	21,400	23,200	22,075		
Source	AU 2	AU 2			

Notes:

See Table AU–1.
Tabulation excluding pensioners is available only for M & F combined.

828158   U

AUSTRIA: Table AU-4

Per-centiles	1926	1947	1953	1960		
1	..	191	183	..	Area: Vienna	4
2	..	176	170	..	Industry: All	1
5	..	154	154	..	Ages: Adults	2
10	140	137	142	(145)	Sex: M	1
20	124	122	125	126	Occupation: Manual	2
75	80	88	85	85	Income: W & S	1
85	70	81	79	77	Intensity: All	1
95	55	68	69	65	Period: Week	3
					Limits: Trade-union firms	3

Median Schillings	54·4	107·0	372	558

Source	AU 1	AU 1	AU 1	AU 1

Notes:

Data collected by union officials from employers. W & S for main occupation only. A bias towards larger firms (which are more often unionized).

Coverage varies, but similar in 1953 and 1960.

AUSTRIA: Table AU-5

Per-centiles	1926	1947	1953	1960		
1	190	176	164	170	Area: Vienna	4
2	168	165	157	158	Industry: All	1
5	144	148	144	141	Ages: Adults	2
10	131	132	130	130	Sex: F	2
20	113	117	117	116	Occupation: Manual	2
75	88	87	91	88	Income: W & S	1
85	74	79	86	83	Intensity: All	1
95	(36)	66	77	71	Period: Week	3
					Limits: Trade-union firms	3

Median Schillings	29·7	69·9	262	354

Source	AU 1	AU 1	AU 1	AU 1

Notes:

See Table AU-4.

AUSTRIA: TABLE AU–6

Per-centiles	1926	1947	1953	1960		
1	..	200	200	..	Area: Vienna	4
2	..	184	186	..	Industry: All	1
5	171	160	166	..	Ages: Adults	2
10	155	141	149	160	Sex: M & F	3
20	138	125	129	136	Occupation: Manual	2
75	70	79	83	79	Income: W & S	1
85	61	70	76	71	Intensity: All	1
95	45	57	66	62	Period: Week	3
					Limits: Trade-union firms	3
Median Schillings	46·3	97·7	324	454		
Source	AU 1	AU 1	AU 1	AU 1		

Notes:

See Table AU–4.

BELGIUM: Table BE–1

Per-centiles	1964 M	F	M & F		
1	..	..	..	Area: Belgium	1
2	..	222	..	Industry: Private	7
5	(206)	187	(205)	Ages: All	1
10	164	158	165	Sex: M, F, M & F	1, 2, 3
20	132	131	134	Occupation: All	1
75	84	82	78	Income: W & S	1
85	76	71	65	Intensity: F/P	2
95	56	(30)	47	Period: Month	2
				Limits:	0
Median Francs	8,210	5,190	7,465		
Source	BE 1	BE 1	BE 1		

Notes:

Based on social security taxation statistics.

Excludes mines and government employees.

Earnings in quarter are divided by number of days employed and multiplied by 25 to give notional monthly rate. This is equivalent to a full-period measurement.

Earnings exclude end-of-year bonus.

Employees who moved to a different firm during the quarter appear twice (but on a daily rate basis).

Manual workers based on a sample of those receiving up to 8,000 francs and extrapolated above that level on the basis of estimates for 1955, after allowing for changes in total number employed and in mean earnings.

Other employees estimated directly for earnings up to 11,275 francs and extrapolated above that level on the basis of 1947 data, after allowing for changes in number employed and mean earnings.

BELGIUM: TABLE BE–2

Por centiles	1964 M	F	M & F		
1	186	177	192	Area: Belgium	1
2	171	161	178	Industry: Private	7
5	150	144	158	Ages: All	1
10	135	132	142	Sex: M, F, M & F	1, 2, 3
20	121	120	126	Occupation: Manual	2
75	86	83	77	Income: W & S	1
85	78	71	65	Intensity: F/P	2
95	57	(47)	47	Period: Month	2
				Limits:	0
Median Francs	7,760	4,745	7,120		
Source	BE 1	BE 1	BE 1		

Notes:

See Table BE–1.

BELGIUM: TABLE BE–3

Per- centiles	1896 M	F	M & F		
1	218	222	(222)	Area: Belgium	1
2	191	204	(195)	Industry: MMB	5
5	164	178	(167)	Ages: All (16+)	1
10	145	158	(149)	Sex: M, F, M & F	1, 2, 3
20	129	136	131	Occupation: Manual	2
75	80	(78)	75	Income: W & S	1
85	69	(68)	61	Intensity: F/P F/T	3
95	49	(52)	41	Period: Day	4
				Limits:	0
Median Francs	3·16	1·65	3·01		
Source	ZA 2 428	ZA 2 428	ZA 2 428		

Notes:

Data from report of industrial census of 1896. Wage taken from payrolls by managers, using last normal payment before date of census. Wage intended to be amount earned in a normal working day.

BRAZIL: TABLE BR–1

Per-centiles	1953 M	F	M & F		
1	625	..	635	Area: Brazil	1
2	588	562	592	Industry: Government	6
5	389	334	386	Ages: All	1
10	252	207	242	Sex: M, F, M & F	1, 2, 3
20	158	151	160	Occupation: All	1
75	..	..	..	Income: W & S	1
85	..	..	..	Intensity: F/P	2
95	..	..	..	Period: Month	2
				Limits:	0
Median Cruzeiros	1,395	1,460	1,385		
Source	BR 1	BR 1	BR 1		

Notes:

Based on official data for employees in the Federal Public Service, numbering 180,112 in all.

Interpolations are rough and cannot be made below median.

CANADA: TABLE CA-1

Per-centiles	1930–1	1940–1	1950–1	1960–1		
1	567	..	..	..	Area: Canada	1
2	442	369	258	(283)	Industry: All	1
5	317	271	194	214	Ages: 10+ (1930)	
					14+ (1940 &	
					1950), 15+	
					(1960)	1
10	243	215	164	176	Sex: M	1
20	186	(173)	137	145	Occupation: All	1
75	49	(47)	65	64	Income: W & S	1
85	34	(27)	44	41	Intensity: All	1
95	17	(8)	(15)	15	Period: Year	1
					Limits:	0

Median $	771	868	2,120	3,610

Source	CA 4	CA 3	CA 2	CA 1
	78	24–5	19–1	T 19
			and	
			19–2	

Notes:

1930–1: Covers all wage-earners (as reported in Census) except those with zero earnings in the year because of complete unemployment and those whose earnings were not stated.

1940–1 and 1950–1: Same as 1930–1. Income includes all W & S but no allowance for value of board or room.

1960–1: Covers all 15+ reporting a full or part-time job as employee (or looking for work) in the week prior to enumeration (in first half of June). Gross cash earnings with no allowance included for free room or board, or reimbursements for travel or other expenses.

CANADA: TABLE CA–2

Per-centiles	1930–1	1940–1	1950–1	1960–1		
1	405	419	266	312	Area: Canada	1
2	352	358	237	267	Industry: All	1
5	284	283	203	221	Ages: See CA–1	1
10	238	234	179	188	Sex: F	2
20	187	(185)	153	159	Occupation: All	1
75	57	(46)	48	50	Income: W & S	1
85	40	(26)	(27)	28	Intensity: All	1
95	18	(8)	(8)	(9)	Period: Year	1
					Limits:	0

Median $	476	424	1,190	1,990

Source	CA 4	CA 3	CA 2	CA 1
	78	24–5	19–1 and 19–2	T 19

Notes:

See Table CA–1.

CANADA: TABLE CA–3

Per-centiles	1930–1	1940–1	1950–1	1960–1		
1	594	517	(341)	..	Area: Canada	1
2	467	414	270	299	Industry: All	1
5	332	305	209	230	Ages: See CA–1	1
10	259	242	175	189	Sex: M & F	3
20	196	183	146	154	Occupation: All	1
75	51	(47)	59	56	Income: W & S	1
85	35	(27)	36	34	Intensity: All	1
95	16	(9)	(10)	(11)	Period: Year	1
					Limits:	0

Median $	674	710	1,840	3,100

Source	CA 4	CA 3	CA 2	CA 1
	78	24–5	19–1 and 19–2	T 19

Notes:

See Table CA–1

CANADA: TABLE CA–4

Per-centiles	1940–1	1950–1	1960–1	1960–1 Ontario	1960–1 Quebec		
1	..	..	..	..	..	Area: All, Ontario & Quebec	1,2
2	..	..	..	..	..	Industry: Non-farm	2
5	235	..	212	210	222	Ages: 14+, 15+	1
10	201	157	173	169	178	Sex: M	1
20	155	133	143	139	146	Occupation: All	1
75	55	68	67	71	67	Income: W & S	1
85	(34)	49	46	51	47	Intensity: All	1
95	(12)	(17)	(16)	(16)	(17)	Period: Year	1
						Limits:	0

Median						
$	975	2,230	3,720	4,000	3,430

Source	CA 3 90	CA 2 21–2	CA 1 T 21	CA 1 T 21	CA 1 T 21

Notes:

   See Table CA–1

CANADA: TABLE CA–5

Per-centiles	1940–1	1950–1	1960–1	1960–1 On-tario	1960–1 Que-bec		
1	413	268	..	..	289	Area: All, Ontario and Quebec	1, 2
2	356	241	268	264	253	Industry: Non-farm	2
5	280	206	218	213	213	Ages: 14+, 15+	1
10	229	180	188	181	187	Sex: F	2
20	169	155	159	154	156	Occupation: All	1
75	(58)	49	51	50	57	Income: W & S	1
85	(36)	(29)	(30)	(29)	(37)	Intensity: All	1
95	(12)	(9)	(10)	(9)	(13)	Period: Year	1
						Limits:	0

Median						
$	435	1,180	2,000	2,160	1,910

Source	CA 3 90	CA 2 21–1 21–3	CA 1 T 21	CA 1 T 21	CA 1 T 21

Notes:

   See Table CA–1.

CANADA: TABLE CA-6

Per-centiles	1940–1	1950–1	1960–1	1960–1 On-tario	1960–1 Que-bec		
1	..	..	..	..	..	Area: All, Ontario	1, 2
						and Quebec	
2	..	..	294	290	312	Industry: Non-farm	2
5	288	206	225	220	230	Ages: 14+, 15+	1
10	227	172	187	182	189	Sex: M & F	3
20	177	143	152	148	152	Occupation: All	1
75	(49)	61	58	60	60	Income: W & S	1
85	(29)	38	35	(37)	39	Intensity: All	1
95	(9)	(12)	(11)	(10)	(13)	Period: Year	1
						Limits:	0
Median $	778	1,900	3,160	3,400	2,960		
Source	CA 3	CA 2	CA 1	CA 1	CA 1		
	90	21–1	T 21	T 21	T 21		
		21–3					

Notes:
   See Table CA–1.

CANADA: TABLE CA-7

Per-centiles	1940–1	1950–1	1960–1	1960–1 On-tario	1960–1 Que-bec		
1	292	..	229	209	229	Area: All, Ontario	1, 2
						and Quebec	
2	256	184	203	191	205	Industry: Non-farm,	3
						non-service	
5	215	157	177	168	179	Ages: 14+, 15+	1
10	184	144	158	151	159	Sex: M	1
20	150	131	138	133	137	Occupation: Manual	2
75	57	68	66	71	65	Income: W & S	1
85	(37)	48	44	51	45	Intensity: All	1
95	(14)	(17)	(15)	(17)	(16)	Period: Year	1
						Limits:	0
Median $	925	2,140	3,470	3,780	3,220		
Source	CA 3	CA 2	CA 1	CA 1	CA 1		
	T 6	T 21	T 21	T 21	T 21		

Notes:
   See Table CA–1.
   Covers manual workers in mining, manufacturing, construction and transport, and other non-farm labourers.

CANADA: TABLE CA–8

Per-centiles	1940–1	1950–1	1960–1	1960–1 On-tario	1960–1 Que-bec		
1	310	209	242	230	246	Area: All, Ontario	1, 2
						and Quebec	
2	252	195	218	206	223	Industry: Non-farm,	3
						non-service	
5	196	172	192	182	194	Ages: 14+, 15+	1
10	160	157	171	163	173	Sex: F	2
20	130	136	145	142	143	Occupation: Manual	2
75	(56)	64	59	60	65	Income: W & S	1
85	(34)	40	38	(38)	(45)	Intensity: All	1
95	(12)	(13)	(12)	(12)	(16)	Period: Year	1
						Limits:	0

Median $	500	1,270	1,880	2,040	1,800

Source	CA 3 T 6	CA 2 T 21	CA 1 T 21	CA 1 T 21	CA 1 T 21

Notes:

See Table CA–7.

CANADA: TABLE CA–9

Per-centiles	1940–1	1950–1	1960–1	1960–1 On-tario	1960–1 Que-bec		
1	315	..	233	221	243	Area: All, Ontario	1, 2
						and Quebec	
2	275	193	212	201	217	Industry: Non-farm,	3
						non-service	
5	226	166	185	175	190	Ages: 14+, 15+	1
10	192	151	163	157	168	Sex: M & F	3
20	159	135	142	137	143	Occupation: Manual	2
75	57	65	62	65	62	Income: W & S	1
85	(35)	45	(41)	45	43	Intensity: All	1
95	(12)	(16)	(14)	(15)	(15)	Period: Year	1
						Limits:	0

Median $	850	2,010	3,270	3,560	2,970

Source	CA 3 T 6	CA 2 T 21	CA 1 T 21	CA 1 T 21	CA 1 T 21

Notes:

See Table CA–7.

CANADA: TABLE CA–10

Per-centiles	1950–1		1960–1			
	40+ weeks	50+ weeks	40–52 weeks	40–52 weeks & 35+ hours		
1	..	..	..	..	Area: Canada	1
2	212	..	(267)	(264)	Industry: All	1
5	184	189	203	203	Ages: All	1
10	157	156	167	166	Sex: M	1
20	132	132	137	137	Occupation: All	1
75	78	80	77	77	Income: W & S	1
85	65	67	64	65	Intensity: F/P, and F/P F/T	2, 3
95	44	45	42	46	Period: Year	1
					Limits:	0
Median $	2,335	2,380	4,080	4,110		
Source	CA 2 T 19	CA 2 T 19	CA 1 T 19	CA 1 T 19		

Notes:
  See Table CA–1.

CANADA: TABLE CA–11

Per-centiles	1950–1		1960–1			
	40+ weeks	50+ weeks	40–52 weeks	40–52 weeks & 35+ hours		
1	233	230	275	264	Area: Canada	1
2	209	207	239	228	Industry: All	1
5	179	177	195	187	Ages: All	1
10	158	156	168	163	Sex: F	2
20	137	136	143	139	Occupation: All	1
75	70	70	69	75	Income: W & S	1
85	49	48	53	61	Intensity: F/P, and F/P F/T	2, 3
95	(17)	(15)	28	39	Period: Year	1
					Limits:	0
Median $	1,415	1,445	2,370	2,474		
Source	CA 2 T 19	CA 2 T 19	CA 1 T 19	CA 1 T 19		

Notes:
  See Tables CA–1.

CANADA: TABLE CA–12

	1950–1		1960–1			
Per-centiles	40+ weeks	50+ weeks	40–52 weeks	40–52 weeks & 35+ hours		
1	..	..	..	..	Area: Canada	1
2	255	255	278	(275)	Industry: All	1
5	192	193	214	209	Ages: All	1
10	161	161	176	173	Sex: M & F	3
20	135	134	144	142	Occupation: All	1
75	71	73	70	72	Income: W & S	1
85	57	58	56	59	Intensity: F/P, and F/P F/T	2, 3
95	31	31	31	39	Period: Year	
					Limits:	0
Median $	2,115	2,158	3,565	3,670		
Source	CA 2 T 19	CA 2 T 19	CA 1 T 19	CA 1 T 19		

Notes:
See Table CA–1.

CHILE: TABLE CH–1

Percentiles	1960		
1	650	Area: Chile	1
2	517	Industry: All	1
5	358	Ages: All	1
10	261	Sex: M & F	3
20	185	Occupation: Non-manual	5
75	70	Income: W & S	1
85	60	Intensity: All	1
95	45	Period: Month	2
		Limits:	0
Median Escudos	101		
Source	CH 1		

Notes:
Based on inquiry sent to persons covered by the Caja de Previsión de Empleados Particulares de Chile, asking for earnings in month of November 1960. Active depositors 171,300, of whom 116,327 replied. Caja covers mainly administrative, technical, and clerical employees, but also some personal service, e.g. chauffeurs, tailors, automobile mechanics, hairdressers, and cinema attendants.

CHILE: TABLE CH–2

Percentiles	1964		
	M	F	M & F
1	..	433	..
2	..	361	..
5	(349)	278	362
10	277	228	279
20	196	178	195
75	53	59	53
85	41	49	42
95	29	34	(31)
Median Escudos	2·81	1·83	2·55
Source	CH 1	CH 1	CH 1

Area: Chile — 1
Industry: Non-farm — 2
Ages: All — 1
Sex: M, F, M & F — 1, 2, 3
Occupation: Manual — 2
Income: W & S — 1
Intensity: All — 1
Period: Day — 4
Limits: — 0

Notes:

Data relate to manual workers (obreros) belonging to the Social Security System. Probably excludes farm workers. Earnings are given as daily earnings in source. Refers to workers who made a claim, as a result of temporary unemployment, during the year. Of a total of 1,340,000 covered by Social Security 99,036 made a claim.

CEYLON: TABLE CN–1

Percentiles	1962	1963
1	(783)	(769)
2	(578)	(567)
5	(387)	(378)
10	(277)	(273)
20	194	193
75	72	71
85	61	60
95	41	45
Median Rupees	72·9	74·4
Source	CN 1	CN 1

Area: Ceylon — 1
Industry: Central Government — 6
Ages: All — 1
Sex: M & F — 3
Occupation: All — 1
Income: W & S — 1
Intensity: F/P F/T — 3
Period: Month — 2
Limits: — 0

Notes:

Basic monthly salary at 30 September. Number of persons covered:

1962   270,449
1963   282,152.

Some smoothing of graph required.

CZECHOSLOVAKIA: Table CZ-1

Percentiles	1962	1964		
1	221	218	Area: Czechoslovakia	1
2	198	196	Industry: Non-farm	2
5	171	170	Ages: All	1
10	152	150	Sex: M & F	3
20	132	131	Occupation: All	1
75	79	79	Income: W & S	1
85	70	70	Intensity: F/P F/T	3
95	57	58	Period: Month	2
			Limits:	0
Median				
Kčs	1,464	1,469		
Source	CZ 1	CZ 1		
	130	130		

Notes:

Employees in socialized sector only (i.e. excludes agricultural co-operatives). Relates to employees working at least 180 h in May (160 h in some industries). Earnings are for that month.

Not clear if apprentices included, but they probably are.

DENMARK: Table DK-1

Per-centiles	Pre-tax 1956	Post-tax 1956	1958	1962		
1	359	314	317	325	Area: Denmark	1
2	287	259	261	264	Industry: All	1
5	218	205	207	209	Ages: All	1
10	185	176	175	177	Sex: M & F	3
20	148	144	145	146	Occupation: All	1
75	65	67	66	69	Income: Total	2
85	48	51	49	52	Intensity: All	1
95	27	28	27	28	Period: Year	1
					Limits: Taxpayers	2
Median						
Kroner	10,320	8,240	8,990	13,280		
Source	DK 4	DK 1	DK 2	DK 3		

Notes:

Post-tax data are income 'assessments', which means 'income after legal deduction for payment of direct taxes, insurance premiums, etc.' Direct taxes are income and net property taxes paid during the year of assessment.

Covers all industries except household service.

1956 pre-tax estimates made by applying tax rates computed from DK 4 to 1956 post-tax percentiles.

DENMARK: TABLE DK-2

Per-centiles	Pre-tax 1956	Post-tax 1956	1958	1962		
1	302	271	277	229	Area: Denmark	1
2	257	236	238	212	Industry: All	1
5	209	197	199	187	Ages: All	1
10	176	169	171	166	Sex: M & F	3
20	145	141	142	140	Occupation: Manual	2
75	66	68	67	69	Income: Total	2
85	48	51	50	51	Intensity: All	1
95	27	29	27	27	Period: Year	1
					Limits: Taxpayers	2
Median Kroner	10,110	8,080	8,810	11,990		
Source	DK 4	DK 1	DK 2	DK 3		

Notes:

See Table DK-1,

EL SALVADOR: TABLE ES-1

Percentiles	1954		
1	..	Area: Three towns	4
2	..	Industry: All	1
5	216	Ages: All	1
10	183	Sex: M & F	3
20	150	Occupation: Manual	2
75	80	Income: Household	3
85	65	Intensity: All	1
95	(39)	Period: Month	2
		Limits:	0
Median Colones	135,500		
Source	ES 1 8		

Notes:

Working-class families in the City of San Salvador and neighbouring cities of Mejicanos and Villa Delgado.

Limited to families of three or more, living in special buildings (mesones), in which head is a manual worker in full employment.

Data based on 'Microcenso' of May 1954.

FINLAND: TABLE FN-1

Percentiles	1960 M	F	M & F		
1	515	405	524	Area: Finland	1
2	390	344	402	Industry: All	1
5	273	272	286	Ages: All	1
10	211	218	227	Sex: M, F, M & F	1, 2, 3
20	167	168	177	Occupation: All	1
75	53	44	51	Income: Total	2
85	34	(25)	30	Intensity: All	1
95	(12)	(8)	(10)	Period: Year	1
				Limits:	0
Median Old marks (000)	411	264	340		
Source	FN 1	FN 1	FN 1		

Notes:

Based on income-tax statistics but exemption limit is only 1,000 old marks. Covers persons whose major source was W & S. Family allowances and interest on bank deposits excluded.

Data based on sample.

FRANCE: TABLE FR-1

Percentiles	1951	1952	1954	1956		
1	510	520	..	554	Area: France	1
2	376	383	..	419	Industry: Non-farm	2
5	253	258	265	274	Ages: All (except 1951)	1
10	190	193	197	201	Sex: M	1
20	146	147	149	151	Occupation: All	1
75	76	75	76	74	Income: W & S	1
85	65	63	65	63	Intensity: F/P F/T	3
95	48	43	46	46	Period: Year	1
					Limits:	0
Median Francs (000)	290	334	366	477		
Source	FR 2 56-7	FR 3 58-9	FR 4 51-2	FR 5 64		

Notes:

Data derived from returns from employers. Covers 'permanent' employees only, i.e. those employed for the whole 12 months full-time. Excludes agriculture, domestic service, and public administration.

1951 data exclude apprentices. Income excludes income in kind and is net of social security contributions.

FRANCE: TABLE FR–2

Per-centiles	1951	1952	1954	1956		
1	312	320	..	316	Area: France	1
2	261	266	..	263	Industry: Non-farm	2
5	203	208	209	209	Ages: All (except 1951)	1
10	171	174	173	175	Sex: F	2
20	141	144	143	143	Occupation: All	1
75	78	78	80	78	Income: W & S	1
85	67	67	69	69	Intensity: F/P F/T	3
95	(46)	43	(48)	(52)	Period: Year	1
					Limits:	0
Median Francs (000)	208	235	268	332		
Source	FR 2 56–7	FR 3 58–9	FR 4 51–2	FR 5 64		

Notes:

See Table FR–1.

FRANCE: TABLE FR–3

Per-centiles	1951	1952	1954	1956		
1	491	507	..	552	Area: France	1
2	363	376	..	403	Industry: Non-farm	2
5	247	254	..	265	Ages: All (except 1951)	1
10	188	193	196	197	Sex: M & F	3
20	146	148	157	151	Occupation: All	1
75	74	73	75	72	Income: W & S	1
85	63	62	65	62	Intensity: F/P F/T	3
95	45	42	46	46	Period: Year	1
					Limits:	0
Median Francs (000)	267	306	337	435		
Source	FR 2 56–7	FR 3 58–9	FR 4 51–2	FR 5 64		

Notes:

See Table FR–1.

FRANCE: TABLE FR–4

Per-centiles	1957	1959	1961	1963		
1	567	..	610	..	Area: France	1
2	419	445	463	441	Industry: Non-farm	2
5	276	287	295	293	Ages: All	1
10	201	205	210	211	Sex: M	1
20	150	152	154	154	Occupation: All	1
75	74	74	76	74	Income: W & S	1
85	63	62	63	62	Intensity: F/P F/T	3
95	44	43	44	39	Period: Year	1
					Limits:	0
Median Francs (000)[1]	526	615	721	883		
Source	FR 6 295	FR 7 431	FR 9 156	FR 11 56		

Notes:

See Table FR–1.

An inquiry in 1961 showed that some non-permanent employees were included in error.

In 1963 covers those *paid* for whole 12 months. This shift eliminated about 5 per cent of employees who were on books for whole year but not paid in one or more months—for reasons of sickness, holiday, etc. Average income of remainder is 1·5–2 per cent higher as a result, and dispersion is probably reduced.

Growing dispersion below median in 1963 attributed to influx of apprentices and young people in post-war population bulge.

---

[1] In 1961 and 1963, 10 new francs.

FRANCE: Table FR–5

Per-centiles	1957	1959	1961	1963		
1	339	355	367	363	Area: France	1
2	278	288	292	288	Industry: Non-farm	2
5	213	218	222	219	Ages: All	1
10	178	181	183	181	Sex: F	2
20	145	147	147	148	Occupation: All	1
75	78	78	76	76	Income: W & S	1
85	68	67	67	65	Intensity: F/P F/T	3
95	(49)	49	46	43	Period: Year	1
					Limits:	0
Median Francs (000)[1]	360	423	504	618		
Source	FR 6 295	FR 7 431	FR 9 156	FR 11 56		

Notes:

See Table FR–4.

[1] In 1961 and 1963, 10 new francs.

FRANCE: Table FR–6

Per-centiles	1957	1959	1961	1963		
1	547	598	582	562	Area: France	1
2	408	437	436	418	Industry: Non-farm	2
5	270	278	280	282	Ages: All	1
10	199	202	202	205	Sex: M & F	3
20	151	152	152	152	Occupation: All	1
75	73	72	72	72	Income: W & S	1
85	61	61	60	60	Intensity: F/P F/T	3
95	43	42	43	39	Period: Year	1
					Limits:	0
Median Francs (100)[1]	477	559	665	813		
Source	FR 6 295	FR 7 431	FR 9 156	FR 11 56		

Notes:

See Table FR–4.

[1] In 1961 and 1963, 10 new francs.

FRANCE: Table FR–7

Per-centiles	1951	1952	1954	1956		
1	225	227	..	252	Area: France	1
2	205	206	..	228	Industry: Non-farm	2
5	178	178	194	192	Ages: All (except	1
					1951, 1952)	
10	157	157	166	165	Sex: M	1
20	134	134	139	139	Occupation: Manual	2
75	78	78	77	76	Income: W & S	1
85	67	68	67	64	Intensity: F/P F/T	3
95	49	52	46	47	Period: Year	1
					Limits:	0
Median Francs (000)	267	309	341	436		
Source	FR 2 56–7	FR 3 58–9	FR 4 51–2	FR 5 64		

Notes:

See Table FR–1.
Apprentices excluded in 1951 and 1952.

FRANCE: Table FR–8

Per-centiles	1951	1952	1954	1956		
1	210	211	..	233	Area: France	1
2	189	192	208	205	Industry: Non-farm	2
5	165	167	173	175	Ages: All (except	1
					1951, 1952)	
10	147	147	149	152	Sex: F	2
20	128	128	128	130	Occupation: Manual	2
75	81	82	82	83	Income: W & S	1
85	69	72	72	74	Intensity: F/P F/T	3
95	(50)	(50)	(48)	(54)	Period: Year	1
					Limits:	0
Median Francs (000)	187	214	241	294		
Source	FR 2 56–7	FR 3 58–9	FR 4 51–2	FR 5 64		

Notes:

See Table FR–7.

FRANCE: Table FR–9

Per-centiles	1951	1952	1954	1956		
1	236	236	..	268	Area: France	1
2	213	215	245	236	Industry: Non-farm	2
5	185	186	202	199	Ages: All (except	1
					1951, 1952)	
10	162	162	171	170	Sex: M & F	3
20	137	137	141	142	Occupation: Manual	2
75	76	76	77	74	Income: W & S	1
85	66	66	67	63	Intensity: F/P F/T	3
95	48	51	(45)	(48)	Period: Year	1
					Limits:	0

Median Francs (000)	246	287	316	402

Source	FR 2	FR 3	FR 4	FR 5
	56–7	58–9	51–2	64

Notes:

See Table FR–7.

FRANCE: Table FR–10

Per-centiles	1957	1959	1961	1963		
1	247	257	262	..	Area: France	1
2	221	227	231	230	Industry: Non-farm	2
5	187	190	191	190	Ages: All	1
10	163	164	163	162	Sex: M	1
20	138	138	138	135	Occupation: Manual	2
75	76	76	77	76	Income: W & S	1
85	65	65	65	64	Intensity: F/P F/T	3
95	46	44	44	40	Period: Year	1
					Limits:	0

Median Francs (000)[1]	483	562	656	804

Source	FR 6	FR 7	FR 9	FR 11
	295	431	156	56

Notes:

See Table FR–4.

[1] In 1961 and 1963, 10 new francs.

FRANCE: TABLE FR–11

Per-centiles	1957	1959	1961	1963		
1	229	236	254	255	Area: France	1
2	204	209	221	219	Industry: Non-farm	2
5	172	177	181	179	Ages: All	1
10	152	154	157	155	Sex: F	2
20	131	132	133	133	Occupation: Manual	2
75	83	82	83	81	Income: W & S	1
85	72	70	73	70	Intensity: F/P F/T	3
95	(51)	(51)	50	(46)	Period: Year	1
					Limits:	0
Median Francs (000)[1]	315	365	426	526		
Source	FR 6 295	FR 7 431	FR 9 156	FR 11 56		

Notes:

See Table FR–4.

[1] In 1961 and 1963, 10 new francs.

FRANCE: TABLE FR–12

Per-centiles	1957	1959	1961	1963		
1	261	271	266	..	Area: France	1
2	233	239	239	241	Industry: Non-farm	2
5	195	200	200	197	Ages: All	1
10	170	170	169	166	Sex: M & F	3
20	142	142	141	139	Occupation: Manual	2
75	75	74	74	74	Income: W & S	1
85	63	63	63	62	Intensity: F/P F/T	3
95	45	43	43	(39)	Period: Year	1
					Limits:	0
Median Francs (000)[1]	443	516	608	743		
Source	FR 6 295	FR 7 431	FR 9 156	FR 11 56		

Notes:

See Table FR–4

[1] In 1961 and 1963, 10 new francs.

FRANCE: TABLE FR–13

Per-centiles	1963					
	Male		Female			
	PA	FT	PA	FT		
1	..	575	363	366	Area: France	1
2	441	424	288	292	Industry: Non-farm	2
5	293	282	219	226	Ages: All	1
10	211	205	181	185	Sex: M, F	1, 2
20	154	151	148	149	Occupation: All	1
75	74	73	76	75	Income: W & S	1
85	62	60	65	64	Intensity: F/P F/T	3
95	39	36	(43)	(37)	Period: Year	1
					Limits:	0
Median Francs 10	883	828	618	578		
Source	FR 11 56	FR 11 56	FR 11 56	FR 11 56		

Notes:

    PA = 'permanent', as defined previously.

    FT = each employee's earnings converted to an equivalent full-time basis. Those paid for less than full year are given a weight proportional to the period paid.

FRANCE: TABLE FR–14

Per-centiles	1963					
	Male		Female			
	PA	FT	PA	FT		
1	..	248	255	255	Area: France	1
2	230	223	219	219	Industry: Non-farm	2
5	190	190	179	178	Ages: All	1
10	162	163	155	155	Sex: M, F	1, 2
20	135	137	133	133	Occupation: Manual	2
75	76	75	81	79	Income: W & S	1
85	64	63	70	68	Intensity: F/P F/T	3
95	(40)	(37)	(46)	(37)	Period: Year	1
					Limits:	0
Median Francs 10	804	753	526	502		
Source	FR 11 56	FR 11 56	FR 11 56	FR 11 56		

Notes:

    See Table FR–13.

FRANCE: Table FR–15

Percentiles	1955	1956		
1	278	266	Area: France	1
2	248	237	Industry: Non-farm, non-service	3
5	207	207	Ages: All	1
10	173	172	Sex: M & F	3
20	144	143	Occupation: Manual	2
75	73	73	Income: Household	3
85	63	62	Intensity: All	1
95	46	45	Period: Year	1
			Limits:	0
Median Francs (000)	590	627		
Source	FR 1 232	FR 1 233		

Notes:

Covers Metropolitan France, except Corsica. Excludes institutions.
Four groups of 5,700 households approached at quarterly intervals.
1955 data based on three quarterly groups interviewed in 1956.
1956 data based on one quarter's interviews early in 1957.
Classified by occupation of head of household.
Covers contremaîtres, ouvriers, and manœuvres. Excludes domestic and other service trades and farm workers.

FRANCE: Table FR–16

Per-centiles	1891–5 Tobacco		Railways			
	M	F	M			
1	167	207	302	Area: France	1
2	149	189	253	Industry: Tobacco, Railways	9
5	141	173	194	Ages: Adults	2
10	131	154	161	Sex: M, F	1, 2
20	120	130	137	Occupation: Manual	2
75	88	82	82	Income: W & S	1
85	81	74	76	Intensity: F/P F/T	3
95	70	61	66	Period: Day	4
				Limits:	0
Median Francs	5.03	3.00	3.81		
Source	ZA 1 196–7	ZA 1 196–7	ZA 1 196–7		

GUATEMALA: Table GA–1

Percentiles	1952–3		
1	..	Area: Urban	3
2	431	Industry: All	1
5	327	Ages: All	1
10	263	Sex: M & F	3
20	194	Occupation: All	1
75	64	Income: Household	3
85	53	Intensity: All	1
95	(29)	Period: Year	1
		Limits:	0

Median Quetzals	1,015

Source	ZA 3 29

Notes:

Based on sample survey of 776 households.

GERMANY: Table GE–1

Percentiles	1950	1957	1961		
1	317	365	350	Area: Germany (F.R.)	1
2	260	295	290	Industry: All	1
5	201	225	222	Ages: All	1
10	166	181	180	Sex: M & F	3
20	138	148	147	Occupation: All	1
75	69	58	59	Income: W & S	1
85	54	(38)	35	Intensity: All	1
95	(31)	(14)	(10)	Period: Year	1
				Limits:	0

Median Marks	2,880	4,345	5,880

Source	GE 1 413	GE 3 445	GE 4 464

Notes:

Based on wage tax statistics, which, in principle, cover all with wage or salary earnings in the year. But some part-year workers do not send in their cards to the Finansamt, and some high-income people need to use them for their income-tax declarations.

Notes to 1957 statistics say that 85 per cent of all employees are covered. Those with less than 16,000 DM are sampled at 1·3 per cent rate. Others are taken in total.

GERMANY: TABLE GE–2

Percentiles	1957		
	M	F	
1	342	359	Area: Germany (F.R.) 1
2	279	303	Industry: All 1
5	211	242	Ages: All 1
10	170	199	Sex: M, F 1, 2
20	138	159	Occupation: All 1
75	74	(59)	Income: W & S 1
85	51	(36)	Intensity: All 1
95	(15)	(12)	Period: Year 1
			Limits: 0
Median Marks	5,170	2,710	
Source	GE 3 445	GE 3 445	

Notes:

See Table GE–1.

GERMANY: TABLE GE–3

Percentiles	1957		
	All	F/P	
1	365	346	Area: Germany (F.R.) 1
2	295	282	Industry: All 1
5	225	213	Ages: All 1
10	181	173	Sex: M & F 3
20	148	141	Occupation: All 1
75	58	67	Income: W & S 1
85	38	49	Intensity: All & F/P 1, 2
95	14	(23)	Period: Year 1
			Limits: 0
Median Marks	4,345	4,820	
Source	GE 3 445	GE 3 445	

Notes:

See Table GE–1.
F/P means employed 11 months or more.

GERMANY: TABLE GE–4

Percentiles	1957	1962		
1	178	184	Area: Germany (F.R.)	1
2	165	166	Industry: Industry, trade,	3
			and services	
5	148	147	Ages: Excl. apprentices	2
10	135	134	Sex: M	1
20	121	120	Occupation: Manual	2
75	86	87	Income: W & S	1
85	79	81	Intensity: F/P F/T	3
95	67	70	Period: Month	2
			Limits:	0

Median			
Marks	502	740	

Source	GE 3	GE 4
	512	517,
		520

Notes:

Sample inquiry covering about 25 per cent of employees in establishments with 10+ employees. Excludes any who were absent for reasons of sickness or accident during the month.

Covers industry, trade, and services, but not agriculture, transport, or government.

Relates to month of October.

Manual workers are distinguished by type of pension scheme to which they belong.

GERMANY: TABLE GE-5

Percentiles	1957	1962
1	169	166
2	159	156
5	143	142
10	132	130
20	120	118
75	86	88
85	79	81
95	63	69

Area: Germany (F.R.) — 1
Industry: Industry, trade, and services — 3
Ages: Excl. apprentices — 2
Sex: F — 2
Occupation: Manual — 2
Income: W & S — 1
Intensity: F/P F/T — 3
Period: Month — 2
Limits: — 0

Median Marks	302	472
Source	GE 3 512	GE 4 517, 520

Notes:
   See Table GE-4.

GERMANY: TABLE GE-6

Percentiles	1957	1962
1	186	(189)
2	172	171
5	154	151
10	140	138
20	125	123
75	80	82
85	68	71
95	54	58

Area: Germany (F.R.) — 1
Industry: Industry, trade, and services — 3
Ages: Excl. apprentices — 2
Sex: M & F — 3
Occupation: Manual — 2
Income: W & S — 1
Intensity F/P F/T — 3
Period: Month — 2
Limits: — 0

Median Marks	468	697
Source	GE 3 512	GE 4 517, 520

Notes:
   See Table GE-4.

GERMANY: TABLE GE-7

Per-centiles	1962					
	M	F	M & F			
1	..	162	..	Area: Germany (F.R.)		1
2	154	153	159	Industry: Industry, trade, and services		3
5	138	139	142	Ages: Excl. apprentices		2
10	128	129	131	Sex: M, F, M & F		1, 2, 3
20	117	118	119	Occupation: Manual		2
75	89	89	84	Income: W & S		1
85	83	83	75	Intensity: F/P F/T		3
95	73	72	62	Period: Hour		5
				Limits:		0

Median Marks	3·53	2·39	3·35

Source	GE 4 517	GE 4 517	GE 4 517

Notes:

See Table GE-4.

Hourly earnings obtained by dividing week's earnings by number of hours worked.

GERMANY: TABLE GE-8

Percentiles	Dortmund mining 1896	33 cities municipal 1907			
1	204	154	Area: Urban and Dortmund		3, 4
2	168	147	Industry: Municipal and Mining		9
5	138	136	Ages: Adults		2
10	129	127	Sex: M		1
20	119	117	Occupation: Manual		2
75	79	90	Income: W & S		1
85	68	85	Intensity: F/P F/T		3
95	50	75	Period: Day		4
			Limits:		0

Median	Fr. 4.98	Mk. 3.72

Source	ZA 1 196–7	ZA 2 431

Notes:

Dortmund: Daily wages in mining in third quarter of 1896.

33 cities: Daily wages of male municipal workers in 33 cities of over 50,000 inhabitants.

GREECE: TABLE GR–1

Percentiles	1962	1963		
1	497	460	Area: Greece	1
2	392	355	Industry: All	1
5	284	255	Ages: All	1
10	219	200	Sex: M & F	3
20	166	157	Occupation: All	1
75	70	71	Income: Family	3
85	58	62	Intensity: All	1
95	45	50	Period: Year	1
			Limits: Taxpayers	2
Median Drachmas (000)	52·1	64·8		
Source	GR 1	GR 1		

Notes:

Family income of families whose main source of income was wages, salaries, or pensions.

Covers only a small proportion (probably less than 10 per cent) of employee families. Actual numbers covered:

| 1962 | 84,231 |
| 1963 | 70,632 |

Employees subject to taxation are those with some non-employment income or with more than 60,000 Drs. of wages, salary, or pension.

GREECE: TABLE GR–2

Percentiles	1962	1963		
1	475	402	Area: Greece	1
2	385	333	Industry: All	1
5	286	255	Ages: Adults	2
10	227	206	Sex: M	1
20	170	159	Occupation: All	1
75	62	69	Income: W & S	1
85	47	54	Intensity: All	1
95	24	24	Period: Year	1
			Limits: Taxpayers	2
Median Drachmas (000)	36·8	46·3		
Source	GR 1	GR 1		

Notes:

See Table GR–1.
Wages, salary, or pension of husband, in families reporting for tax.
Coverage: 1962   140,760
          1963   117,829

APPENDIX 7

HUNGARY: TABLE HU–1

Percentiles	1962				
	M	F	M & F		
1	..	219	..	Area: Hungary	1
2	..	195	..	Industry: Non-farm	2
5	181	163	190	Ages: 14+	1
10	156	144	162	Sex: M, F, M & F	1, 2, 3
20	132	126	137	Occupation: All	1
75	81	82	78	Income: W & S	1
85	71	71	68	Intensity: All	1
95	56	(49)	(51)	Period: Year	1
				Limits:	0
Median Forints per month	1,767	1,231	1,545		
Source	HU 1 28–33	HU 1 28–33	HU 1 28–33		

Notes:

Based on household survey covering 14,996 employees. In 94 per cent of cases the employee's annual income was verified from the employer's records.

Includes a small number of farm workers who are employees, presumably on State farms.

Data expressed at average monthly rates.

HUNGARY: TABLE HU–2

Percentiles	1962				
	M	F	M & F		
1	..	182	..	Area: Hungary	1
2	..	168	206	Industry: Non-farm	2
5	163	151	173	Ages: All	1
10	144	136	153	Sex: M, F, M & F	1, 2, 3
20	127	123	133	Occupation: Manual	2
75	82	82	79	Income: W & S	1
85	73	71	69	Intensity: All	1
95	58	(48)	(52)	Period: Year	1
				Limits:	0
Median Forints per month	1,692	1,159	1,496		
Source	HU 1 28–33	HU 1 28–33	HU 1 28–33		

Notes:

See Table HU–1.

All farm workers excluded in this table.

HUNGARY: TABLE HU–3

Percentiles	All	Budapest		
1	..	..	Area: All and Budapest	1, 2
2	..	..	Industry: Non-farm	2
5	190	..	Ages: All	1
10	165	167	Sex: M & F	3
20	140	140	Occupation: All	1
75	72	68	Income: Household	3
85	59	53	Intensity: All	1
95	40	38	Period: Year	1
			Limits:	0

Median		
Forints per month	2,825	3,105

Source	HU 2	HU 2
	58	55

Notes:

Same sample survey as in Table HU–1.
A few farm employee households included.

HUNGARY: TABLE HU–4

Percentiles	All	Budapest		
1	..	..	Area: All and Budapest	1, 2
2	213	..	Industry: Non-farm	2
5	181	185	Ages: All	1
10	159	162	Sex: M & F	3
20	136	139	Occupation: Manual	2
75	73	69	Income: Household	3
85	60	56	Intensity: All	1
95	41	40	Period: Year	1
			Limits:	0

Median		
Forints per month	2,685	2,805

Source	HU 2	HU 2
	58	55

Notes:

See Table HU–3.
No farm employees included.

828158 Y

IVORY COAST: TABLE IC–1

Percentiles	1956		
1	. .	Area: Abidjan	4
2	. .	Industry: All	1
5	246	Ages: All	1
10	214	Sex: M & F	3
20	171	Occupation: All	1
75	71	Income: Household	3
85	59	Intensity: All	1
95	43	Period: Month	2
		Limits: Africans	1
Median			
Francs	13,680		
Source	IC 1		
	48		

Notes:

Total expenditure, not income. Families covered are those of which the head received a wage or salary, excluding single persons and households of more than 3 adults or with more than 2 wage or salary earners.

Covers urban districts of Adjamé and Treichville in commune of Abidjan. 560 budgets collected in July–September 1956.

INDONESIA: TABLE ID–1

Percentiles	1957		
1	. .	Area: Djakarta	4
2	298	Industry: All	1
5	226	Ages: All	1
10	196	Sex: M & F	3
20	153	Occupation: Manual	2
75	77	Income: Household	3
85	66	Intensity: All	1
95	47	Period: Month	2
		Limits:	0
Median			
Rupiahs	495		
Source	ZA 7		
	578		

Notes:

Based on sample survey of 935 households.

INDIA: Table IN–1

Percentiles	1958–9			
	All	F/P		
1	(482)	(404)	Area: Urban	3
2	394	342	Industry: Manufacturing and building	5
5	297	263	Ages: All	1
10	240	212	Sex: M & F	3
20	190	168	Occupation: Manual	2
75	54	70	Income: W & S	1
85	35	57	Intensity: All and F/P F/T	1, 3
95	12	31	Period: Week	3
			Limits:	0
Median Rupees	11·4	13·6		
Source	IN 1 135–7	IN 1 135–7		

Notes:
Based on sample survey.
Covers workers in 'crafts and production processes' only. *Includes self-employed* and their income.
F/P = working 43–56 hours in the week.
Excludes those whose earnings were 'not recorded' (16·6 per cent of 'all' and 6·1 per cent of F/P).

INDIA: Table IN–2

Percentiles	1954–6				
	M	F	M & F		
1	729	476	695	Area: Bombay City	4
2	493	406	485	Industry: All	1
5	315	308	313	Ages: All	1
10	225	233	222	Sex: M, F, M & F	1, 2, 3
20	156	172	153	Occupation: All	1
75	78	(35)	75	Income: W & S	1
85	61	(19)	53	Intensity: All	1
95	(19)	(6)	(17)	Period: Month	2
				Limits:	0
Median Rupees	101·5	63·6	99·7		
Source	IN 2	IN 2	IN 2		

Notes:
Based on a survey of a 3 per cent sample drawn from the Electoral Rolls. All households in each selected tenement were to be interviewed. Number of males with employment earnings was 17,354, and females 1,730.

INDIA: Table IN–3

Percentiles	1954–6				
	M	M & F			
1	269	277	Area: Bombay City	4
2	226	233	Industry: All	1
5	184	187	Ages: All	1
10	156	156	Sex: M, M & F	1, 3
20	130	131	Occupation: Manual	2
75	76	71	Income: W & S	1
85	(52)	39	Intensity: All	1
95	(14)	10	Period: Month	2
			Limits:	0
Median Rupees	94·0	91·0		
Source	IN 2	IN 2		

Notes:

See Table IN–2. Manual workers include skilled, semi-skilled, and unskilled workers. Foremen and supervisors excluded. Covers 11,614 males and 1,301 females. Female percentiles not given because median unreliable.

ISRAEL: Table IS–1

Percentiles	1962–3				
	M	F	M & F		
1	..	..	..	Area: Israel	1
2	..	..	..	Industry: All	1
5	..	..	..	Ages: All	1
10	..	268	..	Sex: M, F, M & F	1, 2, 3
20	166	209	176	Occupation: All	1
75	(41)	(42)	(39)	Income: W & S	1
85	(22)	(24)	(20)	Intensity: All	1
95	(6)	(7)	(6)	Period: Year	1
				Limits:	0
Median IL	3,860	2,130	3,380		
Source	IS 3	IS 3	IS 3		

Notes:

Data estimated by collating income from all employments of each employee. May not have included every job because of difficulties of collation.

ISRAEL: TABLE IS–2

Percentiles	1962–3				
	M	F	M & F		
1	..	..	..	Area: Israel	1
2	..	..	..	Industry: All	1
5	..	..	..	Ages: All	1
10	..	197	..	Sex: M, F, M & F	1, 2, 3
20	(152)	157	153	Occupation: All	1
75	69	63	66	Income: W & S	1
85	51	(42)	47	Intensity: F/P	2
95	(21)	(14)	(18)	Period: Year	1
				Limits:	0
Median					
IL	4,755	3,330	4,445		
Source	IS 3	IS 3	IS 3		

Notes:

See Table IS–1.

Limited to those working 10 months or more in the year.

ISRAEL: TABLE IS–3

Per-centiles			1963–4			
	1956–7	1959–60	Pre-tax	Post-tax		
1	..	..	..	..	Area: Urban	3
2	..	..	..	..	Industry: All	1
5	194	..	..	..	Ages: All	1
10	166	192	..	..	Sex: M & F	3
20	136	150	158	144	Occupation: All	1
75	71	76	75	76	Income: Household	3
85	(64)	62	62	(65)	Intensity: All	1
95	(40)	(35)	35	(38)	Period: Year	1
					Limits: Jewish	1
Median						
IL per month	228	336	525	482		
Source	IS 1 122–3	IS 4	IS 4	IS 2 204		

Notes:

Based on sample surveys.

Income for whole year, expressed at a monthly rate. Families are urban Jewish headed by wage or salary earner, defined by major source of income. Head is husband of married couple or oldest earner. Household excludes boarders.

Post-tax is pre-tax minus income tax, consolidated loan and National Insurance fees payable by the family. These deductions were estimated at the editing stage of the survey.

ITALY: TABLE IT-1

Percentiles	1953–4		
1	..	Area: Italy	1
2	236	Industry: Non-farm	2
5	192	Ages: All	1
10	162	Sex: M & F	3
20	136	Occupation: Manual	2
75	79	Income: Household	3
85	70	Intensity: All	1
95	(52)	Period: Month	2
		Limits:	0
Median			
Lire	54,700		
Source	IT 1		
	27		

Notes:

Families whose heads are 'lavoratori dipendenti' amongst 3,137 households in a sample survey.

Data refer to total monthly *expenditure* per family.

JAPAN: TABLE JA-1

Per-centiles	1951	1953	1955	1956		
1	489	509	531	556	Area: Japan	
2	394	397	415	435	Industry: Private	7
					non-farm	
5	293	291	302	308	Ages: All	1
10	230	222	236	238	Sex: M & F	3
20	174	170	180	179	Occupation: All	1
75	67	(60)	61	61	Income: W & S	1
85	53	(40)	50	49	Intensity: F/P F/T	3
95	(24)	(13)	35	34	Period: Year	1
					Limits: Excludes firms	4
Median					with no taxpayers	
Yen (000)	119	161	162	179		
Source	JA 3	JA 3	JA 3	JA 3		
	165–8	165–8	165–8	165–8		

Notes:

Data derived from annual survey by tax authorities. Covers only employees working for the whole year in establishments in which at least one person is subject to tax. More than half of labour force is excluded by this rule and virtually all agricultural workers.

JAPAN: TABLE JA–2

Per-centiles	1955		
	M	F	M & F
1	475	350	530
2	376	298	415
5	270	235	303
10	211	193	237
20	162	150	179
75	64	(76)	61
85	50	(67)	49
95	35	(50)	35
Median Yen (000)	202	92·7	161
Source	JA 2 1955 18	JA 2 1955 18	JA 2 1955 18

Area: Japan   1
Industry: Private non-farm   7
Ages: All   1
Sex: M, F, M & F   1, 2, 3
Occupation: All   1
Income: W & S   1
Intensity: F/P F/T   3
Period: Year   1
Limits: Excludes firms with   4
  no taxpayers

Notes:
  See Table JA–1.

JAPAN: TABLE JA–3

Per-centiles	1957	1959	1961	1963	1965
1	568	583	605	550	506
2	450	456	453	416	403
5	316	321	318	296	280
10	246	249	241	229	217
20	185	187	181	171	165
75	60	60	62	66	66
85	48	48	51	54	54
95	33	34	37	37	38
Median Yen (000)	190	206	258	329	407
Source	JA 2 1957 22	JA 2 1959 22	JA 2 1961 23	JA 2 1963 40	JA 2 1965 51

Area: Japan   1
Industry: Private non-farm   7
Ages: All   1
Sex: M & F   3
Occupation: All   1
Income: W & S   1
Intensity: F/P F/T   3
Period: Year   1
Limits: Excludes firms with   4
  no taxpayers

Notes:
  See Table JA–1.

JAPAN: TABLE JA–4

Percentiles	1955	1962	1963			
1	..	..	..	Area: Urban	3
2	301	..	..	Industry: All	1
5	238	244	..	Ages: All	1
10	196	194	196	Sex: M & F	3
20	155	152	152	Occupation: All	1
75	71	74	74	Income: Household	3
85	57	61	62	Intensity: All	1
95	35	37	39	Period: Month	2
				Limits:	0

Median			
Yen	23,600	39,200	43,300

Source	ZA 3	JA 5	JA 1
	29–30	99	400

Notes:

1955 and 1962

No details in source but presumably the same as in 1963.

1963

Survey covering January to November 1963. Each household, in principle, keeps records for 6 months. Households included are those headed by wage or salary earner, i.e. principal earner in household is of this type. Excludes one-person households, farmers and fishermen, restaurants and boarding-houses.

KOREA (Rep.): TABLE KO–1

Percentiles	1963	1964			
1	..	..	Area: Urban	3
2	..	..	Industry: All	1
5	(296)	..	Ages: All	1
10	224	211	Sex: M & F	3
20	169	163	Occupation: All	1
75	69	70	Income: Household	3
85	56	57	Intensity: All	1
95	33	40	Period: Month	2
			Limits:	0

Median		
Won	4,900	6,130

Source	KO 1	KO 1
	96	97

Notes:

Based on 955 households in 1963 and 974 in 1964.

No details in source on survey technique. Data relate to 'wage and salary earner families' in 'all cities'.

MEXICO: Table ME–1

Per-centiles	1960, All		1960, Fed. District			
	All	Mfg.	All	Mfg.		
1	1,670	1,197	1,306	1,304	Area: All and Fed. District	1, 4
2	1,242	841	1,039	1,033	Industry: All and Manufacturing	1,4
5	599	506	597	598	Ages: All	1
10	349	299	327	333	Sex: M & F	3
20	212	185	214	192	Occupation: All	1
75	(57)	(66)	62	69	Income: W & S	1
85	(34)	(47)	44	54	Intensity: All	1
95	(10)	(18)	(18)	(31)	Period: Month	2
					Limits:	0
Median Pesos	364	472	559	552		
Source	ME 1	ME 1	ME 1	ME 1		

Notes:

Census data for month of May 1960.

Covers all receiving income from employment in that month.

Persons covered are fewer than those economically active because some persons working without pay, unwilling to give income, temporarily not at work, etc.

NETHERLANDS: Table NL–1

Percentiles	1949	1952	1953		
1	449	466	481	Area: Netherlands	1
2	343	344	356	Industry: All	1
5	242	241	245	Ages: All	1
10	189	189	189	Sex: M & F	3
20	147	151	150	Occupation: All	1
75	54	57	57	Income: Total	2
85	33	37	37	Intensity: F/P	2
95	(11)	(12)	(12)	Period: Year	1
				Limits: Tax-assessed persons	2

Median Guilders	2,230	2,630	2,740

Source	NL 1	NL 2	NL 3
	T 27	T 4	T 5

Notes:

Based on income-tax assessments which cover almost all full-period employees. Those who worked for only part of the year have been allocated to the income class corresponding to their annual rate of earning.

Married women's income included with their husbands'.

Income net of social security contributions and life annuity premiums.

Employees defined as persons whose major source is W or S, including managing directors of companies.

NETHERLANDS: Table NL–2

Per-centiles	1952	1954	1957	1959		
1	437	458	450	445	Area: Netherlands	1
2	325	336	337	336	Industry: Non-farm	2
5	232	236	232	231	Ages: All	1
10	184	183	180	180	Sex: M & F	3
20	149	145	144	143	Occupation: All	1
75	(56)	58	55	54	Income: Total	2
85	(36)	40	38	36	Intensity: F/P	2
95	(12)	(18)	22	21	Period: Year	1
					Limits: Tax-assessed persons	2

Median Guilders	2,673	3,212	4,125	4,410

Source	NL 2	NL 4	NL 5	NL 7
	T 4	T 5	T 1	T 1

Notes:

See Table NL–1.

COUNTRY TABLES 331

NETHERLANDS: TABLE NL–3

Per-centiles	1952	1954	1957	1959		
1	227	215	207	202	Area: Netherlands	1
2	205	196	189	186	Industry: Non-farm	2
5	181	171	167	164	Ages: All	1
10	162	151	150	148	Sex: M & F	3
20	145	133	132	130	Occupation: Manual	2
75	(56)	60	56	55	Income: Total	2
85	(35)	41	39	38	Intensity: F/P	2
95	(11)	(15)	24	23	Period: Year	1
					Limits: Tax-assessed persons	2
Median Guilders	2,475	3,063	3,930	4,190		
Source	NL 2 T 4	NL 4 T 5	NL 5 T 1	NL 7 T 1		

Notes:

See Table NL–1.

NETHERLANDS: TABLE NL–4

Percentiles	1957	1958	1959		
1	406	404	405	Area: Netherlands	1
2	313	314	315	Industry: Non-farm	2
5	222	225	223	Ages: All	1
10	177	178	177	Sex: M & F	3
20	143	142	142	Occupation: All	1
75	56	55	54	Income: W & S	1
85	38	37	39	Intensity: F/P	2
95	22	22	22	Period: Year	1
				Limits: Tax-assessed persons	2
Median Guilders	4,338	4,460	4,620		
Source	NL 5 T 5	NL 6 T 5	NL 7 T 5		

Notes:

See Table NL–1.

Based on tabulation of 'kerninkomen', which means income typical of group. It includes social insurance contributions, which are excluded from total income.

NETHERLANDS: TABLE NL–5

Per-centiles	1957	1958	1959		
1	193	193	199	Area: Netherlands	1
2	179	180	183	Industry: Non-farm	2
5	159	161	162	Ages: All	1
10	145	143	146	Sex: M & F	3
20	129	128	129	Occupation: Manual	2
75	61	61	55	Income: W & S	1
85	42	41	37	Intensity: F/P	2
95	25	25	23	Period: Year	1
				Limits: Tax-assessed persons	2
Median Guilders	4,190	4,350	4,410		
Source	NL 5 T 5	NL 6 T 5	NL 7 T 5		

Notes:

See Table NL–1. Workers in 'industry' only.

NORWAY: TABLE NO–1

Per-centiles	1960				
	M	F	M & F		
1	..	175	..	Area: Norway	1
2	(146)	161	150	Industry: Manufacturing and mining	4
5	134	143	139	Ages: Adult	2
10	126	133	130	Sex: M, F, M & F	1, 2, 3
20	117	121	120	Occupation: Manual	2
75	88	88	84	Income: W & S	1
85	83	83	76	Intensity: F/P F/T	3
95	75	74	61	Period: Hour	5
				Limits:	0
Median Kroner	6·17	4·10	5·88		
Source	NO 1	NO 1	NO 1		

Notes:

Total earnings for the quarter of adult workers employed for at least 45 h per week, divided by number of hours worked. Where normal hours of a worker were less than 45 the quotient was multiplied by a factor equal to 45 over the normal hours (to offset variations in overtime premiums).

NORWAY: TABLE NO–2

Percentiles	1962		
1	336	Area: Norway	1
2	284	Industry: All	1
5	228	Ages: All	1
10	189	Sex: M & F	3
20	149	Occupation: All	1
75	56	Income: Household	3
85	36	Intensity: All	1
95	(13)	Period: Year	1
		Limits:	0
Median Kronor	14,180		
Source	NO 2 T 8		

Notes:

Based on tax records. Husbands and wives (and some children) matched from assessments. Sample of about 1 per cent of households covered.

Income as defined for tax purposes, excluding some transfers.

NEW ZEALAND: TABLE NZ–1

Per- centiles	1935	1944–5	1950–1	1960–1		
1	..	..	..	..	Area: New Zealand	1
2	..	..	..	..	Industry: All	1
5	(253)	190	(171)	183	Ages: All	1
10	200	159	149	152	Sex: M	1
20	166	134	127	129	Occupation: All	1
75	51	69	76	79	Income: Total	2
85	34	50	59	63	Intensity: All	1
95	(12)	26	31	36	Period: Year	1
					Limits:	0
Median £	146	332	462	877		
Source	NZ 2 37, 42	NZ 3 T 2	NZ 4 108, 110	NZ 5 8		

Notes:

Based on Census data. Persons covered are 'employees' as recorded in the Census.

In principle, income includes income in kind. Maoris excluded in 1935 and 1944–5 but included later.

NEW ZEALAND: TABLE NZ–2

Per-centiles	1935	1944–5	1950–1	1960–1		
1	454	293	261	273	Area: New Zealand	1
2	397	255	230	234	Industry: All	1
5	311	203	192	194	Ages: All	1
10	239	170	165	167	Sex: F	2
20	177	142	140	141	Occupation: All	1
75	(51)	70	70	70	Income: Total	2
85	(31)	49	53	51	Intensity: All	1
95	(11)	18	21	20	Period: Year	1
					Limits:	0

Median £	65	159	242	450

Source	NZ 2 37, 42	NZ 3 T 2	NZ 4 108, 110	NZ 5 8

Notes:

    See Table NZ–1.

NEW ZEALAND: TABLE NZ–3

Per-centiles	1935	1944–5	1950–1	1960–1		
1	..	..	..	..	Area: New Zealand	1
2	..	..	..	258	Industry: All	1
5	296	221	..	191	Ages: All	1
10	240	184	158	161	Sex: M & F	3
20	199	152	135	137	Occupation: All	1
75	51	59	64	65	Income: Total	2
85	(33)	45	48	50	Intensity: All	1
95	(11)	(21)	26	25	Period: Year	1
					Limits:	0

Median £	113	268	407	767

Source	NZ 2 37, 42	NZ 3 T 2	NZ 4 108, 110	NZ 5 8

Notes:

    See Table NZ–1.

NEW ZEALAND: Table NZ–4

Per-centiles	1925–6	1935	1944–5	1950–1	1960–1		
1	..	..	..	..	..	Area: New Zealand	1
2	..	..	..	..	..	Industry: Non-farm	2
5	..	..	188	(159)	180	Ages: All	1
10	155	179	156	138	150	Sex: M	1
20	130	147	132	122	129	Occupation: All	1
75	71	54	74	80	82	Income: Total	2
85	54	36	50	65	66	Intensity: All	1
95	29	(14)	23	36	39	Period: Year	1
						Limits:	0
Median £	215	174	347	464	887		
Source	NZ 1 T 8	NZ 2 T 7 & 8	NZ 3 T 5	NZ 4 T 13	NZ 5 T 4		

Notes:

1925–6: Excludes agriculture, forestry, and fishing. Omits 'no income' and 'not specified'. Income for 12 months preceding Census. Excludes unemployed at time of Census (April 1926) and Maoris.

1935 and 1944–5: Same as 1925–6 but includes, in principle, income in kind.

1950–1 and 1960–1: Income for year ending 31 March. All sources except social security benefits and war pensions. Includes income in kind. Excludes agriculture, services, commerce, government.

NEW ZEALAND: Table NZ–5

Per-centiles	1925–6	1935	1944–5	1950–1	1960–1		
1	298	451	294	251	264	Area: New Zealand	1
2	261	396	257	218	229	Industry: Non-farm	2
5	207	309	205	180	191	Ages: All	1
10	166	239	172	154	166	Sex: F	2
20	136	175	141	135	138	Occupation: All	1
75	(61)	(49)	66	73	71	Income: Total	2
85	(40)	(29)	(47)	55	52	Intensity: All	1
95	(13)	(9)	(17)	21	20	Period: Year	1
						Limits:	0
Median £	111	64·7	157	228	456		
Source	NZ 1 T 8	NZ 2 T 7 & 8	NZ 3 T 5	NZ 4 T 13	NZ 5 T 4		

Notes:

See Table NZ–4.

NEW ZEALAND: Table NZ–6

Per- centiles	1925–6	1935	1944–5	1950–1	1960–1		
1	..	..	..	..	..	Area: New Zealand	1
2	..	..	..	..	250	Industry: Non-farm	2
5	..	276	212	(161)	187	Ages: All	1
10	172	224	179	142	159	Sex: M & F	3
20	147	184	151	124	135	Occupation: All	1
75	62	49	56	71	65	Income: Total	2
85	46	(30)	41	54	49	Intensity: All	1
95	(21)	(10)	15	30	13	Period: Year	1
						Limits:	0

Median £	180	126	275	446	779

Source	NZ 1 T 8	NZ 2 T 7 & 8	NZ 3 T 5	NZ 4 T 13	NZ 5 T 4

Notes:

See Table NZ–4.

NEW ZEALAND: Table NZ–7

Per- centiles	1945–6	1949–50	1954–5	1956–7		
1	305	280	262	268	Area: New Zealand	1
2	234	222	212	219	Industry: All	1
5	177	173	166	171	Ages: All	1
10	150	148	143	147	Sex: M	1
20	128	127	126	127	Occupation: All	1
75	(83)	83	84	83	Income: Total	2
85	(73)	74	75	74	Intensity: All	1
95	(51)	56	62	58	Period: Year	1
					Limits: Taxpayers	2

Median £	391	475	747	824

Source	NZ 6 19	NZ 6 19	NZ 11 18	NZ 13 20

Notes:

Total assessable income of persons whose principal source was wages or salaries.

Exemption limits: 1945–6 and 1949–50, £200; 1954–5 and 1956–7, £375.

NEW ZEALAND: Table NZ–8

Per-centiles	1945–6	1949–50	1954–5	1956–7		
1	338	235	213	232	Area: New Zealand	1
2	292	206	192	207	Industry: All	1
5	244	173	165	170	Ages: All	1
10	211	149	142	148	Sex: F	2
20	(184)	127	123	126	Occupation: All	1
75	(45)	(53)	88	86	Income: Total	2
85	(26)	(31)	84	81	Intensity: All	1
95	(10)	(10)	79	76	Period: Year	1
					Limits: Taxpayers	2
Median £	184	311	490	513		
Source	NZ 6 19	NZ 6 19	NZ 11 18	NZ 13 20		

Notes:

See Table NZ — 7.

PHILIPPINES: Table PH–1

Per-centiles	All	Total urban	Metro. Manila	1961	
1	..	..	..	Area: All; Total urban; Metro. Manila	1, 3, 4
2	590	..	..	Industry: All	1
5	392	397	..	Ages: All	1
10	300	293	286	Sex: M & F	3
20	195	205	202	Occupation: All	1
75	56	64	61	Income: Household	3
85	40	48	48	Intensity: All	1
95	18	27	35	Period: Year	1
				Limits:	0
Median Pesos	1,670	2,120	3,020		
Source	PH 1 T 9	PH 1 T 9	PH 1 T 9		

Notes:

Survey of 6,977 households, of which 3,541 in urban areas and 849 in Metropolitan Manila. Covers families whose main source of income was wages and salaries (both agricultural and non-agricultural).

APPENDIX 7

POLAND: TABLE PO-1

Per- centiles	1956	1957	1958	1960		
1	325	329	308	308	Area: Poland	1
2	277	279	267	263	Industry: Non-farm	2
5	221	224	215	210	Ages: All	1
10	184	185	180	176	Sex: M & F	3
20	148	149	147	145	Occupation: All	1
75	75	74	74	75	Income: W & S	1
85	64	62	62	63	Intensity: F/P F/T	3
95	50	45	45	45	Period: Month	2
					Limits:	0

Median Zloty	1,084	1,246	1,410	1,552

Source	PO 1 332	PO 1 332	PO 1 332	PO 3 430

Notes:

Employees in the socialist economy (i.e. excluding private and co-operative employees). Very few in agriculture.

Covers only those who worked full-time and throughout whole month of September.

POLAND: TABLE PO-2

Per- centiles	1960	1961	1963	1964		
1	302	297	..	..	Area: Poland	1
2	257	256	260	253	Industry: Non-farm	2
5	209	207	212	208	Ages: Excludes apprentices	2
10	176	175	178	176	Sex: M & F	3
20	144	144	145	143	Occupation: All	1
75	75	75	75	74	Income: W & S	1
85	64	64	64	63	Intensity: F/P F/T	3
95	47	48	48	47	Period: Month	2
					Limits:	0

Median Zloty	1,564	1,608	1,730	1,808

Source	PO 4 469	PO 4 469	PO 4 469	PO 4 469

Notes:

See Table PO-1.

POLAND: TABLE PO–3

Per-centiles	1950	1957	1958	1960		
1	321	327	308	281	Area: Poland	1
2	274	279	268	247	Industry: Non-farm	2
5	223	225	219	204	Ages: All	1
10	186	187	184	174	Sex: M & F	3
20	149	150	149	145	Occupation: Manual	2
75	74	73	73	73	Income: W & S	1
85	63	60	60	60	Intensity: F/P F/T	3
95	48	44	42	41	Period: Month	2
					Limits:	0
Median Zloty	1,058	1,219	1,370	1,519		
Source	PO 1 332	PO 1 332	PO 1 332	PO 3 431		

Notes:

See Table PO–1.
Covers 'physical' workers.

POLAND: TABLE PO–4

Per-centiles	1960	1961	1963	1964		
1	279	276	271	272	Area: Poland	1
2	244	243	239	239	Industry: Non-farm	2
5	202	203	202	200	Ages: Excludes apprentices	2
10	172	172	173	172	Sex: M & F	3
20	143	144	144	143	Occupation: Manual	2
75	74	74	74	73	Income: W & S	1
85	62	62	61	61	Intensity: F/P F/T	3
95	44	46	46	45	Period: Month	2
					Limits:	0
Median Zloty	1,532	1,573	1,684	1,769		
Source	PO 4 470	PO 4 470	PO 4 470	PO 4 470		

Notes:

See Tables PO–1 and 3.

POLAND: TABLE PO–5

Per-centiles	1957	1958	1961	1962		
1	301	282	267	264	Area: Poland	1
2	264	248	235	234	Industry: Non-farm	2
5	216	205	195	195	Ages: All	1
10	181	174	167	168	Sex: M	1
20	147	144	140	140	Occupation: Manual	2
75	74	74	75	75	Income: W & S	1
85	62	63	63	63	Intensity: F/P F/T	3
95	45	46	44	40	Period: Month	2
					Limits:	0

Median Zloty	1,372	1,560	1,760	1,783

Source	PO 1 336–7	PO 1 336–7	PO 2 398–9	PO 3 434–5

Notes:

See Tables PO–1 and 3.

POLAND: TABLE PO–6

Per-centiles	1957	1958	1961	1962		
1	236	225	221	219	Area: Poland	1
2	214	203	201	199	Industry: Non-farm	2
5	180	178	175	174	Ages: All	1
10	158	157	157	156	Sex: F	2
20	136	137	137	136	Occupation: Manual	2
75	(74)	73	74	73	Income: W & S	1
85	(63)	(60)	63	62	Intensity: F/P F/T	3
95	(49)	50	(40)	(39)	Period: Month	2
					Limits:	0

Median Zloty	925	1,003	1,133	1,140

Source	PO 1 342–3	PO 1 342–3	PO 2 398–9	PO 3 434–5

Notes:

See Tables PO–1 and 3.

POLAND: TABLE PO-7

Percentiles	1958		
1	307	Area: Poland	1
2	273	Industry: Government	6
5	229	Ages: All	1
10	196	Sex: M & F	3
20	160	Occupation: All	1
75	70	Income: W & S	1
85	60	Intensity: F/P F/T	3
95	48	Period: Month	2
		Limits:	0
Median			
Zloty	1,241		
Source	PO 1		
	332		

Notes:

See Table PO–1.
Employees in 'administration'.

PUERTO RICO: TABLE PR-1

Per- centiles	1953			
	All areas	Urban only		
1	..	..	Area: All and urban	1, 3
2	..	..	Industry: All	1
5	..	..	Ages: All	1
10	188	..	Sex: M & F	3
20	150	146	Occupation: Manual	2
75	70	66	Income: Household	3
85	61	55	Intensity: All	1
95	(39)	40	Period: Year	1
			Limits:	0
Median				
$	1,042	1,227		
Source	PR 1	PR 1		

Notes:

Sample survey in April–July 1954.

Special definition of 'wage earner families', which allowed some subsidiary earnings from agriculture. Income includes lump sums (inheritance, gifts, lottery winnings, etc.) but not income in kind.

SPAIN: TABLE SP–1

Percentiles	1964		
1	..	Area: Spain	1
2	303	Industry: Non-farm, non-service	3
5	239	Ages: All	1
10	196	Sex: M & F	3
20	156	Occupation: All	1
75	72	Income: W & S	1
85	57	Intensity: All	1
95	35	Period: Month	2
		Limits:	0
Median			
Pesetas	3,270		
Source	SP 1		

Notes:

Based on stratified sample of establishments. Each establishment gives data for one month in each quarter. The above results are the sum of three quarters' results January–September 1964. Each establishment occurs three times.

Establishments employing less than 10 manual workers excluded. Also all government employees. Salaries include family allowances but not income in kind.

SWEDEN: TABLE SW–1

Per-centiles	1930	1945	1951	1960		
1	581	543	396	(392)	Area: Sweden	1
2	441	406	301	300	Industry: All	1
5	303	270	211	222	Ages: All	1
10	229	199	166	175	Sex: M	1
20	177	151	135	138	Occupation: All	1
75	(55)	66	67	75	Income: Total	2
85	(35)	49	48	57	Intensity: All	1
95	(12)	29	25	31	Period: Year	1
					Limits: Tax-assessed persons	2

Median Kronor	1,740	3,865	6,820	13,000

Source	SW 2 102	SW 3 10–11	SW 4 6–7	SW 5 50–1

Notes:

Census data matched with tax returns. Estimates exclude persons for whom no tax return discovered.

1930 income is net of general deductions, such as insurance and pension contributions, local taxes, etc.

Exemption limit was Kr. 600 in earlier years and Kr. 1,200 in 1960.

In 1960 the persons covered were those at work at time of census (October 1960) and those normally at work but temporarily out of work for not more than previous 4 months.

SWEDEN: Table SW–2

Per-centiles	1930	1945	1951	1960		
1	477	361	402	327	Area: Sweden	1
2	402	301	332	274	Industry: All	1
5	302	233	268	219	Ages: All	1
10	235	194	220	183	Sex: F	2
20	178	156	177	148	Occupation: All	1
75	(44)	66	53	63	Income: Total	2
85	(25)	53	(35)	48	Intensity: All	1
95	(8)	36	(15)	(25)	Period: Year	1
					Limits: Tax-assessed persons	2

Median Kronor	1,013	2,435	3,110	7,565
Source	SW 2 226	SW 3 10–11	SW 4 8–9	SW 5 52–3

Notes:

See Table SW–1.

SWEDEN: Table SW–3

Per-centiles	1930	1945	1951	1960		
1	598	539	411	392	Area: Sweden	1
2	453	400	318	307	Industry: All	1
5	316	271	228	228	Ages: All	1
10	241	204	183	181	Sex: M & F	3
20	184	156	152	144	Occupation: All	1
75	(49)	62	53	64	Income: Total	2
85	(28)	47	35	47	Intensity: All	1
95	(9)	30	16	26	Period: Year	1
					Limits: Tax-assessed persons	2

Median Kronor	1,485	3,397	5,550	11,315
Source	SW 2 102, 226	SW 3 10–11	SW 4 6–9	SW 5 50–3

Notes:

See Table SW–1.

SWEDEN: Table SW-4

Per-centiles	1920	1930	1945	1951	1960		
1	325	491	452	309	339	Area: Sweden	1
2	250	361	335	233	261	Industry: MMB	5
5	196	253	222	176	197	Ages: All	1
10	167	197	176	150	161	Sex: M	1
20	143	156	142	129	133	Occupation: All	1
75	67	62	74	76	79	Income: Total	2
85	53	(44)	59	57	64	Intensity: All	1
95	33	(18)	36	29	36	Period: Year	1
						Limits: Tax-assessed persons	2

Median Kronor	2,768	1,970	4,040	7,120	13,180

Source	SW 1 406	SW 2 120–4	SW 3 10–11	SW 4 6–7	SW 5 50–1

Notes:
See Table SW–1.

SWEDEN: Table SW-5

Per-centiles	1920	1930	1945	1951	1960		
1	268	314	285	285	260	Area: Sweden	1
2	234	263	241	252	230	Industry: MMB	5
5	195	210	195	199	188	Ages: All	1
10	169	176	164	178	160	Sex: F	2
20	141	144	137	153	136	Occupation: All	1
75	68	(53)	74	52	70	Income: Total	2
85	(46)	(33)	58	33	55	Intensity: All	1
95	(16)	(10)	38	(12)	(30)	Period: Year	1
						Limits: Tax-assessed persons	2

Median Kronor	1,613	1,180	2,460	3,380	7,300

Source	SW 1 406	SW 2 232–6	SW 3 10–11	SW 4 8–9	SW 5 52–3

Notes:
See Table SW–1.

SWEDEN: Table SW–6

Per-centiles	1930	1945	1951	1960		
1	344	234	202	201	Area: Sweden	1
2	297	211	183	184	Industry: All	1
5	243	183	161	160	Ages: All	1
10	207	160	146	144	Sex: M	1
20	168	139	130	127	Occupation: Manual	2
75	(53)	65	65	73	Income: Total	2
85	(31)	49	47	55	Intensity: All	1
95	(10)	31	25	30	Period: Year	1
					Limits: Tax-assessed persons	2
Median Kronor	1,603	3,368	6,305	11,910		
Source	SW 2 102	SW 3 10–11	SW 4 6–7	SW 5 50–1		

Notes:

See Table SW–1.

SWEDEN: Table SW–7

Percentiles	1945	1951	1960		
1	261	310	229	Area: Sweden	1
2	228	283	211	Industry: All	1
5	189	248	187	Ages: All	1
10	165	219	168	Sex: F	2
20	141	182	146	Occupation: Manual	2
75	70	55	64	Income: Total	2
85	57	36	48	Intensity: All	1
95	41	14	(20)	Period: Year	1
				Limits: Tax-assessed persons	2
Median Kronor	1,915	2,324	5,948		
Source	SW 3 10–11	SW 4 8–9	SW 5 52–3		

Notes:

See Table SW–1.

SWEDEN: TABLE SW–8

Per-centiles	1930	1945	1951	1960		
1	384	255	240	218	Area: Sweden	1
2	330	230	220	198	Industry: All	1
5	272	198	192	174	Ages: All	1
10	234	173	174	155	Sex: M & F	3
20	178	148	151	136	Occupation: Manual	2
75	(49)	63	52	63	Income: Total	2
85	(27)	48	35	45	Intensity: All	1
95	(8)	32	15	25	Period: Year	1
					Limits: Tax-assessed persons	2

Median Kronor	1,335	3,008	5,055	10,590

Source	SW 2 102, 226	SW 3 10–11	SW 4 6–9	SW 5 50–3

Notes:
  See Table SW–1.

SWEDEN: TABLE SW–9

Per-centiles	1930	1945	1951	1960		
1	320	223	194	199	Area: Sweden	1
2	274	202	176	179	Industry: MMB	5
5	217	173	155	158	Ages: All	1
10	183	152	140	142	Sex: M	1
20	151	132	125	126	Occupation: Manual	2
75	62	75	75	79	Income: Total	2
85	(43)	59	55	63	Intensity: All	1
95	(15)	36	28	37	Period: Year	1
					Limits: Tax-assessed persons	2

Median Kronor	1,900	3,720	6,850	12,480

Source	SW 2 120–4	SW 3 10–11	SW 4 6–7	SW 5 50–1

Notes:
  See Table SW–1.

SWEDEN: TABLE SW–10

Per-centiles	1930	1945	1951	1960		
1	250	199	232	195	Area: Sweden	1
2	224	180	217	179	Industry: MMB	5
5	196	160	197	160	Ages: All	1
10	170	144	179	147	Sex: F	2
20	139	128	157	132	Occupation: Manual	2
75	(57)	73	51	70	Income: Total	2
85	(34)	58	32	55	Intensity: All	1
95	(11)	38	(10)	(31)	Period: Year	1
					Limits: Tax-assessed persons	2

Median Kronor	1,110	2,280	3,032	6,810

Source	SW 2 236	SW 3 10–11	SW 4 8–9	SW 5 52–3

Notes:

See Table SW–1.

SWEDEN: TABLE SW–11

Per-centiles	1954	1959	1964		
1	357	369	367	Area: Sweden	1
2	280	286	289	Industry: All	1
5	205	212	215	Ages: All	1
10	164	169	172	Sex: M	1
20	134	137	138	Occupation: All	1
75	71	69	71	Income: Total	2
85	50	46	51	Intensity: All	1
95	29	24	26	Period: Year	1
				Limits: Tax-assessed persons	2

Median Kronor	8,870	11,680	17,370

Source	SW 6 T 11	SW 7 T 11	SW 8 T 13

Notes:

Based on tax reports.
Exemption limit in 1954 and 1959 was Kr. 1,200, and in 1964 Kr. 2,400.

SWEDEN: TABLE SW–12

Percentiles	1954	1959	1904		
1	379	387	372	Area: Sweden	1
2	313	326	317	Industry: All	1
5	252	259	255	Ages: All	1
10	210	214	213	Sex: F	2
20	169	172	169	Occupation: All	1
75	55	51	51	Income: Total	2
85	39	35	33	Intensity: All	1
95	18	(15)	(12)	Period: Year	1
				Limits: Tax-assessed persons	2

Median				
Kronor	4,245	5,480	8,260

Source	SW 6	SW 7	SW 8
	T 11	T 11	T 13

Notes:

See Table SW–11.

SWEDEN: TABLE SW–13

Percentiles	1954	1959	1964		
1	375	397	390	Area: Sweden	1
2	300	309	312	Industry: All	1
5	223	232	233	Ages: All	1
10	180	186	189	Sex: M & F	3
20	148	152	154	Occupation: All	1
75	55	52	53	Income: Total	2
85	37	34	35	Intensity: All	1
95	20	17	16	Period: Year	1
				Limits: Tax-assessed persons	2

Median				
Kronor	7,280	9,390	13,885

Source	SW 6	SW 7	SW 8
	T 11	T 11	T 13

Notes:

See Table SW–11.

UNITED KINGDOM: TABLE UK–1

Per-centiles	1954–5	1958–9	1960–1	1961–2		
1	370	366	375	379	Area: United Kingdom	1
2	274	275	280	284	Industry: All	1
5	195	197	199	203	Ages: All	1
10	160	161	162	164	Sex: M	1
20	134	134	136	135	Occupation: All	1
75	78	77	75	75	Income: W & S	1
85	66	63	61	62	Intensity: All	1
95	45	44	41	41	Period: Year	1
					Limits: Tax-assessed persons	2
Median £	477	608	678	713		
Source	UK 1 T 55	UK 2 T 68	UK 2 T 68	UK 3 T 67		

Notes:

Schedule E income (major source only). Covers wages, salaries, pensions, and miscellaneous fees.

Exemption limits: 1954–5, £165; 1955–6 onwards, £190. A definite fall in dispersion occurs in 1955–6 which may well reflect this change. And some of the increasing dispersion thereafter may be the result of rising money incomes and a constant exemption limit.

UNITED KINGDOM: TABLE UK–2

Per-centiles	1954–5	1958–9	1960–1	1961–2		
1	283	320	335	338	Area: United Kingdom	1
2	249	274	283	286	Industry: All	1
5	202	214	218	225	Ages: All	1
10	166	174	176	180	Sex: F	2
20	137	140	142	142	Occupation: All	1
75	82	81	78	76	Income: W & S	1
85	74	72	69	67	Intensity: All	1
95	(66)	64	59	57	Period: Year	1
					Limits: Tax-assessed persons	2
Median £	266	325	352	367		
Source	UK 1 T 55	UK 2 T 68	UK 2 T 68	UK 3 T 67		

Notes:

See Table UK–1.

UNITED KINGDOM: TABLE UK–3

Per-centiles	1954–5	1958–9	1960–1	1961–2		
1	372	372	382	390	Area: United Kingdom	1
2	275	281	291	296	Industry: All	1
5	203	206	214	215	Ages: All	1
10	169	171	176	177	Sex: M & F	3
20	142	142	147	148	Occupation: All	1
75	69	67	66	65	Income: W & S	1
85	57	54	53	52	Intensity: All	1
95	45	42	40	39	Period: Year	1
					Limits: Tax-assessed persons	2
Median £	422	533	578	605		
Source	UK 1 T 55	UK 2 T 68	UK 2 T 68	UK 3 T 67		

Notes:

See Table UK–1.

UNITED KINGDOM: TABLE UK–4

Per-centiles	1911–12				
	M	F	M & F		
1	462	231	459	Area: Great Britain	1
2	321	205	322	Industry: All	1
5	214	165	230	Ages: All	1
10	179	142	198	Sex: M, F, M & F	1, 2, 3
20	153	125	162	Occupation: All	1
75	72	73	74	Income: W & S	1
85	58	57	57	Intensity: All	1
95	28	36	31	Period: Year	1
				Limits:	0
Median £	67·3	44·8	56·6		
Source	UK 11 52	UK 11 52	UK 11 52		

Notes:

Estimates by Routh, using income-tax data for 451,000 employees and other partial data for the remaining 16 million. Data adjusted to relate to Great Britain only.

UNITED KINGDOM: TABLE UK–5

Percentiles	1958–9				
	M	F	M & F		
1	372	340	380	Area: Great Britain	1
2	278	287	285	Industry: All	1
5	198	227	210	Ages: All	1
10	160	184	176	Sex: M, F, M & F	1, 2, 3
20	134	146	146	Occupation: All	1
75	79	74	60	Income: W & S	1
85	65	(59)	47	Intensity: All	1
95	43	(33)	(31)	Period: Year	1
				Limits:	0
Median					
£	588	268	489		
Source	UK 11	UK 11	UK 11		
	52	52	52		

Notes:

Estimates by Routh, based on Schedule E tax distribution for United Kingdom (from Inland Revenue *103rd Report*) adjusted for Northern Ireland and number below exemption limit.

UNITED KINGDOM: TABLE UK–6

Per-centiles	1906 All	1938		1960 F/T		
		All	F/T			
1	..	..	..	198	Area: United Kingdom	1
2	207	..	..	182	Industry: Non-farm, non-service	3
5	174	156	155	161	Ages: Adults	2
10	153	140	139	145	Sex: M	1
20	133	124	124	128	Occupation: Manual	2
75	79	83	85	83	Income: W & S	1
85	70	74	78	75	Intensity: All, & F/P F/T	1,3
95	54	55	67	65	Period: Week	3
					Limits:	0

Median					
£	1·42	3·39	3·67	14·15

Source	UK 8 549	UK 9 49	UK 9 49	UK 7 139

Notes:

Covers manufacturing, mining (except coal, and in 1906 all mining and quarrying), building, transport (except railways in 1938 and 1960), gas, electricity and water, local authority services and government industrial establishments, and a few service trades, such as laundries, garages, and boot and shoe repair.

Earnings are for a specified week in October, when the establishment was working normally.

1906: Males 20 and over. Includes Eire.
1938: Males 21 and over. Full-time means working over 48 h.
1960: Males 21 and over normally working 30 or more hours per week.

354   APPENDIX 7

UNITED KINGDOM: Table UK-7

Per-centiles	1960		
	M	F	M & F
1	198	186	208
2	182	172	192
5	161	153	169
10	145	138	152
20	128	123	133
75	83	85	77
85	75	78	65
95	65	67	49
Median £	14·15	7·55	13·04
Source	UK 7 139–49	UK 7 139–49	UK 7 139–49

Area: United Kingdom 1
Industry: Non-farm, non-service 3
Ages: Adults 2
Sex: M, F, M & F 1, 2, 3
Occupation: Manual 2
Income: W & S 1
Intensity: F/P F/T 3
Period: Week 3
Limits: 0

Notes:

See Table UK-6.

UNITED KINGDOM: Table UK-8

Percentiles	1960		
	M	F	M & F
1	193	179	208
2	177	166	191
5	158	149	169
10	143	136	152
20	126	122	133
75	83	86	73
85	75	79	61
95	64	67	47
Median £	14·85	7·56	13·32
Source	UK 7 142–3, 149	UK 7 142–3, 149	UK 7 142–3, 149

Area: United Kingdom 1
Industry: Manufacturing 4
Ages: Adults 2
Sex: M, F, M & F 1, 2, 3
Occupation: Manual 2
Income: W & S 1
Intensity: F/P F/T 3
Period: Week 3
Limits: 0

Notes:

See Table UK-6.
For combination of M and F all males 'under £7' treated as '£6–7' and females earning '£16 and over' were spread smoothly from £16 to £22.

UNITED KINGDOM: TABLE UK–9

Percentiles	1953–4					
	M	F	M & F			
1	(347)	(295)	352	Area: Great Britain	1
2	(270)	(257)	268	Industry: All	1
5	199	208	200	Ages: 18+	2
10	161	166	164	Sex: M, F, M & F	1, 2, 3
20	133	134	136	Occupation: All	1
75	85	75	74	Income: W & S	1
85	77	63	57	Intensity: F/P	2
95	54	45	36	Period: Year	1
				Limits:	0
Median					
£	444	238	403		
Source	UK 6	UK 6	UK 6		

Notes:

Based on sample survey, covering Great Britain only.
Full-period means 48 weeks or more at work (not including paid holidays).

UNITED KINGDOM: TABLE UK–10

Percentiles	1964				
	All	Manual			
1	..	..	Area: United Kingdom	1
2	..	..	Industry: All	1
5	..	..	Ages: Adults	2
10	180	167	Sex: M & F	3
20	144	142	Occupation: All and Manual	1, 2
75	75	77	Income: Household	3
85	65	67	Intensity: All	1
95	48	50	Period: Week	3
			Limits:	0
Median				
£	23·0	21·35		
Source	UK 20	UK 20		
	8	8		

Notes:

Survey of 3,244 households, of which 2,275 were headed by employees.
Of the latter, 1,652 were headed by manual workers (including 'other ranks'
in defence, police, and fire services).

U.S.S.R.: TABLE UR–1

Per-centiles	1914 Day	1928 Day	1928 Month	1934 Month		
1	..	..	296	..	Area: U.S.S.R.	1
2	408	..	265	291	Industry: Manufacturing	4
5	314	226	224	234	Ages: All	1
10	248	191	189	194	Sex: M & F	3
20	179	153	152	153	Occupation: Manual	2
75	70	74	72	72	Income: W & S	1
85	57	62	60	61	Intensity: F/P F/T	3
95	(30)	(41)	(43)	42	Period: Day, Month	4, 2
					Limits: Large establish-ments	4
Median Rubles	0·90	2·47	66·0	139·6		
Source	UR 1 226–8	UR 1 226–8	UR 1 226–8	UR 1 226–8		

Notes:

1914: Eight industry groups covered. Earnings include overtime.
　　　Average daily wages in month of June.
1928: Daily wages as above for month of March. Excludes overtime.
　　　Monthly wages are for employees on payroll throughout the month.
　　　Includes overtime.
1934: Monthly wages as in 1928, for month of October. Seasonal differences
　　　not considered important.

U.S.S.R.: TABLE UR–2

Percentiles	1928	1934		
1	329	415	Area: U.S.S.R.	1
2	288	344	Industry: Manufacturing	4
5	234	268	Ages: All	1
10	194	213	Sex: M & F	3
20	154	163	Occupation: All	1
75	71	71	Income: W & S	1
85	59	59	Intensity: F/P F/T	3
95	(42)	40	Period: Month	2
			Limits: Large establishments	4
Median Rubles	68·8	149		
Source	UR 1 226–8	UR 1 226–8		

Notes:
　　See Table UR–1.

COUNTRY TABLES 357

UNITED STATES: TABLE US–1

Percentiles	1939	1949	1959		
1	..	371	..	Area: United States	1
2	424	279	287	Industry: All	1
5	286	211	214	Ages: 14+	1
10	218	175	176	Sex: M	1
20	169	144	144	Occupation: All	1
75	53	64	61	Income: W & S	1
85	35	41	36	Intensity: All	1
95	18	(15)	(10)	Period: Year	1
				Limits:	0

Median $	1,055	2,695	4,670

Source	US 1	US 2	US 3
	T 72	T 22	T 27

Notes:

Based on census data.
1939: Persons in the experienced labour force reporting $100 or more of wage or salary income in 1939.
1949: Persons in the experienced civilian labour force reporting $1 or more of W & S income in 1949. 3⅓ per cent sample.
1959: Same definition. 5 per cent sample.

UNITED STATES: TABLE US–2

Percentiles	1939	1949	1959		
1	426	300	320	Area: United States	1
2	345	259	281	Industry: All	1
5	268	213	237	Ages: 14+	1
10	217	186	204	Sex: F	2
20	170	155	169	Occupation: All	1
75	54	50	(42)	Income: W & S	1
85	37	(29)	(24)	Intensity: All	1
95	(22)	(9)	(6)	Period: Year	1
				Limits:	0

Median $	649	1,576	2,290

Source	US 1	US 2	US 3
	T 72	T 22	T 27

Notes:

See Table US–1.

UNITED STATES: TABLE US-3

Percentiles	1939	1949	1959		
1	..	382	394	Area: United States	1
2	442	293	316	Industry: All	1
5	302	228	238	Ages: 14+	1
10	238	188	197	Sex: M & F	3
20	179	153	160	Occupation: All	1
75	54	57	50	Income: W & S	1
85	35	35	27	Intensity: All	1
95	(20)	(11)	(8)	Period: Year	1
				Limits:	0
Median					
$	901	2,296	3,740		
Source	US 1	US 2	US 3		
	T 72	T 22	T 27		

Notes:

  See Table US-1.

UNITED STATES: TABLE US-4

Percentiles	1939	1949	1959		
1	..	..	..	Area: United States	1
2	..	270	278	Industry: All	1
5	267	206	206	Ages: 14+	1
10	199	168	168	Sex: M	1
20	155	135	137	Occupation: All	1
75	65	74	74	Income: W & S	1
85	48	61	59	Intensity: F/P	2
95	24	34	33	Period: Year	1
				Limits:	0
Median					
$	1,352	3,111	5,330		
Source	US 1	US 2	US 3		
	T 72	T 23	T 28		

Notes:

  Full-period means: in 1939, those who worked full-time throughout the year; in 1949 and 1959, those who worked 50–2 weeks, whether full-time or part-time.

UNITED STATES: TABLE US–5

Percentiles	1939	1949	1959		
1	367	252	248	Area: United States	1
2	294	215	216	Industry: All	1
5	231	177	182	Ages: 14+	1
10	191	157	161	Sex: F	2
20	156	134	139	Occupation: All	1
75	67	71	70	Income: W & S	1
85	45	55	52	Intensity: F/P	2
95	(24)	27	(23)	Period: Year	1
				Limits:	0

Median				
$	788	1,994	3,140	

Source	US 1	US 2	US 3
	T 72	T 23	T 28

Notes:

See Tables US–1 and 4.

UNITED STATES: TABLE US–6

Percentiles	1939	1949	1959		
1	..	..	..	Area: United States	1
2	403	278	288	Industry: All	1
5	271	209	215	Ages: 14+	1
10	205	173	176	Sex: M & F	3
20	160	141	144	Occupation: All	1
75	61	72	68	Income: W & S	1
85	45	56	52	Intensity: F/P	2
95	22	30	27	Period: Year	1
				Limits:	0

Median				
$	1,201	2,750	4,660	

Source	US 1	US 2	US 3
	T 72	T 23	T 28

Notes:

See Tables US–1 and 4.

UNITED STATES: TABLE US–7

Percentiles	1939	1949	1959		
1	..	..	..	Area: United States	1
2	414	278	286	Industry: Non-farm	2
5	277	208	212	Ages: 14+	1
10	211	172	174	Sex: M	1
20	163	142	143	Occupation: All	1
75	58	66	63	Income: W & S	1
85	40	44	40	Intensity: All	1
95	21	16	(11)	Period: Year	1
				Limits:	0

Median					
$	1,132	2,770	4,750		

Source	US 1	US 2	US 3
	T 72	T 22	T 27

Notes:

   See Table US–1.

UNITED STATES: TABLE US–8

Percentiles	1939	1949	1959		
1	424	301	319	Area: United States	1
2	348	257	279	Industry: Non-farm	2
5	269	211	235	Ages: 14+	1
10	217	184	203	Sex: F	2
20	169	154	169	Occupation: All	1
75	54	51	43	Income: W & S	1
85	37	30	(23)	Intensity: All	1
95	(22)	10	(7)	Period: Year	1
				Limits:	0

Median					
$	651	1,590	2,310		

Source	US 1	US 2	US 3
	T 72	T 22	T 27

Notes:

   See Table US–1.

UNITED STATES: Table US–9

Percentiles	1939	1949	1959		
1	..	375	390	Area: United States	1
2	429	288	311	Industry: Non-farm	2
5	291	225	235	Ages: 14+	1
10	229	185	195	Sex: M & F	3
20	172	151	158	Occupation: All	1
75	57	58	52	Income: W & S	1
85	38	37	28	Intensity: All	1
95	20	12	(8)	Period: Year	1
				Limits:	0

Median				
$	959	2,350	3,800	

Source	US 1	US 2	US 3
	T 72	T 22	T 27

Notes:
    See Table US–1.

UNITED STATES: Table US–10

Percentiles	1939	1949	1959		
1	..	..	..	Area: United States	1
2	..	275	278	Industry: Non-farm	2
5	264	199	206	Ages: 14+	1
10	197	166	167	Sex: M	1
20	153	135	137	Occupation: All	1
75	70	76	75	Income: W & S	1
85	54	63	60	Intensity: F/P	2
95	34	38	35	Period: Year	1
				Limits:	0

Median				
$	1,408	3,140	5,370	

Source	US 1	US 2	US 3
	T 72	T 23	T 28

Notes:
    See Tables US–1 and 4.

UNITED STATES: TABLE US-11

Percentiles	1939	1949	1959		
1	367	252	246	Area: United States	1
2	295	217	215	Industry: Non-farm	2
5	231	178	183	Ages: 14+	1
10	191	158	161	Sex: F	2
20	156	135	139	Occupation: All	1
75	66	72	70	Income: W & S	1
85	45	55	52	Intensity: F/P	2
95	24	28	(23)	Period: Year	1
				Limits:	0
Median					
$	788	1,990	3,140		
Source	US 1	US 2	US 3		
	T 72	T 23	T 28		

Notes:

See Tables US-1 and 4.

UNITED STATES: TABLE US-12

Percentiles	1939	1949	1959		
1	..	..	..	Area: United States	1
2	398	278	287	Industry: Non-farm	2
5	267	209	215	Ages: 14+	1
10	202	173	176	Sex: M & F	3
20	159	142	144	Occupation: All	1
75	64	73	68	Income: W & S	1
85	50	57	53	Intensity: F/P	2
95	26	31	28	Period: Year	1
				Limits:	0
Median					
$	1,240	2,770	4,690		
Source	US 1	US 2	US 3		
	T 72	T 23	T 28		

Notes:

See Tables US-1 and 4.

UNITED STATES: TABLE US–13

Por centiles	1030*	1040*	1040	1050	
1	313	237	242	237	Area: United States 1
2	272	215	217	212	Industry: Non-farm 2
5	224	185	185	183	Ages: 14+ 1
10	193	161	162	162	Sex: M 1
20	157	138	138	140	Occupation: Manual 2
75	59	68	67	62	Income: W & S 1
85	41	46	45	40	Intensity: All 1
95	23	19	18	(12)	Period: Year 1
					Limits: 0
Median					
$	1,009	2,640	2,585	4,385	
Source	US 1	US 2	US 2	US 3	
	T 72	T 22	T 22	T 27	

Notes:

See Table US–1.

1939* }
1949* } Craftsmen, operatives, and labourers.

1949 }
1959 } Above categories plus service workers other than household.

UNITED STATES: TABLE US–14

Per- centiles	1939*	1949*	1949	1959	
1	270	242	268	287	Area: United States 1
2	235	214	239	263	Industry: Non-farm 2
5	197	187	207	228	Ages: 14+ 1
10	171	165	181	197	Sex: F 2
20	141	144	155	163	Occupation: Manual 2
75	64	62	56	(50)	Income: W & S 1
85	48	40	(35)	(29)	Intensity: All 1
95	(29)	(14)	(12)	(9)	Period: Year 1
					Limits: 0
Median					
$	589	1,560	1,370	1,940	
Source	US 1	US 2	US 2	US 3	
	T 72	T 22	T 22	T 27	

Notes:

See Tables US–1 and 13.

364 APPENDIX 7

UNITED STATES: TABLE US–15

Per- centiles	1939*	1949*	1949	1959		
1	340	252	261	268	Area: United States	1
2	292	229	235	239	Industry: Non-farm	2
5	243	195	199	207	Ages: 14+	1
10	205	170	174	182	Sex: M & F	3
20	165	143	147	154	Occupation: Manual	2
75	60	64	60	54	Income: W & S	1
85	43	44	40	32	Intensity: All	1
95	23	18	(15)	(10)	Period: Year	1
					Limits:	0
Median $	913	2,440	2,315	3,735		
Source	US 1 T 72	US 2 T 22	US 2 T 22	US 3 T 27		

Notes:
 See Tables US–1 and 13.

UNITED STATES: TABLE US–16

Per- centiles	1939*	1949*	1949	1959		
1	267	218	219	216	Area: United States	1
2	234	197	198	195	Industry: Non-farm	2
5	194	171	171	169	Ages: 14+	1
10	167	150	150	149	Sex: M	1
20	140	130	130	131	Occupation: Manual	2
75	72	77	76	74	Income: W & S	1
85	56	65	63	60	Intensity: F/P	2
95	38	40	39	38	Period: Year	1
					Limits:	0
Median $	1,311	3,030	2,972	5,035		
Source	US 1 T 72	US 2 T 23	US 2 T 23	US 3 T 28		

Notes:
 See Tables US–1, 4, and 13.

UNITED STATES: TABLE US–17

Per-centiles	1939*	1949*	1949	1959		
1	247	206	221	229	Area: United States	1
2	213	181	195	210	Industry: Non-farm	2
5	177	161	172	183	Ages: 14+	1
10	154	145	153	162	Sex: F	2
20	133	127	134	140	Occupation: Manual	2
75	83	77	73	72	Income: W & S	1
85	73	66	60	56	Intensity: F/P	2
95	52	47	37	(31)	Period: Year	1
					Limits:	0
Median $	748	1,950	1,778	2,654		
Source	US 1 T 72	US 2 T 23	US 2 T 23	US 3 T 28		

Notes:
  See Table US–16.

UNITED STATES: TABLE US–18

Per-centiles	1939*	1949*	1949	1959		
1	274	225	232	229	Area: United States	1
2	241	204	209	207	Industry: Non-farm	2
5	200	176	180	178	Ages: 14+	1
10	174	154	157	157	Sex: M & F	3
20	143	133	135	137	Occupation: Manual	2
75	68	75	74	69	Income: W & S	1
85	55	62	59	54	Intensity: F/P	2
95	38	39	36	31	Period: Year	1
					Limits:	0
Median $	1,247	2,880	2,747	4,630		
Source	US 1 T 72	US 2 T 23	US 2 T 23	US 3 T 28		

Notes:
  See Table US–16.

UNITED STATES: TABLE US-19

Per- centiles	United States		Central cities		1959	
	All	Whites	All	Whites		
1	..	..	..	..	Area: All and Urban	1, 3
2	..	..	279	..	Industry: All	1
5	213	212	204	207	Ages: All	1
10	170	170	166	164	Sex: M	1
20	139	139	136	135	Occupation: All	1
75	71	73	74	76	Income: W & S	1
85	54	58	60	62	Intensity: F/P	2
95	27	29	34	35	Period: Year	1
					Limits: All and Whites only	0, 1
Median $	5,224	5,380	5,240	5,470		
Source	US 5 T 25	US 5 T 25	US 5 T 25	US 5 T 25		

Notes:

Males aged 14 and over who worked for 50 to 52 weeks and received $1 or more in wage or salary in 1959.

Urban means central cities of urbanized areas.

UNITED STATES: TABLE US-20

Per- centiles	1939 All	1949 All	1959			
			All	NE		
1	..	(400)	..	..	Area: All and Northeast	1, 2
2	436	292	..	..	Industry: All	1
5	297	217	(223)	(219)	Ages: All	1
10	231	182	179	178	Sex: M	1
20	176	151	145	141	Occupation: All	1
75	51	59	59	68	Income: W & S	1
85	(34)	38	34	48	Intensity: All	1
95	(17)	15	12	17	Period: Year	1
					Limits:	0
Median $	988	2,624	4,630	4,840		
Source	US 5 T 24	US 5 T 24	US 5 T 24	US 5 T 24		

Notes:

Persons aged 14 and over in the experienced labour force with wage or salary income of $100 or more in the previous year.

NE means north-eastern region of the United States, which comprises about one-quarter of the total population.

UNITED STATES: TABLE US-21

Per-centiles	1939 All	1949 All	1959 All	NE		
1	448	306	319	308	Area: All and Northeast	1, 2
2	367	266	280	268	Industry: All	1
5	281	218	236	222	Ages: All	1
10	229	187	201	190	Sex: F	2
20	179	156	167	156	Occupation: All	1
75	(56)	52	45	52	Income: W & S	1
85	(40)	33	27	33	Intensity: All	1
95	(23)	(16)	(11)	(13)	Period: Year	1
					Limits:	0
Median $	610	1,570	2,317	2,533		
Source	US 5 T 24	US 5 T 24	US 5 T 24	US 5 T 24		

Notes:

See Table US 20.

UNITED STATES: TABLE US-22

Per-centiles	1939 All	1949 All	1959 All	NE		
1	..	398	..	..	Area: All and Northeast	1, 2
2	452	301	..	..	Industry: All	1
5	309	231	240	237	Ages: All	1
10	243	193	197	191	Sex: M & F	3
20	182	156	159	153	Occupation: All	1
75	52	56	50	58	Income: W & S	1
85	(36)	34	29	36	Intensity: All	1
95	(19)	14	11	13	Period: Year	1
					Limits:	0
Median $	863	2,283	3,780	3,970		
Source	US 5 T 24	US 5 T 24	US 5 T 24	US 5 T 24		

Notes:

See Table US-20.

UNITED STATES: TABLE US–23

Per-centiles	1890 M	1892 M	1899 M	F	M & F	
1	258	289	..	222	..	Area: United States, 1, 2
						Massachusetts
2	229	242	..	201	..	Industry: See notes –
5	194	194	193	169	201	Ages: Adults 2
10	165	169	169	148	175	Sex: M, F, M & F 1, 2, 3
20	136	147	144	130	146	Occupation: Manual 2
75	85	71	79	81	75	Income: W & S 1
85	79	59	69	(70)	65	Intensity: F/P F/T 3
95	67	42	53	(51)	(47)	Period: Day, Week 4, 3
						Limits: 0

Median					
$ per week..	..	10·14	6·78	9·11	

Source	ZA 1	ZA 1	ZA 2	ZA 2	ZA 2
	197	197	431	431	431

Notes:

1890: Railways, United States, daily wages.
1892: Textiles, United States, daily wages.
1899: Manufacturing, Massachusetts, weekly earnings.
The data for 1890 and 1892 have been smoothed before interpolation.

YUGOSLAVIA: TABLE YU–1

Percentiles	Persons 1963	Households 1963		
1	292	..	Area: Yugoslavia	1
2	253	..	Industry: Non-farm	2
5	207	..	Ages: All	1
10	174	..	Sex: M & F	3
20	143	153	Occupation: All	1
75	76	72	Income: W & S, household	1, 3
85	66	59	Intensity: F/P	2
95	(52)	42	Period: Year	1
			Limits:	0
Median Dinars (000)	297·4	572		
Source	YU 1 299	YU 2 12		

Notes:

Persons: Some farm employees probably covered, e.g. in State farms. Income is wages and salaries net of taxes (probably not very high or progressive) for the whole year.

Household: Survey of 16,567 households in December 1963. Data for year 1963. Data relate to 'available household resources', which include all income sources plus net credit, withdrawals from bank deposits, etc. Households covered are 'workers', which excludes agricultural workers, craftsmen, liberal professions, and pensioners. Excludes income in kind.

YUGOSLAVIA: Table YU–2

Percentiles	1963	1964	June 1964		
1	341	..	331	Area: Yugoslavia	1
2	289	294	282	Industry: Non-farm	2
5	230	231	223	Ages: All	1
10	188	189	185	Sex: M & F	3
20	150	151	149	Occupation: All	1
75	75	74	76	Income: W & S	1
85	65	64	65	Intensity: F/P F/T	3
95	(50)	50	52	Period: Month	2
				Limits:	0

Median Dinars	25,280	31,580	30,200

Source	YU 1 296	YU 1 296	YU 1 296

Notes:

Income collected each month for employees paid for 180 to 230 h in the month (or in some cases 160 to 200 h). Income is net of taxes. A few farm employees probably included.

Annual figures are based on distributions which average the monthly distributions.

Monthly earnings fluctuate widely, as a result of quarterly and annual bonuses, so that these distributions are more widely dispersed than true annual data would be.

APPENDIX 8

Statistical Sources

AL 1.   *Reports of the Commissioner of Taxation, Australia*, Canberra, Annual.

AL 2.   Special tabulation provided by the Deputy Commonwealth Statistician of New South Wales.

AL 3.   *Labour report*, Commonwealth Bureau of Census and Statistics, Canberra, Annual.

AR 1.   'Cuentas Nacionales y Distribución del Ingreso en Argentina.' Extracts sent by Mr. Alberto Fracchia of the Instituto Torcuato di Tella, Buenos Aires.

AU 1.   *Die Langfristige Entwicklung von Löhnen und Gehältern in Wien*, Kammer für Arbeiter und Angestellte für Wien, 1963. Supplemented by data from Dr. E. Weissel, of the Kammer.

AU 2.   Data supplied by Dr. H. Kramer, derived from *Steuerstatistiken 1957*.

BE 1.   Data supplied by M. Claude Carbonelle.

BR 1.   *Anuario estatistica do Brasil 1955*.

CA 1.   *Tenth census of Canada, 1961*, vol. iii, Part 3, Series 3.3, *Labour force, earnings, hours and weeks of employment of wage-earners by occupations, provinces*, Dominion Bureau of Statistics, Ottawa, 1963.

CA 2.   *Ninth census of Canada, 1951*, vol. v, *Labour force, earnings and employment of wage-earners*, Dominion Bureau of Statistics, Ottawa, 1953.

CA 3.   *Eighth census of Canada, 1941*, vol. vi, *Earnings, employment and unemployment of wage-earners*, Dominion Bureau of Statistics, Ottawa, 1946.

CA 4.   *Seventh census of Canada, 1931*, vol. v, *Earnings of wage-earners, dwellings, households, families, blind and deaf-mutes*, Dominion Bureau of Statistics, Ottawa, 1935.

CA 5.   *Tenth census of Canada, 1961*, vol. vii, part 1, Series 7.1, *General review, educational levels and school attendance*, Dominion Bureau of Statistics, Ottawa, 1965.

CA 6.   *Eighth census of Canada, 1941*, vol. vii, *Gainfully occupied by occupations, industries, etc.*, Dominion Bureau of Statistics, Ottawa, 1944.

CA 7.   *Ninth census of Canada, 1951*, vol. iv, *Labour force: occupations and industries*, Dominion Bureau of Statistics, Ottawa, 1953.

372 APPENDIX 8

CA 8.   *Tenth census of Canada, 1961*, vol. iii, Part 1, *Labour force: occupations*, Dominion Bureau of Statistics, Ottawa, 1962–4.

CH 1.   Data supplied by Mr. Sergio Chaparro Ruiz.

CN 1.   *Statistical abstract of Ceylon 1964.*

CZ 1.   *Czechoslovak statistical yearbook 1965.*

DK 1.   *Statistisk Årbog Danmark 1958.*

DK 2.   Same series, *1960.*

DK 3.   Same series, *1965.*

DK 4.   *Statistiske Efterretninger*, no. 49, pp. 665–7.

ES 1.   *Costo y condiciones de vida en San Salvador 1954*, Dirección General de Estadistica y Censos, San Salvador, June 1956.

FN 1.   Data supplied by Professor Raoul Brummert, University of Oulu.

FR 1.   *Budgets des Français en 1956, dépenses et niveaux de vie*, Extrait de la Revue *Consommation*, INSEE et CREDOC, Dunod, 1960.

FR 2.   *Bulletin mensuel de statistique, Supplément*, I.N.S.E.E., October–December 1953.

FR 3.   Same series, October–December 1954.

FR 4.   *Études statistiques*, Supplément Trimestriel du Bulletin Mensuel de Statistique, July–September 1956.

FR 5.   Same series, October–December 1958.

FR 6.   Same series, July–September 1959.

FR 7.   Same series, October–December 1961.

FR 8.   Same series, April–June 1962.

FR 9.   Same series, April–June 1963.

FR 10.   Same series, April–June 1964.

FR 11.   *Études et conjoncture*, November 1965.

GE 1.   *Statistisches Jahrbuch für die Bundesrepublik Deutschland, 1955.*

GE 2.   Same series, *1959.*

GE 3.   Same series, *1961.*

GE 4.   Same series, *1965.*

GR 1.   Data supplied by Mr. P. Couvelis.

HU 1.   *A Munkások és Alkalmazottak Száma, Keresete a Munka Jellege Szerint*, Központi Statisztikai Hivatal, Budapest, 1966.

HU 2.   *A Népesség Jövedelmi Helyzete 1962*, Központi Statisztikai Hivatal, Budapest, 1964.

IC 1.   *Les budgets familiaux des salariés africains en Abidjan (août–septembre 1956)*, Service de la Statistique Générale et de la Mécanographique, Territoire de la Côte d'Ivoire, août 1958.

IN 1.   *National sample survey report no. 85, 14th round, 1958–59*, Indian Statistical Institute, Calcutta.

IN 2.   Data supplied by Professor D. T. Lakdawala, University of Bombay.

IS 1.   *Family expenditure surveys (1950/51–1956/57–1959/60)*, Central Bureau of Statistics, Special Series No. 148, Jerusalem, 1963.

IS 2.   *Family Expenditure survey 1963/64, First results*, Central Bureau of Statistics, Jesusalem, 1965.

IS 3.   Information supplied by Dr. A. Nizan of the National Insurance Institute, Jerusalem.

IT 1.   *Annali di statistica*, anno 89, serie viii–vol. ii, *Indagine statistica sui bilanci di famiglie non agricole negli anni 1953–54*, Istituto Centrale di Statistica, Roma, 1960.

JA 1.   *Japan statistical yearbook 1964*, Bureau of Statistics, Tokyo. 1965.

JA 2.   *Report on salaries and wages in private firms*, National Taxation Board, Tokyo. Series relating to years 1953 to 1965 respectively.

JA 3.   Chotaro Takahashi, *Dynamic changes of income and its distribution in Japan*, Tokyo, 1959.

JA 4.   *Japan's growth and education*, Ministry of Education, Tokyo, 1963.

JA 5.   *Statistical handbook of Japan, 1964*, Bureau of Statistics, Tokyo, 1964.

JA 6.   *Population of Japan, 1960, Summary of the results of 1960 population census of Japan*, Bureau of Statistics, Tokyo, 1963.

JA 7.   *Japanese economic statistics*, Economic Planning Agency, Tokyo. Monthly publication.

KO 1.   *Monthly statistics of Korea, 1965, 4*, Bureau of Statistics, Economic Planning Board, Republic of Korea.

ME 1.   *Ingresos por trabajo de la poblacion economicamente activa y jefes de familia (VIII Censo de Poblacion de 1960)*, Direccion General de Estadistica, Mexico, 1964.

NL 1.   *Maandstatistiek van het financiewezen*, October 1954, Centraal Bureau voor de Statistiek, 's-Gravenhage.

NL 2.   *Inkomensverdeling 1952 en vermogensverdeling 1953*, as above, 1957.

NL 3.   Same series for 1953 and 1954, 1957.

NL 4.   Same series for 1954 and 1955, 1959.

NL 5.   Same series for 1957 and 1958, 1962.

NL 6.   Same series for 1958 and 1959, 1963.

NL 7.   Same series for 1959 and 1960, 1963.

NO 1.   Data supplied by Mrs. Turid Sletten, of Statistisk Sentralbyrå, Oslo.

NO 2.   P. Myklebust, 'Hovedresultater fra intektsstatistikken 1958 og 1962,' *Arbeidsnotater*, February 1966, Statistisk Sentralbyrå, Oslo.

NZ 1. *New Zealand population census, 1926*, vol. xi, *Incomes of the population*, Census and Statistics Office, Wellington, 1930.

NZ 2. *New Zealand population census, 1936*, vol. xii, *Incomes*, Census and Statistics Department, Wellington, 1945.

NZ 3. *New Zealand population census, 1945*, vol. x, *Incomes*, Census and Statistics Department, Wellington, 1952.

NZ 4. *New Zealand population census, 1951*, vol. iv, *Industries, occupations and incomes*, Census and Statistics Department, Wellington, 1954.

NZ 5. *New Zealand population census, 1961*, vol. 5, *Incomes*, Department of Statistics, Wellington, 1964.

NZ 6. *Report on the income and income-tax statistics of New Zealand, 1946–50*.

NZ 7. Same series, *1950–1*.

NZ 8. Same series, *1951–2*.

NZ 9. Same series, *1952–3*.

NZ 10. Same series, *1953–4*.

NZ 11. Same series, *1954–5*.

NZ 12. Same series, *1955–6*.

NZ 13. Same series, *1956–7*.

NZ 14. Same series, *1957–8*.

NZ 15. Same series, *1958–9*.

NZ 16. Same series, *1959–60*.

PH 1. The *Philippine statistical survey of households*, Bulletin Series No. 14, *Family income and expenditures April 1961*, Bureau of the Census and Statistics, Manila, 1964.

PH 2. 'Wages and working conditions in the Philippines, 1938 and 1939', *Monthly Labor Review*, March 1940.

PO 1. *Polish statistical yearbook 1959*.

PO 2. Same series, *1962*.

PO 3. Same series, *1963*.

PO 4. Same series, *1965*.

PR 1. *Income and expenditures of the families, Puerto Rico, 1953*, vol. ii, Bureau of Labor Statistics, Commonwealth of Puerto Rico, June 1960.

SP 1. *Estadística salarios*, Instituto Nacional de Estadística, Madrid, 1965.

SW 1. *Folkräkningen den 31 December 1920*, v, Statistiska Centralbyrå, Stockholm, 1927.

SW 2. *Folkräkningen den 31 December 1930*, vii, Statistiska Centralbyrå, Stockholm, 1937.

SW 3. *Folkräkningen den 31 December 1945*, iii: 1, Statistiska Centralbyrå, Stockholm, 1949.

STATISTICAL SOURCES 375

SW 4. *Folkräkningen den 31 December 1950*, vii, Statistiska Centralbyrå, Stockholm, 1956.

SW 5. *Folkräkningen den 1 November 1960*, xi, Statistiska Centralbyrå, Stockholm, 1965.

SW 6. *Skattetaxeringarna samt fördelningen av inkomst och förmögenhet, Taxeringsåret 1954*, Statistiska Centralbyrå, Stockholm, 1955.

SW 7. Same series, *1959*.

SW 8. Same series, *1964*.

UK 1. *Inland revenue report, no. 100*, H.M.S.O., London.

UK 2. Same series, *no. 105*.

UK 3. Same series, *no. 106*.

UK 6. Results of 1954 Savings Survey, supplied by Oxford University Institute of Statistics.

UK 7. *Ministry of Labour Gazette*, April 1961, H.M.S.O., London.

UK 8. E. H. Phelps Brown and M. H. Browne, 'Earnings in industries of the United Kingdom, 1948–59', *Economic Journal*, September 1962, 72, 517–49.

UK 9. R. B. Ainsworth, 'Earnings and working hours of manual wage-earners in the United Kingdom in October 1938', *Journal of the Royal Statistical Society, Series A*, Part I, 1949, 92, 35–66.

UK 10. *Family expenditure survey, report for 1964*, Ministry of Labour. H.M.S.O., London, 1965.

UK 11. G. Routh, *Occupation and pay in Great Britain 1906–1960*. Cambridge: University Press, 1965.

UK 12. *Ministry of Labour Gazette*, October 1960, H.M.S.O., London.

UR 1. A. Bergson, *The structure of Soviet wages*. Cambridge, Mass.: Harvard University Press, 1944.

US 1. *United States census of population 1940*, vol. iii, *The labor force, Part I, United States summary*, Bureau of the Census, Washington, 1943.

US 2. *United States census of population 1950, Report P-E No. 1B, Occupational characteristics*, Bureau of the Census, Washington, 1956.

US 3. *United States census of population 1960, Final report PC(2)-7A, Occupational characteristics*, Bureau of the Census, Washington, 1963.

US 4. *United States census of population 1960, Final report PC(2)-7B, Occupation by earnings and education*, Bureau of the Census, Washington, 1963.

US 5. *United States census of population 1960, Final report PC(2)-4C, Sources and structure of family income*, Bureau of the Census, Washington, 1964.

US 6. *Occupational trends in the United States, 1900 to 1950*, Bureau of the Census, Working Paper no. 5, U.S. Department of Commerce, Washington, 1958.

376 APPENDIX 8

US 7. *The statistical history of the United States from colonial times to the present.* Stamford, Conn.: Fairfield, 1965.

YU 1. *Statistički Godišnjak SFRJ 1965.*

YU 2. *Anketa o Ličnoj Potrošnji Stanovništva 1963, I Deo*, Statistički Bilten Broj 314, Savezni Zavod za Statistiku, Belgrade, 1964.

ZA 1. Lucien March, 'Quelques exemples de distribution des salaires', *Journ. de la Société de Statistique de Paris*, June 1898, **39**, 193–206.

ZA 2. L. Dugé de Bernonville, 'Distribution de salaires et de revenus en divers pays', *Bull. de la Statistique Générale de la France*, 1912–13, **2**, 400–36.

ZA 3. *Bulletin of family budget surveys, 1950–1960*, International Labour Office, Geneva, 1961.

ZA 4. *Demographic yearbook 1963*, United Nations, New York, 1964.

ZA 5. *Demographic yearbook 1964*, United Nations, New York, 1965.

ZA 6. *Statistical yearbook 1964*, Unesco, Paris, 1966.

ZA 7. *Compendium of social statistics: 1963*, United Nations, New York, 1963.

ZA 8. *Yearbook of national accounts statistics 1964*, United Nations, New York.

ZA 9. *Yearbook of labour statistics 1965*, International Labour Office, Geneva, 1966.

ZA 10. *The state of food and agriculture 1955*, Food and Agriculture Organization, Rome, 1955.

ZA 11. *Demographic yearbook 1956*, United Nations, New York, 1956.

ZA 12. *Bulletin of labour statistics*, International Labour Office, Geneva, 1965.

BIBLIOGRAPHY

AITCHISON, J., and BROWN, J. A. C. (1954). 'On criteria for descriptions of income distribution', *Metroeconomica*, **6**, 88–107.
—— —— (1957). *The lognormal distribution*. Cambridge: University Press.
ALLEN, G. C. (1965). *Japan's Economic Expansion*. London: Oxford University Press.
ANASTASI, A. (1958). *Differential psychology*. New York: Macmillan.
ANDERSON, C. A. (1961). 'A skeptical note on the relation of vertical mobility to education', *Amer. Journ. of Sociology*, **66**, 560–70.
—— and BOWMAN, M. J. (1966). (Eds.), *Education and economic development*. London: Frank Cass.
BAHRAL, U. (1962). 'Wage differentials and specification bias in estimates of relative labor prices', *Rev. Econ. Stats.* **44**, 473–81.
BARNA, T. (1945). *Redistribution of incomes through public finance in 1937*. Oxford: Clarendon Press.
BAUMOL, W. J. (1959). *Business behavior, value and growth*. New York: Macmillan.
BAYLEY, N. (1955). 'On the growth of intelligence', *Amer. Psychologist*, **10**, 805–18.
BECKER, G. S. (1957). *The economics of discrimination*. Chicago: University Press.
—— (1964). *Human capital*. New York: Columbia University Press for NBER.
—— and CHISWICK, B. R. (1966). 'Education and the distribution of earnings', *Amer. Econ. Rev.* **56**, 358–69.
BELL, P. W. (1951). 'Cyclical variations and trend in occupational wage differentials in American industry since 1914', *Rev. Econ. Stats.* **33**, 329–37.
BELLERBY, J. R. (1956). *Agriculture and industry: relative income*. London: Macmillan.
BERGSON, A. (1944). *The structure of Soviet wages*. Cambridge, Mass.: Harvard University Press.
BERLINER, J. S. (1966). Discussion on contributed papers at the conference of the American Economic Association. *Amer. Econ. Rev.* **56**, 156–8.
BLOOM, B. S. (1964). *Stability and change in human characteristics*. New York: Wiley.
BOALT, G. (1954). 'Social mobility in Stockholm: a pilot investigation', in *Transactions of the Second World Congress of Sociology*, **2**, International Sociological Association.
BOGUE, D. J. (1959). *The population of the United States*. Glencoe, Ill.: Free Press.

BOISSEVAIN, C. H. (1939). 'Distribution of abilities depending upon two or more independent factors', *Metron*, 15, 48–58.

BOWLEY, A. L. (1933). 'The action of economic forces in producing frequency distributions of income, prices, and other phenomena: a suggestion for study', *Econometrica*, 1, 358–72.

BRISTOL, R. B. (1958). 'Factors associated with income variability', *Amer. Econ. Rev., Papers and Proceedings*, 48, 279–90.

BROWN, E. H. P. (1949). 'Prospects for Labour', *Economica*, 16, 1–10.

Bureau of the Census (1964). *Accuracy of data on population characteristics as measured by reinterviews*, Evaluation and Research Program of the U.S. Census of Population and Housing, 1960, Series ER 60, No. 4. Washington: Government Printing Office.

BURT, C. (1943). 'Ability and income', *Brit. Journ. Educ. Psychol.* 13, 83–98.

—— (1955). 'The evidence for the concept of intelligence', ibid. 25, 158–77.

—— (1958). 'The inheritance of mental ability', *Amer. Psychol.* 13, 1–15.

—— (1959). 'Class differences in general intelligence: III', *Brit. Journ. Statist. Psychol.* 12, 15–33.

—— (1961). 'Intelligence and social mobility', ibid. 14, 3–23.

CHAMPERNOWNE, D. G. (1953). 'A model of income distribution', *Econ. Journ.* 68, 318–51.

CLARK, C. (1951). *The conditions of economic progress*, 2nd ed. London: Macmillan.

CONWAY, J. (1959). 'Class differences in general intelligence: II', *Brit. Journ. Statist. Psychol.* 12, 5–14.

CRAMÉR, H. (1946). *Mathematical methods of statistics*. Princeton: University Press.

DAVIS, H. T. (1941a). *The analysis of economic time series*. Bloomington: Principia Press.

—— (1941b). *The theory of econometrics*. Bloomington: Principia Press.

DEANE, P. (1965). *The first industrial revolution*. Cambridge: University Press.

DE GROOT, A. D. (1951). 'War and the intelligence of youth', *Journ. Abnorm. Soc. Psychol.* 46, 596–7.

DENISON, E. F. (1962). *The sources of economic growth in the United States and the alternatives before us.* New York: Committee for Economic Development.

DESCARTES, R. (1912). *A discourse on method.* Everyman edition. London: Dent.

DE WOLFF, P., and HÄRNQUIST, K. (1961). 'Reserves of ability: size and distribution', in Halsey (1961).

DOUTY, H. M. (1953). 'Union impact on wage structures', *Proc. Indust. Rel. Res. Assoc.* 61–76.

DUNLOP, J. T. (1939). 'Cyclical variations in the wage structure', *Rev. Econ. Stats.* 21, 30–9.

BIBLIOGRAPHY379

DUNLOP, J. T., and ROTHBAUM, M. (1955). 'International comparisons of wage structures', *Internat. Lab. Rev.* **71**, 347–63.

ÉLTETŐ, Ö. (1965). 'Large-sample lognormality tests based on new inequality measures', 35th Session of the International Statistical Institute, Belgrade.

FELDMESSER, R. A. (1966). 'Towards the classless society ?', in Bendix, R., and Lipset, S. M. (Eds.), *Class, status, and power*, 2nd ed. New York: Free Press.

FITZGERALD, C. P. (1964). *The birth of communist China*. London: Penguin.

FLANAGAN, J. C., and others (1964). *Project talent—the American highschool student*. Pittsburgh: University of Pittsburgh.

FLEMING, C. M. (1943). 'Socio-economic level and test performance', *Brit. Journ. Educ. Psychol.* **13**, 74–82.

FLOUD, J. E., and HALSEY, A. H. (1958). 'Measured intelligence is largely an acquired characteristic', ibid. **28**, 290–1.

—— —— and MARTIN, F. M. (1966). *Social class and educational opportunity*. London: Heinemann.

FORSTER, E. M. *Abinger Harvest*. London: Penguin, 1967.

FOULDS, G. A., and RAVEN, J. C. (1948). 'Normal changes in the mental abilities of adults as age advances', *Journ. Ment. Sci.* **94**, 133–42.

FRASER, E. (1959). *Home environment and the school*. London: University of London Press.

FRÉCHET, M. (1939). 'Sur les formules de répartition des revenus', *Revue de l'Institut International de Statistique*, **7**, 32.

—— (1945). 'Nouveaux essais d'explication de la répartition des revenus', ibid. **13**, 16.

FRIEDMAN, M. (1957). *A theory of the consumption function*. Princeton: University Press.

—— and KUZNETS, S. (1945). *Income from independent professional practice*. New York: N.B.E.R.

FUCHS, V. R. (1967). *Differentials in hourly earnings by region and city size, 1959*. New York: Columbia University Press for National Bureau of Economic Research.

GALENSON, W. (1962). (Ed.), *Labor in developing economics*. Berkeley: University of California Press.

GIBRAT, R. (1931). *Les inégalités économiques*. Paris: Librairie du Recueil Sirey.

GINZBERG, E. (1943). 'The occupational adjustment of 1000 selectees', *Amer. Sociolog. Rev.* **8**, 256–63.

GOLDMAN, M. I. (1965). 'The reluctant consumer and economic fluctuations in the Soviet Union', *Journ. Pol. Econ.* **73**, 366–80.

GOODE, W. J. (1966). 'Family and mobility', in Bendix, R., and Lipset, S. M. (Eds.), *Class, status, and power*, 2nd ed. New York: Free Press.

GORDON, H. (1923). *Mental and scholastic tests among retarded children*. Education Pamphlet no. 44. London: Board of Education.

GÜNTER, H. (1964). 'Changes in occupational wage differentials', *Internat. Lab. Rev.* **89**, 136–55.

HALDANE, J. B. S. (1942). 'Moments of the distribution of powers and products of normal variates', *Biometrika*, **32**, 226–42.

HALSEY, A. H. (1961). (Ed.), *Ability and educational opportunity*. Paris: O.E.C.D.

—— FLOUD, J., and ANDERSON, C. A. (1961). (Eds.), *Education, economy and society—a reader in the sociology of education*. Glencoe, Ill.: Free Press.

HANNA, F. A., PECHMAN, J. A., and LERNER, S. M. (1948). *Analysis of Wisconsin income*. Conference on Research in Income and Wealth, **9**. New York: N.B.E.R.

HARBISON, F., and MYERS, C. A. (1964). *Education, manpower, and economic growth*. New York: McGraw-Hill.

—— —— (1965). (Eds.), *Manpower and education*. New York: McGraw-Hill.

HARRELL, T. W. and M. S. (1945). 'Army general classification test scores for civilian occupations', *Educational and Psychological Measurement*, **5**, 229–40.

HICKS, J. R. (1935). *The theory of wages*. London: Macmillan.

HILL, T. P., and KNOWLES, K. G. J. C. (1956). 'The variability of engineering earnings', *Bull. Oxford Inst. Stats.* **18**, 97–140.

HOUTHAKKER, H. S. (1959). 'Education and income', *Rev. Econ. Stats.* **41**, 24–8.

HUSÉN, T. (1951). 'The influence of schooling upon IQ', *Theoria*, **17**, 61–88.

—— (1961). 'Educational structure and the development of ability', in Halsey (1961).

INKELES, A. (1966). 'Social stratification and mobility in the Soviet Union', in Bendix, R., and Lipset, S. M. (Eds.), *Class, status, and power*, 2nd ed. New York: Free Press.

JOHNSON, D. G. (1953). 'Comparability of labor capacities of farm and non-farm labor', *Amer. Econ. Rev.* **43**, 296–313.

KAHL, J. A. (1953). 'Educational and occupational aspirations of "common man" boys', *Harvard Educational Review*, **23**.

KALECKI, M. (1945). 'On the Gibrat distribution', *Econometrica*, **13**, 161–70.

KANNINEN, T. P. (1953). 'Occupational wage relationships in manufacturing, 1952–53', *Monthly Lab. Rev.* **76**.

KAPTEYN, J. C. (1903). *Skew frequency curves in biology and statistics*. Groningen: Nordhoff.

KEAT, P. G. (1960). 'Long-run changes in occupational wage structure, 1900–1956', *Journ. Pol. Econ.* **68**, 584–600.

KEATING, M. (1967). 'Australian wages, employment and average earnings, 1947–48 to 1962–63', *Econ. Record*, **43**, 65–87.

KEMP, L. C. D. (1955). 'Environmental and other characteristics determining attainments in primary schools', *Brit. Journ. Educ. Psychol.* **25**, 67–77.

KNOWLES, K. G. J. C., and ROBERTSON, D. J. (1951a). 'Differences between the wages of skilled and unskilled workers, 1880–1950', *Bull. Oxford Inst. Stats.* **13**, 109–27.

—— —— (1951b). 'Earnings in engineering, 1926–1948', ibid. 179–200.

1BIBLIOGRAPHY 381

KRAVIS, J. B. (1962). *The structure of income*. Philadelphia: University of Pennsylvania.

KUZNETS, S. (1966). *Economic growth and structure: selected essays*. London: Heinemann.

LANGE, O. (1959). *Introduction to econometrics*. Oxford: Pergamon Press.

LANSING, J. B., GINSBURG, G. P., and BRAATEN, K. (1961). *An investigation of response error*. Urbana: University of Illinois.

LAYARD, P. R. G., and SAIGAL, J. C. (1966). 'Educational and occupational characteristics of manpower: an international comparison', *Brit. Journ. Indust. Rel.* **4**, 222–66.

LEBERGOTT, S. (1959). 'The shape of the income distribution', *Amer. Econ. Rev.* **49**, 328–47.

—— (1964). *Manpower in economic growth: the American record since 1800*. New York: McGraw-Hill.

LEE, E. S. (1951). 'Negro intelligence and selective migration: a Philadelphia test of the Klineberg hypothesis', *Amer. Sociolog. Rev.* **16**, 227–33.

—— and others (1957). *Population redistribution and economic growth, 1870–1950, Vol. I, Methodological considerations and reference tables*. Philadelphia: The American Philosophical Society.

LEISERSON, M. W. (1959). *Wages and economic control in Norway, 1945–1957*. Cambridge, Mass.: Harvard University Press.

LESTER, R. A. (1952). 'A range theory of wage differentials', *Indust. and Lab. Rel. Rev.* **5**, 483–500.

LIPSET, S. M., and BENDIX, R. (1954). 'Ideological equalitarianism and social mobility in the United States', in *Transactions of the Second World Congress of Sociologists*. vol. ii. International Sociological Association.

—— (1959). *Social mobility in industrial society*. Berkeley and Los Angeles: University of California Press.

LOCKWOOD, W. W. (1954). *The economic development of Japan. Growth and structural change 1868–1938*. Princeton: University Press.

LYDALL, H. F. (1955). 'The life cycle in income, saving, and asset ownership', *Econometrica*, **23**, 131–50.

—— (1959). 'The distribution of employment incomes', ibid. **27**, 110–15.

—— (1965). 'The dispersion of employment incomes in Australia', *Econ. Record*, **41**, 549–69.

MCALISTER, D. (1879). 'The law of the geometric mean', *Proc. Roy. Soc.* **29**, 367–76.

MCAULEY, M. (1966). 'Some observations on labor and wages in Czechoslovakia', *Co-existence*, 173–88.

MCGUIRE, J. W., CHIU, J. S. Y., and ELBING, A. O. (1962). 'Executive incomes, sales and profits', *Amer Econ. Rev.* **52**, 753–61.

MCKINSEY & COMPANY, Inc. (1965). *Survey of executive compensation overseas*. New York. (circulated privately).

MCNEMAR, Q. (1942). *The revision of the Stanford–Binet scale*. Boston: Houghton Mifflin.

MANDELBROT, B. (1960). 'The Pareto-Lévy law, and the distribution of income', *Internat. Econ. Rev.* 1, 79–106.

—— (1961). 'Stable Paretian random functions and the multiplicative variation of income', *Econometrica*, 29, 517–43.

MARRIS, R. (1964). *The economic theory of 'managerial' capitalism.* Glencoe, Ill.: The Free Press.

MARX, K., *Critique of the Gotha programme.* London: Lawrence & Wishart, 1938.

MAYER, T. (1960). 'The distribution of ability and earnings', *Rev. Econ. Stats.* 42, 189–95.

MILL, J. S. *Utilitarianism, liberty, and representative government.* Everyman edition. London: Dent, 1936.

MILLER, H. P. (1955). *Income of the American people.* New York: Wiley.

—— (1966). *Income distribution in the United States.* Washington: U.S. Government Printing Office.

MINCER, J. (1958). 'Investment in human capital and personal income distribution', *Journ. Pol. Econ.* 66, 281–302.

MINER, J. B. (1957). *Intelligence in the United States.* New York: Springer.

MOORE, H. L. (1911). *Laws of wages, an essay in statistical economics.* London: Macmillan.

MORGAN, J. (1962). 'The anatomy of income distribution', *Rev. Econ. Stats.* 44, 270–83.

—— and LININGER, C. (1964). 'Education and income: comment', *Quarterly Journ. Econ.* 78, 346–7.

MUNTZ, E. E. (1955). 'The decline in wage differentials based on skill in the United States', *Internat. Lab. Rev.* 71, 575–92.

MYRDAL, J. (1965). *Report from a Chinese village.* London: Heinemann.

National Bureau of Economic Research (1958). *An appraisal of the 1950 census income data,* Studies in income and wealth, 13. Princeton: University Press.

NICHOLSON, J. L. (1964). 'Redistribution of income in the United Kingdom in 1959, 1957, and 1953' in Clark, C., and Stuvel, G., *Income and wealth, series X, Income redistribution and the statistical foundations of economic policy.* New Haven, Conn.: International Association for Research in Income and Wealth.

NOVE, A. (1966). 'Wages in the Soviet Union: a comment on recently published statistics', *Brit. Journ. Ind. Rel.* 4, 137–53.

OBER, H. (1948). 'Occupational wage differentials 1907–1947', *Monthly Lab. Rev.* 67, 127–34.

O.E.C.D. (1964). *The residual factor and economic growth,* Paris: O.E.C.D.

—— (1965). *Wages and labour mobility.* Paris: O.E.C.D.

ORLEANS, L. A. (1961). *Professional manpower and education in Communist China.* Washington: National Science Foundation.

OSTRY, S. W., COLE, H. J. D., and KNOWLES, K. G. J. C. (1958). 'Wage differentials in a large steel firm', *Bull. Oxford Inst. Stats.* 20, 217–64.

OZANNE, R. (1962). 'A century of occupational differentials in manufacturing', *Rev. Econ. Stats.* 44, 292–9.

PARETO, V. (1897). *Cours d'économie politique.* vol. ii. Lausanne.

—— (1927). *Manuel d'économie politique,* 2nd ed. Paris.

PASTERNAK, B., *Doctor Zhivago.* New York: Pantheon, 1958.

PATTON, A. (1901). *Men, money and motivation.* Now York: McGraw-Hill.

PERKINS, J. A. (1966). 'Foreign aid and the brain drain'. *Foreign Affairs,* **44,** 608–19.

PERLMAN, R. (1958). 'Forces widening occupational wage differentials', *Rev. Econ. Stats.* **40,** 107–15.

PIGOU, A. C. (1932). *The economics of welfare,* 4th ed. London: Macmillan.

REDER, M. (1955). 'A theory of occupational wage differentials', *Amer. Econ. Rev.* **45,** 833–52.

—— (1957). *Labor in a growing economy.* New York: Wiley.

REYNOLDS, L. G. (1951). *Structure of labor markets wages: and labor mobility in theory and practice.* New York: Harper.

—— (1959). *Labor economics and labor relations,* 3rd ed. Englewood Cliffs, N.J.: Prentice-Hall.

—— and TAFT, C. H. (1956). *The evolution of wage structure.* New Haven: Yale University Press.

ROBERTS, D. R. (1959) *Executive compensation.* Glencoe, Ill.: The Free Press.

ROBINSON, E. A. G., and VAIZEY, J. E. (1966). (Eds.), *The economics of education.* London: Macmillan.

ROUSSEAU, J. J., *The social contract.* Everyman edition. London: Dent, 1935.

ROUTH, G. (1965). *Occupation and pay in Great Britain.* London: Cambridge University Press for the National Institute of Economic and Social Research.

ROY, A. D. (1950a). 'The distribution of earnings and of individual output', *Econ. Journ.* **60,** 489–505.

—— (1950b). 'A further statistical note on the distribution of individual output', ibid. 831–6.

—— (1951). 'Some thoughts on the distribution of earnings', *Oxford Econ. Papers,* **3,** 135–46.

RUBNER, A. (1962). *Fringe benefits: the golden chains.* London: Putnam.

RUTHERFORD, R. S. G. (1955). 'Income distributions: a new model', *Econometrica,* **23,** 277–94.

SCOVILLE, J. G. (1966). 'Education and training requirements for occupations', *Rev. Econ. Stats.,* **48,** 387–94.

SEERS, D. (1964). (Ed.), *Cuba: the economic and social revolution.* Chapel Hill: University of North Carolina Press.

—— (1966). 'The transmission of inequality', paper presented at the Haile Selassie Prize Trust Conference, Addis Ababa. To be published.

SIMON, H. A. (1955). 'On a class of skew distribution functions', *Biometrika,* **42,** 425–40. Reprinted in Simon, H. A., *Models of man.* New York: Wiley, 1957.

—— (1957). 'The compensation of executives', *Sociometry,* **20,** 32–5.

SLICHTER, S. H. (1950). 'Notes on the structure of wages', *Rev. Econ. Stats.* **32,** 80–91.

SMITH, A., *The wealth of nations*. Everyman edition. London: Dent, 1947.

SOLTOW, L. (1965). *Toward income equality in Norway*. Madison: University of Wisconsin Press.

STAEHLE, H. (1943). 'Ability, wages, and income', *Rev. Econ. Stats.* 25, 77–87.

SVENNILSON, I., EDDING, F., and ELVIN, J. (1961). *Targets for education in Europe*. Report for the Washington Policy Conference on Economic Growth and Investment in Education. Paris: O.E.E.C.

TAEUBER, I. B. (1958). *The population of Japan*. Princeton, N.J.: Princeton University Press.

TAIRA, K. (1961). *The dynamics of Japanese wage differentials, 1881–1959*. Ph.D. dissertation, Stanford.

TAWNEY, R. H. *Equality*. New edition. London: Allen & Unwin, 1964.

THOMAS, B. (1954). *Migration and economic growth*. Cambridge: University Press.

THORELLI, H. B. (1965). 'Salary span of control', *Journ. Manag. Studs.* 2, 269–302.

TUDDENHAM, R. D. (1948). 'Soldier intelligence in World Wars I and II', *Amer. Psychologist*, 3, 54–6.

TURNER, H. A. (1952). 'Trade unions, differentials and the levelling of wages', *Manchester School*, 20, 227–82.

—— (1965). *Wage trends, wage policies, and collective bargaining*. Cambridge: University Press for Department of Applied Economics.

TYLER, L. E. (1965). *The psychology of human differences*. New York: Meredith.

United States Department of Labor, Bureau of Employment Security, *Dictionary of Occupational Titles*, 2nd ed., 1 and 2. Washington, D.C., 1949.

VAN UVEN, M. J. (1917). 'Logarithmic frequency distributions', *Proceedings of the Academy of Science*, Amsterdam.

WECHSLER, D. (1958). *The measurement and appraisal of adult intelligence*, 4th ed. Baltimore: Williams & Wilkins.

WELFORD, A. T. (1958). *Ageing and human skill*. London: Oxford University Press.

WISEMAN, S. (1964). *Education and environment*. Manchester: University Press.

WOLFLE, D. (1954). *America's resources of specialized talent*. New York: Harper.

—— and SMITH, J. G. (1956). 'The occupational value of education for superior high-school grades', *Journ. Higher Education*, 27, 201–32.

WOODS, H. D., and OSTRY, S. (1962). *Labour policy and labour economics in Canada*. Toronto: Macmillan.

YAMAMURA, K. (1965). 'Wage structure and economic growth in post-war Japan', *Indust. and Lab. Rel. Rev.* 19, 58–69.

YANOWITCH, M. (1963). 'The Soviet income revolution', *Slavic Review*, 22, 683–97.

ZIPF, G. K. (1949). *Human behavior and the principle of least effort*. Cambridge, Mass.: Addison-Wesley.

Children and their primary schools. A report of the Central Advisory Council for Education (England). Vol. i. London: H.M.S.O., 1967.
Higher education. Report of the Robbins Committee on Higher Education. Cmnd. 2154. London: H.M.S.O., 1963.
15 to 18. Report of the Central Advisory Council for Education (England). Vol. i. London: H.M.S.O., 1959.

INDEX

Ability, factors responsible for, 8, 10, 36, 41, 69–88; distribution of, 25–9, 32, 68; variation within occupations, 102–3, 105; correlation with education, 106–8; variation with age, 113–17. *See also* Intelligence.

Age, effect on ability, 8, 70; changes in variance of income with, 39; effects on income distribution, 57–8; variation of earnings with, 112–25.

Agriculture, proportion engaged in as influence on dispersion of earnings, 10, 215–19; environmental effects of, 204–7.

Aitchison, J., 33, 37, 41, 105, 138n., 176, 377.

Allen, G. C., 230, 231, 232, 233n., 377.

Anastasi, A., 80n., 250, 377.

Anderson, C. A., 107, 108, 109n., 210n., 236n., 255n., 256n., 259n., 265n., 377, 380.

Argentina, dispersion of earnings in, 142–5, 158; 'class differential' in, 150–1; dispersion of Standard Distribution in, 152–7; dispersion of manual workers in, 158; changes in dispersion in, 198, 250; dispersion related to: inequality of education, 211–12, proportion in agriculture, 216–17, *per capita* G.D.P., 216, 218; appendix tables, 287–8.

Attainment, correlations of twins, 74; factors determining, 81–8, 274; distribution of, 85–8.

Augsburg, City of, 14.

Australia, distribution of award rates in, 99–100; dispersion of earnings in, 142–5; dispersion of Standard Distribution in, 152–8; changes in dispersion in, 190–3, 237, 250; dispersion related to: proportion in agriculture, 216–17, *per capita* G.D.P., 216, 218; appendix tables, 283–6.

Austria, dispersion of earnings in, 142–5; dispersion of Standard Distribution in, 152–7; changes in dispersion in, 187–8, 234–5; dispersion related to: proportion in agriculture, 216–17, *per capita* G.D.P., 216, 218; appendix tables, 288–91.

Bahral, U., 168, 377.

Barna, T., 45n., 377.

Baumol, W. J., 131, 132n., 377.

Bayley, N., 116n., 377.

Becker, G. S., 90n., 96n., 112, 243n., 377.

Belgium, dispersion of earnings in, 142–5; 'class differential' in, 151; dispersion of Standard Distribution in, 152–7; dispersion of manual workers in, 158–9; changes in dispersion in, 188, 235–6; dispersion related to: proportion in agriculture, 216–17, *per capita* G.D.P., 216, 218; appendix tables, 292–3.

Bell, P. W., 171n., 377.

Bellerby, J. R., 204n., 377.

Bendix, R., 106, 107, 108, 379, 381.

Bergson, A., 161, 377.

Berliner, J. S., 127n., 377.

Blitz, R. C., 212.

Bloom, B. S., 75n., 377.

Boalt, G., 107, 108, 377.

Bogue, D. J., 250–1, 378.

Boissevain, C. H., 40n., 88n., 378.

Bowley, A. L., 28, 378.

Bowman, M. J., 109n., 210n., 255n., 256n., 265n., 377.

Braaten, K., 30n., 381.

Brain drain, 252–3.

Brazil, dispersion of earnings in, 142–5; dispersion of Standard Distribution in, 152–7; dispersion related to: inequality of education, 211, proportion in agriculture, 216–17, *per capita* G.D.P., 216, 218; appendix table, 294.

394   INDEX

PRINTED IN GREAT BRITAIN
AT THE UNIVERSITY PRESS, OXFORD
BY VIVIAN RIDLER
PRINTER TO THE UNIVERSITY